D0153337

THE FORMER YUGOSLAVIA'S DIVERSE PEOPLES

Other Titles in
ABC-CLIO's
ETHNIC DIVERSITY WITHIN NATIONS
Series

Canada's Diverse Peoples, J. M. Bumsted

Nigeria's Diverse Peoples, April A. Gordon

FORTHCOMING

Australia's Diverse Peoples, Andrew Wells and Julia Theresa Martínez

The Former Soviet Union's Diverse Peoples, James Minahan

THE FORMER YUGOSLAVIA'S

DIVERSE PEOPLES

A REFERENCE SOURCEBOOK

*Matjaž Klemenčič
and Mitja Žagar*

A B C 🞄 C L I O

Santa Barbara, California   Denver, Colorado   Oxford, England

Library of Congress Cataloging-in-Publication Data
Klemenčič , Matjaž, 1955–
  The former Yugoslavia's diverse peoples: a reference sourcebook /
Matjaž Klemenčič and Mitja Žagar.
    p. cm. — (ABC-CLIO's ethnicity within nations series)
Includes bibliographical references and index.
  ISBN 1-57607-294-0 (hardcover : alk. paper) 1-85109-547-0 (eBook)
  1. Yugoslavia—History. 2. Yugoslavia—Emigration and
immigration—History. 3. Yugoslavia—Ethnic relations—History.
4. Yugoslavia—Race relations—History. 5. Former Yugoslav
Republics—History. I. Žagar, Mitja. II. Title. III. Series: Ethnic
diversity within nations.
DR1246.K59 2003
949.7'004—dc22

                                                    2003018390

07 06 05 04 🙙 10 9 8 7 6 5 4 3 2 1

This book is also available on the World Wide Web as an e-book.
Visit abc-clio.com for details.

ABC-CLIO, Inc.
130 Cremona Drive, P.O. Box 1911
Santa Barbara, California 93116-1911

This book is printed on acid-free paper.
Manufactured in the United States of America

Contents

Series Editor's Foreword

We think of the United States as a nation of peoples, with some describing it as a mosaic, a stew, an orchestra, and even yet as a melting pot. In the American vision of diversity the whole is perceived as greater than the sum of its parts—groups of peoples unify into a national identity. Not all Americans have shared that vision, or, to the extent that they initially did, they considered diversity as groups of people with shades of difference—such as shades of whiteness or variants of Protestantism. Many of the early newcomers would come to represent the core of an American society wherein distinctions were expected to fade by and large because a unity was anticipated that would be greater than any one homogeneous racial or ethnic national community. That unity would be forged through a common commitment to the American system of republicanism and a shared set of political principles and values—collectively, America's civic culture. For decades the diversity that was recognized (essentially in terms of religion and nationality) did not appear to be so formidable as to constitute a barrier to nationhood—as long as one did not look beyond the whiteness to the African and Native American (and later Latino and Asian) peoples. By rendering such groups invisible, if not beyond the pale, majority groups did not perceive them as representing a challenge to, or a denial of, the national unity. They were simply left out of the picture until, eventually, they would compel the majority to confront the nation's true composition and its internal contradictions. And, even before that more complex confrontation took place, streams of (mostly) European newcomers steadily stretched the boundaries of the nation's diversity, requiring a reexamination of the bonds of nationhood, the elements of nationality, and the core society and values. By World War II and in the ensuing two decades it became more and more difficult to ignore the impact of a dual development—the expanding Latino and Asian immigration and the arrival of far more diverse groups of European newcomers. To secure their national vision, Americans had (albeit reluctantly and not without conflict) to make rather profound and fundamental adjustments to many of those components that had served as the nation's bonds, particularly the perception of America as a multicultural society and the belief that pluralism was a legitimate and inherent part of American society and culture.

To what extent has this scenario of a nation of peoples been present elsewhere in the world? Where have others struggled to overcome racial, religious, tribal, and nationality differences in order to construct—or to preserve—a nation? Perhaps one might even ask where, by the late twentieth century, had others *not* experienced such struggles? In how many of the principal nations has there long been present a homogeneity of people around which a nation could be molded and shaped with little danger of internal discord threatening the overall fabric of national unity? On the other hand, in how many countries has there been present a multiplicity of peoples, as in the United States, who have had to forge a nation out of a disparate array of peoples? Was that multiplicity the product of in-migrations joining a core society as it has been in the United States, or was there a historic mosaic of tribes, bands, and other more-or-less organized entities that eventually adhered together as their discovered commonalities outweighed their differences? Or, do we see invasions from without and unity imposed from above, or the emergence of one group gradually extending its dominance over the others—installing unity from below? Did any of these variations result in nation-states comparable to the United States—the so-called first new nation—and, if so, what have been the points of similarity and difference, the degrees of stability or unrest? Have their diversities endured, or have they been transmuted, absorbed, or suppressed? How much strain have those states experienced in trying to balance the competing demands among majority and minority populations? In other words, where nation-states have emerged by enveloping or embracing (or subjugating) diverse peoples, what have been the resulting histories in terms of intergroup relations and intergroup strains as well as the extent of effective foundations of national unity?

The challenges of coexistence (voluntarily or otherwise) remain the same whether two or twenty people are involved. The issue is what traditions, institutions, concepts, principles, and experiences enable particular combinations of peoples to successfully bond and what factors cause others to fall prey to periodic unrest and civil wars? Finally, many upheavals have taken place over the past 150 years, during which in-migrations have penetrated nations that were previously homogenous or were sending nations (experiencing more out-migration than in-migration) and were less prepared to address the rather novel diversities. Have theses nations had institutions, values, and traditions that enabled them to take on success-fully such new challenges?

Examples abound beyond the borders of the United States that require us to examine the claims of American exceptionalism (that America's multiculturalism has been a unique phenomenon) or, at the very least, to understand it far better. Canada and Australia have had indigenous peo-ples but have also long been receiving nations for immigrants—however, usually far more selectively than has the United States. Brazil and Argentina were, for decades in the late nineteenth and early twentieth centuries, important immigrant-receiving nations, too, with long-term consequences for their societies. Long before there were Indian and Yugo-slavian nation-states there were myriad peoples in those regions who struggled and competed and then with considerable external pressures, strained to carve out a stable multiethnic unity based on tribal, religious, linguistic, or racial (often including groups labeled "racial" that are not actually racially different from their neighbors) differences. Nigeria, like other African countries, has had a history of multiple tribal populations that have competed and have endured colonialism and then suffered a lengthy, sometimes bloody, contest to cement those peoples into a stable nation-state. In the cases of South Africa and Russia there were a variety of native populations, too, but outsiders entered and eventually estab-lished their dominance and imposed a unity of sorts. Iran is representa-tive of the Middle Eastern/Western Asian nations that have been for cen-turies the crossroads for many peoples who have migrated to the region, fought there, settled there, and been converted there, subsequently having to endure tumultuous histories that have included exceedingly complex struggles to devise workable national unities. In contrast, England and France have been tangling with about two generations of newly arrived diverse populations from the Asian subcontinent, the West Indies, and Africa that are particularly marked by racial and religious differences (apart from the historic populations that were previously wedded into those nation-states), while Germans and Poles have had minorities in their communities for centuries until wars and genocidal traumas took their toll, rendering those ethnic stories more history than on-going con-temporary accounts—but significant nonetheless.

The point is that most nation-states in the modern world are not like Japan, with its 1 percent or so of non-Japanese citizens. Multiethnicity and multiculturalism have become more the rule than the exception, whether of ancient or more recent origins, with unity from below or from above. Moreover, as suggested, the successes and failures of these experiments in multiethnic nation-states compel us to consider what traditions, values, institutions, customs, political precedents, and historical encounters have contributed to those successes (including that of the United States) and failures. What can Americans learn from the realization that their own history—by no means without its own conflicts and dark times—has parallels elsewhere and, as well, numerous points of difference from the experiences of most other nations? Do we come away understanding America better? Hopefully.

An important objective of the Ethnic Diversity Within Nations series is to help readers in America and elsewhere better appreciate how societies in many parts of the world have struggled with the challenges of diversity and, by providing such an understanding, enable all of us to interact more effectively with each other. Thus, by helping students and other readers learn about these varied nations, our goal with this series is to see them become better-informed citizens that are better able to comprehend world events and better able to act responsibly as voters, officeholders, teachers, public officials, and businesspersons, or simply when interacting and co-existing with diverse individuals, whatever the sources of that diversity.

Elliott Robert Barkan

Preface

This book on the history of the territory, peoples, and nations of the former Yugoslavia (which has borne the names Kingdom of Serbs, Croats, and Slovenes; Kingdom of Yugoslavia; Federal People's Republic of Yugoslavia; and Socialist Federative Republic of Yugoslavia) presents a very complex story, actually several historically interwoven stories, of this region's peoples and ethno-nations.

The ethnic communities that developed into these various Yugoslav nations have throughout their histories undergone many transformations. Initially they emerged as peoples of South Slavic origin between the fifth and ninth centuries, during the migration of peoples who later developed medieval feudal states ruled by local rulers (from the seventh century on). After the collapse of these states, the western part of the territory of the former Yugoslavia was ruled by the Habsburgs (later the Austro-Hungarian Monarchy), and the eastern part belonged to the Ottoman Empire. The histories of the medieval states as predecessors of modern nations shaped their national identities and consciousness from the middle of the eighteenth century. In the nineteenth century these communities started to transform into modern nations that formulated national(ist) programs and immediate demands, such as the right to education in their own language. These programs reflected the fact that the actual ethnic boundaries did not correspond to the existing administrative borders. The introduction of dualism in the Habsburg Monarchy transformed this empire into Austria-Hungary in 1867 and resulted in its formal division into two units—Austrian and Hungarian. Within the Ottoman Empire, vassal states of Serbs and Montenegrins were established (still under suzerainty of the Ottoman Empire) that gained their independence in the nineteenth century.

World War I changed the picture. The "unification" of the kingdoms of Serbia and Montenegro with the South Slavic territory of the former Austria-Hungary resulted in the formation of a new state—the Kingdom of

Serbs, Croats, and Slovenes—in 1918. This state was renamed the Kingdom of Yugoslavia in 1929. In 1941 its territory was occupied and divided
by Axis forces. The formation of the "new" Yugoslav federation within the
national liberation movement started during World War II when the
Democratic Federal Yugoslavia was established in 1943. The Federal People's Republic of Yugoslavia was formally established in 1945. It was renamed the Socialist Federative Republic of Yugoslavia in 1963. This country existed until 1991, when it disintegrated into five independent states:
the Republic of Slovenia, the Republic of Croatia, the State of Bosnia and
Herzegovina, the Federal Republic of Yugoslavia (including Serbia and
Montenegro), and the Republic of Macedonia.

The development of the country, usually called the former Yugoslavia,
can be divided into two main stages. In the first stage, the establishment of
the Yugoslav monarchy initially brought hopes of a democratic development that soon proved unrealistic. This unitary (and unitaristic) monarchy denied the very existence of ethnic pluralism and limited political
pluralism, which became especially evident after the introduction of the
(fascist) dictatorship of King Alexander (Aleksandar) in 1929. In the second stage, after World War II, the existence of ethnic pluralism was recognized, and the Yugoslav federation was declared a multinational state.
Nevertheless, the "communist" dictatorship of President Tito, who was at
first a harsh ruler but was later (after his split with Stalin) described as a
benign dictator in the West, limited the political pluralism that is considered a precondition of a (Western-type) democracy.

The post–World War II period can be divided into two stages: The first
stage was the period of administrative socialism until 1950–1953. This
stage was characterized by the introduction of a centralized Soviet-type
federation and system of command economy, based on the state ownership of means of production; following the nationalization of private
property, especially industry, companies, and larger farms, the state became the sole owner of means of production and directed a centralized national "planned" economy. The beginning of the second stage was marked
by the introduction of workers' self-management in 1950, which in 1953
was transformed into socialist self-management. In the second stage, state
property was formally transformed into a social ownership of means of
production that was supposed to be controlled by organized workers. The
initial slogan was "Factories to the workers," but this social ownership was
soon introduced in other fields as well. The same model of the participation of workers and citizens was also introduced in politics. Although this
system never functioned as envisioned, it changed the previous system and

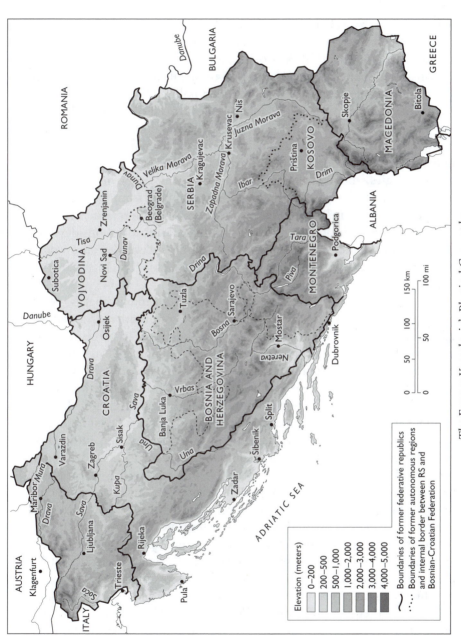

The Former Yugoslavia's Physical Geography

From the point of view of physical geography the territory of the former Yugoslavia is not unified. The plains to the north provide some open areas, but among the chains of mountains, the plateaus and basins are sharply divided.

opened space for pluralism and democratization, which made it substantially different from all other "communist" systems in Eastern Europe.

The political history of the territory, peoples, and nations of the former Yugoslavia is only a part of the story. Ethnic histories of these peoples and nations were shaped parallel with this political history. Both histories were interwoven: the previously mentioned political history affected ethnic histories and, in turn, ethnic histories influenced the political history. Specific political and ethnic histories also shaped endemic terminology used in the former Yugoslavia to describe diverse phenomena. This terminology was influenced by contemporary politics and (political and ethnic) ideologies—nationalism(s), the unitary monarchy, Soviet-type communism, and the system of socialist self-management from the 1950s.

In the Significant People, Places, and Events section of each chapter readers can find brief explanations of specific terms that we considered to be unfamiliar to an average reader in the West. However, here we would like to present a few key terms (and theoretical concepts) used in this book.

The term ethnicity can have several different meanings, that is, being ethnic, belonging to a certain ethnic group or community, or an ethnic group and/or community itself. Ethnicity is based on (a perception of) common historic origins or of shared culture, religion, and/or language. Ethnicity also implies shared ethnic identity. The perception of ethnicity in Europe differs from the one in the United States. In Europe it is traditionally defined not only with a common history, culture, ethnic identity, religion, and/or language, but also includes the traditional territory of settlement of a certain ethnic community. In this context, the autochthonous settlement is usually considered an important element in defining a certain ethnicity. In this book the term ethnic community is used as a general term that describes all types of social organization based on ethnicity (ethnically determined groups and communities).

Premodern culturally and ethnically determined communities (those that existed before the formation of modern nations and nation-states) are described as historic peoples (according to Hegel, it was by definition those nations that had their own states). Historic peoples, as with all types of ethnic communities, were characterized by common historic origins and by shared culture, religion, and/or language. Their existence did not necessarily depend on the existence of common states. Nevertheless, their identity was traditionally connected with a territory of their autochthonous settlement. Such a territory was often declared to be the "sacred lands" of a certain nation during the historic process of the formation of modern (European) nations in the nineteenth century. This perception denied the traditional existence of multiethnic societies everywhere in Europe and also in other parts of the world. Especially in cases in which different ethnic communities all claimed the same territory as their (exclusive) sacred lands, this perception became a possible source of (ethnic) conflicts—which proved tragically true in southeastern Europe. Although the populations of the Medieval Balkan states (between the sixth and fifteenth centuries) were linguistically and ethnically very diverse, they are nowadays often perceived as ethnically based states and as predecessors of modern nations and nation-states in the region.

As a specific type of ethnic community, a modern (European) nation (by some also called ethno-nation) is defined as "a stable, historically developed community of people with a territory (specific) economic life, distinctive culture, and language in common" (*Webster's New Universal Unabridged Dictionary*, 1983, 1196). Besides the previously mentioned criteria, we will add to this definition the existence of a national identity as an important element: individuals have a will to be a member of a certain nation, and an individual wants to be recognized by other members of such an ethnic community as its member. In most environments, especially in local communities, ethnicity still plays a central role in political socialization and self-identification. Ethnic identities often remain the strongest collective identities in plural societies and have proven to be able, in specific circumstances, to override individual identities or other collective identities.

One factor contributing to this is the prevailing perception that the existing states are, or should be, ethnically based nation-states. Although modern societies are ethnically diverse, nation-states are perceived as ethnically homogenous states of their "titular nations," defined in ethnic terms, and as the most effective tool for the realization of their "national interests." In this context, the existing ethnic diversity, especially the existence of ethnic minorities, is often considered a problem. The emergence of modern nations went hand in hand with the process of formation of modern nation-states. This emergence of nations was often conditioned on the existence of nation-states, and sometimes vice versa, as was usually the case in southeastern Europe. In this process states that were established and perceived as single nation-states of titular nations acquired an ethnic identity. This concept could be explained by a simple equation: State = nation = people (Hobsbawm, 1990, 23).

We should note that in (South) Slavic languages the term "nation" does not necessarily imply political statehood. An ethnic community can also become a nation without establishing a state of its own as a prerequisite. Such a definition of a nation was also developed by the leading Slovene and Yugoslav Marxist ideologue Edvard Kardelj, who stressed the importance of historical and cultural criteria in defining a nation as a specific historic ethnic community (Kardelj 1977).

The emergence of ethnically based nation-states also resulted in the creation of (traditional) national (ethnic) minorities as we know them today. When a state as a nation-state of a titular nation acquired its ethnic identity, all its citizens who did not belong to this ethnicity became members of ethnic minorities. Francesco Capotorti defines an ethnic minority as a group "numerically inferior to the rest of the population of a state; in a non-dominant position; whose members—being nationals of the state—possess ethnic, religious or linguistic characteristics differing from those of the rest of the population; and show, if only implicitly, a sense of solidarity, directed towards preserving their culture, traditions, religion or language" (Capotorti 1991, 96).

An additional element in the definition of traditional national minorities is that they live as distinct autochthonous communities in the territory of their traditional settlement. This differentiates them from other ethnic minorities. The Constitution of the Socialist Federal Republic of Yugoslavia of 1963 replaced the traditional term "national minority" with the term "nationality." The term "nationality" was intended to express a new ethnic policy that established these minorities as equal communities, ensuring their equal status and rights. This new terminology was also meant to abolish the possible pejorative connotations of the traditional term "minority," which might have implied inequality (unequal status).

For the presentation of ethnic relations in the former Yugoslavia it is necessary to explain the federal structures and arrangements after World War II. Post–World War II constitutions defined Yugoslavia as a federation consisting of six republics. The status of republics within the federation was constantly changing. Their autonomy and independence were growing with the process of decentralization that increased, especially after the adoption of the second Constitution of the Socialist Federal Republic of Yugoslavia of 1974. Nevertheless, the constituent elements of the Yugoslav federation were also autonomous regions and provinces that were simultaneously constituent parts of the (Socialist) Republic of Serbia. These specific federal units were established to ensure the equality and special rights of traditional national minorities that traditionally lived in the territories of Vojvodina and Kosovo (Kosovo and Metohia or Kosmet) and represented a local majority, or at least a substantial share of the local population. The federal constitution of 1974 equalized the status of both autonomous units, defined as autonomous provinces.

One also cannot explain ethnic relations in the territory of the former Yugoslavia without reference to internal and external migrations, which, to a large extent, shaped ethnic diversity in this region. Reasons for migrations and the nature of those migrations were changing over time. Wars, the search for adequate territory for settlement, and natural disasters (including famine) were typical reasons for migrations in earlier historic periods. Economic and political reasons later started to play more important roles, especially in the past two centuries. Constantly changing administrative conditions and borders especially complicate the definition of internal and external migrations. All migrations within the existing historic states (i.e., Ottoman Empire, Habsburg Empire and Austria-Hungary, Yugoslavia) could be defined as internal migrations during the existence of these states. Migrations across internationally recognized borders should be considered external migrations. In this context, migration within the former federal Yugoslavia, even if people crossed republic borders, should be considered internal migrations. When the former republics became independent states after the disintegration of the Yugoslav federation, such migrations became external migrations.

This book would not have been possible without the generous assistance during the past three years of numerous individuals and institutions. We cannot name all here. However, we would like thank all of them and express special thanks to some.

The idea for the Ethnic Diversity Within Nations series came from Elliot Barkan at the history department at the University of California at San Bernardino. Once this book was conceived he offered his advice first on how to start and then offered his guidance chapter by chapter and contributed his expertise in editing the manuscript, without which this book would not be possible. Judith Rosenblatt from the Immigration History Research Center at the University of Minnesota helped us by contributing linguistic editing of the text. She tried to understand our nonnative speakers' English and helped us clarify the meanings of some words and concepts.

We thank Zmago Drole for creating the maps and helping us gather statistical and other materials. Nada Vilhar and others from the Specialized Documentation and Information Center of the Institute for Ethnic Studies in Ljubljana helped tremendously by gathering bibliographies and literature, but especially by collecting materials from contemporary newspapers. The staffs of the National and University Library in Ljubljana and the Library of the Institute for Ethnic Studies in Ljubljana were also helpful.

We would like to thank the staff of ABC-CLIO for their contribution. Alicia Meritt was very helpful in the initial phases of creating this book. Her coordinating effort was then taken over by Carol Smith. Our copy editor, Raven Moore Amerman, also gave her important contribution, providing us with more than 700 questions and remarks in order to make the text of the book more understandable and readable for a general audience. Scott Horst, the media editor from ABC-CLIO, helped us in gathering the artwork for the book.

Samo Kristen of the Institute for Ethnic Studies in Ljubljana helped us by reading the final version of the text and helped us further improve the manuscript and correct some factual errors. His contribution is invaluable. We would like to thank also the leadership of the University of Maribor and University of Ljubljana as well as the Institute for Ethnic Studies.

In thanking everybody for their contribution and help that, no doubt, made this book a much better text, we need stress that the blame for all possible errors, mistakes, and shortcomings is exclusively on us.

We would like to thank our families for the nuisances they had to put up with in various stages of making of this book.

Bibliography

Capotorti, Francesco. *Study on the Rights of Persons Belonging to Ethnic, Religious, and Linguistic Minorities.* (New York: United Nations, 1991).

Gellner, Ernest. *Nations and Nationalism.* (Ithaca, NY: Cornell University Press, 1983).

Hobsbawm, Eric J. *Nations and Nationalism since 1789: Programme, Myth, Reality.* (Cambridge, UK: Cambridge University Press, 1990).

Jenkins, Richard. *Rethinking Ethnicity: Arguments and Explorations.* (London: SAGE Publications, 1997).

Kardelj, Edvard (Spcrans). *Razvoj slovenskega narodnega vprašanja* (The Development of the Slovene National Question). (Ljubljana, Slovenia: Državna Založba Slovenije, 1977).

Macartney, C. A. *National States and National Minorities.* (Humprey Milford, U.K.: Oxford University Press, 1984).

Seton-Watson, Hough. *Nations and States.* (London: Methuen, 1977).

Smith, Anthony D. *The Ethnic Origins of Nations.* (Oxford: Basil Blackwell, 1986).

Webster's New Universal Unabridged Dictionary, 2nd ed. (New York: Dorset & Baber, 1983).

List of Maps

CHAPTER ONE

The South Slavic Peoples

Sixth Century to the Early Nineteenth Century

ALTHOUGH WE COULD START THIS BOOK much farther back in history, we begin this review of ethnic history with the settlement of the South Slavs, who are considered predecessors of modern nations, in the territory of the former Yugoslavia. This settlement occurred during the second period of the great east-to-west migrations of peoples in the sixth and seventh centuries, following the first wave of migrations during which Germanic peoples had been on the move from east to west. However, we do take into account relevant earlier developments that influenced the history of South Slavic peoples.

The medieval states of the South Slavic peoples and the impact of powerful empires of the time, such as the Byzantine Empire, were important for the creation of historic lands, their social and political institutions, and consequently for the emergence of the modern South Slavic nations. These medieval states, reinterpreted by myths of various ethnic groups, became the foundation of the South Slavic people's ethnic identity. Although these mythical interpretations often do not correspond to reality, they form the identities of the modern Slovene, Croatian, Bosniak, Serb, Montenegrin, and Macedonian nations and continue to have an impact on social and political processes and events in the beginning of the twenty-first century.

Settlement of South Slavs

Before the second period of great migrations of the peoples in Europe in the sixth and seventh centuries, the Slavs settled in the region between the Carpathian Mountains in the south and the Baltic Sea in the north and between the eastern river basin of Oder to the west and the Dnieper River to the east. (During the first migrations, starting in the fourth century, Germanic peoples had moved into this area and later into central and western Europe.) The first credible reports on Slavs were written by Greek and Roman writers (Plinius Sr., Tacitus, and Ptolomeius). According to Ptolomeius, the Slavs represented a great people—around 1.35 million Slavs lived in the region, which encompassed around 300,000 square miles.

Until the end of the fifth century, the Slavs lived north and east of the Carpathian Mountains. Linguists theorize that three dialects could be found among the Slavs of the region: Western-, Eastern- and South-Slavic. By the sixth century, the Slavs could be divided into three groups: Venetians (ancestors of the Western Slavs), Ants (ancestors of the Eastern Slavs), and Slavenes (ancestors of the South Slavs). At the beginning of the mid-sixth century Slavs migrated in various directions and in a number of waves, moving toward their future settlements. The Avars, a nomadic soldier people with a developed societal organization, pushed the Slavs, predominantly farmers, from the coasts of the Black Sea toward central and southeastern Europe. The Avars temporarily subjugated some Slavic tribes and, together with them, mounted military expeditions against the Byzantine Empire toward Dalmatia, Greece, and Constantinople. As nomads, the Avars then returned from these expeditions and migrated to the region between Tisa and the Danube River. Some Slav peasants and cattle breeders also started to settle permanently in this newly occupied region.

During the period of Slav-Avaric alliance, the South Slavs learned the art of war from the Avars and started to attack Byzantine regions south of the Danube. After the fall of Syrmium (today the town of Sremska Mitrovica in Serbia) into Slavic hands in 582 as the result of a Slav military victory, the Slavs began moving across and along the Danube River more frequently. In 614 they conquered Salona (today Split, a seaport in Croatia), which was the center of Dalmatia. The Slavic attacks went as far as Peloponnese and even Crete. The Slavic populations that settled permanently in these regions were later Hellenized. Until 620 the Slavs settled the vast regions of the Balkans. Croatian and Serb tribes settled the central Balkans (along the Morava River and south of the Sava River) between 622 and 640. Migratory waves were also coming from the areas of western and eastern Slavic settlements. The Slavic population mixed with the indigenous population between the Balkan Mountains and the Danube River; after 680, they also mixed with the ancestors of the Bulgarians (Protobulgarians).

With the settling of the Slavs in the vast regions of the Balkans, their economic activities, which had almost ceased during the previously men-

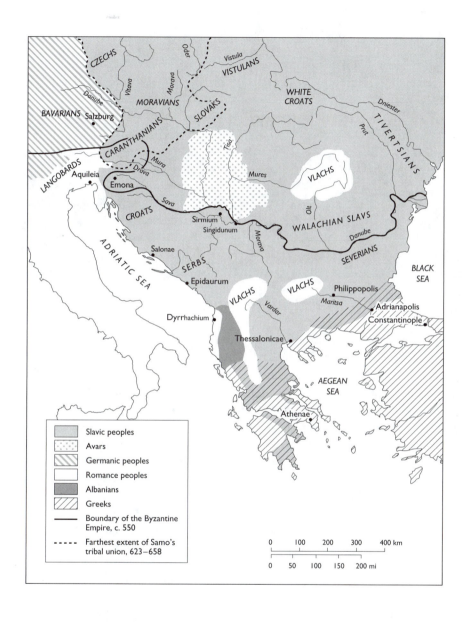

CZECHS

Oder

Vistula

VISTULANS

Vltava

Morava

MORAVIANS

SLOVAKS

WHITE
CROATS

Dniester

BAVARIANS Salzburg

Danube

CARANTHANIANS

Prut

T I V E R T S I A N S

LANGOBARDS

Drava

Mura

Tisa

Mures

VLACHS

Aquileia

Emona

Sava

CROATS

Sirmium

Singidunum

Morava

Olt

WALACHIAN SLAVS

Danube

ADRIATIC SEA

Salonae

SERBS

Epidaurum

VLACHS

VLACHS

Vardar

SEVERIANS

BLACK
SEA

Philippopolis

Maritsa

Adrianapolis

Constantinople

Dyrrhachium

Thessalonicae

AEGEAN
SEA

Athenae

Slavic peoples
Avars
Germanic peoples
Romance peoples
Albanians
Greeks

Boundary of the Byzantine
Empire, c. 550

Farthest extent of Samo's
tribal union, 623–658

0   100   200   300   400 km

0   50   100   150   200 mi

Southeastern Europe after Slav Settlement (Eighth Century)
The period of great migrations of Slavic tribes began after 500.
By 620, Slavs had settled the eastern Alps, the Pannonian and Walachian Plains,
and most of the Balkans. Only the Greeks, the Romanic population,
and the ancestors of the Albanians were preserved.

Roman amphitheater in Pula, Istria (Corel)

tioned military expeditions, were renewed. By the eighth century, the people again lived as farmers and cattle breeders. Byzantines reigned, but only at the shores of the Mediterranean. Of course, the indigenous peoples did not disappear after the Serbs moved into the region. The Greeks lived in the region of Constantinople, on the Greek peninsula, and on the shores of the Aegean and Ionian Seas. The Romanic peoples remained in mid-Greece, on the shores of the Adriatic Sea, and in some mountainous regions of the Balkan Peninsula. They are today known as Vlachs. The ancestors of today's Albanians persevered in the southeastern Adriatic and in the mountains of what is today Albania.

During the period of the first Slavic successes, when they occupied the regions south of the Danube, they also settled the regions of the eastern Alps and Pannonia, where the ancestors of today's Slovenes started to move through the so-called Moravian Pass around 550. Soon after, the Germanic tribe of the Langobards moved westward to the Friuli Plain (north of the Gulf of Trieste). After 568 the Slavs started to move into Pannonia (up to the Balaton Lake in today's Hungary). The Alpine Slavs (ancestors of the Slovenes) settled as far as the springs of the Zilja, Mura, Drava, and Traun Rivers and up to the Danube in the north and the west; to Chiemsee Lake in Bavaria; and up to Balaton Lake in the east. Until 620 they also settled the hinterland of Romanic cities in Istria and today's border regions between Italy and Slovenia (Resia, Venetian Slovenia, and Goriška Brda). Geographically, the region of settlement of the Alpine Slavs in the ninth century encompassed 70,000 square kilometers. As historic maps show, it has become substantially smaller during the intervening centuries. At the springs of Drava and the Danube River, the Alpine Slavs bordered the land of the Bavarians; between the Drava River and the Istrian Peninsula they bordered the ancestors of today's Croatians.

The Slavic settlement in the region south of the Danube River substantially influenced the course of European history. Large regions of eastern and southeastern Europe were settled with Slavs. The Germanic tribes who settled the same regions (during the first migrations of historic peoples) moved west, and the Slavic settlements in these regions persist until today. Also, the fact that the Slavs created different states helped them to preserve their hold over large parts of the conquered territories.

Prior to the settlement of the South Slavs, the frontier between the western and eastern parts of the Roman Empire had been drawn in the same territories as the ones the Slavs eventually settled in. Later, during the Middle Ages, here lay the frontier between the Muslim Ottoman Empire and Christian Europe. And in still later periods, these same lands marked the borderline between the Eastern and Western worlds. Periods of peace did not occur too often there, and because of the many wars there was always uncertainty among the population.

South Slavic Territories from the Ninth to the Fourteenth Century

The geographic expanse of South Slavic settlement was reduced during later periods, especially in the Pannonian Plain (because of new Hungarian settlements after 896); between the Danube and Drava Rivers in the Eastern Alps (due to German colonization between the ninth and fifteenth centuries); and in the southernmost part of the Balkan Peninsula (as a result of Greek colonization and the influence of the civilization of the Greek cities that resulted in the Hellenization of the Slavs in the Greek Peninsula).

The most important factor in changing the situation of the South Slavs was the Hungarian settlement in the Middle Danubian Basin. On one hand, the Hungarians destroyed Frankish rule and the German ring, which, in the ninth century, had started to enclose the nucleus of future Slovene territory in the Eastern Alps from the north and east. German settlements cut the Slovenes off from the Western Slavs and made

Germanization of this territory possible. On the other hand, by conquering what were the Slavic territories, the Hungarians succeeded in interrupting the connection among the territories of Western Slavic and South Slavic settlements.

The period from around 900 until 1200 saw substantial changes in the cultural development of the South Slavs, which resulted in the formation of several ethnic nuclei. In the ninth century, the first Slavic literary language came into being as a result of the missionary action of Constantine (Cyril) and Methodius. This language was based on the Slavic language spoken in the vicinity of Salonika, where the ancestors of today's Macedonians lived.

Because of influences from neighboring political and cultural areas (the German Empire, Hungary, and Italy), the unity of South Slavs started to dissipate. Especially important was the schism of the Eastern and Western Christian churches into Orthodoxy and Roman Catholicism in 1054, which meant, among other things, the division of the Catholic South Slavs (modern Slovenes and Croats) from the Orthodox South Slavs (modern Serbs, Montenegrins, Macedonians, and Bulgarians).

As results of these events and processes, frontiers emerged in the region of South Slavic settlements during the course of the eleventh and twelfth centuries that caused different historical developments and substantial cultural and religious differences among South Slavic peoples. As the following chapters will show, these differences resulted in the emergence and development of the modern South Slavic ethnic nations. The border of the German Empire at the Kolpa and Sotla Rivers helped to determine the ethnic frontier between Slovenes and Croats (with the exception of Istria). To the north, Croatia succeeded in establishing a border on the Drava River that later ethnically divided Croats and Hungarians, even though they lived in the same state.

With permanent settlements, South Slavic tribes started the process of transforming their tribal units into individual ethnic nuclei that developed into their first feudal states (principalities). These first feudal principalities strengthened their positions in the ninth century but did not succeed in retaining their independence. They were forced to capitulate to their more powerful neighbors (the German Empire, the Hungarian Kingdom, Venice, and the Ottoman Empire). However, some of them survived as vassals of those powerful neighbors for many centuries.

Parallel to this process of gradually losing their independence, the South Slavic principalities also experienced the beginning of the spread of Christianity, especially during the eighth and ninth centuries. It spread

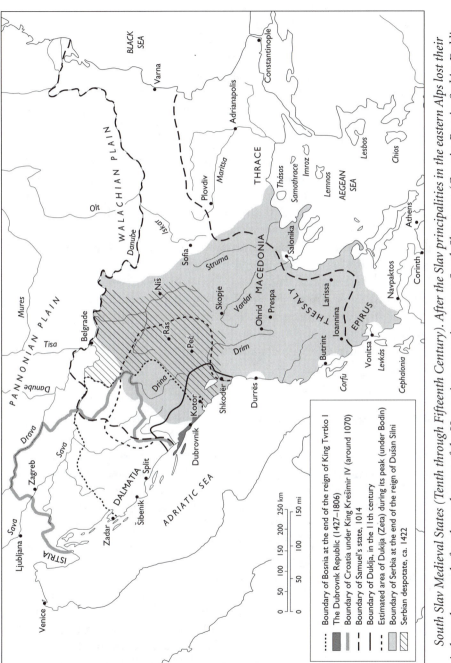

South Slav Medieval States (Tenth through Fifteenth Century). After the Slav principalities in the eastern Alps lost their independence and after the settlement of the Hungarians, some important South Slav states (Croatia, Bosnia, Serbia, Duklja, Samuel's state) came into being in the center of the region. Until the beginning of the fifteenth century these states lost their independence. Dubrovnik Republic remained independent from 1358 to 1808, but it paid taxes to powerful neighbors.

Boundary of Bosnia at the end of the reign of King Tvrtko I
The Dubrovnik Republic (1427–1806)
Boundary of Croatia under King Krešimir IV (around 1070)
Boundary of Samuel's state, 1014
Boundary of Duklja, in the 11th century
Estimated area of Duklja (Zeta) during its peak (under Bodin)
Boundary of Serbia at the end of the reign of Dušan Silni
Serbian despotate, ca. 1422

BLACK SEA
Varna
WALACHIAN PLAIN
Constantinople
Adrianopolis
Olt
Plovdiv
Maritsa
THRACE
Danube
Iskar
Thásos
Samothrace
Imroz
Lemnos
Lesbos
Chios
AEGEAN SEA
Sofia
Struma
MACEDONIA
Salonika
Niš
Skopje
Vardar
Ohrid
Prespa
THESSALY
Larissa
Navpaktos
Athens
Corinth
Belgrade
Ras
Peć
Drim
Ioannina
EPIRUS
Mureş
Tisa
PANNONIAN PLAIN
Butrint
Vonitsa
Levkás
Corfu
Cephalonia
Drina
Kotor
Shkodër
Durrës
Danube
Drava
Sava
Zagreb
Sava
Split
Šibenik
DALMATIA
Zadar
Dubrovnik
ADRIATIC SEA
Ljubljana
Sava
ISTRIA
Venice

250 km
200
150
100
50
0

150 mi
100
50
0

from Constantinople in its eastern version and from Rome in its western version, so that the old border between the former western and eastern halves of the Roman Empire began to reappear—this time as a new religious and cultural border between people of otherwise rather ethnically unified Christianized South Slavic populations. As a consequence, from the beginning of the tenth century on, individual South Slavic ethnic nuclei developed in fundamentally different ways that strengthened after the schism of 1054.

Also, the Crusades (from the eleventh to the thirteenth century) were very important events in the development of the South Slavic states. On the one hand, the influence of Western European culture and civilization strengthened in the western part of the Slavic states, while the eastern regions felt themselves to be even more under the influence of Constantinople. On the other hand, the Crusades strengthened religious fanaticism and deepened the differences between the Catholic and Orthodox churches. In this context we should mention especially the Fourth Crusade, when the Catholic Crusaders (with the help of Venice), instead of going toward Jerusalem to liberate the Holy Land, went toward Zadar and in 1204 against Constantinople, which marked the beginning of the end of the Byzantine Empire. This changed the status of almost all South Slavic states, especially Serbia, as these medieval Slavic states played the roles of regional powers.

South Slavic Territories from the Fourteenth to the Nineteenth Century

During the second half of the fourteenth century, the South Slavic territories began to be threatened by the Turks, a threat that had a great impact on the history of South Slavs and the rest of Europe. For almost five centuries all South Slavic lands experienced Turkish conquests or wars with the Turkish army. The Turkish occupation of the southeastern South Slavic territories left especially deep imprints. Although the Turkish army did not actually occupy the northwestern South Slavic territories, it threatened them—at least with occasional incursions that they had to fight off. It is often said that these territories were fighting the Turkish threat not only for themselves but also for Europe. The Turkish danger and constant fighting put the brakes on the area's natural economic and cultural development and were among the reasons that, in later historic epochs, the South Slavic territories lagged behind the more developed parts of Europe.

The Turks came into Europe for the first time during the years 1354–1357, when they occupied Gallipoli. During the next two centuries they slowly but surely conquered the Balkans. The Turkish Ottoman Empire reached its climax in the middle of the sixteenth century when it occupied Syria, Egypt, Mesopotamia, Hungary, and parts of the Arabian Peninsula. In 1529 the Turkish Army came before Vienna for the first time.

However, in 1683 the Austrian Imperial Army defeated the Turks outside Vienna, signaling the beginning of the end of the Ottoman Empire. By 1699, the Austrians had reconquered all the Hungarian plains and established the frontier with the Ottoman Empire on the Sava and Danube Rivers.

Many parts of what is now the former Yugoslavia fell victim to the Turkish conquest. The Turks ruled Macedonia for more than 500 years, Serbia and Bosnia for 400 years, and some areas north of Sava and the Danube and Dalmatia for 150 years. During this period the ethnic structure of certain areas was completely altered; Turkish conquests caused changes such as had not happened since the first settlements of South Slavs during the sixth and seventh centuries.

At the outset, the Turks colonized their newly conquered territories with settlers from other parts of the Ottoman Empire of different ethnic origins (Yuruks, Armenians, and others). Significant numbers of the Christian peoples of Macedonia, Serbia, Bosnia, and Dalmatia fled north. They were settled in the military border regions, where they accepted military duties to guard the border. In exchange they were given their land for farming without feudal obligations. The Serbs who fled north settled vast territories of southern Hungary, especially Slavonia, western Croatia, and the interior of Dalmatia; they also settled western Bosnia. This colonization was organized by the Ottoman Empire as well as by the Habsburg Monarchy. Many of the descendants of the relocated peoples moved back to their peoples' original settlements in the nineteenth century, but others remained in their "new" settlements until the 1990s.

At the end of the fifteenth century, for military purposes, the Turkish authorities started to resettle these vast areas (which had been deserted because of the wars between the Ottoman Empire and the Habsburg Empire and Russia) with Orthodox Christian farmers, who in exchange for their military service were exempted from feudal obligations. The Turkish authorities employed this population as the first line of defense of the Ottoman Empire, and they were given special privileges in so-called military Krajinas. (The word *krajina* comes from the Serbo-Croatian word *kraj*, meaning end, or edge. The name of the region, *Vojna krajina*, means military frontier zone.) A similar defense system was organized by the Habsburgs beginning in the second half of the sixteenth century in a military frontier region (Vojna krajina) on their borders with the Turkish Empire. Their sources of soldiers were mostly the Serbs, who had fled the Turks. In exchange for military service, they got farmland and some other privileges. For centuries, both the Habsburgs and Turks included tens of thousands of inhabitants from their respective sides of their border in their military expeditions, so that the Orthodox Serbs from the Austrian side of the border were fighting the Orthodox Serbs from the Turkish side.

After the Turks failed to conquer Vienna during the years 1683–1699, the Austrian army went on to conquer vast regions of the Balkans (northern Bosnia, Serbia, Kosovo, and northern Macedonia). The non-Muslim Slavic population there welcomed them as liberators. When the Austrian army had to retreat, the non-Muslim Slavic population retreated with them. As a result, the Serbs moved from Kosovo to Vojvodina (which remained under Austrian occupation). These were the so-called "Great Migrations." The leader of this population was Vladika (Orthodox Bishop) Arsenius III Crnojević. The Turks settled Albanian cattle breeders in the previous Serb settlements in Kosovo and Metohia.

During the course of the eighteenth century, the greatest changes in ethnic structure of the population occurred in Vojvodina, which was by then almost completely deserted due to the ravages of war. After the war ended and Vojvodina fell into Austrian hands they resettled this territory with the Serbs, Hungarians, and Romanians. In spite of this colonization of the region, Vojvodina had a very low population density until the Austrian authorities started to colonize it with members of all the ethnic groups that lived in the Monarchy, mostly Germans and Hungarians. They also settled many Czechs, Slovaks, Ukrainians, and Ruthenians here. Thus, Vojvodina (today's northern Serbia-Montenegro) became one of the most ethnically mixed regions in Europe, and this ethnic mix remains even today. Greater movements of populations occurred during the same period into modern Bosnia and Herzegovina, Serbia, Montenegro, and Macedonia. These migrations thus changed the ethnic structure and ethnic frontiers in the Balkans.

The most important consequence of the Turkish rule is that even today there are large numbers of Muslims in Macedonia, Kosovo, Sandžak, and Bosnia and Herzegovina. The Muslims (with the exception of those in Kosovo and Macedonia) spoke Serbo-Croatian but had a separate cultural identity from the others in the region. In fact, although under foreign occupation for so many years, the South Slavic peoples succeeded in retaining their languages and other ethnic characteristics. They also retained a feeling of mutual interrelationship. During the modern period of national awakening from the end of the eighteenth century onward these feelings were strengthened, and national movements led to the establishment of separate national consciousnesses. However, this feeling of mutual relationship and brotherhood contributed to the creation of a common state in the twentieth century.

Histories of the South Slavic Nations

Slovenes

During the first decades after their settlement in the Eastern Alps around the year A.D. 600, the ancestors of the Slovenes were still under the rule of the Avars, a nomadic tribe. In the seventh century a substantial independent region of Slavs, Marca Vinedorum, developed in the region of what is today southern Carinthia. Under Prince Valuk it became a part of Prince Samo's tribal union, which, under Prince Samo of Moravia, spread from

Primož Trubar, Slovene protestant minister who published the first books in the Slovene language (Enciklopedija Slovenije. *Ljubljana, Slovenia: Mladinska knjiga, 1999, p. 373)*

what is today southwestern Poland to the Julian Alps and Drava River and from Chiemsee to Balaton Lake. The ancestors of the Slovenes escaped the Avars' rule and, together with other Slavic tribes that were part of Samo's tribal union, successfully fought off German attacks and German attempts to spread Christianity. During this time a new name developed for the region of South Slavic settlement in the Eastern Alps—Carantania (named after the Roman settlement Civitas Carantana in today's Zollfeld/Gosposvetsko polje (field) in southern Carinthia/Austria). After Samo's tribal union collapsed, Carantania remained free. When the pressure of the Avars again increased, Carantanians, under their prince, Borut, had to seek help from the Bavarians and, consequently, had to accept their supreme authority. Yet, in spite of Bavarian and, later (after 788), Frankish rule, the Carantanians were still ruled by their own princes. They retained their ritual of installation of the prince (and later the duke), which, although the ceremony changed, was performed in the Slovene language until 1414. This ritual installation of the dukes of Carinthia, who received their power from the peasants, suggests that Slovenes enjoyed one of the oldest traditions of democratic autonomy in Europe.

At the end of the eighth century, south of the Karavanke Mountains in what is today central Slovenia, another Slavic principality developed, Carniola, which retained its freedom until 791. When Corinthia and Carniola came under Bavarian rule, Christianity started to spread in this territory from the mid-eighth until the mid-tenth century, leading to the strengthening of the foreign rule and the development of a feudal order. The Slavic population initially reacted to these changes with numerous uprisings. One of the best-known uprisings involving Carantanians and Carniolans started in 819 in what is today Slavonia in northern Croatia. This rebellion, however, was stifled in 820. Some years after this, the Frankish King Ludwig of Germany gave this territory as fief to a Slavic prince, Pribina, and his son Kocelj. In 862, Kocelj freed himself from the Frankish rule and developed the almost independent state of Lower Pannonia. However, it was reconquered by the Franks in 876 and again became part of the Frankish Kingdom.

The process of feudalization of the future Slovene territory under the Frankish rule was halted when Hungarian tribes rode their horses into these territories and conquered most of the Pannonian Plain. After they lost a battle near Augsburg in 955, a period of relative stability followed. During this period the feudal order was finally strengthened in this territory. Large land possessions and functions in the feudal order were given to church and temporal lords who were not of Slavic descent and who were interested in developing a system in which they would have princely authority over the lands. This started the process of the development of new administrative units, the so-called historic lands (Carniola, Styria, Carinthia, Görz/Gorizia, etc.), which occurred in the fourteenth century.

The common ethnic identity of Carantanians began to be replaced by different regional identities based on the newly developed historic lands. This period was also characterized by the decline and decay of numerous noble dynasties as well as a short period of rule by Czech king Otokar Premysl, who was defeated by the Habsburgs. Until 1235, the Habsburgs were a little and insignificant noble family who resided in Switzerland (in canton Aargau). In 1273 Rudolph of Habsburg was given the title of German Emperor by the German state princes. After that, he gave to his relatives in fief the lands that were conquered by the German Empire. Among those lands were the ethnic territories of the Slovenes. The only competitors with the Habsburgs for the Slovene ethnic territories from the second third of the fourteenth century were the counts of Celje/Cilli, the only noble family that originated in Slovene ethnic territory and had risen to the ranks of the state princes. After the death of the last member of the family of Cilli, the Habsburgs expanded their authority over the whole Slovene ethnic territory by 1460.

The period of the dynastic fights was also the period of the Turkish invasions and raids, which reached their peak in the 1470s and 1480s. The already bad conditions were worsened by the wars with Venice and the discontent of the peasantry, which led to an open, armed peasant rebellion. During the 150 years following this first great rebellion in Carinthia in 1478, three other major peasant rebellions broke out in Slovene ethnic territory. The largest one was the rebellion of 1515. Best known was the Croatian-Slovene rebellion under the leadership of Matija Gubec and Ilija Gregorić, which, because of its strength, left the strongest impact in the minds of the people. This Croatian-Slovene peasant rebellion ended with the "crowning" of Matija Gubec as peasant "king" in Zagreb (Croatia). He was brought to an iron seat and crowned with an iron crown that had been made red-hot in a fire, so that Matija Gubec died in great pain.

The rebellions had as their aim the bettering of the position of the peasants, who wanted to be under the immediate rule of the emperor and not under their feudal lords. The rebellions also had some characteristics of national uprisings, as the peasants were of Slovene (and, in the case of the common rebellion, also of Croat) ethnic background and the feudal lords were of German and Italian ethnic background. Although they were primarily fought for social justice and fewer feudal burdens, the peasant rebellions were justified in the name of *stara pravda* (old justice), under which peasants claimed they should not have to pay more tribute than was written in the old records (*urbar*).

Because of the Turkish raids, the princes of historical lands, the Habsburgs, had to collect large sums of money to defend their lands against the Turks. The land estates had to give concessions allowing higher taxes in order to pay for defense. In exchange, they were allowed to keep their Protestant faith. At the same time, the Protestant Reformation Movement also developed in Slovene lands. In accordance with the Religious Peace of Augsburg (1555), which gave the princes of the provinces in historic lands the right to decide on the religious affiliation of their subjects, in the Slovene lands the Habsburgs demanded that the Protestant nobility give up their Protestant faith. This had severe consequences for the Slovenes. Namely, one of the very important teachings of the evangelical churches was that the ordinary people had to read the Bible in order to be saved. Therefore, the ordinary people had to be provided with the Bible in their own language. For the Slovenes, the evangelical (Protestant) movement was more important as a cultural rather than as a religious movement. Some of the greatest achievements of the evangelical church in Slovene ethnic territory were the publication of the first Slovene books by Rev. Primož Trubar, the first Slovene grammar book in 1584 by Adam Bohorić, and the first translation of the Bible into the Slovene language by Jurij Dalmatin. These books were important contributions to the development of the Slovene language and cultural consciousness.

After the defeat of the Turks near Sisak in 1593, the Habsburgs succeeded in the re-Catholicization of the nobility as well as the peasantry in Slovene lands. In accordance with the Religious Peace of Augsburg, they forced people in the Slovene lands to go back to Catholicism. Later, the second half of the seventeenth century brought the development of commerce, energizing economic activities and modernizing transportation. The Austrian War for Succession brought young Empress Maria Theresa to power in 1740. Her reforms and those of her son Joseph II focused on modernization of administration, the fiscal system, and the army. These reforms substantially bettered the conditions of the peasantry. Of special importance was school reform, which introduced compulsory schooling for children in which each nationality group's own language was used. This, too, was important for the creation and development of the modern Slovene nation.

During the second half of the eighteenth century, such intellectuals as Marko Pohlin and baron Žiga Zois, under the influence of the European

Enlightenment, started a national awakening in Slovene lands. They became interested in the Slovene language and in its development as the language of culture. With the publication of the works of Anton Tomaž Linhart (*Geschichte von Krain und den übrigen Ländern der südlichen Slaven Österreichs—The History of Carniola and the Other South-Slavic Lands of Austria*, 1789–1791) and Jernej Kopitar, who served as librarian in the Viennese court (*Grammatik der slavischen Sprache in Krain, Kärnten und Steiermark—The Grammar of the Slavic Language in Carniola, Carinthia, and Styria*, 1808), the ethnic unity of Slovenes—the people of the inner Austrian lands of Carniola, Styria, Carinthia, Görz/Gorizia/Gorica, Triest/Trieste/Trst, and Istria—started to develop and was being recognized by the turn of the nineteenth century.

Croats

The lands that Croats settled during the first half of the seventh century had different physical/geographical characteristics (Pannonian Plain, Dinaric Ranges, Adriatic Karst), because of which people experienced different conditions of living that affected their political and social development. The Croatian lands were divided in different political units that existed at the beginning of the ninth century: Croatia (between the Velebit Mountains and Cetina River), the Principality of Neretva or Pagania (between Cetina and the Neretva River), and the Principality of Slovinje or Slavonia (on the Pannonian Plain). Coastal cities and the Adriatic islands, which were settled by Romanic populations, were under the rule of Byzantium.

Although Slavonia and Croatia were at first under the Avars and from 803 were under the Frankish rule, the Principality of Neretva developed relatively independently until the eleventh century. In the mid-ninth century, the influence of the Frankish and Byzantine states over the Croatian lands started to vanish because of internal troubles of the Frankish and Byzantine Empires. During the period of Prince Trpimir (845–864), Croatia started to strengthen its position. In 878 it liberated itself from the Frankish rule, and it reached its peak in political strength and territorial expansion during the rule of Tomislav (910–930). He fought the Hungarians and succeeded in uniting Slavonia and Croatia. He made good use of the weakness of Serbia (which was being pressured by the Bulgarians) and succeeded in annexing part of what was then Bosnia (for which Serbia also fought). To defend against the "Bulgarian danger," Tomislav became an ally of Byzantium. This enabled him to both mount a successful defense against the Bulgarians and extend his rule to the coastal cities, in spite of the fact that formally they stayed under the Byzantine rule.

After the end of Emperor Samuel's government in Macedonia and the fall of his state in 1014, Croatia became one of the strongest states in the Balkans outside of the renewed Byzantine Empire. As a result of the fights between Byzantium and the Bulgarians for territory and influence in the Balkans, Byzantium was weakened and Dalmatia came under the religious control of authorities of the Roman Catholic Church, with religious services now being conducted in the Latin language. In spite of that, the Ancient Church Slavonic language, written in the Glagolic alphabet (*glagolica*), was retained in Roman Catholic services in addition to Latin.

After the death of Tomislav, Croatia lived through crises caused by battles for succession to the throne and to the small landholdings of Croatian kings. Croatian strength was renewed again during the rule of King Krešimir IV (1058–1073) and his successor Zvonimir (1075–1089). Zvonimir promised vassal faithfulness to Pope George VII, which enabled him to occupy Dalmatian cities. After Zvonimir died in 1089, Croatia was thrown into anarchy. The newest research has discovered that he died of natural causes and that the legends that he had been killed were created much later (Tanner, 1997, 13–14). Part of the nobility, along with the widow of King Zvonimir (who was sister to the Hungarian king), called upon Hungarian King Louis I Anjou to become the Croatian king, but he did not succeed in occupying the Croatian throne. The Croatian nobility elected Petar as the Croatian king. King Petar, the last Croatian king, was defeated by Hungarian King Koloman in 1097. Croatian historians maintained for a very long time that the Croatian nobility obtained an agreement (the so-called Pacta Conventa) under which Croatians became vassals of the Hungarians. Hungarian historiography maintained, however, that Croatia was conquered by the Hungarians with fire and sword. The historical truth is somewhere in between. Koloman was crowned as a Croatian king in Biograd, with long-lasting consequences for Croatia. The Pacta Conventa never existed, but the story about it was important for the Croatian position in the Habsburg Empire in the eighteenth and nineteenth centuries, when the Croats claimed their rights to statehood on the basis of this agreement. Although Croatia ceased to exist as an independent state, the Croatian nobility retained relatively strong powers. The princes of Bribir (a settlement 15 miles northwest of Šibenik in Dalmatia), or Šubići, who conquered the coastland of Croatia (Šibenik, Trogir, Split, Omiš) and Bosnia in the thirteenth century and at the beginning of the fourteenth century, became especially strong. Their strength was broken in 1322 by Hungarian King Karl I Robert of Anjou.

Finally, all Croatian nobility came under Hungarian rule with the ascent of Robert of Anjou's successor, Louis I (1342–1382), who also conquered Venice. With the peace of Zadar (1358), Venetians had to relinquish their authority over the territories between the Gulf of Kvarner and Durrës (in modern Albania). Dalmatian cities were now able to penetrate the hinterland with their economic activities, allowing for freer development. The change was for the better for the City Republic of Dubrovnik (the Republic of Ragusa), which was given complete autonomy in return for paying a yearly contribution or tax to the Hungarian king and for symbolically being under his rule. This made it possible for Dubrovnik to develop into a city-state and make use of the economic advantages of its connections with the Balkan hinterlands. During the next decades Dubrovnik was able to spread its control, and these territories were retained as possessions of Dubrovnik until 1808, when Napoleon occupied Dubrovnik and ended the Republic.

In the fifteenth century, Croatia was at first threatened by the Venetian Republic, which succeeded in occupying Dalmatia again, and then by the Turks, who occupied most of Croatia and stopped its economic, cultural, and legal development for three centuries. Hungarian-Croatian armies were defeated at the battle of Mohács in 1526. The organization of the defense of European Christian civilization against the Turks was in the hands of the Habsburg dynasty. By 1535 they had developed as a defense territory the so-called Military Frontier Region (*Vojna krajina*), with its seat in Karlovac (a city northwest of Zagreb), which in many instances held off Turkish robber attacks into Christian territories as late as the seventeenth century. Service in the Military Frontier Region was taken over by Orthodox Serb refugees (from Bosnia and Serbia), who fled from the Turkish oppression and reprisal. They were given land in exchange for military service. They had a special position, did not pay taxes, and were not under the feudal rule of the Hungarian nobility.

With these circumstances, Croatia, under the rule of the *ban* (viceroy and the representative of the Hungarian king), was limited to the territory from Rijeka to Varaždin and the border between Croatia and Carniola. The Habsburgs wanted to introduce absolute rule in Croatian lands, but the Croatian nobility secretly opposed this, especially the Zrinjski and Frankopan families. The Habsburgs found out about the conspiracy and foiled the coup. Both leaders, Petar Zrinjski and Franjo Krsto Frankopan, were sentenced to death.

The Habsburg monarchy regained its Hungarian and Croatian lands and its rule of Slavonia in 1699. Nearly a century later, following the death of Austrian Emperor Joseph II in 1790, Hungarian feudal lords wanted to create from Hungary and Croatia one state with Hungarian majority rule. They succeeded in this at the meeting of the Hungarian-Croatian diet (*sabor*) in Posszony (today Bratislava, in Slovakia) in 1790–1791, when Croatia, with the consent of its nobility, became administratively subordinated to Hungary. Because of threats of Hungarization and attempts by the Hungarian nobility to establish a Hungarian national state (from the Carpathian Mountains to the Adriatic Sea), national movements soon began to spread among Croats, aimed at uniting all Croatian lands into one state. This movement against the Hungarization and Austrian rule in Istria and Dalmatia spread, especially during the nineteenth century, and after World War I this movement made it possible for the Croats to be included in the new South Slav state.

Bosnians

The name "Bosnia" first was used in the tenth century. The Bosnia region's old nucleus (the Sarajevo-Zenica Basin and the region of the Upper Vrbas River) retained its tribal order for the longest time of all South Slavic lands because of its physical geography: It was enclosed by the mountains, far away from important commercial routes and, therefore, less exposed to outside influences. From the beginning of the twelfth century, rule over the territory of today's Bosnia changed hands among the Croatian and medieval Serb states and Byzantium.

Soon after the fall of Croatia, Hungarian kings also took over rule in Bosnia. Even though the Hungarian king was represented in Bosnia by a special official (*ban*), some autonomous if not independent inner development of Bosnia was possible. The most important Bosnian ban, Kulin (1180–1204), began trading with Dubrovnik during his rule, while other countries in the region fought wars. In addition, a heresy based on the teaching of Balkan Bogomils started to appear during this period in Bosnia. The Bogomil religious movement, which had emerged in Macedonia during the first half of the tenth century, taught that the world was created by Sataneal (God's older son, a symbol of evil) and that the good beginnings were given to mankind by the second, younger son, Jesus Christ. This was the reason for the constant dualistic fight between good and evil, the Bogomils taught.

The appearance of Bogomils in Bosnia made the Papal hierarchy nervous, and they began a large-scale persecution of the Bogomils. Because of the intense outside pressure, Ban Kulin gave up his Bogomilism in front of a representative of the pope in 1203 and became a friend of the Crusades. These acts of allegiance to the pope did not stop the spread of Bogomilism in Bosnia, which even provoked military intervention by the papal hierarchy after 1221. The Bosnians fought against this intervention under the leadership of Ban Matej Ninoslav (1233–1250). In the end, the Catholic Church's attempt to crush Bogomilism failed, and Bogomils began to rule over the Old Bosnian Diocese, which became the dualistic Bosnian Church. The Bosnian Church was then the only one in Europe that did not belong to either the Roman Catholic or the Byzantine Orthodox Christian Church.

After its fall to the Hungarians, Bosnia rose again in the fourteenth century after the Hungarian crises, the breakdown of the Serb Dušan's empire, and the collapse of the Croatian noble family of Šubić, who had ruled Bosnia for two decades. Bosnian ban Štefan I Kotromanić successfully used the political situation to move the Bosnian borders toward the west and south and created solid economic foundations for the state. Bosnia reached its largest size, however, during the rule of Tvrtko I, who strengthened central rule in Bosnia even more, and its territorial borders spread toward the Lim River (1373) and the bay of Boka Kotorska (1377) in Montenegro. In 1377 Tvrtko was crowned King of Serbia and Bosnia and expanded his rule into the territory of Zeta, occupying Kotor in 1384. After the death of Hungary's King Louis I, internal feudal fights broke out, and Tvrtko I sided with the Croatian nobility against the new Hungarian king, Sigismund. Tvrtko thereby started a war, occupied Croatian and Dalmatian cities, and added to his titles that of King of Croatia and Dalmatia. At the same time he was an ally of the Serb Prince Lazar and sent Lazar a unit of soldiers who, in 1389, cooperated in the battle of Kosovo polje against the Turks.

After the death of Tvrtko I (1391), Bosnia very quickly weakened. The main voices in leading the country were those of the nobility, who, at will, set up and deposed Bosnian kings and even entered into alliances with their own adversaries. As a consequence, Tvrtko's successors fell more and more under the influence of the Turks and Hungarians over the next three decades. After king Stjepan Tomaš tried to halt the anarchy in the state, fights between the peasant population and the nobility reached a critical state, and there were also further tensions between the Catholic Church and Bogomils. The Turks started interfering in internal affairs of state. In

1463, under the leadership of Mehmed II the Conqueror, the Turks occupied Bosnia and organized a special administrative frontier unit, "sandžak," from which they continued their conquests of Europe. Bosnia became a part of the Ottoman Empire, with a similar social and administrative regime to that in the other parts of the Empire. Moreover, Turkish-Byzantine civilization started to spread in Bosnia and was especially evident in the life of the cities. During this period, a majority of the local population also accepted Islam.

Feudal anarchy—which arose after the death of the Turkish emperor Sultan Suleiman I the Magnificent in 1566—spread to Bosnia. The situation of the peasantry worsened, which at first provoked brigandage (*hajduštvo*). By the end of the sixteenth and the beginning of the seventeenth century this escalated into the first uprisings of the peasantry. Because of the wars with Austria-Hungary (1716–1718, 1737–1739, and 1788–1791) and even greater feudal anarchy, the Bosnian nobility began disseminating the idea of autonomy, which later formed the basis for Bosnian Muslim nationalism and resulted in a Bosniak (Muslim) ethnic nation. Bosnian Muslims fought against reforms in the Turkish Empire initiated by Sultan Selim III (1789–1807). Their rebellions soon became continuous. At first they fought for autonomy against the Turkish authorities and, after 1878, for unification with other South Slavs and against Austria-Hungary.

Serbs

The ancestors of the Serbs settled in the Balkans during the first half of the eighth century. They settled the hinterlands of the Principality of Neretva, Zahumlje, Travunia, and Duklja, which meant the territories from the Croatian border on the west to the town of Ras on the east. The center was in the so-called Serblia (later called Raška), which had had to fight already in the ninth century against attempts by Byzantium to conquer it; it fought also with the Bulgarian state. In spite of the fact that Bulgarian Emperor Simeon succeeded in conquering some Serb territories, in 924 Prince Časlav was able to renew the Serb state, whose territory spread from the Western Morana River to the Vrbas River; Travunia was annexed to it also. This was a very tumultuous period of history for the Serb state, which, after the decay of the First Bulgarian Empire (971), was first under the Byzantine rule, later under the rule of Samuel's Macedonian Empire, and then after 1018 was again under the rule of Byzantium. These political changes did not, however, affect Serbia's inner development.

Beginning in the mid-eleventh century, the center of Serb political life was in Duklja, during this period called Zeta. Because of its successful conquest of new territories, Zeta became more important during the rule of Prince Mihailo and his successor Bodin, who succeeded in annexing Raška (inner Serbia) and Bosnia, in addition to the already annexed Travunia and Zahumlje. After Bodin's death, fights occurred among members of the king's family, and Zeta began to lose its political importance.

During the twelfth century, the center of Serb statehood again became Raška. Serb princes, or Great Mayors (*veliki župani*), who were formally vassals of Byzantium, were able to consolidate their power by successfully taking advantage of conflicts between Byzantium and Hungary. By the end of the twelfth century, during the rule of the great mayor Štefan Nemanja, Serbia succeeded in ridding itself of the influence of Byzantium. The youngest son of Štefan Nemanja, Sava, an Orthodox priest, played an important role by achieving the independence of the Serb Orthodox Church from the Byzantine Orthodox Church. The Serb Orthodox Church became the guardian of the Serb state idea and also carried out Serb state traditions after the end of the Serb medieval state.

Štefan Nemanja's successor was his son Štefan Nemanjić. He became the foremost Great Mayor and, in 1217, he accepted the title of king and added to his title *Prvovencani* (First Crowned). During the rule of his son, Štefan Uroš I (1243–1276), mining began to develop in Serbia with the help of miners from Saxony. The first mines soon developed into townships and centers of commerce. Precious metals (silver and gold) acted as promoters of trade and connected Serbia with trade in the Mediterranean. At the same time, these mines were important sources of the king's income or state revenues. After Uroš I left the throne in 1276 and was followed by his son Dragutin, further development of the Serb state was interrupted by fights for succession to the throne. In spite of these internal fights, Serbs succeeded in conquering some territories in Macedonia and along the Hungarian border in the north. The Serb state reached its peak during the rule of Dušan (Dušan Šilni)—known as Dušan the Mighty. At that time Serbia occupied all of Albania and Macedonia up to Saloniki and the Maritsa River, and in 1346 Dušan was crowned Emperor of Serbia and Greece. Exploiting the weakness of the Byzantine Empire, he also occupied Epirus and Thessalia and spread the frontiers of his state to the Gulf of Corinth. During the rule of Dušan Šilni, Serb feudal society reached its complete maturity.

Consolidation of the feudal order in Serbia was sanctioned also by the development of a law code called Dušan's Code of Laws (1349 and 1354), which was based on the Laws of Byzantium. Dušan enacted the rights of the emperor, nobility, and traders and also the duties of peasants. This constitution of medieval Serbia was also the first written law code developed among the South Slavs. More than one-third of the articles of Dušan's Code of Laws dealt with the rights, privileges, and duties of estates (classes and their mutual relations and duties). The first articles dealt with the church and clergy. Marriage in the Orthodox Church was the only valid type of marriage. Everyone had to obey the bishop in religious matters. Catholic propaganda was forbidden, and those distributing it would be persecuted. Marriage between a Catholic man and an Orthodox woman was not valid if the man did not become an Orthodox believer. In religious matters, only the church had the right of judgment.

Feudal property was secure under this code; the nobility had the right to own slaves and to have serfs and to use their labor. The nobility also had special rights in penal proceedings. Dušan's Code of Law prescribed lesser punishment for nobles than for serfs for the same offenses. The nobility had to pay tribute to the emperor and provide an army to fight his wars. The nobility also had to organize and pay for the transport of the emperor, for his properties, for building and rebuilding cities and towns—even outside of their properties—and to help the emperor materially in certain situations. According to Dušan's Code of Laws, the serfs had to work for their lord two days per week, to cut grass once per year, and to work in the vineyard (altogether, 106 days annually). Serfs had to pay certain taxes (so-called *soće*), provide housing for guards and food for the emperor, cooperate in building and guarding the towns, and fight together with their nobles in guarding themselves. The emperor, his family, the nobility, and the townships were forbidden to take into their custody foreign "merops" (peasants who had to stay on the lord's lands), as those who provided them with custody would be punished as unbelievers. "Sebres" (serfs) were not allowed to meet in public places. A merop had the right to sue his lord in court if his lord broke the Code, even if it were the emperor being sued.

Of interest here are also those parts of Dušan's Code of Laws that were rewritten on the basis of the Byzantine Code, which stated that judges had to rule in accordance with the emperor's orders. If those orders were not in accordance with the law, however, judges had to give judgments according to the law. They did not have to obey the orders of the emperor given out of anger or love or mercy to anyone (Krstić, 1989, 3–8). The penal code was a significant part of Dušan's Code; there were punishments prescribed for those who worked against the feudal, social, or state order, or against the church and religion, or in disrespect of foreign property or persons.

After Dušan's death, all the weaknesses of his empire surfaced. During the rule of his son Uroš V, the state very quickly fell apart into numerous territories with independent rulers. These rulers fought each other, and their lands soon became the booty of the Turks, who from 1354 onward were spreading their state onto European soil. Individual Serb rulers attempted to fight the Turks, but they were finally defeated in the famous battle of Kosovo polje, which lasted from 15 June 1389 until 28 June 1389. Although some historical records claim that the Turks actually withdrew after the death of their emperor and that the Serbs might have even won the battle, they definitively lost the war. In any case, this battle had dramatic consequences. Members of Serb nobility became vassals of the Turks. However, the battle of Kosovo polje became the symbol of the long fight between the Turks and the Serbs and was glorified in numerous people's songs. The story grew to mythic proportions—a myth that was used by the Serb nationalists in establishing the Serb nation in the nineteenth century and again in the 1990s.

Out of the once-great Dušan's empire, only three regions were preserved, led by Prince Štefan Lazarević, Vuk Branković, and the Balšić family. Under the foreign Turkish supreme authority, unification came to these regions. The most important role in this process was played by Štefan Lazarević, who succeeded in uniting the three territories until 1421. During the period 1435–1459, however, the Turks completely occupied the Serb territories (with the exception of Zeta), bringing to an end the continuous economic, social, and political development of Serbia. During this period of Turkish rule, the Serb ethnic territories were enlarged because the Serb population, out of fear, fled in great numbers from the Turks over the Sava and Danube Rivers into Hungary. On those territories that were now emptied of Serbs, the Turkish authorities settled Valachs or Vlachs (indigenous people), who were included in the Turkish feudal order. The Vlachs settled the so-called "Vallachian territory" from Herzegovina (a region in today's Bosnia and Herzegovina) to Lika, Krbava, and Bania up to Slavonia (regions in today's Croatia), from which the Christian population also fled to Christian lands in the Habsburg Empire, especially to Croatia. Austrian military authorities systematically settled these refugees from the Turkish Empire on the frontiers and included them in their Anti-Turkish defense system (Military Frontier Region).

After they occupied Serbia, the Turks did not at once abolish its church organizations or force the population to accept Islam. The Serb Patriarchy was abolished at the beginning of the fifteenth century; it was, however, renewed in 1557 with the seat in Peć because of the state interest of the Ottoman Empire. Its jurisdiction was larger than all former Serb state and church territories combined. It included Macedonia, western Bulgaria, Serbia, Montenegro, Bosnia, and the Serb-settled regions in Hungary, Croatia, and Venetian Dalmatia. The Patriarchy unified all the Serbs from these territories into one religious community and preserved the old Serb state tradition. And yet, after the sixteenth century when the Ottoman Empire started to show its first serious signs of decay, it was the Serb Church that led the discontented Serb population in its open fight against the Turks. After the Turks were defeated on the outskirts of Vienna in 1683, the rebellions of the Serb population in the Ottoman Empire became more and more numerous. The Serbs rebelled especially during the wars of European powers against Turkey (1737–1739, 1788–1791). The numerous rebellions of the Serb population compelled the Turkish authorities to give the Serbs local self-management and religious freedom after the peace in Svištov (1791).

Peace in the border area with Austria-Hungary and relative security in Serb lands were decisive factors in the economic development of Serbia. Export of livestock and animal products to Austria enabled a part of the Serb population to become traders and members of the village-bourgeoisie, who then became an important political factor and led the later Serb uprisings in the nineteenth century.

Montenegrins

The territory of what is today Montenegro (*Crna gora*) was mentioned for the first time in the fourteenth century; the name was in common use by the fifteenth century. The region was first named Duklja (after the Roman township Diocleia), but from the eleventh century, it was called Zeta (after the River Zeta).

The history of Duklja is, until the tenth century, little known. From this period, only "Sovereign of Doclea" (*arhont Dioklije*) Peter is known, as his name appears in Greek letters on one leaded rubber stamp. The history of Duklja becomes better known at the end of the tenth century, when Zeta became more and more used as the name of the region. It is known that the then-prince, Vladimir, out of fear of the Macedonian Emperor Samuel, tried to make contact with Byzantium. In 998 Samuel conquered Zeta, which, after the end of his empire, again came under the rule of Byzantium. After the death of Byzantine Emperor Basil II, Prince Štefan Vojislav in 1042 defeated the Byzantine army and expanded the territory of Zeta up to the Vijosë River in what is today Albania. With that, he created the first foundations of the state of Zeta. It became even more significant in the second half of the eleventh century, after Pope George VII gave Vojislav's son Mihailo the title of king. Zeta came to its height under Bodin.

After the death of Bodin, Zeta started to decay because of internal fights among members of the kings' family and the nobility. The fights for power took place until the 1180s, when Štefan Nemanja was able to annex Zeta to Raška. Zeta then represented the most developed territory of Raška. Its coastal towns (Skadar, Ulcinj, Bar, Kotor), having developed commerce, were an important part in the Serb feudal state.

After the death of Dušan in 1335, the Balšić family started their independent rule in Zeta. During this period the first fights with the Turks took place (1385 near Berat in Albania). As the Turks became more and more dangerous, the family of Crnojević exploited the situation and, with the support of Bosnian king Tvrtko I, ruled as independent rulers in so-called Upper Zeta (with its seat in Žabljak). Djuradj II Balšić then was forced to fight on two fronts, both against the Crnojevićs and against the Turks. To do this, he asked for help from Venice. When the Venetian influence in Zeta became too strong, Balša III later tried to stop it as soon as he came to power in 1403. Finally he had to give up, as the influence of Venice in Zeta was supported by the Crnojević family. When Balša III died in 1421, he gave Zeta to Serb ruler Štefan Lazarević and his successor Djuradj Branković. Until the Turks later occupied Zeta there were constant fights for rule over it between successors of Štefan Lazarević, on the one hand, and Venice and its allies, the Crnojevićs, on the other.

Further fights were ended in 1457 by the Turkish occupation of the territories of Zeta. After the Turks occupied also the territories of the Crnojevićs in 1479, they completed their occupation of Zeta in 1499 by annexing Zeta to the Sandžak (Turkish administrative unit) of Skadar. It remained part of Skadar's Sandžak until 1514, when Zeta became an independent sandžak with the name of Montenegro (or *Crna gora*). As the vassal of the Turkish sultan, Staniša Crnojević became the ruler of Montenegro (sandžak-beg)—having renamed himself Skender-beg—and Montenegro became a Turkish region (sandžak) with wide self-management. Its population had no other masters but Staniša Crnojević and so was free in relation to the other nobility. After the death of Skender-beg in 1528, Montenegro again became part of the Sandžak of Skadar. This, however, did not stop its autonomous development, especially in its local judiciary. Montenegrins were paying relatively lower taxes than the other subjects of the Ottoman Empire, and they had to help the Turkish army only when it fought on the Montenegrins' own territory. Turkish officials, except for the Sultan's official who collected flat rate duties, were forbidden to enter Montenegro. This wide autonomy enabled free life to prevail almost everywhere in the region.

When the Turks started to limit the extent of Montenegrin autonomy in the second half of the seventeenth century, they ran into a convincing rebellion from the Montenegrins. Representatives of Zeta Diocese, together with its *vladika* (Orthodox bishop of the Zeta Diocese), were the leaders of this defense. *Vladikas* later played a decisive role in uniting Montenegrin tribes and organizing a defense against the spread of Islam and of Turkish feudalization. From the end of the seventeenth century on, *vladikas* were always elected from the tribe of Njegoš and Petrović's lineage, which later became the royal family of Montenegro.

The end of the seventeenth century and the beginning of the eighteenth century brought a decisive turning point in the history of Montenegro, because, from the War of Morea (1685–1699) on, decisive anti-Turkish fights did not stop. With the help of the Russians, *vladika* Danilo Petrović Njegoš defeated the Turks in July 1712 and did away with the Turkish supreme authority in the battle of Carev Laz. After Bosnian Grand Vizier Numan-paša Köprülü (Ćuprilić) threatened Montenegro in 1714, *vladika* Danilo looked to Venice for help. In return for this help, Danilo gave the Venetians the supreme authority in Montenegro, and the Venetians gave Danilo the supreme church authority over the Orthodox population in the Bay of Kotor (Boka Kotorska). Because the Turks could not stop the spread of Venetian influence in Montenegro with military action, they persuaded some of the Montenegrin tribal leaders to start fighting the Venetians, who had fomented conflict among the Montenegrin tribes. Peace among the tribes and order in the country were finally imposed by a foreigner, Šćepan Mali, who represented himself as Russian emperor Peter III. The Turks and Venetians did not like his rule in Montenegro, and the Turks bribed his servant to kill him. Despite all these upheavals, in the eighteenth century Montenegro became an important political and strategic factor in international relations, especially in the antagonisms between great powers in the Balkans.

Macedonians

The Slavs who settled in the seventh century in the former Roman province of Macedonia were divided into numerous tribes. They lived in determined territories, which developed into principalities known as

Sclavinias. Macedonian *Sclavinias* were under the influence of Byzantium, especially under the influence of the town of Salonika. In the seventh century, Sclavinias failed to unite and their forces failed to occupy the town of Salonika, although several attempts were made. By the end of the eighth century, Sclavinias came under the Byzantine rule and, from 864 onward, under the Bulgarian rule. After that, Christianity came to the Macedonian Slavs, in connection with the work of pupils of Methodius. Among the pupils of Methodius, especially important were Kliment and Naum from Ohrid, who succeeded in introducing the language of Macedonian Slavs into the church and literature.

During the period of the Bulgarian rule, the number of serfs increased. Under the influence of the continuous wars that the Bulgarians fought against Byzantium, the living conditions of Macedonian Slavs (especially the serfs) worsened. Under these conditions, in the mid-tenth century the heretical Bogomil movement appeared. Because Bogomils fought especially against the nobility, rich people, and the Christian Church, the movement spread widely among the poor. The church authorities were able to stop the Bogomil movement among Macedonian Slavs relatively quickly, but it later had a strong influence in other parts of the Balkans, especially in Bosnia and Herzegovina.

In 971 Byzantium succeeded in renewing its authority in the Balkans and in Macedonia. Because the situation of the subject population worsened as feudal conditions developed further, the subject population started to rebel more and more. One such Macedonian rebellion was in 976 under the leadership of Samuel. Byzantium was paralyzed at the time because of civil war and Arab wars. Samuel was able to conquer the whole of the territories of historic Macedonia (with the exception of Salonika), Thessalia, Epirus, and a part of Albania with Durrës, Duklja, Zahumlje, Raška, Srem, Bosnia, and Bulgaria. Samuel, who proclaimed himself "emperor of Bulgarians and the Macedonians," did not forget about the organization of his own state. He moved his capital from Prespa to Ohrid, and the diocese of Ohrid became the Patriarchy. Byzantine Emperor Basil II attacked Samuel's state around the year 1000. In a battle near Belasica (situated near Strumica) in 1014, Basil II defeated Samuel's army. After the victory, according to legends, Basil II ordered the blinding of 14,000 of Samuel's soldiers and brought them to Samuel. He left one eye to every one hundred soldiers. When he saw this army Samuel died of a stroke. For the first time since Slavic settlements had begun, Byzantium ruled almost the whole Balkans. However, many Slavic rebellions against Byzantium were organized in the territories of the Macedonian Slavs.

After the Fourth Crusade in 1204, Byzantium was ruined. Macedonian territories then became part of Epirus and later part of a renewed Bulgaria and the Latin Empire, and then, during the fourteenth century (during the rule of the last Nemanjićs), part of Serbia. From 1282 on, Skopje was the capital of Serbia. After the death of Dušan Šilni (1335), when the Serb Empire was divided, numerous noble families ruled Macedonia.

Because of constant fights among them, Macedonians became victims of the Turkish occupation. The Turks first conquered Gallipoli (Gelibolu) in 1354 and then continued to conquer parts of the Balkans. All the Macedonian members of nobility became Turkish vassals after a battle on the Maritsa River in 1371. Among them was King Marko (son of King Vukašin), about whom numerous folk songs were written that portrayed him as a Serb national hero and, contrary to his actual role, a symbol of rebellion against the Turks. After the death of King Marko, who died as a Turkish vassal, the Turks occupied Macedonia. It shared the fate of other conquered regions in the Ottoman Empire. However, in addition to the Turkish authorities, the Macedonians were oppressed by the Greek Church as well. Consequently, the population started to rebel against the Turkish authorities by the sixteenth century (near Ohrid, Prilep, Bitola, etc.).

In the seventeenth century, conditions in the Turkish Ottoman Empire worsened. The Austrian army started to penetrate deep into the Turkish Empire, and rebellions became even more numerous. One of the best-known rebellions started in northwestern Macedonia, where the rebels under the leadership of Karpoš were very successful. The Austrian army went to the region of the rebellion, but later had to leave the Balkans to pursue a war with France. After the Austrians left, the Turks succeeded in putting down the rebellion. Karpoš was impaled and thrown into the Vardar River. Macedonians then fled these territories because they were afraid of Turkish revenge; these territories of Macedonia were then settled by the Albanians and Turks.

Cultural History from the Settlement of the Slavs until 1800

During the period of the Slav settlement in Europe, feudalism reigned. This period of Christianization also brought literacy among the South Slavs and a written Slavic language. It was spread by two Greek monks, brothers Constantine (Cyril) and Methodius, who went from Salonika to the northwest in the second half of the ninth century to teach Slavic peoples Christianity in their own language. This language was written in a specific script, the Glagolic alphabet (*glagolica*). Later it was replaced with the Cyrillic alphabet (*cirilica*), named after Cyril (Constantine), which is still used—in a slightly evolved version—by the Serbs, Macedonians, Montenegrins, Russians, and some other Eastern European nations (e.g., Bulgarians). (The Glagolic alphabet was used by the Croats until the fourteenth century.) The formation of this so-called Old Church Slavonic written language became a cornerstone of cultural development in the region, especially with the Orthodox South Slavic peoples, but also in coastal Croatia and Bosnia.

Different influences from the East and West marked the life and diverse cultural developments of the South Slavic peoples. Those differences were further increased by the Schism of 1054, which divided South Slavs into two large cultural areas. Among the Slovenes and most of the Croats, influences of the German state, Hungary and the Venetian Republic, with the Catholic Church, prevailed; among the Serbs, Montenegrins, and Macedonians, the influence of Byzantium and the Orthodox Church prevailed. Those influences were significant in arts in architecture as well as in literature.

Official culture in the Middle Ages mostly served the churches and the nobility. However, at the beginning of the thirteenth century, oral literature started to develop among the people. Slovenes and Croats composed folk poetry, myths, fairy tales, etc. During the period of the Turkish rule in the Balkans, the Serbs and Montenegrins also created such folk literature. The beginning of the end of the Middle Ages (the beginning of the fifteenth century) in Europe was marked by the Renaissance—a cultural revolution that saw the development of the bourgeoisie and the introduction of capitalism. However, until the beginning of the nineteenth century European society was still largely agrarian, with two main classes—feudal landlords and peasant subjects. Concussions from the Turkish occupation of the Balkan Peninsula and of foreign rule (by the Habsburgs) in the latter Middle Ages marked the life of South Slavic peoples.

During the Turkish rule cultural life developed, especially in Serb Orthodox monasteries and in Franciscan monasteries in Bosnia and Herzegovina. In territories ruled by the Ottoman Empire mostly Turkish culture developed, which produced numerous—but not overly inventive—works. In science the Turks were influenced by the Arabs; in historiography and poetry they followed the Persians; in architecture they followed Byzantium. This mix produced some cultural achievements and foundations that were admired in the West.

In the South Slav areas of settlement that were not under the Turkish rule (Slovene lands, Croatia, Slavonia, Dalmatia, Vojvodina, Dubrovnik), the values of the Renaissance and of humanism were adopted. At the end of the fifteenth century, the first books appeared in Glagolic (1482) and Cyrillic (1493). Numerous works from Dalmatian cities and the architectural art of Dalmatia from this period now belong among the most valued works of Renaissance art of the fifteenth century in Europe.

With humanistic culture, which laid the cornerstones of modern science and scholarship, the desire for religious renewal was also present. One of the consequences of this was the Reformation (the fight for reform within the Catholic Church that caused the split within the Catholic Church and the establishment of the Protestant churches). Religious leaders of some South Slavic nations were influenced by the ideas of Slavism, a political philosophy based on the idea of Slavic greatness and unity. Some Slovene (e.g. Primož Trubar) and Croatian (e.g., Petar Pavao Vergerij) adherents of the Protestant Church, together with some Serb adherents, tried to develop a unified South Slavic language, but they were not successful. The Protestants wanted people to read the Bible by themselves. This is why they provided for translations and printings of the Bible in national languages, and also in Slovene and Croatian. So, the Protestants in the Slovene lands developed the literary Slovene language. Their success forced the proponents of the Counter-Reformation (a movement led by the Catholic Church hierarchy to suppress Protestantism) to continue to print their writings in the "national" languages after the victory of the Counter-Reformation. Although the influence of the Catholic Church increased again, Europe in the seventeenth and eighteenth centuries was rocked by great social and economic changes, including numerous wars that ruined the feudal order and strengthened the bourgeoisie. The Peace of Westphalia of 1648, which ended the Thirty Years' War, opened the door to numerous new developments. One of its consequences was also the development of a new Baroque culture (beginning in the mid-seventeenth century) that flourished more in visual arts and music than in literature.

The increasing political might of the bourgeoisie marked the end of the seventeenth century and led to the development of a new movement—the Enlightenment. Ideas that spread among South Slavs from the French Revolution resulted in their awakened national consciousness—leading to the creation of modern South Slavic nations.

Slovenes

In the Slovene ethnic territories during the Middle Ages, manuscripts, mainly in German and Latin, appeared. In the Slovene language, though, only some prayers were written. Among them, the most important were *Brižinski spomeniki* (around the year 1000)—the first written text in one of the Slavic languages, *Rateški* or *Celovški rokopis* (at the end of the fourteenth century), and *Stiški rokopis* (in the first half of the fifteenth century). The Slovene language was in most cases preserved through oral folk literature. The most used forms were folk songs. In prose, as with other parts of Europe, myths, fairy tales, and narrations were created. In architecture, until the sixteenth century—under the influence of Middle European and Mediterranean cultural currents—buildings and churches constructed in the form of Romanesque country churches prevailed. In culture, paintings, figural arts, and wall murals with religious motifs, or in some cases also with motifs of everyday life, prevailed. Also, most of the music was meant for religious use.

Printed literature in the Slovene language developed during the Reformation period. Primož Trubar's *Katekizem* (*Catechisms*, 1550) and *Abecedarij* (*ABC*, 1550); Jurij Dalmatin's translation of the Bible into the Slovene language (1584), which was among the first ones in Europe; Adam Bohorič's first Slovene grammar, *Arcticae horulae* (1584); and Sebastjan Krelj's *Postilla Slovenska* (1564) provided the basis for the future developments of Slovene literature. Although known Slovene composers (Jakobus Gallus, Jurij Prenner, Daniel Laghkner) worked abroad, important developments occurred in music in Slovene ethnic territories as well. During the Reformation the first portraits were painted in addition to altar pictures. Although the period of the Counter-Reformation was a certain setback for Slovene culture, its development did continue.

In 1693 Janez Vajkard Valvazor published in the German language his *Die Ehre der Herzogthums Krain* (*The Glory of the Carniola Dukedom*), which was the first description of geography, history, and cultural achievements in Carniola. The first public library was opened in 1701. The establishment of the Academia Operosorum (1693) and Philharmonical Society (1701) marked new developments in music. In the arts, workshops of the painters appeared in the Baroque period. Anton Tomaž Linhart wrote the first Slovene plays, *Županova Micka* (influenced by a Viennese play, J. Ricter's *Die Feldmühle*) and *Matiček se ženi* (influenced by C. de Beaumarchais's *Le mariage de Figaro ou la folle journée*), which started the development of the Slovene theater. At the end of this period, the first scholarly work on the Slovene language, Jernej Kopitar's *Grammatik der slavischen Sprache in Krain, Kärnten, und Steiermark* (Grammar of the Slavic Language from Carniola, Carinthia, and Styria), was published in 1809.

Nave of Trogir Cathedral (Hans Georg Roth/Corbis)

Croats

Until the beginning of the twelfth century the so-called Old Croatian architecture consisted mostly of small churches in which barbaric art and the relics of antiquity mixed. The well-known Rotunda (rotunda means round building or hall) of St. Donat was built in Zadar in Dalmatia. As centers of architecture, literature, and the arts, Dalmatian coastal cities continued to play the most important role in Croat cultural life throughout the Middle Ages, Renaissance, and Gothic periods. The most important monuments were cathedrals in Split, Šibenik, Trogir, and Zadar, but also palaces of nobility and rich bourgeoisie built during the Renaissance and Gothic periods. Probably the most important monument was Radovan's portal in the Trogir Cathedral (1240), which made Croatian figural sculpture known worldwide.

An important European center of culture, especially of literature and architecture, in the medieval years and the Renaissance was the Republic of Ragusa (Dubrovnik). In the Baroque period, religious and secular monuments, including palaces with Baroque parks, were built in the northern parts of Croatia, especially Croatian Zagorje and Slavonia. Until the four-

Bridge at Mostar (built in 1556) by Franklin McMahon
(Franklin McMahon/Corbis)

teenth and fifteenth centuries, literature was written in the Croatian form of the Old Church Slavonic language or under the strong influence of it. Short stories and novels were written on the basis of Greek-Byzantine stories. Religious anthologies and city statutes represented the most important written works from this period (*Vinodolski zakonik, Misal kneza Novaka, Misal vojvoda Hrvoja*). During that period dramas for religious use were written (e.g., Marko Marulić's work *Judita*). At the same time singers' lyrics (Šiško Menčetić, Džore Držić, Hanibal Lučić) and moralistic poetry (Predator Hektorović's *Ribanje i ribarsko prigovaranje*) were being written. The old Croatian literature reached its peak with the Renaissance comedies of Marin Držić (e.g., *Dundo Maroje*) and the work of Ivan Gundulić, *Osman,* which describes the Turkish treatment of Croats.

Under the influence of Slovene Protestant literature, the literature in the Kaikavian dialect started to develop in northern Croatia in the sixteenth century. The first book in this dialect (*Kronika*) was published by Anton Vremac. During the period of the Enlightenment the most important Croatian writer was Tito Brezovački, who dealt with the social backwardness of the period. Most known are his plays *Grabanciaš* and *Diogeneš i Grabanciaš.*

Bosniaks (Bosnian Muslims)

Being far away from larger cultural centers and because of the religious movement of Patarens, Bosnia retained its originality in the arts until the end of the fifteenth century. The religious movement of Patarens was a dualistic heretic movement, which had its source in Bogomilism. Bogomilism, which emerged in Macedonia during the first half of the tenth century, taught that the world was created by Sataneal (God's older son, a symbol of evil); the good beginnings were given to mankind by the second, younger son, Jesus Christ. This was the reason for the constant dualistic fight between good and evil. The most typical examples of Bosniak art are Bogomil monumental tombstones—*stećki*. Altogether, around 50,000 were made in the period from the thirteenth until the sixteenth century. They are made in the form of a sarcophagus, house, or coffin, with names of the deceased on some of them, and they are decorated with different motifs.

This isolation, however, hindered development of church architecture, and only a few examples of Romance architecture (the church tower of St. Luka in Jajce) and Gothic architecture (Jajce, Srebrenica, Bihać) can be found from this period.

Architecture developed quickly after the Turkish occupation of Bosnia and Herzegovina in 1463. Some well-known mosques (Aladža Mosque in Foča, 1550; Ali-paša and Husref-beg Mosque in Sarajevo; Šarena Mosque in Travnik) and some bridges in Višegrad and Mostar were built. Influenced by Islamic traditions, this period was marked by development of artisan activities, especially filigree, by silversmiths and goldsmiths. The literature served mostly religious Islamic purposes, in spite of the fact that it was written in Slavic language and Arabic script. However, the literature started by the first Christian religious *Anthologies* was also significant. With the arrival of the Franciscans, the Catholic literary tradition was strengthened. We should mention especially Matija Divković's work *Narod kristjanski za narod slovinski*.

Serbs

The strong medieval Serb state gave the Serbs the best opportunities among all the South Slavic nations for independent cultural development. Although influenced by Greek-Byzantine culture, the literature marked the interdependence of the Orthodox national church and the state. In Serb prose of the Middle Ages this could be seen especially in the biographies of Serb rulers (*Žitije*) and church dignitaries, and in chronicles. Of special importance is *Dušan's Code of Laws* (1349 and 1354). After the Turkish occupation, cultural life was significantly curtailed. It developed only in Orthodox monasteries in Serbia and in the Hilandar Monastery on Atos Mountain (on the Halkidika Peninsula) in Greece. The most significant cultural achievement of the Turkish era was the folk poetry. It was based on real or mythical historical events (for example, about Prince Marko and his heroic deeds or about Prince Lazar and his defeat in Kosovo polje in 1389) and was created in the people's language in the following centuries. These poems never reached a high artistic quality. However, they played an important role in preserving historic memories and national myths, and they contributed to the awakening of national consciousness, leading to the ideas of Serb statehood and freedom.

Serb literature developed faster during the Enlightenment. The most important literary figure of this period was Dositej Obradović, who wanted to educate simple people and help them out of their backwardness. His attempts were hindered by the Serb Orthodox Church but had a strong echo among the people, as he wrote in the people's language. Especially well known is his autobiography, *Život i priključenija* (*Life and Stories*).

The Greek-Byzantine culture also influenced the arts. From the end of the twelfth century on many important monuments of the Middle Ages were built on the territories of Raška. In the architecture of the churches and monasteries, the influence of Romance style is also shown (the monastery Djurdjevi stupovi; churches of St. Mary Assumption and of St. Nicholas in Kuršumlija, Church of St. Mary Assumption in Studenica monastery). Of special importance are wall murals from this period, which represented valuable examples of Christian iconography of the Middle Ages. In discussing decoration of churches, icons (holy images painted on wood) from the end of the fourteenth century deserve to be mentioned. After the fall of Smederevo in 1459, the old Serb art of the court was discontinued. However, Byzantine traditions remained in spite of Turkish rule (at Fruška gora, Hilandar, Piva). After the great migration of the Serbs in the 1690s, Western influences began. Although in architecture (the cathedral in Sremski Karlovci) and the iconostasis wall (a wall in Orthodox churches with icons that divided the altar from the place for believers), Baroque influences began to be accepted, church and icon paintings remained under the Byzantine influence.

Montenegrins

Montenegrin literature in the Middle Ages was a part of Serb literature. It started to differ from the Serb literature during the Turkish occupation of the Balkans. The folk poetry in the common language of the people told about historic events and created myths.

In the Middle Ages, art in Montenegro was mostly simple (one-nave and three-nave churches prevailed on the coast, but also some basilicas were built with three naves, e.g., the Cathedral of St. Tripun in Kotor). For the later development in the Gothic period (Svač, Bar, Ulcinj, Kotor), Dominican and Franciscan fathers can take credit, but the Turkish occupation hindered development of Baroque architecture. In Montenegro, art developed under the influence of Serbia and Byzantium. Monasteries (Djurdjevi stupovi in Ivangrad, 1220; Morača, 1252) are important monuments of the Raška school of architecture, and frescoes in Morača could be counted among works in the old Serb monumental style. The tradition of monumental paintings was preserved until the beginning of the nineteenth century.

Macedonians

The historic development of Macedonian language and literature differs from others in the Slavic world. Its beginnings were the oldest, if one agrees with the thesis that the promoters of Slavic literacy, Fathers Constantine (Cyril) and Methodius, were at the same time the beginners of the Macedonian literature. Many scholars do not agree with this thesis. However, there is no doubt that pupils of Constantine and Methodius, who later worked in the Macedonian ethnic territories, fostered Macedonian literature. Because the Macedonians were dominated by neighboring ethnic groups (Bulgarians, Serbs, Greeks, Turks), development of a distinctive Macedonian culture was hindered. In the Middle Ages Christianity brought changes in church architecture, which until the ninth century had been influenced by the Roman Western style. From the ninth century on, the church started to adjust to Eastern influences. The Byzantine style prevailed in church architecture during the period of Samuel's state (tenth until the eleventh century).

The most important and famous monument of the early architecture is the Church of St. Sophia in Ohrid, which had a deterring influence on ar-

The ancient monastery at Ohrid (Corel)

chitecture of the Eastern Church. Its facade belongs among the greatest creations of its time. Other church builders of the time copied its style. According to one source it was Byzantine Archbishop Leon who built this church, but according to another source he only renewed a church constructed by Emperor Samuel around 1000. The church was rebuilt many times over the course of centuries, and different parts were built until the fourteenth century.

When Macedonia became a part of Serbia, the building of churches continued under the Serb rulers and local lords (Church of St. Nicolas in Skopska Črna gora near Skopje, church in Štip, etc.). The Turkish occupation in the fourteenth and fifteenth centuries halted the development of Slavic feudal society and its architecture with it. Of definite importance for the development of architecture was the change of the official religion: In monumental architecture the Christian churches were replaced by mosques. The need for fortresses disappeared; instead, open settlements and towns developed where the Turkish administration built its structures. However, the native creativity was retained and developed, especially in the building of houses, where the builders made autochthonous architecture adjusted to the Macedonian environment, climate, and building materials.

Conclusion

The migration of Slavic peoples (tribes) changed the ethnic situation in the territory of the former Yugoslavia and influenced its political and administrative development. In a way, the settlement of South Slavs in these territories and the establishment of their medieval states started—at least in mythical outlooks—the process of development of modern South Slavic ethnic nations. The "memories" and glory of their ancient states represent not only the mythical foundations of these (ethnic) nations but also historical foundations of their present nation-states. Although specific circumstances and historic developments of different parts of this territory included foreign rule by different hegemonic empires—resulting in specific ethnic identities and the formation of distinct modern ethnic nations—strangely enough, the myths and memories of common ethnic origins and ethnic kindred survived and found their reflection in the emergence of the "Yugoslav idea" in the nineteenth century and were present (although often contested) throughout the existence of Yugoslav state(s) in the twentieth century.

Timeline

546–620	Invasions of the Slavic tribes to the Balkan Peninsula resulting in Slavs settling Eastern Alps, Pannonian and Walachian Plain, and most of the Balkan Peninsula
623–658	Samo's tribal union
783	Macedonian Slavs came under Byzantine rule
788	Carantanians subjugated to the Franks
803	Croatia and Slavonia subjugated to the Franks
818–820	The anti-Frankish rebellion of Ljudevit Posavski in Lower Pannonia; Carantanians and Carniolans joined
862–874	Kocelj reigned in Lower Pannonia as an independent ruler; Lower Pannonia was the last medieval independent Slovene principality
864	Macedonian Slavs came under Bulgarian rule
878	Croatia liberated itself from Frankish rule
881–896	Hungarian settlements in the Pannonian Plain between the Danube and Drava Rivers in the Eastern Alps
910–930	The rule of Tomislav in Croatia; Croatia reached its peak in political strength and territorial expansion

971	Byzantium renewed its authority in Macedonia
976–1014	The Macedonian Empire of the Emperor Samuel
995	In the battle near Augsburg the German army defeated the Hungarians, and the Hungarian attacks toward the west ended
1014	The battle near Belasica; Byzantine Emperor Basil II defeated Samuel's army
1042	Prince Štefan Vojislav defeated the Byzantine army and created the first foundations of the state of Zeta
1054	Schism of Eastern and Western Christian churches into Orthodoxy and Roman Catholicism
1097	Hungarian King Koloman defeated the last Croatian king, Petar
1102	*Pacta Conventa?;* Croatians became vassals of the Hungarians
1166–1196	The great mayor Štefan Nemanja; Serbia succeeded in ending the rule of Byzantium
1183	Štefan Nemanja annexed Zeta to Raška
1204	End of the Byzantine Empire
1331–1355	The rule of Dušan Šilni—Dušan the Mighty
1354–1357	Turks occupied Gallipoli
1371	Battle on the Maritsa River; Slavic nobility in Macedonia became Turkish vassals
15–28 June 1389	Battle of Kosovo polje
1435–1459	Turks occupied the Serb territories
1456–1526	Habsburgs united the majority of the Slovene ethnic territories under their rule
1457	Turkish occupation of the territories of Zeta
1463	Turks, under the leadership of Mehmed II the Conqueror, occupied Bosnia
1478	The first great peasant rebellion in Carinthia
1515	Croatian-Slovene peasant rebellion under the leadership of Matija Gubec and Ilija Gregorić
1526	Turks defeated Hungarian-Croatian army in the battle at Mohács
1529	Turkish army reaches Vienna for the first time
1535	Habsburgs developed as a defense territory, the so-called Military Frontier Region (*Vojna krajina*)
1670	Conspiracy of Croatian feudal lords of Zrinjski and Frankopan against Habsburgs

1683	Austrian Imperial Army defeated the Turks outside Vienna
1689	Karpoš's rebellion in northwestern Macedonia
1689–1690	"Great Migrations" of Serbs from Kosovo to Vojvodina under the leadership of *Vladika* Arsenius III Crnijević
1699	The Habsburg Monarchy regained Hungarian and Croatian lands and Slavonia from Turks
July 1712	*Vladika* Danilo Petrović Njegoš defeated the Turks and did away with the Turkish supreme authority
1737–1739	Serbs' rebellion against the Turks
1740	Beginning of the reign of Empress Maria Theresa
1788–1791	Serbs' rebellion against the Turks
1790–1791	Croatia, with the consent of its nobility, became administratively subordinated to Hungary
1791	Peace of Svištov; the Turkish authorities had to give the Serbs local self-management and religious freedom

Significant People, Places, and Events

CRNOJEVIĆ, IVAN Ruler of Zeta during the years 1465–1490 and known as Ivan-beg. Ivan acknowledged the supreme authority of Venice and fought the Turks. In 1479, when they made peace with Venice, the Turks occupied Upper Zeta and Skadar. Under Turkish pressure Ivan had to flee to Italy. In 1481 he succeeded in renewing his authority in part of Zeta but had to acknowledge the supreme Turkish authority. The smaller area of Zeta under his rule was the same as the territory of later Montenegro. Its capital became Cetinje, to which Ivan moved the seat of the old Orthodox Zetan Diocese.

SAMUEL Macedonian emperor during the period from 976 until 1014. In fights against Byzantium, Samuel established a Macedonian Empire (with its seats in Prespa and later in Ohrid) and by the end of the tenth century had conquered Macedonia, Thessalia, Epirus, Albania, Duklja, Zahumlje, Raška, Srem, Bosnia, and Danubian Bulgaria. Emperor Basileus II of Byzantium conquered one-half of this state during the period 1001–1004, but it took him another ten years to finally conquer Samuel's troops in the battle of Belasica near Strumica, on 29 July 1014. Samuel himself escaped to Prilep, but later died of a stroke.

SKENDER-BEG (*Staniša Crnojević*) Youngest son of Ivan Crnojević, brought to power in Montenegro by the Turks. Montenegro was organized as a special entity—"sandžak" (a Turkish administrative unit), with the seat in Žabljak, the old capital of Crnojević's Montenegro. A combination of the medieval Serb rulers and Turkish rulers, he listened to both Christian and Muslim religious leaders.

SOKOLOVIĆ, MEHMED-PAŠA (c. 1505–1579) Turkish statesman and military leader of Bosnian Slavic descent. Sokolović was born in a Christian family but became a *yanitsar* (soldier) as a part of *dervishma* (blood tax, i.e., the Turks took young boys from their Christian parents and educated them as soldiers of the Turkish army). In 1565 he became prime minister of Turkey. He became famous in numerous wars (Austrian-Turkish, 1551–1561 and 1566; in Persia, Sudan, Cyprus etc.). He rebuilt the Turkish navy, which was destroyed at Lepant. He worked on development of education, literary works, and arts and even planned the building of the Suez and Don–Volga canals. There was conservative opposition against him, and he was killed by a dervish.

ŠTEFAN, DUŠAN Also called Dušan Šilni (Dušan the Mighty), ca. 1308–1355 Serb king from 1331, czar of the Serbs and Greeks from 1345. In his wars against Byzantium, Dušan Štefan established a great Serb state that spread from Belgrade to the Gulf of Patras (Macedonia, Albania, Epirus, Thessalia). He even tried to conquer Constantinople and become the ruler of all of Byzantium. He was crowned emperor, and the Serb Church became a patriarchy, a supreme Orthodox Church administrative unit within its national community in 1345. He proposed to the pope a crusade against the Turks in which he wanted to be "supreme commander." He also initiated administrative reforms and published Dušan's Code, a collection of laws that was the most important legal document of medieval Serbia.

TOMISLAV I Croatian prince and first Croatian king (*dux and rex Croatorum*) of the Trpimirović dynasty. Tomislav I reigned from 910 to 928. During the years 914–925 he united under his rule all of historic Croatia, Dalmatia, and Slavonia and stopped Hungarian invaders. The Christian Church in Croatia remained under an archbishop with its seat in Split. During Tomislav's rule the old Romance population of Dalmatian cities began to be Croatized. In 926 he won the battle against Bulgarian Czar Simeon and stopped a Bulgarian invasion from the southeast. Two years later, Tomislav died of natural causes.

TRUBAR, PRIMOŽ (1508–1586) Protestant minister, the author of the first printed book in the Slovene language and translator of the Bible into Slovene. Trubar served as Catholic priest. However, he followed Lutheran ideas, became a Protestant, and was forced to leave for

Germany. In exile he wrote *Catechismus* and *Abecedarium* (ca. 1550) and wrote and translated some religious works (altogether, twenty-four books and ten forewords). He also wrote some religious songs. In his work *Slovenska cerkvena ordninga* (*Slovene Religious Order*) he wrote about a plan for the organization of Slovene churches and schools.

TVRTKO I KOTROMANIĆ (1338–1391) Bosnian ban and king under whose rule Bosnia became the largest and the leading state of the Balkan Peninsula. In 1353 Tvrtko I became the ban and fought against the feudal separatism of numerous Bosnian nobles. After the death of Serb czar Dušan (1355), Tvrtko extended the territory of his state eastward and, after the death of Uroš of Serbia, was crowned "King of Bosnia and Serbia." After the death of Hungarian King Ladislav I, he extended his rule to Dalmatian cities. He succeeded in uniting a majority of the Croats and Serbs. In 1388 he won the Battle of Bileća against the Turks, and his troops also took part in the Battle of Kosovo.

Bibliography

Arnakis, G. C. "The role of religion in the development of Balkan nationalism." In Jelavich, Charles, and Jelavich, Barbara (eds.). *The Balkans in Transition: Essays on the Development of Balkan Life and Politics since the Eighteenth Century.* (Berkeley: University of California Press, 1963): 115–144.

Carter, Francis W. *Dubrovnik (Ragusa): A Classic City-State.* (London: Seminar Press, 1972).

Fine, John V. A., Jr. *The Bosnian Church: A New Interpretation.* (New York: Columbia University Press, 1975).

Jelavich, Barbara. *History of the Balkans.* (Cambridge, U.K.: Cambridge University Press, 1983).

Krstić, Djurdjica. *Dušan's Code of Law.* (Beograd, Serbia-Montenegro: Vajat, 1999).

Rogić, V. "Croatian Military Border: Fundamental, Historical-Geographical Problems." *Geographical Papers 8* (1991): 167–190.

Rothenberg, Günther E. *The Austrian Military Border in Croatia, 1522–1747.* (Urbana: University of Chicago Press, 1960).

Sugar, Peter F. *Southeastern Europe under Ottoman Rule 1453–1803.* (Seattle: University of Washington Press, 1977).

Tanner, Marcus. *Croatia: A Nation Forged in War.* (New Haven and London: Yale University Press, 1997).

Turnock, David. *The Making of Eastern Europe from the Earliest Times until 1815.* (London: Routledge, 1988).

Vlasto, A. P. *The Entry of the Slavs into Christendom.* (Cambridge, U.K.: Cambridge University Press, 1970).

Vucinich, Wayne S., and Emmert, Thomas A. (eds.). *Kosovo: Legacy of a Medieval Battle.* (Minneapolis: Minnesota Mediterranean and East European Monographs, 1991).

CHAPTER TWO

The Yugoslav Nations,
from 1800 to World War I

THE BEGINNING OF THE NINETEENTH CENTURY was the period when the ideas of the Enlightenment spread to the masses. In Europe those ideas inspired desires for national unification and the development of nation-states from these unified nations. In the "Yugoslav nations" as in other nations, fights against foreign feudal lords and masters and against townspeople who were of foreign ethnic origin strengthened these ideas and dreams the natives had of creating nation-states of their own.

This period of nationalistic movements found the Yugoslav nations scattered in many territorial units and states. The "Yugoslav Idea," a political ideology and program to unify all South Slavs politically and economically, appeared among all South Slavic nations. The idea was to improve their conditions under the foreign rule, but especially to help the oppressed Slav Christians in the Ottoman Empire. The Serb uprisings against the Turks in the nineteenths century, Garašanin's *Načertanie,* and Illyrism were important impulses to this idea. Initially, the territory of their autochthonous settlement was divided among many countries: the Habsburg Monarchy (after 1867 Austria-Hungary), the Turkish Ottoman Empire, the Republic of Dubrovnik, and the Republic of Venice. This geopolitical situation was changed by the wars of Napoleon I Bonaparte. As a result of his conquests, the independent republics of Dubrovnik and Venice disappeared from the political map of Europe, the Republic of Venice in 1797 and the Republic of Dubrovnik in 1806. Napoleon also occupied many territories of the southern regions of the Habsburg Monarchy (Istria, Gorizia, Trieste, western Carinthia, Carniola, and Croatia, including the Frontier Military Zone on the right bank of the Sava River) and established a special geopolitical unit, the Illyrian Provinces (1809–1813). It is important to note that the French occupation did not change the status of peasants in those territories. In other words, the French did not abolish the feudal order in Yugoslav lands.

After the French left, the Habsburg rule was renewed. The despotic rule of the Ottoman Empire continued, which affected the Macedonians, but also the Serbs and Montenegrins, who managed to establish their (more or less) independent states but were also dependent upon a resolution of the so-called "Eastern Question," that is, the outcome of the fight among European powers for supreme rule over the Balkans.

This situation compelled the Croat and Serb bourgeoisie (middle class) to create their spheres of influence over as wide a region as possible. Based on the idea of national unification, Croat, Serb, and Slovene bourgeoisie developed their own grand national ideologies and nationalism. However, the Yugoslav idea of establishing a common state of all South Slavic nations also emerged and was developed. The competing nature and differences between great Croat and great Serb ideas provoked conflicts and fights between Croat and Serb leaders for supremacy in the region (i.e., Yugoslav lands) or, at least, in certain parts of it. Austria-Hungary and Turkey used and even stimulated these conflicts to stop the spread of the Yugoslav idea and to stop any strengthening of other nationalistic ideas that could have fatal consequences for the Ottoman or Austro-Hungarian empires. It was the policy of the Habsburg Monarchy, especially of the leading politicians of Hungarian and Austrian-German origin, to provoke strife among the Serb and Croat bourgeoisie and political leaders so that the Monarchy would be able to survive.

Distribution of "Ethnic" Groups and Growth of Populations

As they had also been in the past, in the mid-nineteenth century the Yugoslav lands were politically, territorially, ethnically, and culturally divided. Until World War I the territories of today's Slovenia, Croatia, Vojvodina, and (after 1878) Bosnia and Herzegovina were parts of Austria-Hungary. Serbia and Montenegro were formally parts of the Ottoman Empire until 1878, and Macedonia was part of the Ottoman Empire until 1912. People identified mostly with their historic regions or lands until the nineteenth century, when the development of capitalism and integration processes caused the birth of modern national identities—so that Slovenes, Croats, Serbs, Bosnian Muslims (present-day Bosniaks), Macedonians, and Montenegrins each started to identify themselves as ethnic nations.

TABLE 2.1   DEVELOPMENT OF POPULATION IN THE REGIONS OF THE FORMER YUGOSLAVIA, 1870–1910

Region	1870*	1910*	Percentage Change
Serbia	1,302	2,912	+ 123.7
Croatia-Slavonia	1,838	2,732	+ 48.6
Bosnia and Herzegovina	1,042	1,898	+ 82.1
Dalmatia	457	625	+ 31.6
Slovenia	1,134	1,064	− 6.2
Macedonia	N/A	1,665	——
Montenegro	65.5	238	+ 63.4
Vojvodina	N/A	1,353	——

*in thousands

SOURCE: Lampe, John R. *Yugoslavia as History. Twice There Was a Country.* (Cambridge: Cambridge University Press, 1996): 73.

There were three main characteristics in the demographic development in this territory. First, there was a large increase of population, especially in the regions abandoned by the Turks, due to the return of a large part of the Slavic population that had fled from the Turks in the past.

Second, there were voluminous internal migrations from the rural areas to the cities (urbanization) and international migrations comprising emigration to the western European countries and overseas. These migrations, mostly spurred by bad economical and social conditions, were a part of worldwide simultaneous migrations from poorer rural regions to richer industrialized areas. Emigration was especially intensive from Slovene and Croat ethnic territories. According to U.S. statistics, between 1898 and 1915 more than 485,000 immigrants to the United States claimed to be of Slovene and Croat "race or people."

Third, the above-mentioned factors influenced the evolving, ethnically mixed structure of the population in most of the regions of the former Yugoslavia. Because of the immigration of Germans and Hungarians into the territories settled by the Slovenes and Croats and the forced Germanization and Hungarization of the Croats and Slovenes, the degree of ethnic mixture became even greater during the decades before World War I in the regions of Austria-Hungary.

We can follow the evolving ethnic structure on the basis of official statistical data, especially in Austria-Hungary.

The population surveys of 1846 and 1850 were based on available information of local authorities on the language situations of each village or township. The first such censuses were made in 1773 for Hungary (without Croatia and Transylvania) and in 1830 for Styria. The results of the survey in Austrian lands in 1846 (as published in 1857) are quite accurate regarding the population in general; however, this inquiry did not take into account migrants who moved into certain regions where other languages were spoken.

Similar statistical inquiries on ethnicity in certain places were made also for the Hungarian part of the Monarchy in 1850.

The first census in the Habsburg Monarchy in which the language of each person was actually determined was that of 1880. In the Austrian part census takers tried to determine the language of communication ("Umgagssprache"), while in the Hungarian part they counted population by mother tongue. Wilhelm Winkler later compiled the census data for 1910 and adjusted them based on the new borders in Europe, so that his data for 1910 are comparable to the 1921 and 1931 data for Yugoslavia (see table 4.2). However, the ethnic structure of the population was not examined and determined by the censuses in Serbia and Montenegro before World War I.

Political Histories of the South Slavic Ethno-Nations

Slovenes

At the beginning of the nineteenth century, Slovenes lived in Austrian lands (Carniola, Gorizia, Trieste, the north of Istria, southern Carinthia, and southern Styria). The most northeastern part of the Slovene ethnic territory, Prekmurje, was part of the Hungarian counties of Zala and Vas. At that time most of the west and south of the Slovene ethnic territories (western Carinthia, Gorizia, Trieste, Carniola) were conquered during the "coalition wars" by Napoleon I Bonaparte, who created a new territorial entity, the Illyrian Provinces, which also included southern Croatia, Dalmatia, Istria, and Boka kotorska.

After the French left in 1813, the Austrian authorities took over again. The Austrian chancellor, Metternich, was successful in his attempt to restrict nationalist political movements in the empire, with the help of the police and with censorship. This period was marked by the accelerated development of the Slovene language as the language of culture, education,

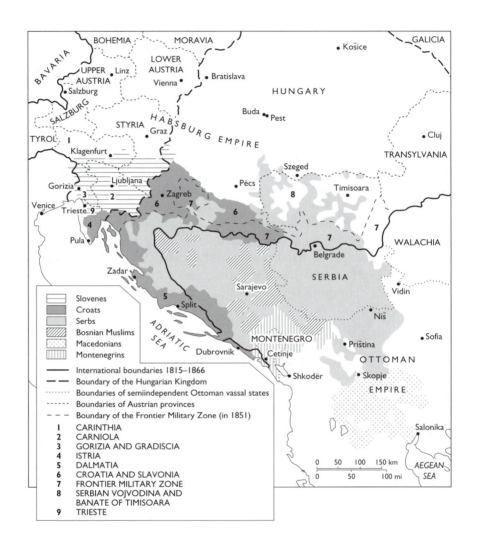

South Slavs in the Mid-Nineteenth Century
In the mid-nineteenth century, South Slav settlement was divided between
the Habsburg Monarchy and the Ottoman Empire. The first statistical data on
population based on inquiries and censuses of the population are from this period.
These sources also provide data on the ethnic and language structure of
the population in the Habsburg Monarchy.

and, gradually, politics. It was the period when France Prešeren, who is considered the greatest Slovene poet in history, wrote his *Poezije*. This book of poems includes *Zdravljica* (*A Toast*), today's Slovene national anthem:

> Anew the vines have fruited
> And borne us, my good friends, sweet wine
> To charge our blood diluted,
> To clear our heart, our eye define,
> To suppress
> All distress
> And waken hope in saddened breast.
> Let's drink that every nation
> Will live to see that bright day's birth
> When 'neath the sun's rotation
> Dissent is banished from the earth,
> All will be
> Kinfolk free
> With neighbors none in enmity.
>   (Prešeren, 1999: 159–161)

Especially in Carniola, but also in other Slovene lands, a primary and secondary school system was developed that taught in the Slovene language. A Slovene newspaper (*Kmetijske in rokodelske novice*) was also published. As a consequence, Slovene national consciousness started to develop. However, one could not define it as a political consciousness—as a Slovene national identity—in the modern sense before the March 1848 revolution.

During the March revolution of 1848 (called the Spring of Nations), the Slovenes were among the groups who defined a national program. With this program, called Združena Slovenija (United Slovenia), the Slovenes demanded unification of all the territories of their autochthonous settlement in one unit under the Austrian emperor, a region in which the Slovene language would be the official language in schools and public offices. The demands for United Slovenia were declared by Matija Majar Ziljski, a Carinthian Slovene Catholic priest, and by a group of Slovene students in Vienna, who were united as *Društvo Slovenija* (Association Slovenia). These demands were also supported in peasants' petitions signed during 1848–1849. During the next decades this set of demands became a cornerstone of all Slovene nationalist movements. The demands for the United Slovenia were confirmed during the period of large meetings, called *taborsko gibanje* (mass meetings movement), between 1868 and 1871.

During this period the Slovene nationalist movement became a mass movement, and modern Slovene national consciousness started to spread to the masses—peasants and townspeople alike. During the next decades, the Slovene political leaders and middle class did not want to aggravate the political situation, as everyone was aware that it was impossible to change the nature of the Habsburg Empire. In attempts to improve the position of Slovenes in the empire, Slovene politicians developed a strategy of resolving some minor problems first. Despite the continued pressures by the Austrian authorities for Germanization of the Slovenes, this policy succeeded in increasing the use of the Slovene language in schools, in the judicial system, and in the administration of the Slovene historic lands. It also succeeded in opening up the electoral system so that the lower classes could also vote, which meant that the majority of the Slovenes could then vote. Meanwhile, the Austrian Germans were intensifying the Germanization of the Slovenes.

During the last quarter of the nineteenth century, the Slovene people were victims of an economic crisis, particularly in agriculture and in crafts from artisans, due to the coming of the railroad. The Southern Railroad Trieste-Vienna brought new products, and Slovene artisans' products could not compete with them. As a consequence, many Slovenes had to emigrate: more than one-fifth of the population (some 250,000) left for the Americas and western Europe.

In the last years before World War I, Slovene politicians continued the policy of making changes in small steps, and the Slovene political and economic situation within the monarchy was steadily improving. However, the Slovene politicians ceased their demands for thorough reforms of the political system in the monarchy. At the same time, internal political diversification occurred, and Slovene politicians became divided along political lines. As a result, the first Slovene political parties were formed. Apart from certain influences of "Illyrian," "Pan-Slavic" and "Yugoslav" ideas (see the following sections), their policy debates were initially confined to historic Slovene lands in the empire and did not reach across those borders. However, in the decades before World War I some groups were formed, especially within the liberal political camp, which were convinced that the "Slovene national question" could not be solved within the Habsburg monarchy but only with its dissolution and the establishment of a new Yugoslav state in which Slovenia would be one of the equal units.

On the other hand, although the situation of Slovenes in Austria-Hungary was deteriorating following the outbreak of World War I, some political parties of Slovenes, especially the Catholic Slovene People's Party, remained loyal to the monarchy.

Croats

For Croats, the first half of the nineteenth century was marked by fights against the policies of Hungarization promulgated by Hungarian authorities, which were aimed at destroying Croatia as a political entity. During this period, Croats lived divided in their historical lands, where their situations differed. The northern part of Croatia and Slavonia, including the capital, Zagreb, was under Hungarian rule, and Dalmatia and Istria belonged to Austria. Also, many Croats lived in Bosnia and Herzegovina, which was under the Ottoman rule until the Austrian occupation in 1878. The aim of Croat nationalist movements was to unite the historic lands with Croat populations into one unit. Occasional and specific problems of the Croat nationalist movement were relations with those Serbs who lived scattered in different parts of this territory and formed one-quarter of its population.

From this fight against foreign Hungarian and Austrian rule, the "Illyrian idea" of the unification of Croat and South Slavic peoples into one cultural unit on the basis of a common written language (a kind of mixture of all written languages of South Slavs) and a common national consciousness was born in the 1830s. The Illyrian movement under the leadership of Ljudevit Gaj supported political unification of the Southern Slavs. For this reason the Habsburg officials thought of it as an anti-Habsburg revolutionary movement, and, in January 1843, the Viennese court forbade political Illyrism in Croatia. Although the Illyrian movement's social programs were reasonable, they also provoked resistance and the opposition of the feudal Croat nobility. In spite of Vienna's attempts to suppress it, however, this movement provided the cornerstone of an idea of solidarity among the Southern Slavs.

In the revolutionary year of 1848, Croats under the leadership of ban (viceroy-governor of Croatia) Josip Jelačić fought for statehood. In March 1848, deputies from all Croat lands convened in Zagreb, and three months later the Croat Sabor (Parliament) started to operate, formed by representatives of the Croat nobility as well as representatives of pro-liberal and democratic townspeople. However, further development of democratic institutions in Croatia was interrupted by the victory of the counterrevolution and the restoration of the absolute power of the monarchy in 1851. It is interesting to note that Ban Jelačić and his forces later helped the Viennese throne crush the Hungarian revolution in Budapest. They feared Hungarian nationalism and the possible consequences of the victory of the Hungarian revolution more than they feared the Austrian monarchy.

During the period of absolutism that followed, the authorities introduced many reforms in the judicial system and administration that abolished the feudal order in Croatia. These reforms helped to solidify the centralized power of the Habsburg monarchy and create a unified Austrian Empire. In 1861 the constitutional order was restored. The emperor proclaimed the February Patent, with a new enacted electoral system and centralist administration. The Croats were too weak to start the fight for federalization of the Habsburg monarchy and introduction of Trialism, which demanded a reorganization of the monarchy into three units (Austrian, Hungarian, and South Slav). If the Croats had been successful, one of the units of the monarchy could have united the South Slavs of the monarchy. The (confederated) constitutional reforms and the introduction of dualism in 1867 divided the Habsburg monarchy into two parts—Austria and Hungary—and established only the following common institutions: the monarch, who was simultaneously Austrian emperor and Hungarian king; a common army; and a common foreign policy. These reforms actually worsened the political position of Croats in the empire: the Hungarian-Croat *Nagodba* (agreement) brought Croats completely under Hungarian political and economic domination and eroded political freedoms that the Croats had previously enjoyed.

The foreign rule, division, and (economic and social) backwardness of Croat lands fostered the development of two main national ideas: the Yugoslav idea and *pravaštvo*, the Greater Croat idea. Representatives of the Yugoslav idea, such as Stjepan Rački and Josip Juraj Strossmayer, thought that Yugoslavism was the only solution for the further existence of "Yugoslav nations." They even thought of a possible Balkan Federation. Whereas this idea was initially adopted by only a small part of the bourgeoisie, *pravaštvo* or Greater Croatia (the idea and movement for an independent Croatia, seen as the fight for Croat rights based on historical law) was adopted by most of the Croat bourgeoisie, the intelligentsia, part of the Catholic clergy, and a large number of the peasantry. Ante Starčević, a key proponent, and other ideologists who embraced the idea of Greater Croatia and initiated the movement developed the concept of independent Croatia on the basis of Croat historical law and traditions of the Medieval Croat state. *Pravaštvo* envisioned the unification of South Slavs based on the belief that all South Slavs belonged to the Croat people. Additionally, this clashed sharply with Serb policy and the idea of "Greater Serbia." The proponents of Greater Croatia subsequently tried to gather support from the Croat people by opposing the "Greater Serbia" idea.

Croat politicians were unhappy with the Nagodba. However, because of their opportunist politics and because they were not united, they were unable to prevent Croatia's complete dependence on Hungary and the processes of Hungarization of Croat lands and peoples.

Still, at the turn of the century some Croat political parties and, in particular, certain Dalmatian politicians led by Ante Trumbić, believed that cultural autonomy in the spirit of "Austroslavism" was not satisfactory. They promoted the idea of an independent South Slav state that would break its ties with Austria-Hungary. This became the cornerstone of the so-called *politika novog kursa* (Policy of a New Course). It was led by Franjo Supilo and was made up of the broad coalition of most of the Croat and Serb parties before World War I. During the next years, the coalition under Supilo pursued anti-Habsburg policies. Within the coalition the influence of the opposition of the petit bourgeoisie led by the Serb politician Svetozar Pribičević was growing. Eventually, Supilo, who demanded an independent Croatia, left the coalition, as it did not support his ideas. However, the ideas concerning Croat-Serb unity were adopted by a younger generation of politicians, who, on the basis of Supilo's philosophy, developed new ideas about a state of Serbs, Croats, and Slovenes outside of Austria-Hungary.

Bosniaks (Bosnians, Bosnian Muslims)

Bosnia and Herzegovina had a special position in the Ottoman Empire because most of the Slavic population there became Muslims. We cannot define this phenomenon as forced Islamization of the Slavic population; however, we can also not deny that the Turks tried in as many ways as they could to ensure that their religion would be adopted by a great many people in the lands they occupied. It was believed that the conversion to Islam would connect people with the state and would symbolize their love for the Sultan, the Turkish emperor. Islam spread in particular among the peasant population, but it was adopted also by most of the Slavic nobility. The reasons for such a successful Islamization of the population can be found in the socioeconomic and legal privileges that Muslims in the Turkish Empire were given in comparison with other, non-Muslim, populations.

Although the central authority in the Ottoman capital of Istanbul developed its strength from the Muslim populace, during the course of the nineteenth century it no longer controlled its large empire. Feudal anarchy was a fact of life. More and more among Bosnian landlords, the idea of an autonomous Bosnia developed. Therefore, it is not surprising that Bosnian landlords fought against the reforms and modernization attempts of Sultan Mahmud II. This resistance group of Bosnian landlords, under the leadership of Husein kapetan-Gradaščević, was crushed only after their military defeat in 1832 and the military expedition of Omer-pasha Latas in 1850–1851. (*Kapetan* was a leader of a territorial unit of defense in Bosnia. *Pasha* was a supreme military and administrative leader of a pashdom, a supreme military and administrative unit in the Ottoman Empire.) The Bosnian landlords wanted to return "what the state had stolen from them" with its reforms that imposed higher taxes on the peasantry.

Several unconnected uprisings by the Christian population also occurred. The largest was the 1875 outbreak in Nevesinje, which showed many signs of a national liberation movement. Christian rabble armies fought successfully against the Turks for three years. The situation did not develop in favor of the Bosnian Christians, however, but in favor of Austria-Hungary, which, with the help of the German Empire, initiated very successful diplomacy with its allies against the Turks to further its political and military aims, first in Bosnia and Herzegovina and later in other Balkan states. Consequently Austria-Hungary achieved its aims. The Congress of Berlin (13 June 1878) allowed Austria-Hungary to occupy Bosnia and Herzegovina. Austria-Hungary did not change the Turkish feudal order, and the peasants did not get the land, which meant that the peasant uprising did not succeed in its aims. At the same time, the Muslim population of Bosnia fought against Austro-Hungarian occupation because they were afraid to lose the privileged position they had held under Turkish rule. The Austro-Hungarian occupation army had to fight against armed Muslim resistance under the leadership of Hadži Loja. It took the imperial army three months to crush this resistance. After that Bosnia and Herzegovina became a "colony" of German and Hungarian interests.

The Austro-Hungarian occupation of Bosnia and Herzegovina also meant the beginning of an industrial revolution and the economic development of Bosnia and Herzegovina, which brought great social changes. The Muslim landlords began to lose their power as the influence of for-

A street scene in Sarajevo where Archduke Francis Ferdinand was assassinated
(Underwood and Underwood/Corbis)

eign investment capital increased and, with this, also the influence of the
Bosnian bourgeoisie. Meanwhile, the peasant population continued to be
unhappy because of unresolved agrarian issues. Social changes, together
with the increasing number of intellectuals, who became the leaders of
social and national movements, sparked intensified national and social

unrest among the Bosnian population that resulted an uprising in Herze-govina in 1882, a continuous struggle for the religious and cultural auton-omy of Serbs in the country (1896–1905), and uprisings among Muslims (1899–1909), as well as other movements of the peasantry and workers.

The tensions within the Ottoman Empire and among the great world powers at the beginning of the twentieth century also impacted Bosnia and Herzegovina. The revolution of the Young Turks, a movement of Turkish bourgeoisie, broke out in 1908. The Young Turks wanted to trans-form the Ottoman Empire into a modern western-type centralized state based on a democratic constitutional order. Austria-Hungary wanted to settle the unclear international legal status of Bosnia and Herzegovina. On 5 October 1908, Austro-Hungarian Emperor Francis Joseph declared the annexation of Bosnia and Herzegovina to Austria in spite of the great powers' and the Bosnian populace's protestations against the annexation. Austria-Hungary succeeded in annexing Bosnia and Herzegovina, with the help of the German Empire. The influence of the Balkan Wars (1912–1913) (see the next section of this chapter) further amplified the growing resistance against Austria-Hungary that was already being fueled by the repressive policies of the existing police regime. That resistance and the fight for religious/cultural autonomy, which were at the heart of the nationalist politics of the Bosnian Muslim population, likewise emerged in opposition to Serb and Croat nationalists who wanted Bosnian Mus-lims to identify either with the Serbs or Croats. And yet, even before World War I, part of the Muslim population had joined the political movement for the creation of Yugoslavia, which was to be a state of equal peoples and nations, with Bosnian Muslims being one of the nations. In Bosnia, the Yugoslav idea was embraced by the youth, who wanted to stop the nationalist fights among the Bosnian Serbs, Bosnian Muslims, and Bosnian Croats. The most radical among them joined the revolutionary movement of *Mlada Bosna* (Young Bosnia). One of its members was Gavrilo Princip, who on 28 June 1914 in Sarajevo, shot the Austrian suc-cessor to the throne, Archduke Francis Ferdinand. Austria-Hungary ac-cused Serbia of plotting with the assassins. This assassination was used by Austria-Hungary as a pretense to attack Serbia, which escalated into the beginning of World War I.

Serbs

The beginning of the nineteenth century is a great landmark in the his-tory of the Serbs' struggles for liberation of their lands from Turkish occupation. From these fights emerged the Serb nation-state. In the beginning the Serbs wanted only wider autonomy because of the violence of Turkish authorities in the Belgrade Pashdom (see map 2.1) and the killings of many members of the Serb nobility (Serb village princes). In 1804 the First Serb Uprising started. Serbs under the leadership of Djordje Petrović (nicknamed Karadjordje) liberated the whole Pashdom in a few months and started to create their own civil administration. The Turks, who were busy in a war with Russia after 1806, were unable to put down the uprising until 1813.

Because of the cruel Turkish revenge against the rebels, the Second Serb Uprising started in spring 1815, under the leadership of Miloš Obrenović. Due to pressure from Russia, which proclaimed itself protector of the Orthodox South Slavs of the Ottoman Empire, and due to unrest in every corner of the Ottoman Empire, the Turkish government decided in autumn 1815 to promise self-government to the Serbs. In 1830 the Turks officially recognized the autonomy and self-government of the Serbs. Although still under Ottoman suzerainty, Serbia thus became an autonomous principality under Russian protection.

The Serb monarchy was, however, a state where the feudal order was still intact, a situation fought against by Serb liberals, who wanted to improve social conditions in Serbia. Until 1903 the official policy of the Serb governments under the Obrenović dynasty (1815–1842 and 1859–1903) and the Karadjordjević dynasty (1842–1858) was to fight to improve the social situation in Serbia—and in particular to improve the status of the Obrenović and Karadjordjević dynasties. On the other hand, the politics and policies of these governments encouraged the liberation of all the South Slav lands in which the Serbs lived and their inclusion in a Greater Serbia. However, in this so-called Greater Serbia Philosophy it was initially questionable whether Greater Serbia could include those lands that were ethnically mixed, for example, Bosnia and Herzegovina, Dalmatia, Macedonia, Kosovo, and Metohija. In 1844 the Serb minister of the interior, Ilija Garašanin, wrote a document, *Naćertanie* (Plan), in which he demanded the unification and liberation of the Serbs and the other South Slavic "nations" who still lived under Turkish rule. He also opposed the Great Powers' rejecting of Serb (national) interests. But because Serb policy was the policy of unification, under which the economically more developed South Slavic lands would become part of a centrally ruled Greater Serbia, it was not at all attractive to the other South Slavs.

The official policy of Serbia was directed toward keeping the monarchy and the dynasty intact, regardless of the price. Serbia lost some opportunities for its national liberation and remained passive as far as foreign policy was concerned until the uprising in Bosnia and Herzegovina (1875–1878). In 1876 Serbia, together with Montenegro, declared war on Turkey to help the uprising of the Bosnian Christians. A weak, disorganized Serb army was defeated by the Turks in March 1877. After Russia, as self-proclaimed protector of the South Slavs of the Ottoman Empire, declared war on Turkey in April 1877, Serbia followed at once. The Peace of San Stefano and the Congress of Berlin (1878) that concluded this war formally recognized the independence of Serbia, which finally ended Turkish suzerainty over that nation. It also gave more land to Serbia, as Niš, Pirot, Toplica, and Vranje counties were annexed (encompassing 6,835 square miles). In the broader picture, the Congress of Berlin divided the entire Balkan area into Russian and Austro-Hungarian spheres of interest. Most of the regions settled by South Slavs came into the Austro-Hungarian sphere of interest.

After Serbia became independent it was inactive in foreign policy for some decades. Prince Milan II Obrenović signed a secret agreement with Austria-Hungary in 1881, under which Serbia committed itself not to spread any anti-Austro-Hungarian propaganda in Bosnia and Herzegovina or to make any agreements without informing Austria-Hungary, which would have to sign off on such agreements. In return Austria-Hungary promised Serbia its diplomatic help in spreading Serb territories toward the south and promised to support the prince (who renamed himself king in 1882) and his dynasty on the Serb throne. In what was a bad economic setup, Milan II Obrenović was the largest capitalist in Serbia and also controlled its foreign commerce (which depended almost entirely on selling pigs and prunes). He put the dynasty's interests above the interests of the people, and therefore the Serb people felt betrayed by the dynasty. The result was a successful attempt on the life of Milan's heir, Aleksandar I Obrenović, on 29 May 1903, and a change of the dynasty on the Serb throne.

After the dethroning of the Obrenović dynasty, the throne of Serbia was occupied by Petar I Karadjordjević. Under his leadership a bourgeois regime and parliamentary democracy were introduced. Serbia also changed its foreign policy away from that of looking only to Austria-Hungary. With its independent policy toward Austria-Hungary, Serbia regained its reputation among the South Slavs in Austria-Hungary. However, the changes in Serb foreign policy became a great obstacle to Austro-Hungarian imperialistic interests in the Balkans. The Austro-Hungarian authorities tried to hinder Serbia by all means. At first, Austria-Hungary tried to geographically encircle Serbia by occupying

*Petar I, king of Serbia, ruled
the country from 1903 to 1921.
He served as king of the Serbs,
Croats, and Slovenes from
1918 to 1921. (Corbis)*

Kosovo. Then Austria-Hungary, with the so-called Customs War, put economic pressure on Serbia and economically ruined it during the period 1906–1910. Because of such imperialist Austro-Hungarian policies and in an attempt to finally liberate all South Slavic lands (especially Macedonia, which was considered South Serbia) from the Turkish rule, the Serbs developed a political alignment with Montenegro and Greece, creating the so-called Balkan Alliance in 1912. The signatories, among other things, obligated themselves to military cooperation with each other. The First Balkan War broke out in October 1912 with an attack on the Turkish Ottoman Empire, and the member states of the Balkan Alliance liberated most of the Turkish possessions in the Balkans within a month. European powers at first wanted to prevent changes in political borders, but after the Turkish defeat they had to recognize the new situation. With the Peace of London on 30 May 1913, Turkey had to cede to the members of the Balkan Alliance all the territories west of a line from Enos/Enez (150 miles southwest of Istanbul) and Midiia/Kiyiköy (55 miles northwest of Istanbul).

Among the members of the Balkan Alliance many differences existed on the question of how to divide the newly "liberated" territories among themselves (especially on how to divide Macedonia). These differences were sharpened by Austria-Hungary, which tried by all means to prevent the establishment of any strong Slavic state on its eastern borders. Austria-Hungary believed that such a state would pose a direct threat to South Slavic territories within the empire. Different interests led to the Second Balkan War, when Bulgaria, which wanted the whole of Macedonia's territory, attacked Serbia at the end of June 1913. After Greece, Montenegro, and Romania entered the war on the Serb side, Bulgaria was defeated very quickly. The Peace of Bucharest on 10 August 1913 again made Serbia larger and stronger. Kosovo and what is today the (former Yugoslav) Republic of Macedonia became a part of Serbia, which was enlarged by 19,885 square miles. With these developments the Balkan Wars brought important changes to the political map of the Balkans just before World War I.

After the Serb success, which for some time stopped Austro-Hungarian penetration in the Balkans, Austria-Hungary started to look for occasions to attack Serbia. It found a pretext to do this following the assassination of Archduke Francis Ferdinand by Gavrilo Princip in Sarajevo (28 June 1914), but what they thought would be a local war exploded into World War I within a few weeks.

Montenegrins

At the beginning of the nineteenth century, Montenegrins enjoyed wide local autonomy. The wars they successfully fought against the Turks resulted in complete internal autonomy and a vanishing Turkish influence in Montenegro. Montenegrins also became an important political and strategic factor in international relations. Parallel with that, the role of the Montenegrin religious leader, the *vladika* (leader of the Montenegrin Orthodox Church), also became stronger.

The Montenegrins had finally formed their tribal union in the eighteenth century and also achieved territorial unity. In the nineteenth century they started to address questions of setting up their state apparatus and achieving formal independence from the Ottoman Empire. Substantial financial aid, however, was needed for this operation. Montenegrin *vladika* Petar I Petrović could not gather those finances without the help of the European Powers. He asked Russia for help, and from then on Montenegrin policy became dependent on Russia. In 1830, Montenegrin *vladika* Petar II Petrović-Njegoš (1813–1851), who with Russian help created the senate and organized the police and judicial authorities, became a prince. In 1841 he succeeded in reaching a mutual understanding on the

border with Austria, which also entailed recognition of Montenegro's independence by Austria. Moreover, in addition to being the religious and
political leader, Njegoš was an important Montenegrin poet. He wrote
about Montenegrin fights again the Turks. The most important of these
works was his epic poem *Gorski vijenac* (*The Mountain Wreath*) in which
he expressed faith in the Christian God and resistance to change. The following passage, in which *Vojvoda* (duke) Batrić, one of the Montenegrin
chiefs, urges the Turks (actually Muslim Montenegrins) to return to the
ancestral faith, illustrates his attitude:

> So tear down minarets and mosques
> also kindle the Serb yule logs
> and paint our Easter eggs,
> the two fasts observe honestly;
> as for the rest, do as you will.

Although Batrić's conception of Christianity may be rudimentary, he is
willing to kill for it:

> Should you not listen to Batrić,
> I swear to you by Obilić's faith
> and by my arms, my trusty weapons,
> our faiths will be immersed in blood,
> the better one will not sink!
> Bairam cannot make peace with Christmas!
> (From Banac, 1984, 60)

Njegoš was succeeded in 1851 by prince Danilo, who did not become
vladika because he wanted to separate religious from state authority in
Montenegro. He also wanted to sign a treaty with the Turkish authorities,
but the Turks did not recognize the independence of Montenegro. This
led to Turkish-Montenegrin wars in the years 1852–1853, 1858–1862, and
1876–1878. The war with Turkey during 1876–1878, into which Montenegro entered together with Serbia after the beginning of the uprising in
Bosnia and Herzegovina, brought formal independence to Montenegro.
Territorially, Montenegro wanted to include its seashore. This was upheld
by the Peace of San Stefano and the Congress of Berlin, which regulated
the newly created conditions in the Balkans.

The state territory of Montenegro doubled. Besides annexing Podgorica
and Nikšić, Montenegro also extended to the seashore at Bar and Ulcinj,

The arrival of the post in Cetinje, ca. 1890. The town has been the capital of Montenegro (in all its political iterations) for centuries. (Underwood and Underwood/Corbis)

thus achieving its territorial goals. Along with the territorial enlargement, as early as 1879, Montenegrin authorities began reforms aimed at turning Montenegro from a patriarchal tribal structure into a state. The judiciary was separated from administration and was better organized. The badly organized and undisciplined people's army was replaced by an organized state army. Reforms, however, did not improve the bad economic situation and the opposition (intelligentsia and peasants) demanded a constitution that would limit the absolute power of princes. As all these changes were taking place, prince Nikola (who had succeeded Danilo) had to give the state a constitution in 1905. Montenegro became a constitutional but not parliamentary monarchy. The prince, who named government and other high officials, still had most of the power in his hands, but the constitution made it possible for an opposition to be created.

This was also the period when Serbia and Montenegro competed for leadership in the nationalist movement. On the one hand, some Montenegrins fought for leadership in the national movement of Montenegro and, on the other, some Montenegrins embraced the idea of unification with Serbia in order to make it easier for the state to unite with other South Slavs. The idea of unification was hindered at first by the conflict of interests between two royal dynasties—the Petrovićs of Montenegro and the Karadjordjevićs of Serbia. However, the unification idea became realistic after the victory and liberation of substantial territories in the Balkan Wars, after which Montenegro and Serbia became neighbors. Once Austria-Hungary declared war on Serbia in 1914, Montenegro fought on Serbia's side. It did so although Austria-Hungary offered Montenegro substantial advantages if it would remain neutral, such as financial aid, territorial expansion in Albania and Sandžak, and guarantees of independence. Thus, Montenegro became one of the first European countries to enter World War I.

Macedonians

Macedonian Slavs awaited the beginning of the nineteenth century under an unstable Turkish rule characterized by fights among economically and socially backward Turkish feudal landowners. They fought against the central Turkish authorities, which resulted in the increasing exploitation of the peasants. These harsh conditions forced Macedonian agricultural peasants to move into the cities, where they started to work as artisans and shopkeepers, and many migrated to North America and some to Australia. Development of commerce and trade also facilitated the growth of the Macedonian bourgeoisie, who—due to commercial connections with central Europe—began to develop a Macedonian national consciousness and to demand self-management in matters of religion and education. In spite of some successes, the Macedonian national awakening during the first half of the nineteenth century remained limited to narrow literary and linguistic questions and did not venture into the field of politics.

Even during the later decades of the nineteenth century, the Macedonian national awakening developed very slowly. One reason was the very ethnically mixed bourgeoisie, comprised of Macedonians, Vlachs, Greeks, Jews, and Turks. Another was that all the national wealth was in the hands of the Turks. Consequently, the Macedonian bourgeoisie and intelligentsia (the so-called Macedonists) directed all their efforts into demands for the renewal of the Patriarchy of Ohrid and use in the church of the Macedonian language, which had begun to be used in literature instead of the Old Church Slavonic language. This was a fight for the independence of the Ohrid Archdiocese. The Ohrid Archdiocese was not abolished; it retained its autonomous status within the Ottoman Empire. However, by the end of sixteenth century the leading positions in the Archdiocese had been taken over by Greek priests. This made Macedonians unhappy and escalated into a fight of Macedonian bourgeoisie against Greek priests in the nineteenth century. In the 1860s the inhabitants of Ohrid, Skopje, and other larger cities abolished their contacts with the Patriarchy in Istanbul and established their own church-school communes. Under the pressure of the Russian diplomacy the Sultan abolished the supremacy of Greek priests in Macedonia. However, he did not agree with the independence of the Ohrid Archdiocese. Consequently, the Bulgarian priests replaced Greek ones.

After the Congress of Berlin in 1878, the politicians of neighboring countries circulated their countries' propaganda in Macedonia because they wanted to annex parts of, if not the whole, Macedonian territory once Turkey fell apart. By 1886 the Serbs had established the St. Sava Society, which disseminated Serb culture in Macedonia. At the same time the Greek government and merchants established many Greek societies and spread Greek culture and literacy in Macedonia. The strongest effort, however, was the large amount of Bulgarian propaganda, aided considerably by the establishment of the Bulgarian (Orthodox) exarchy in Sofia in 1870.

In spite of all the foreign propaganda and the repression by Turkish authorities a national liberation movement developed in Macedonia. In 1893 in Thessaloniki, the VMRO (Vnatrešna makedonskata revolucionarna organizacija)—Inner Macedonian Revolutionary Organization—was established. Its aims were the cessation of foreign propaganda and nationalistic quarrels in Macedonia as well as an independent Macedonian state, initially seen as a distant final objective. Macedonian émigrés in Bulgaria established a "Supreme Committee" to aid the VMRO. Over time, however, this committee became an extended hand of the Bulgarian government in its endeavors to liberate Macedonia from Turkish rule and annex it to Bulgaria.

Even with some reforms in the Turkish Empire the situation in Macedonia under the Turkish feudal order deteriorated, and the Macedonian population was very unhappy. As a result, in August 1903, under the leadership of the VMRO, an organized armed rebellion started (the Ilinden Uprising). Its aim was national liberation of the Macedonian nation and the cessation of the Turkish feudal order. The rebels liberated some territories and proclaimed the Republic of Kruševo, led by Goce Delčev, and they organized a revolutionary government in which Macedonians, Vlachs, and Albanians were represented. However, the Turks were able to crush the Ilinden Uprising quite rapidly. The Republic of Kruševo fell into Turkish hands after ten days.

The Ilinden Uprising in 1903 and the Young Turks Revolution in 1908 did not bring any substantial changes in Macedonia. Both events, however, contributed to the stronger influence of the European great powers in Turkish internal affairs and to these powers' growing interest in the Balkans. This resulted in thousands of documents from the last decades of the nineteenth century and the first decade of the twentieth century being kept, for example, in the British Foreign Office Archive.

Furthermore, because of these developments the Balkan Christian states demanded reforms in Turkey. The Turks did not respond, and Serbia, Montenegro, Bulgaria, and Greece declared war on Turkey in 1912 (the First Balkan War). With the support and agreement of the European great powers, they succeeded in abolishing the Turkish rule in Europe almost completely. And so, after 500 years, Macedonian Slavs were at last liberated from the Turks, although they did not succeed in establishing their own nation-state. After the Second Balkan War the territory of Macedonia was divided between Serbia (Vardar Macedonia), Bulgaria (Pirin Macedonia), and Greece (Aegean Macedonia). The division of Macedonia caused shock waves and great damage to the economic and national political life of the Macedonians. The situation would worsen with the outbreak of World War I.

The Yugoslav Idea in the Nineteenth and Early Twentieth Centuries

Not only did this period, simultaneously with the Spring of Nations in Europe, witness the transformation of South Slav peoples (Slovenes, Croats, Bosniaks, Serbs, Montenegrins, and Macedonians) in the territory of the former Yugoslavia into modern European ethnic nations, it also gave birth to the Yugoslav idea that envisaged a creation of a common state of all South Slav nations.

The creation of a modern ethnic nation required, among other things, development and promotion of a distinct national consciousness and shared collective identity based on loyalty to this new nation. In the process of creating new ethnic nations, nationalist movements usually fought for their own independent nation-states when they did not already possess a state of their own. The creation of their nation-states was understood as the ultimate goal and as the symbol of success of most movements for national unification and liberation.

Considering the existing situation of the Yugoslav nations in this period, the Yugoslav idea should be observed in the context of national liberation. These rather small (by European standards) nations believed that their national liberation and national interests could be best achieved and served in a common state that would be able to resist attempts from large hegemonic European empires to gain control over them and their territories again. However, there were different approaches to the realization of the Yugoslav idea. Some saw the new country as a confederation of equal and free nations, but others—especially some Serb and Croat politicians—saw it as the unification of South Slavs under their supremacy. The nationalistic ideas of, and movements for, a Greater Serbia and/or a Greater Croatia emerged in this context and played an important role in the evolution of ethnic relations and historic developments in this territory in the nineteenth and twentieth centuries.

This period was very important in the historic development of every Yugoslav nation and, in many ways, determined their future development and the present situation. It gave birth to several national myths that still shape the politics in this area. Also, the elaboration of the Yugoslav idea laid historical and political foundations for the creation of the future Yugoslav state that emerged after World War I. This notion contradicts the common misconception that Yugoslavia was just an artificial creation of Great Powers that wanted to ensure stability in the region after the dissolution of Austria-Hungary.

Cultural History from the 1800s until 1918

The ideas of the French bourgeois revolution of 1789 (equality, brotherhood, and freedom) spread quickly around Europe. Even more direct in the territory of the former Yugoslavia was the impact of the Napoleonic wars. The downfall of Napoleon and the victory of reactionary regimes ended everything liberal, which many young and educated people, especially artists, experienced as a nightmare. The optimism of the Enlightenment, with its faith in human sense and might, was replaced by a pessimistic view of life and a disillusionment with bourgeois society. Romantic art—established by 1800 first in England and France—developed in music, literature, and plastic arts in the first half of the nineteenth century. Influenced by social developments and problems in Europe, Realism prevailed in the second half of this century, characterized by a fast development of the capitalist economy, especially natural sciences and technological progresses. If Romanticism meant fleeing from reality, in contrast, Realism was "obsessed" with reality. Observing a contemporary society and social developments, Realism focused on the natural, economic, and social conditions of people. On the same foundations, Naturalism also developed, which deals with human beings especially as a result of biological circumstances. According to Naturalism, human beings were completely dependent on the laws of nature, and their lives were influenced by two factors: inheritance and the influence of the environment.

If Romanticism influenced arts and especially poetry in the territory of the former Yugoslavia in the first half of the century, Realism later prevailed, and the literature of Yugoslav nations caught up with European developments. However, as a consequence of rather different social and economic circumstances it developed differently in different environments. Around 1900 new currents—like Decadence, Impressionism, Symbolism, and New Romanticism—emerged almost simultaneously with contemporary developments in Europe.

Slovenes

The deaths of Baron Žiga Zois (a scholar and patron of arts) and Valentin Vodnik (the most important poet of the time) in 1819 marked the end of the Enlightenment in Slovenia. Matija Čop's work after 1820 began the Romantic period, which ended in the Habsburg Empire with the March Bourgeois Revolution in 1848. The most important author of this period was France Prešeren, recognized as the greatest Slovene poet. He wrote lyric poetry, romances, ballads, and the epic *Krst pri Savici* (*Baptism at the Savica Waterfall*, 1836). Prešeren and his literary circle had contacts with most the important poets and authors of the time and were well integrated in contemporary literary currents in Europe. Prešeren's book *Poezije* (*Poetry*, 1847), a collection of his poems, is considered an important contribution to European Romantic literature. The poetry almanac *Kranjska čbelica*, started in 1830, should also be mentioned from this period.

The developing bourgeois society influenced arts and especially literature in Slovenia after the March Revolution of 1848. Feeling that the Slovene national identity was being jeopardized within the Habsburg empire, Slovene politicians and artists focused on the "national awakening" of Slovenes. They developed the idea of a United Slovenia. During that period the most important authors were Fran Levstik and Josip Stritar, and the most important poets were Simon Gregorčič and Simon Jenko. Gregorčič's patriotic poetry was especially popular for *čitalnice* (reading rooms), which emerged all over the Slovene ethnic territories (beginning in Trieste/Trst in January 1861). Reading rooms were bourgeois social/cultural/political clubs where people read Slovene poetry and sang Slovene home-loving songs. In an environment where more than one-half of the population in Slovenia could read by the mid-nineteenth century, the St. Hermagoras Society (*Družba sv. Mohorja*) published and widely disseminated Slovene books that addressed the practical, aesthetic, religious, and educational needs of the people in villages and towns. During that period Slovene daily newspapers such as *Slovenec* and *Slovenski narod* started to be published.

In the second half of the nineteenth century, important authors were Anton Aškerc, who wrote ballads, and writers Janez Trdina, Fran Levstik, Josip Jurčič, Ivan Tavčar and Janko Kersnik. Also during that period, literary reviews such as *Ljubljanski zvon* (*The Bell of Ljubljana*) and *Dom in svet* (*Home and World*) were published. Around 1900 the so-called Modern period of Slovene literature began. The most important authors of this period were poets Dragotin Kette, Oton Župančič, and Josip Murn and writer, dramatist, and poet Ivan Cankar. Cankar, who wrote *Dream Visions* (*Podobe iz sanj*) in 1917, novels like *Farmhand Yerney's Justice* (*Hlapec Jernej in njegova pravica*, 1907), and dramas such as *Farm Hands* (*Hlapci*, 1910), is considered the greatest Slovene writer. The Modern period in Slovene history ended in 1918 with the death of Ivan Cankar and the dissolution of Austria-Hungary.

After 1848, composers also tried to contribute to the establishment of a Slovene national consciousness and to political demands for a United Slovenia. After the Glasbena Matica (the Slovene Music Publishing House) was established in 1872, Slovene music began to follow contemporary European music. The most important composers were Benjamin Ipavec, Franc Gerbič, Hugo Wolf, and Anton Foerster. The establishment of a professional opera (1892) and the Slovene Philharmonic House (1908; the Philharmonic House was already established in Ljubljana in 1701 as the second oldest in Europe, with Ludvig van Beethoven as honorary member) led to the blossoming of Slovene opera and symphonic music. Important musicians were Risto Savin, Anton Ipavec, Anton Lajovic, and Emil Adamič. Composer Gojimir Gregor Krek published a periodical *Novi Akordi* (*New Accords*).

In architecture, Historicism prevailed in the first half of the nineteenth century. All the important buildings (e.g., the Opera, the National Museum, the National Gallery in Ljubljana, and the little castles Slivnica and Viltuš near Maribor) were built in this style by Czech and Austrian architects. World-renowned Viennese-educated Slovene architects Maks Fabiani and Jože Plečnik, who were cofounders of the artistic trends of Viennese Arts of Secession, also worked in Slovenia later in the nineteenth century. Plečnik, now considered one of the greatest architects of the nineteenth and twentieth centuries, was especially important for the development of contemporary Vienna, Prague, and Ljubljana.

In paintings, at first Realism developed with painters like Ivan Franke, Janez and Jurij Šubic, Anton Ažbe, and Ivana Kobilica, the most important Slovene female painter of her time. Later, important Secessionist-style painters were Maksim Gaspari, Saša Šantl, and Hinko Smerekar, who created especially graphic illustrations and caricatures. Influenced by contemporary European art currents, Rihard Jakopič, who founded an important art gallery in Ljubljana, and other Impressionist painters (Matija Jama, Ivan Grohar, France Slana, etc.) started the Modern arts in Slovenia. Statuary art was also important for the development of Slovene national ideas, as sculptors built monuments of important personalities from Slovene history.

Croats

At the beginning of the nineteenth century, the first Croat newspapers appeared. In the 1830s and 1840s the Illyrian movement started to spread. This movement tried to unite South Slavs within the Habsburg Empire by uniting their languages; it was part of pan-Slavism, a movement that tried to unite all Slavs. Although Ljudevit Gaj (1809–1872), the leader of Illyrism, and others failed to unite South Slavs within the Habsburg Empire by creating a common South Slavic language, they did develop a codified united literary language in Croat historic lands (i.e., Croatia, Dalmatia, Stria, and Slavonia). The poetry of Petar Preradović and Ivan Mažuranić was an important factor in the codification of the Croat language. Especially important was Mažuranić's poem *The Death of Smail Aga Čengić* (*Smrt Smail age Čengića*), which described the Turkish violence against the Christians in the Balkans. An important author in the Illyrian language, a new codified Croat language, was Stanko Vraz, a Slovene writer who joined Illyrism but did not find followers in Slovenia.

Also in Croatia the literature served as the main vehicle of nationalist ideas. August Šenoa, the creator of Croat novels, should especially be mentioned (*Zlatarjevo zlato*/*Goldsmith's Gold*, 1871; *Seljačka buna*/*Peasant Uprising*, 1878). Later Ante Kovačić, Josip Kozarac, Vjenčeslav Novak, Ksaver Šandor Djalski, Silvije Strahimir Kranjčević, and others wrote

Sculptor Ivan Meštrović (1883–1962)
(E. O. Hopps/Corbis)

realistic prose. Although pure lyric poems (e.g., those of Gustav Matoš and Vladimir Vidić) prevailed toward the end of the century, the Yugoslav idea also appeared in the literature (Vladimir Nazor).

As for the development of architecture and music in the nineteenth century, following the end of the independent Republic of Dubrovnik and the Austrian occupation of Dalmatia, northern Croatia, with Zagreb, became the center of Croat national awakening and cultural development. In the beginning of the nineteenth century the bourgeoisie favored Biedermeier styles (an artistic and architectural style popular during the period 1815–1848), especially in interior decoration and furniture. Just before the March Revolution of 1848, the first important Croat painter-portraitist, Vjekoslav Karas, appeared. Croat painting and statuary art developed in the last decades of the century, with painters (Ferdo Quiquerez, Nikola Mašić) and sculptors (Ivan Rendić) educated in Vienna and Paris. In 1892 Vlaho Bukovac came to Zagreb and, together with other painters, after 1898 appeared at shows of the Croat Salon Society. In 1907 an art school was established in Zagreb.

At the beginning of the twentieth century, Impressionism also appeared in Zagreb. Before World War I, Ivan Meštrović became the best-known and most recognized Croat sculptor in the world. Just before the war Munich and Paris became sources of influence for Croat artists.

The establishment of the Music Society in 1827 marked early developments of Croat music. Songs were written to awaken national pride in Croats—including Josip Runjanin's *Lijepa naša domovina* (*Our Beautiful*

Homeland), today the national anthem of the Republic of Croatia. Vatroslav Lissinski composed the first Croat opera, *Ljubav i zloba* (*Love and Malice,* 1846).

After the March Revolution of 1848 Habsburg absolutism silenced the Croat music life until the 1870s, when Ivan Zajec introduced important contemporary and classical works into Croat opera. The first Croat bimonthly publication about music, *Sv. Cecilija* (*St. Cecilia*), appeared and was published until 1944. At the beginning of the twentieth century, some other, younger, musicians became prominent, who—like Blagoje Bersa—introduced current music trends of the time into Croat music.

After 1860 the first demands for the establishment of a Yugoslav university appeared, initiated by Josip Juraj Strossmayer, the bishop of Djakovo in Slavonia, Croatia. The University of Zagreb was established in October 1874 and soon became one of the centers for the idea of the national liberation of Croatia.

Bosniaks

During the period of Turkish rule in Bosnia and Herzegovina (until 1878), the arts developed most especially in the realm of crafts; well known were goldsmiths' handicrafts; different techniques of making ornaments and decorations from stone and wood; and embroidery weaving. These combined Islamic motifs with native ornaments.

The Austro-Hungarian occupation brought changes in architecture with the introduction of Austrian Historicism and later Viennese Secession, the style in which numerous public buildings (schools, railway stations, administrative buildings, etc.) were erected in towns. Many foreign artists immigrated to Bosnia, especially painters, who made numerous descriptive illustrations. The first generation of painters born in Bosnia appeared at the beginning of the twentieth century, having received their education in central Europe, especially in Munich and Prague.

Although disappearing in painting crafts and other arts, the religious content was retained in poetry until the end of the nineteenth century. During the period of 1878–1914, twenty Muslim newspapers were published that contributed to the development of Bosnian literature; some of them were pro-Austrian propaganda (*Vatan, Bošnjak, Rehber*). After 1900, Islamic periodicals with educational and literary content were published (e.g., *Behar,* 1900–1910; *Biser,* 1912–1914). Most of them, with the exception of the proregime ones, disappeared before World War I.

Serbs

Folk epic hero songs, characteristic also in previous periods, developed even more in the first half of the nineteenth century and played a role in the anti-Turkish rebellion and renewal of Serb statehood. With their historic and aesthetic nature, these songs provoked the interest of European, especially German, Romantic poets (J. G. Hoerder, J. Grimm, J. W. Goethe, etc.). Based on the language of folk songs, Vuk Stefanović Karadžić reformed the Serb language with the help of Slovene-Austrian linguist Jernej Kopitar. However, even before him, the comedies and prose of Jovan Sterija Popović and the poetry of Branko Radićević, Jovan Jovanović Zmaj, and Djura Jakšić, written in the people's language, contributed to a national awakening and development of the Serb culture.

A central personality in mid-nineteenth century was Svetozar Markovic, who introduced socialist ideas and Realism in literature. Stevan Sremac wrote funny stories of common life (e.g., *Pop Ćira i pop Spira/ Orthodox Priest Ćira and Orthodox Priest Spira*), and Svetolik Ranković wrote realistic novels (*Seoska učiteljica/Country Teacher*). The most important representative of the Serb realistic prose movement was Simo Matavulj, with his novel *Bakonja Fra Brne* (*Bakonja Rev. Brne*). At the turn of the century Serb writers and poets tried to follow trends in Western Europe. The most important author was Branislav Nušić, who wrote satires and comedies about contemporary life in Serbia (e.g., *Sumljivo lice/Suspicious Face; Pokojnik/The Deceased; Gospodja ministarka/Mrs. Minister*).

At the beginning of the nineteenth century new trends in Serb music also developed. Milan Milovuk authored the first musical theoretical textbooks and established the Belgrade Singing Society. The first Serb professional composer was a piano player and choirmaster, Kornelije Stanković. Other important composers were Josif Marinković, Stevan Mokranjac, Sr., and a Slovene, Davorin Jenko, who composed in Belgrade for more than four decades. Stevan Mokranjac, Sr., with his works *Seoba Serba* (*Migration of the Serbs*), *Markova sablja* (*Marko's Saber*), *Djido, Potjera* (*Driving Out*), etc., built the cornerstones of Serb music theater. He established himself with solo music and screenplay music, especially for Branislav Nušić. His opera *Na uranku* (1903) was the first Serb opera ever performed.

The early nineteenth century saw the beginning of the end of wall paintings and rich illuminated manuscripts in Serbia. Iconography was continued by only a few artists from Prizren. Graphic arts became more and more important; wood engraving and copper plates were especially used (Atanas Jovanović, Ljubomir Ivanović). Developing modern European trends, the first Serb painters gained prominence at the beginning of the nineteenth century. Konstantin Danil, Nikola Aleksić, and Jeftimije Popović had established themselves already in Biedermeier ("stodgy") styles. Also in Serbia, the Romantic period was followed by Realism. Impressionism in Serbia was influenced by artistic movements at the Munich School of Impressionism and by French Impressionism. The first European-educated sculptors appeared in the nineteenth century and adopted Realism. Also during that period, development of civil architecture began, which combined Western influences with the elements of Balkan architecture.

Montenegrins

Narrative poetry on Montenegrin history, based on folk poetry, and other works of Petar I Petrović-Njegoš (e.g., the unfinished *Kratka istorija Crne gore/Short History of Montenegro*) marked the beginning of Montenegrin literature. However, the most important poet was his successor, Petar Petrović-Njegoš, a Montenegrin church and national leader, who wrote the world-renowned epic poem *Gorski vijenac* (*Mountain Wreath*, 1847). This poem was the South Slavic literary work most translated into other languages. Also well known is his collection of folk poems, *Ogledalo srpsko* (*Serb Mirror*), in which he described Montenegrin and Serb fights with the Turks. Other Montenegrin poets of the time wrote about the same themes.

Lyric poetry appeared in the second half of the nineteenth century and did not draw from folk poetry. For the second half of the nineteenth century, memoirs also were important (by Marko Miljanov Popović, Mihael Vukčević, etc.). The first important Montenegrin writer was Stjepan Mitro Ljubiša, who wrote *Pripovjesti* (*Novels*), but the novel *Uskok* (*Renegade*) by Simo Matavulj is considered the best Montenegrin prose before World War I.

The first singing societies and composers appeared after the independence of Montenegro. Czech composer and educator R. Tolinger and Italian composer D. de Sarano San Giorgio (*Balkanska carica, Gorde,* and *Dana*) also wrote works describing life in Montenegro.

Painting developed in Montenegro when the royal court started to order portraits. French graphic artist Théodore Valéiro, Czech painter Jaroslav Čermak, Croat painters Ferdo Quiquerez and Vlaho Bukovac, and Serb painter Paja Jovanović painted them. The beginning of the twentieth century was an important period in painting, as quite a few younger painters returned home during this time after studying at foreign universities. Among them was portraitist and engraver Djoko S. Popović, who studied at the Belgrade Painting School and the academy in Naples. He painted a portrait of himself during the last years of his life and some experimental figures from Ulcinj; his most important realistic work is Maxim Gorki's portrait, which he painted on the Isle of Capri.

Macedonians

The first generation of Macedonian writers (Jovan Krčovski, Kiril Pejčinović, and Teodosije Sinaitski) became known at the beginning of the nineteenth century. They were mostly priests, and they described conditions in contemporary Macedonia, writing in different Macedonian dialects. The fighters for introduction of the Macedonian language into schools and church followed these first writers (in schools, the Turkish or Greek language was used; the Old Church Slavonic language was used in the churches). These writers (Jovan Hadži Konstantinov-Džinot, Dimitrije and Konstantin Miladinovci, Rajko Žiznifov, Grigor Prlićev, etc.) were fighting church authorities, and they were arrested and forced to emigrate. The most talented among them was Grigor Prlićev, who in 1860 received a literary award (first prize) in Athens for his poem *Sirdar* and received the nickname "the second Homer." He was known for his Macedonian translations of the *Iliad,* the *Odyssey,* and the work *Freed Jerusalem.*

At the beginning of the twentieth century, important dramatists were Vojdan Černodrimski and Marko Crvenkov. Krste Popov Misirkov, author of scholarly works on Macedonian literature, became especially known for his work *Za makedonckite raboti,* first published in Sofia in 1903 and reprinted in Skopje in 1946 and 1953. This work on the Macedonian language was written in the Central Macedonian dialect, which he also recommended as a basis for the future literary language. Later (after World War II), the Center for Macedonian Language acted upon his recommendation.

By the end of the nineteenth century, Macedonian music started to develop. Among the musicians from this period was Atanas Badev, who studied in Russia with Rimski-Korsakov. He lectured on Macedonian folk music all over Europe.

In art/architecture, church paintings and architecture prevailed until the withdrawal of the Turks. Contemporary painting started at the beginning of the twentieth century, and the first Western influences in the architecture started to appear during this time.

Conclusion

It was the nineteenth century and the beginning of the twentieth century that in the territory of the former Yugoslavia gave birth to modern Yugoslav ethno-nations—Slovenes, Croats, Bosniaks (Bosnian Muslims), Serbs, Montenegrins, and Macedonians. Based on their histories and folk myths, the key constitutive myths of these nations were established that are still being reproduced and they have fueled nationalistic feelings particularly among the Serbs. This period was equally important for the cultural, social, and political development of individual nations (especially considering the establishment of independent Serb and Montenegrin states). It was also important for the elaboration of the Yugoslav idea and other ideas for linking these nations (in different forms and frameworks, including the Balkan federation) to ensure their very existence and better future. These ideas were developed especially as a defense against the advancing Germanization, Hungarization, and, later, Italization, but also against the decaying Ottoman Empire.

Although these nations lived in geographically different states and empires (and were often divided among them), several connections and links among them were established and/or strengthened in this period. Especially important were connections and links among intellectuals and cultural elites that played important roles in developing their (individual) national identities, but also in establishing grounds for their future collaboration. Political and economic developments in the region, including the changes in borders and in political/administrative status of their historic lands, influenced everyday lives of people, the development of every nation, and the cooperation among these nations in different fields. From the perspective of the future Yugoslav statehood, this period and the cooperation among Yugoslav nations laid important (political) foundations for the establishment of a common state.

Timeline

1773   The first census on language spoken by the inhabitants of eastern part of Habsburg Monarchy (Croatia and Transylvania excluded)

1797   Napoleon I Bonaparte abolished independence of Republic of Venice

1084–1813	The First Serb Uprising under the leadership of Djordje Petrović (Karadjordje)
1806	Napoleon I Bonaparte abolished independence of the Republic of Dubrovnik
1809–1813	Napoleon I Bonaparte occupied many territories of the southern regions of the Habsburg Monarchy and established a special geopolitical unit, the Illyrian Provinces
spring 1815	The Second Serb Uprising started under the leadership of Miloš Obrenović
autumn 1815	Turkish government promised self-government to the Serbs
1830	Beginning of the "Illyrian idea" of the unification of Croat and South Slavic peoples into one cultural unit; Montenegrin vladika Petar II Petrović-Njegoš became a prince
1832	Resistance of Bosnian landlords under the leadership of Husein kapetan-Gradaščević against the Turks
1841	Petar II Petrović-Njegoš succeeded in reaching a mutual understanding on the border with Austria, which also entailed recognition of Montenegro's independence by Austria
January 1843	Viennese court forbade political Illyrism in Croatia
1844	Serb minister of the interior, Ilija Garašanin, wrote a document, "Naćertanie" (Plan), in which he demanded the unification and liberation of the Serbs and the other South Slavic "nations" who lived under Turkish rule
1846	Czoernig's census on the language situation of inhabitants of western part of Habsburg Monarchy
1846	First Croat opera, *Ljubav i zloba* (*Love and Malice*), composed by Vatroslav Lisinski and performed in Zagreb
1847	France Prešeren published his *Poezije* (*Poems*)
1847	Petar Petrović-Njegoš published *Gorski vijenac* (*Mountain Wreath*)
1848	March Revolution (Spring of Nations); Slovenes developed a nationalist agenda (United Slovenia); Croats, under the leadership of ban Josip Jelačič fought for independence from Austria and Hungary
1850	Agreement on the Serbo-Croat literary language was reached
1850–1851	Czoernig's census on the language situation of inhabitants of eastern part of Habsburg Monarchy; military

	expedition of Omer-pasha Latas against rebellious Bosnian landlords
1851	Victory of the counterrevolution; restoration of the absolute power of the Habsburg Monarchy
1852–1853	Turkish-Montenegrin war
1858–1862	Turkish-Montenegrin war
1867	Constitutional reforms and introduction of dualism reorganized the Habsburg Monarchy administratively and politically into two parts—Austria and Hungary
1868	The Hungarian-Croat *Nagodba* (Agreement); Croats came under complete Hungarian political and economic domination
1868–1871	Period of mass meetings, so-called *taborsko gibanje*
1870	Establishment of the Bulgarian (Orthodox) Exarchy
1875	Rebellion of Christian population in the region of Nevesinje against Bosnian landlords
1876	Serbia and Montenegro declared war on Turkey
3 March 1878	Peace of San Stefano
13 June 1878	Congress of Berlin formally recognized the independence of Serbia and Montenegro and allowed Austria-Hungary to occupy Bosnia and Herzegovina; Vardar Macedonia was annexed to Serbia
August 1878	Muslim resistance under the leadership of Hadži Loja against the Austro-Hungarian occupation army
1879	Reforms in Montenegro started to turn the society from a patriarchal tribal structure into a state
1881	Secret agreement between Austria-Hungary and Serbia
1882	Miloš II Obrenović declared himself a king
1886	Serbs established the St. Sava Society, which disseminated Serb culture in Macedonia
1893	The Inner Macedonian Revolutionary Organization (*Vnatrešna makedonskata revoljucionarna organizacija—*VMRO) was established in Thessaloniki
1903	Krste Popov Misirkov published *Za makedonckite raboti* (*Work for Macedonians*), the first scholarly book on Macedonian literary language
29 May 1903	Attempt on the life of Aleksandar I Obrenović succeeded; the throne of Serbia was occupied by the Karadjordjević dynasty
August 1903	Ilinden Uprising in Macedonia

1905	Prince Nikola gave Montenegro a constitution in 1905
5 October 1908	Austro-Hungarian emperor Francis Joseph declared the annexation of Bosnia and Herzegovina to Austria-Hungary
1912	Bulgaria, Greece, Montenegro, and Serbia created "Balkan Alliance" against Turks
October 1912–May 1913	First Balkan War
30 May 1913	Peace of London ended the First Balkan War
June–August 1913	Second Balkan War
10 August 1913	Peace of Bucharest ended the Second Balkan War
28 June 1914	In Sarajevo, Gavrilo Princip killed Archduke Francis Ferdinand, the successor to the Austrian throne

Significant People, Places, and Events

GAJ, LJUDEVIT (1809–1872) Leader of the Croat national movement, or the so-called Illyrian movement. As the leader of the Illyrian movement, Gaj fought for unification of all Croat and other South Slavic lands into one cultural unit, with a unified written language based on the Štokavian dialect. The final aim of Illyrism was political unification. The Illyrian movement was a defense against Hungarian nationalism, but it had pan-Slavist and, in part, Russophile tendencies. He played an important role during the revolutionary period of 1848 and then, during Austrian Chancellor Bach's absolutism, he vanished from the political scene.

KARADŽIĆ, VUK STEFANOVIĆ (1787–1864) Creator of the Serb literary language, reformer of Serb grammar, and historian. Under Jernej Kopitar's mentorship he worked on problems of Serb language and literature. This work led to his introduction of the language as it was spoken by the Serb people as the literary language, replacing Old Church Slavonic. In 1814 he published a Serb grammar, *Pismenica serbskoga jezika,* and in 1818, a Serb-language dictionary. In 1847 he translated the Bible into the Serb language. He also published Serb folk songs. Under the influence of Karadžić, with the help of Kopitar, an agreement was reached on the Serbo-Croat literary language in 1850 in Vienna.

KOPITAR, JERNEJ (1780–1844) Slovene linguist and librarian. Kopitar studied law in Vienna and became a librarian of the Library of the Austrian Court, the private library of the emperor. He also served as head of censorship for the court. In 1808 he published the first scholarly grammar of the Slovene language, with the title *Grammatik der slavischen Sprache in Krain, Kärnten, und Steiermark* (*Grammar of the Slavic Language in Carniola, Carinthia, and Styria*). He helped Serb linguist and folklorist Vuk Stefanović Karadžić.

KOROŠEC, REV. ANTON (1872–1940)Slovene Catholic priest and politician. Korošec became a Catholic priest in 1895. In 1906 he was elected deputy to the Austrian parliament (Reichsrat) as a candidate of the Slovene People's Party. In 1917 he became president of the Austrian parliament's Yugoslav Club, which united deputies from South Slavic lands of the Austrian part of the Habsburg Monarchy, and he read the *Majniška deklaracija* (*May Declaration*—see following chapter) in the parliament. In December 1918, he served as vice president of the first government of the Kingdom of Serbs, Croats, and Slovenes. He served many times as minister and, during the period from June 1928 to January 1929, he also served as president of the Yugoslav government. From 1930 to 1935 he was one of the leaders of an opposition movement; from 1935 on, he was a member of the Yugoslav government again.

OBRENOVIĆ, MILOŠ (1780–1860) Serb prince during the years 1817–1839 and 1858–1860. In 1815 Obrenović led an uprising against Turkish authorities, after which Serbs received their autonomy. He started to organize the state apparatus and was proclaimed a hereditary prince (absolute ruler). In 1817 he ordered the assassination of Karadjordje Petrović, the leader of the first Serb uprising. In 1838 he was forced to adopt a constitution that limited his rule. He had to share authority with a council of seventeen people, which guaranteed freedom of commerce and divided military authorities from civil. Obrenović abdicated the throne the next year. After his successor Aleksandar Karadjordjević was forced to resign, Obrenović returned to the throne again. He reigned until his death in 1860.

PETAR II PETROVIĆ-NJEGOŠ (also called Vladika Rade, 1813–1851) Montenegrin prince and poet. After long, successful fights, Petar II succeeded in defending most of the Montenegrin frontiers against the Turks and in agreeing on a frontier with Austria. He made an alliance with the Serbs and also got help to fight the Turks from Russia. He organized police and judicial systems. Petar II is also considered to be the most important Montenegrin poet. His most important work was *Gorski vjenac* (*Mountain Wreath,* 1847), in which he described one hundred years of fights of Montenegrins against the Turks, in the midst of the mountains and with the interference of different foreign interests, including the Venetians, Austrians, Russians, and the Turks themselves.

PREŠEREN, FRANCE (1800–1849) Slovene poet. Prešeren wrote the work *Poezije* (*Poetry*), which is still considered to be the best poetry in the Slovene language. The main themes are a human individual's freedom and the freedom of a suppressed nation. He also wrote *Sonetni venec* (*Wreath of Sonnets,* 1834), in which he combined lyric poetry with the national idea, and *Krst pri Savici* (*The Baptism at the Savica*), in which he wrote about the Christianization of Slovenes. In *Zdravljica* (*A Toast,* written in 1846, published in 1848), he wrote the most important Slovene political poem, with the ideas of national liberation and democracy. *Zdravljica* is today the Slovene national anthem.

Bibliography

Allcock, John B. "Serbia." In Turnock, David, and Carter, Francis W. (eds.): *The States of Eastern Europe, Volume II: South-Eastern Europe.* (Aldershot, U.K.: Ashgate, 1999): 247–282.

Banac, Ivo. *The National Question in Yugoslavia: Origins, History, Politics* (1984; reprint, Ithaca, NY: Cornell University Press, 1993).

Czoernig, Carl von. *Ethnographie des österreichisches Kaiserstaates* [*Ethnography of the Austrian Imperial Lands*]. (Vienna, Austria: K.u.K. Direction der administrativen Statistik, 1857).

Helmreich, Ernst C. *The Diplomacy of the Balkan Wars, 1912–1913.* (Cambridge, MA: Harvard University Press, 1938).

Lampe, John R. *Yugoslavia as History: Twice There Was a Country.* (Cambridge, U.K.: Cambridge University Press, 1996).

MacKenzie, David. *Ilija Garašanin: Balkan Bismarck.* (New York: Columbia University Press, East European Monographs, 1985).

Murray Despalatović, Elinor. *Ljudevit Gaj and the Illyrian Movement.* (New York: Columbia University Press, East European Quarterly, 1975).

Perry, M. Duncan. *The Politics of Terror: The Macedonian Revolutionary Movements, 1893–1903.* (Durham, NC: Duke University Press, 1988).

Pinson, Mark. (ed.). *The Muslims of Bosnia-Herzegovina: Their Historic Development from the Middle Ages to the Dissolution of Yugoslavia.* (Cambridge, MA: Harvard University Press, 1994).

Prešeren, France. *Poems* (selected and edited by France Pibernik and France Drolc). (Klagenfurt-Ljubljana-Vienna, Austria: Hermagors-Verlag, 1999).

Treadway, John D. *The Falcon and the Eagle: Montenegro and Austria-Hungary, 1908–1914.* (West Lafayette, LA: Purdue University Press, 1983).

Vucinich, Wayne S. (ed.). *The First Serb Uprising, 1804–1813.* (New York: Columbia University Press, East European Monographs, 1982).

CHAPTER THREE

Yugoslav "Nations" during World War I and the Establishment of the Kingdom of Serbs, Croats, and Slovenes

ORLD WAR I CHANGED THE POLITICAL MAP of Europe substantially, and one of its outcomes was the official proclamation of the first common Yugoslav state—the Kingdom of Serbs, Croats, and Slovenes. During the war several events and developments took place that influenced the life of Yugoslav nations in the twentieth century. Especially important was the process of unification, which showed that different and conflicting concepts of the organization and future of the common state had already existed before the state's official establishment. Here, we refer to the confrontation between the federalists and decentralists on the one hand and the unitarists and centralists on the other hand. The former demanded the creation of a federal and decentralized new state that would ensure the equality and wide autonomy of all constituent nations. The latter wanted a new state that would be a strong unitary and centralized state. The unitarists and centralists, who held the position especially favored by the Serb dynasty of Karadjordjevićs and the Serb political elite, won, and this determined the development of the former Yugoslavia at least until World War II.

World War I

It is generally known that World War I started in Sarajevo. Gavrilo Princip, a member of the Young Bosnians group, assassinated the successor to the Austrian throne, Habsburg crown prince Archduke Francis Ferdinand, who was on an official visit to Sarajevo. This was done as a protest against the Austro-Hungarian annexation of Bosnia and Herzegovina.

The suspected assassin of Archduke Francis Ferdinand is hustled into custody in Sarajevo. (The Illustrated London News Picture Library)

This happened on St. Vitus Day, 28 June 1914, which was the anniversary of the historic battle of Kosovo *polje* (see chapter 1). Because the Serb authorities did not allow Austro-Hungarian authorities to investigate the assassination, Austria-Hungary declared war on Serbia, touching off what became World War I, which completely changed the political map of Europe. This period was marked primarily by: (1) the defeat of the old European powers Austria-Hungary, Germany, and Turkey; (2) a socialist revolution in Russia, and (3) the establishment of new European nation states (Finland, Estonia, Lithuania, Latvia, Poland, Hungary, Austria) and multinational states (Czechoslovakia and Yugoslavia) after World War I.

The Austro-Hungarian attack on Serbia and Montenegro, whose national assemblies decided on a joint fight against Austria-Hungary, contributed to the beginning of the unification of the Yugoslav nations into one state. The Serb and Montenegrin army won the first battles of World War I but was soon defeated by the more powerful enemy when the Bulgarian army attacked it without a declaration of war on 14 October 1914 and blocked its path to Thessaloniki/Salonika. In terrible condition and suffering great losses, The Serb and Montenegrin army had to escape to the Greek island of Corfu. Its units joined the forces of the Entente in May

1916 and together with the British, French, and Greek army opened the Front of Salonika against the powerful German and Bulgarian forces. After fierce fights from August to November 1916, a line was formed from Valona, to the Ohrid Lake, to Kajmakčalan, to the Bay of Orfano. It lasted until 15 September 1918, when the Serb army, together with the French under the command of General Franchet d'Esperay, broke through the Bulgarian defense and forced the Bulgarians to cease fire by 30 September 1918. Thus, the recuperated Serb/Montenegrin army returned and contributed to the ending of the war.

Serb politicians who followed the Serb and Montenegrin army pursued their political activities from November 1915 through November 1918 on the island of Corfu. Political leaders of the South Slavic nations (Croats, Slovenes, and Serbs) had difficulties organizing in Austria-Hungary because the authorities put so many restrictions on them during the war. Only the South Slav deputies in the Viennese Parliament, who had immunity as members of Parliament, had the opportunity to engage in political activity. They were united in the Yugoslav Club of the Austrian Parliament. Those pro-Yugoslav intellectuals who succeeded in escaping from Austria-Hungary before the beginning of the war gathered in London as the "Yugoslav Committee." In spite of the worsened political situation with regard to the national rights of South Slavic populations in Austria-Hungary, during the first years of the war some political parties still continued to show loyalty to the Austro-Hungarian state, especially to the institution of the emperor (e.g., Slovenska ljudska stranka [Slovene People's Party], Hrvatska pučka seljačka stranka [Croat People's Peasant Party], Hrvatska stranka prava [Croat Party of Right], and Hrvatsko-srbska koalicija [Croat-Serb Coalition]).

After 1917 many political parties and groups, including those that supported Austria-Hungary at the beginning of the war, promoted the idea of the unification of the South Slav "nations" into one state. However, they eventually had to confront their considerable differences on the issues of the procedures for unification and the future organization of the state.

In the beginning of the process the president of the Serb government, Nikola Pašić, feared that in a future unified country the Serb Orthodox population would become a minority, and he therefore attempted unification only of those South Slavic lands that would not make a Serb majority questionable in the future state. He visualized that state as an enlarged Serbia. Later, he demanded that the Croat and Slovene lands and Bosnia and Herzegovina be included in this enlarged Serbia instead of

Macedonia (which would become part of Bulgaria, if Bulgaria would enter the war on the Allies' side). Still later, however, the Entente decided to give (Vardar) Macedonia to Serbia as a reward for the suffering of its victims and for Serb successes during the war, especially during the fighting on the Front of Saloniki from May 1946 until the end of September 1948. Pašić wanted the future state to be a centralized monarchy, and he did everything possible to ensure the Serb bourgeoisie a leading position in the unified state.

Slovene, Croat, and Serb politicians from Austria-Hungary who gathered in the Yugoslav Committee in London wanted to join with Serbia and Montenegro, believing that it was the best solution for the Habsburg South Slavs to unite into one state with Serbia and Montenegro. They were afraid of the pressure of Germanization from the north as well as the pressure of Italization from the west. The Committee sought the cooperation of Slovene, Croat, and Serb immigrants living in the United States. The Committee asked the U.S. South Slavs to help them with financial contributions and to help persuade the U.S. government that there were the South Slavs in Europe who wanted to unite in a new state. To this end, they called upon leading South Slavs to fight alongside them to found a Yugoslav state. They actually persuaded quite a few American South Slavs to cross the ocean and fight at the Saloniki front.

To reconcile the differences in views among the various camps, representatives of the Serb government and the Yugoslav Committee met on Corfu Island in June 1917 and signed a compromise agreement regarding mutual attempts to establish an independent Yugoslav state. The document, called the Krfska deklaracija (Declaration of Corfu), determined that the new state of Serbs, Croats, and Slovenes ". . . will be a democratic and parliamentary monarchy under the rule of the Karadjordjević dynasty . . ." (Article 1). Most other parts of the declaration were based on the abovementioned principles of the Yugoslav Committee. Article 2 declared that the official name of the state would be "Kingdom of Serbs, Croats, and Slovenes." Article 3 established that the state would have a state coat of arms, one state flag, and a crown. These state emblems would include symbols from each of the three constituent nations' emblems. The country's flag, as a symbol of unity, was to be flown on all the territory of the Kingdom. In Articles 4 and 5 the equality of Serb, Croat, and Slovene flags, coats of arms, and names was spelled out. In Article 6 the equality of the Cyrillic and Latin alphabets was guaranteed. Article 7 stressed the equality of Orthodox, Roman Catholic, and Muslim religions in their relations with the state. Article 8 required a common calendar for the whole of the territory.

Article 9 declared that the territory of the new state had to include the whole traditional ethnic territory of the three constituent nations that formed "our nation of three names." It proclaimed the principle that "our nation" wanted to be liberated and united and added that it should ". . . resolutely exclude any partial solution of its national liberation . . . and unification." This unification would be based on the "principle of national self-determination," and no part of the territory "can be lawfully separated from and united with any other state without consent of the nation itself." However, these principles might not have been realistic considering the upcoming battles for the new country's frontiers and the secret London Agreement. This Agreement promised to Italy that it would get South Tyrol, Dalmatia, Istria, the Kvarner Islands, and western Slovenia, one-third of today's Republic of Slovenia, if it entered the war on the side of the Entente. Article 10 noted that, "in the interest of freedom and equality of all nations," the Adriatic was an open sea. Articles 11–12 established the equality of all citizens before the law and in dealings with the state (Article 11) and the principle of direct, secret, free, and equal elections for the National Assembly and communes (Article 12). Article 13 declared that a Constitution should be prepared and adopted by the directly elected Constitutional Assembly. Article 14 further determined that the Constitution would give the nation the possibility to develop its energy in self-managing units considering their natural, social, and economic conditions. This Article also gave the king the right to veto decisions of the parliament (Šišić 1920, 96–99).

While the Serb government and Yugoslav Committee demanded the establishment of an independent Yugoslav state, thirty-three members of the Viennese parliament joined together in the Yugoslav Club and issued the May Declaration. In this declaration, issued on 30 May 1917, the Slovene and Croat deputies in the Austrian Parliament (Reichsrat) insisted, "based on nationality principle and Croat National Law (hrvatsko narodno pravo) that all territories of the Monarchy in which Slovenes, Croats and Serbs live unite under the sceptre of Habsburg-Lotaring dynasty into an independent state body which should be free of any type of national domination of foreigners and established on the democratic foundations" (Šišić, 1920, 94). Adopted under the strong influence of the Slovene People's Party, this document called only for the unification of South Slavic nations that lived within the Habsburg monarchy and were predominantly Catholic. It did not include any unification with the Serbs and Montenegrins. One could describe this as an attempted "Catholic solution of the national question." The declaration was in contrast with the war aims of Serbia and Montenegro and did not follow the basic principles of the Yugoslav Committee in London, which called for the complete liberation of South Slavic nations from the Habsburg rule and their unification in an independent sovereign South Slavic state.

The May Declaration, which, by spring 1918 had been signed by 200,000 Austrian South Slavs (especially women), provoked a movement for peace that would end the war and that displeased the Austro-Hungarian authorities. When these authorities forbade even this so-called "Declaration Movement," people stopped feeling loyal to the Habsburg dynasty and started to demand the right of the Slavic Habsburg nations to national self-determination. Political leaders of the Yugoslav nations under Austria-Hungary started to organize national councils to help the leaders establish an independent state of Yugoslav nations encompassing all regions in which Slovenes, Serbs, and Croats lived in Austria-Hungary. During the last days of his reign, Emperor Karl granted the demands for reorganization of the Habsburg Empire with the introduction of trialism. The principle of trialism was based on the division of the empire into three—ethnically and culturally based—entities. In addition to the Austrian and Hungarian entities, there would also be one uniting all the South Slavs of the Habsburg Empire, which was the essence of demands written in the May Declaration. Anton Korošec, a Slovene deputy to the Austrian Parliament and chairman of Yugoslav Club of deputies in Austrian Parliament, responded " . . . too late, your Royal Highness." (*Zu spät Majestät*) (Bister, 1992, 258).

It is important to also discuss how Slovenes, Croats, and Serbs in the United States reacted to the events of World War I. American Slovenes, Croats, and Serbs (representing up to 15 percent of these ethnic communities) were able to speak freely on the destiny of their countrymen because they lived in a democratic country. American Slovenes, Croats, and Serbs pursued two kinds of political activity during World War I. One had to do with influencing the actions of the United States. The other tried to influence events in their homeland and took place mostly within American Slovene, Croat, and Serb institutions. This later type of activity can be divided into actions of those who favored a continuation of the Habsburg monarchy; actions of those who supported a unified Yugoslavia created by incorporation of Croat and Slovene ethnic territories into the Kingdom of Serbia (and Montenegro); and actions of those who advocated Yugoslavia as a Federal Republic.

Prior to the entrance of the United States into the war in 1917, many American Slovenes and Croats openly sided with the Habsburg Monarchy. Some continued to support it even later, though secretly. At the outbreak of World War I, pro-Austrian feeling was widespread among American Slovenes and Croats and was promulgated primarily by Austrian diplomacy and some of the Catholic clergy. Although they did not establish an organization, these Slovenes and Croats were active in a part of the press of Slovene and Croat Americans.

The second group of activists was originally based in the Slovenska liga (Slovene League), which was founded in 1915, as well as similar organizatons of American Croats and Serbs; their representatives gathered in Pittsburgh, Pennsylvania, in January 1915 and proclaimed as their aim the unification of all Yugoslavs in the homeland. The representatives of Croat Serb and Slovene immigrants gathered again in Pittsburgh where they accpted the Kardjordjevič's dynasty as the future Yugoslav Royal family and accepted the Yugoslav Committee in London as representative of Slovenes, Croats, and Serbs from Austria Hungary (Čizmić 1974, 300–301).

The third group worked through the Slovene Republican Alliance (founded in 1917), which, after its association with like-minded Croats, was renamed the Yugoslav Republican Alliance in the same year. These activists worked to establish the Federal Republic of Yugoslavia, in which Slovenia and Croatia would be autonomous republics, and wrote the Chicago Declaration proclaiming that goal in May 1917.

This work of the Croats and Slovenes in the South Slavic immigrant movement in the United States also had its opposition. Early in February 1916, Naša izjava (Our Declaration) was published together with an explanation (K Našoj izjavi—A Commentary to Our Declaration), signed by fifteen Croat and Slovene priests. The preamble stated that, since the beginning of the war, Croat priests had not sided with the very intensive Yugoslav propaganda in America. The Declaration said that Croats were not ready to simply renounce their name and history to become Yugoslavs—meaning Serbs, subjects of the Karadjordjević dynasty. To respond to the criticism of the followers of the Yugoslav idea in the United States, these Croat and Slovene priests pointed out the following: "Primarily as the Croats and the sons of our homeland Croatia and the brotherly Slovene countries, we herewith emphasize and declare our political loyalty towards our country in these times of war with its inherent visible and hidden consequences." They claimed that Austria, Hungary, Turkey, and Italy, assisted by England, had always attempted to reduce the freedom and rights of the Croat people, who therefore could not expect to be granted freedom and should achieve it through their own endeavors: "Those doubting the ability of a nation to gain its own freedom disprove its existence. Nations that are given their freedom by others become their inferiors." The Declaration continued: "We do not want to turn either Serb, Yugoslav or Serbo-Croat, but are remaining Croat, Slavic brethren, in our own house, however, with our own rights which had been determining our historical evolution since our ancestors settled down in our present homeland" (Čizmić, Miletić, and Prpić, 2000, 143–145).

Having severely condemned the Italian claims to the Croat Adriatic coast, signatories of Naša izjava faulted the Chicago Declaration for not having called for Croat independence.

The signatories of Naša izjava were not only priests but also some distinguished public workers. Its impact on the Croat immigrant community was very strong. It became a powerful instrument in the struggle against the Yugoslav Committee, and its supporters became known as "Izjavaši" and organized a separate political group.

Narodni list (*The National Gazette*), published in New York City, was one of the most widely read Croat newspapers in the United States at the beginning of World War I. Offering increasing support to pro-Austrian Croat immigrants, the paper attacked immigrants who were in favor of creating a Yugoslav state. This position might have been a consequence of financial donations to the paper by Austro-Hungarian diplomatic representatives.

The State of Slovenes, Croats, and Serbs and the Proclamation of the Kingdom of Serbs, Croats, and Slovenes

In October 1918 the representatives of all three Yugoslav "nations" in Austria-Hungary established in Zagreb a joint political representation, the National Council of the Slovenes, Croats, and Serbs (Narodno vijec Slovenaca, Hrvata i Srba, Narodni svet Slovencev, Hrvatov in Srbov). All political parties and political groups—including those that at the beginning of the war supported the Austro-Hungarian policy—joined the National Council. On 31 October 1918, this Council proclaimed the State of Slovenes, Croats, and Serbs, consisting of the ethnic territories of the South Slavic nations of Austria-Hungary.

The new state soon had to fight many problems in the political and military fields. The state was not internationally recognized. The government of the Kingdom of Serbia initiated diplomatic endeavors against the international recognition of the State of Slovenes, Croats, and Serbs, because Serbia wanted to uphold its position as the only and the predetermined state in the process of the formation of the Kingdom of the Serbs, Croats, and Slovenes. The government of Serbia, however, seemingly agreed to negotiations with a delegation from the National Council. In Geneva on 9 November 1918, Ante Trumbić staged a last stand for the Yugoslav Committee. Following the basic principles of the Yugoslav Committee that demanded the creation of a common state of equal nations, he pressed Nikola Pašić, Serbia's president and its foreign representative, to accept a concept of confederation or federation that would guarantee equality of its constituent nations as the framework for the new government. Both the Serb opposition to Pašić and the Slovene People's Party leader, Korošec, joined forces with Trumbić to secure the tentative so-called Declaration of Geneva (Ženevska deklaracija). But the Belgrade government, headed by Stojan Protić (a member of the Serb Radical Party and regent Aleksandar's favorite), repudiated that agreement two days later by simply resigning with a promise to include the opposition in a new cabinet.

In the end, the Serb government did not recognize the Declaration of Geneva. The articles of this declaration, which ensured the equality of Yugoslav nations within the new state without hegemony of one nation over the others, were never realized. The naïveté of the National Council contributed to this outcome, as it sent its delegation to Belgrade to negotiate the conditions for the uniting in a common state in spite of the opposition of some leaders, such as Stjepan Radić. One must also understand that the National Council worked under pressure, as the Italians were then advancing into the Slovene coastland (Primorska), Istria, and Dalmatia and the socialist revolution started to spread from Hungary.

In the meantime Serbia had already unified with Montenegro. On 26 November 1918, the proclamation of the Montenegrin parliament dethroned Petrović's Montenegrin dynasty and declared the unification of Montenegro with Serbia and other South Slavs who formerly lived in Austria-Hungary. The unification of Serbia with the State of Slovenes, Croats, and Serbs was proclaimed by the regent of the Kingdom of Serbia, Aleksandar Karadjordjević, on 1 December 1918. This proclamation formally completed the process of the establishment of the Yugoslav state and actually determined its monarchic and unitary nature.

Life of the People during the War

On Sunday, 26 July 1914, the Habsburg Monarchy authorities proclaimed to the peoples of the Habsburg Monarchy (with leaflets, ringing of church bells, and drumming) that military units were to be mobilized for an expedition to punish Serbia. This conflict soon grew into World War I. Some military analysts warned that the war would be long and costly, with numerous casualties, but most of the people were convinced that the war would end very quickly.

Therefore, on both sides—in Serbia and Montenegro on the one hand and among the Germans of Austria-Hungary on the other hand—people were enthusiastic to fight against the enemies. Young men volunteered for the army, to fight for their homeland. They were convinced that they would be home in a few months. In reality, the war lasted for four years, and the soldiers endured massive gun and artillery fire, poison gas, starving in the trenches, and despair.

The consequences of the war touched upon substantial parts of the territory of South Slavic ethno-nations. Especially affected were Montenegro and Serbia (together with Macedonia), where one-quarter of the population was killed. Many battles later became part of Serb and Montenegrin war myths. One such battle took place at Kajmakčalan and Grunište at the front of Salonika. In the eyes of Serb politicians, the heroic deeds of Serb soldiers were what enabled the Yugoslav state to come into being.

In the most western part of Slovene ethnic territory, from spring 1915 to autumn 1917, 700,000 soldiers lost their lives at the front of Isonzo/Soča. The fights in the mountains above the river of Isonzo/Soča completely changed the image of the countryside. On the mountains, the scars of the fights may still today be seen; many mountaintops are lower than they were before as a consequence of artillery fire.

The police and security forces increased their efforts, especially in the parts of Austria-Hungary that were settled by South Slavs. The authorities forbade the publishing of all newspapers and the activities of all societies that were publishing or spreading antimilitary or pro-Serb views. Germans and German Austrians were convinced that World War I was the war against all Slavs. Therefore, Slavs of the Habsburg Monarchy were under suspicion as enemies, and stronger controls were imposed. People were imprisoned just on the basis of anonymous denunciations or for suspicious conversations in restaurants. Many Slavic priests, organizers of cultural life, and politicians were imprisoned. Under such conditions, members of the state administration in Austria-Hungary openly showed their hatred toward the Slavic population. It is not surprising, therefore, that some Yugoslav-oriented young men escaped to Serbia and entered its army. Many Slovene, Croat, and Serb soldiers who served in the Austro-Hungarian army on the eastern front (Galicia) very soon surrendered to the Russians on purpose.

Due to violence toward those who thought differently from those in power, and due to shortages in supplies, the strength of the Austro-Hungarians' war effort at the front broke down many times. States engaged in the conflict had to introduce general mobilization. Farmers, workers, the lower strata of the bureaucracy, and students were mobilized into the army. The authorities had trouble convincing intellectuals to fight; many of the resisters were condemned to death and shot by firing squads. The civil population was affected deeply by the war because all industries were producing to meet military needs. Soon shortages of soap, food, civilian clothing, and other necessities appeared. All the men were in the army, so most of the work had to be done by women. The women also organized demonstrations and strikes, after the war brought the situation to the point at which living circumstances became unbearable. This heightened women's importance in the society and strengthened their position in the fights for political and economic rights that followed the war. Soldiers deserted en masse. Many did not return to their units after they went on leave for holidays. They hid in the woods and were named "the green cadre." Some of them robbed civilians to survive.

Cultural History during World War I (1914–1918)

During the years before World War I, architecture prospered as people in Europe built a great deal; there were also many artistic and literary shows. Simultaneously, the various nations armed themselves, and international conflicts caused people to be afraid. The faith in continuous and irrepressible progress, as this situation was described by Austrian writer Stefan Zweig, (Zweig, 1944, 5) started to decrease. The year 1914 marked the beginning of World War I. This war involved and affected tens of millions of people; soon it caused a deep emotional shakeup. Fast-developing technology, which had caused optimism among people before the war, was now used to destroy human beings and their goods. Many intellectuals (philosophers, historians, writers, etc.) foresaw in the war the downfall of European civilization. As in other regions involved in the war, cultural development in the territories where South Slavic nations lived was halted.

In Slovene lands under the rule of Austria-Hungary, any serious cultural activities had been discontinued by censorship from the Austrian authorities. Extraordinary measures temporarily abolished basic personal freedoms, for example, freedom of the press and of opinion. Most of the non-regime newspapers in Austria had to cease publishing. Arrests and calls into the army disposed of those who opposed the war. Only a few people dared to write.

One of them was Slovene writer Fran Maselj Podlimbarski, who was accused of treason and expelled into Lower Austria (an Austrian province near Vienna) because he published a novel, *Gospodin Franjo* (1914), and other works such as *Tovariš Kladivček* (1914), *Romarji* (1915), and *Rex Sodomae* (1916). In spite of the arrests and censorship, some Slovene writers wrote antiwar pieces and published their works in literary reviews like *Dom in svet* (France Bevk, Ivan Cankar, Ferdo Kozak, Ivan Pregelj, etc.); *Slovan* (Alojz Gradnik, Juš Kozak, Ivan Albreht, etc.); and *Ljubljanski zvon* (Cvetko Golar, Fran Milčinski, Ksaver Meško, etc.).

As the authorities in the Hungarian part of Austria-Hungary were more tolerant than those in the Austrian part, the Croats were more fruitful and able to produce. The year 1914 marks the beginning of the Croat modern literature. Vladimir Nazor, who was nicknamed "the poet of the future" during the war, wrote about individual themes (*Intima*). Reflecting the historic moment, many of his poems of the time were pessimistic (*Pabirci*). Writers who accepted the ideas of the socialist (Soviet) October Revolution in Russia in 1917 opened a new period of Croat literature (Miroslav Krleža, August Cesarec). Their works became especially important after the end of World War I.

During World War I, Croat painters and sculptors continued to produce. There were yearly exhibitions of Croat artists called *Proljetni salon,* which from 1916 until 1928 continued to show the development of Croat painting.

World War I interrupted cultural and artistic life in Serbia and Montenegro almost completely. The only exceptions were some painters (Expressionists) who worked outside Serbia. Kosta Milićević, during his sojourn in Thessaloniki and Corfu in 1918, reached his peak. During World War I Milan Milovanović and Nadežda Petrović were also important. In Serb literature of the time, Modernism (a period and an art movement during the first decades of the twentieth century) started to develop; Cosmopolitanism (according to which there is no significant difference among peoples and nations) gained in importance.

World War I stopped cultural and artistic creativity also among Bosnian

Muslims (Bosniaks) and Macedonians completely. The artists and writers in these nations continued their work after the war.

The Creation of the First Yugoslav State

The end of World War I coincided with the actual proclamation of the first Yugoslav state—the Kingdom of Serbs, Croats, and Slovenes. During the war several attempts were made for the establishment of a new, common state for all South Slavs. If during the war such a state had been perceived as the realization of the nationalist aims of all "Yugoslav" nations, these nations had to face a different reality after the war. The idea of a community of equal nations was replaced by a unitary monarchy under the dynasty of the Karadjordjevićs, who had formerly been Serb kings. Although the existence of three "constituent tribes"—Serbs, Croats, and Slovenes—was mentioned formally in the country's documents, the tribes were believed to represent one "Yugoslav nation of three names." At this point, the separate existence of Bosniaks (Bosnian Muslims) and Macedonians was denied, and the Montenegrins had already renounced their sovereignty. Obviously, the Serb king and leading Serb politicians had managed to outwit others who were working toward the establishment of the common state and who wanted to work from a different concept. With the proclamation of the Kingdom of Serbs, Croats, and Slovenes, the Regent Aleksandar realized to a large extent his concept of unification based on the Greater Serbia idea. However, as was mentioned in the previous chapter, the idea to create a new Yugoslav state after World War I was the result of a complex process and was not only in the imaginations of Great Powers that, following the desired dissolution of Austria-Hungary, wanted to prevent further fragmentation and ensure stability in the region.

Timeline

28 July 1914	Austria-Hungary declared war on Serbia; World War I began
1915	Retreat of Serb and Montenegrin forces to the Greek island of Corfu
April 1915	Yugoslav Committee established in London
30 May 1917	Yugoslav Club (thirty-three members of the Viennese parliament) issued the May Declaration

20 July 1917   The Serb government and the Yugoslav Committee signed the Declaration of Corfu

Summer 1918   Fights began on the front of Salonika/Thessaloniki

15 September 1918   Serb/Montenegrin army defeated Bulgarians (the battle of Kajmakcalan)

6 October 1918   Representatives of all three Yugoslav "nations" in Austria-Hungary established a joint political representation, the National Council of the Slovenes, Croats, and Serbs

31 October 1918   The National Council of the Slovenes, Croats, and Serbs proclaimed the State of Slovenes, Croats, and Serbs

9 November 1918   Declaration of Geneva, a French-brokered agreement between the Serb prime minister, Nikola Pašić, and the president of the National Council of Slovenes, Croats, and Serbs, Anton Korošec

26 November 1918   A proclamation of the Montenegrin National Assembly dethroned Petrović's Montenegrin dynasty and declared the unification of Montenegro with Serbia and other South Slavs

28 November 1918   National Council of the Slovenes, Croats, and Serbs sent its delegation to Belgrade to negotiate the conditions for uniting in a common state

1 December 1918   Regent Aleksandar Karadjordjević proclaimed the Kingdom of Serbs, Croats, and Slovenes

Significant People, Places, and Events

CANKAR, IVAN (1876–1918) Slovene writer. Ivan Cankar started to write while he was still attending high school in Ljubljana. He went to Vienna to study Slavic languages but instead switched to contemporary European literature and wrote numerous novels, narratives, and dramas. His most important works are a collection of poems, *Erotika* (*Erotica,* 1899); novels, such as *Hiša Marije pomočnice* (*House of Maria Helper,* 1904) and *Hlapec Jernej in njegova pravica* (*Yerney's Justice,* 1907); and dramas, such as *Pohujšanje v dolini šentflorjanski* (*Scandal in St. Florian Valley,* 1908), *Hlapci* (*Farmhands,* 1910), and *Lepa Vida* (*Beautiful Vida,* 1912). He advocated the unification of the South Slavs into a federation of equal nations. In a lecture entitled Slovenes and

Yugoslavs, he clearly answered the Yugoslav question by saying, among other things, "If political unification of the Yugoslav nations comes—it is not only my wish but I am also convinced that it shall come—then it could not happen any other way than for them to unite as equal nations. . . ."

KREK, JANEZ EVANGELIST (1865–1917) Slovene theologian, sociologist, publicist, and politician. After he was ordained a Catholic priest and had finished his theological studies, Janez Krek became a professor of theology and philosophy at the Theological Faculty in Ljubljana. He founded the Christian Social Movement among the Slovenes and served as a deputy to the Austrian parliament during the periods 1897–1900 and 1907–1918. He was also a vice president of the Catholic National Party (after 1905 renamed the Slovene People's Party). He organized educational workers' societies and agricultural cooperatives. He also published some books; the most important were *Črne bukve kmeckega stanu* (*Black Books of the Farmers' Class*, 1895) and *Socijalizem* (*Socialism*, 1901).

NUŠIĆ, BRANISLAV (1864–1938) Serb comedy writer. Under the influence of Russian writer Nicholas Gogol, Branislav Nušić described the comic, sometime even grotesque, sides of country and city life (the Serb petit bourgeoisie, all types of intrigues, clericalism, and corruption). He devoted special attention to Serb politics, which he said made it possible for simple, uneducated, and unsophisticated people to become "statesmen" while their wives reigned. His works as a whole mirrored the situation in Serbia, which was inherited by the Kingdom of the Serbs, Croats, and Slovenes. His most important works are novels *Narodni poslanik* (*The Peoples' Representative*, 1883), *Sumljivo lice* (*A Suspicious Individual*, 1888) and *Opštinsko dete* (*Child of the Commune*, 1902).

PETROVIĆ-NJEGOŠ, NIKOLA I (1841–1921) Montenegrin prince (1860–1910) and king of Montenegro (1910–1919). Nikola I Petrović-Njegoš received his education in Trieste/Trst and Paris. He succeeded his uncle, Prince Danilo I Petrović-Njegoš, on the throne of Montenegro following Danilo's death in 1860. In 1866 Nikola became a Serb ally. In 1876 he supported a Christian uprising and with Serbia started a war against the Ottoman Empire. By January 1878 he had liberated Nikšić, Bar, and Ulcinj, and ensured access to the sea for Montenegro. At the Berlin Congress in 1879 Montenegro was internationally recognized as an independent state, and its territory was doubled. In 1910 he proclaimed himself king of Montenegro. During the Balkan Wars and during World War I, he served as a supreme commander of the Montenegrin army. He fled to France in 1916 because of the advancing Austro-Hungarian troops. Nikola was deposed in November 1918; Montenegro became a part of Serbia and later of the Kingdom of the Serbs, Croats, and Slovenes. He spent the rest of his life in France. Nikola was also a poet. Among other poems, he wrote the unofficial Montenegrin national anthem, *Onam' Onamo* (*Here and There*).

PRINCIP, GAVRILO (1894–1918) Serb nationalist. Gavrilo Princip was a member of the anti-Austro-Hungarian national/revolutionary organization Mlada Bosna (Young Bosnia), whose goal was the unification of the South Slavic nations into one state. On St. Vitus Day, 28 June 1914, he made a successful attempt on the life of the successor to the throne of Austria-Hungary, Archduke Francis Ferdinand. Austria-Hungary used this as a pretext to attack Serbia, thus setting off World War I. Princip was arrested together with his helpers and was tried in Sarajevo. Because he was not of age when he assassinated the Archduke, he could not be sentenced to death. He was sentenced to twenty years in prison and died in jail in Terezin, Bohemia, in 1918.

TRUMBIĆ, ANTE (1864–1938) lawyer and Croat politician. In 1894 Trumbić was a cofounder of the Party of Law in Dalmatia (a Dalmatian wing of the Croat Party of Law) and was elected to the Dalmatian State Assembly and the Austrian Reichsrat. He served as mayor of Split from 1905 until 1914. He also was instrumental in the creation of the Croat-Serb Coalition, which became the largest party in Croatia after 1906. He emigrated to Italy in 1914. In 1915 he became a President of the Yugoslav Committee and signed the Declaration of Corfu in 1917. After World War I he served as foreign minister of Yugoslavia from 1918–1920, but resigned after the Treaty of Rapallo. Later he supported a confederative solution of the Yugoslav question, or even an independent Croat state.

Bibliography

Banac, Ivo. *The National Question in Yugoslavia: Origins, History, Politics*. (1984; reprint, Ithaca, NY: Cornell University Press, 1993).

Bister, Felix. *Anton Korošec, državnozborski poslanec na Dunaju; Življenje in delo 1872–1918*. (Ljubljana, Slovenia: Slovenska matica, 1992).

Čizmić, Ivan. *Jugoslavenski iseljenički pokret u SAD i stvaranje jugoslavenske države 1918* (Croatia: Sveučilište u Zagrebu, Institute za hrvatsku povijest, 1974).

Čizmić, Ivan, Miletić, Ivan, and Prpić George J. *From the Adriatic to Lake Erie: A History of Croatians in Greater Cleveland.* (Eastlike, OH: American Croat Lodge, Inc., 2000).

Djordjević, Dimitrije. (ed.). *The Creation of Yugoslavia, 1914–1918.* (Santa Barbara, CA: ABC-CLIO, 1980).

Kiraly, Bela K., and Dreiszinger, Nandor F. (eds.). *East European Society in World War I.* (New York: Columbia University Press, East European Monographs, 1985).

Klemenčič, Matjaž. "Immigrant communities and the establishment of new states in East-Central Europe: The case of the Slovenians in North America." In Kaliterna, Ljiljana (ed.). *Srednjoeuropska emigracija i nove demokracije. Društvena istraživanja* 7, no. 1–2 (1998): 43–73.

Šišić, Ferdo. *Dokumenti o postanku kraljevine Srba, Hrvata i Slovenaca 1914–1919.* (Zagreb, Croatia: Matica Hrvatska, 1920).

Zweig, Stefan. *Die Welt von Gestern, Errinerungen eines Europaers* (Stocholm, Sweden: Bermann-Fischer Verlag, 1944).

CHAPTER FOUR

"The First Yugoslavia"

Yugoslav Nations between
the First and Second World Wars (1918–1941)

AFTER THE CREATION of a new state, but especially after World War II, historians from what became Yugoslavia debated vigorously the question of whether there were histories of individual nations in that country. Specifically, Serb historians claimed that the histories of individual peoples ceased to exist after the unification. On the other hand, historians from Slovenia and Croatia insisted that (separate) histories of individual nations, such as Croats, Macedonians, Serbs, Slovenes, etc., continued to exist even after the creation of the common Yugoslav state. This chapter presents a survey of historic developments in the Yugoslav state between World Wars, but (as previous chapters of this book have done) it also presents histories of individual South Slav nations. Moreover, we believe that throughout the common state's existence, ethnic relations played an important role; the history of the Yugoslav state shall in this book be observed as also (and sometimes above all) comprising the history of relations among Yugoslav nations—a history in which relations between the two largest nations, the Serbs and Croats, was the key factor.

The Kingdom of Serbs, Croats, and Slovenes

After the proclamation of the Kingdom of Serbs, Croats, and Slovenes on 1 December 1918, it took quite some time to organize the election for its Constituent Assembly (*ustavotvorna skupština*). During this period a temporary government and a temporary parliament consisting of 270 named deputies (provisional parliament—*Privremeno narodno predstavništvo*) were established to lay a foundation for the work of the Constituent Assembly. In the name of his father, King Petar I, who was 74 years old and in poor health, the Regent Aleksandar named as the first Prime Minister Stojan Protić, a representative of the (Serb) Radical Party. His government consisted of thirteen Serbs, four Croats, two Slovenes, and a Bosnian. Such overwhelming Serb majorities in the government continued during the whole interwar period, as did the Serbs' intent to strengthen the Serb domination and control over institutions of the kingdom. The governments in the first years after the unification set about trying to establish control in the newly united lands and to diminish the largest differences among the lands.

The temporary government had to find solutions to many problems. Above all, it had to harmonize life and institutions in these newly united lands that, before World War I, had belonged to different countries and had undergone very different economic and cultural development. These different backgrounds resulted in very different political, cultural, and economic legacies and different regional and religious characteristics. Out of 12 million inhabitants, 8 million spoke Serb and Croat, which were considered the same literary language, Serbo-Croatian. However, Serbs and Montenegrins wrote in the Cyrillic alphabet, but Croats used the Latin alphabet. Slovenes spoke their own Slovene language and also used the Latin alphabet. The new nation's authorities denied the very existence of Macedonians as being a specific nation that spoke its own language and used the Cyrillic alphabet.

In spite of these differences, there was a feeling of community among the citizens, who generally accepted the belief that they were ethnically related. The official ideology was based on the proclaimed principle that the Serbs, Croats, and Slovenes were tribes of the same unified Yugoslav nation. However, the very complex ethnic structure of the population of the Balkans and the inadequate ethnic relations policy of the new state resulted in ethnic tensions that soon erupted vigorously in the ethnically mixed territories of Vojvodina, Bosnia and Herzegovina, Kosovo, and Macedonia. Complications and tensions also existed between the (central) authorities and the inhabitants in the newly annexed lands. Additionally, economic conditions in the kingdom were very depressed. The former Habsburg lands were economically completely exhausted as a consequence of World War I and its aftermath. During the war, Serbia and Montenegro had lost almost 1.2 million people, more than one-quarter of their total population. The Kingdom of Serbs, Croats, and Slovenes was among the economically least developed and most backward countries in

**TABLE 4.1   LANGUAGES, ALPHABETS, AND RELIGIONS OF MAJOR
ETHNIC GROUPS IN THE KINGDOM OF SERBS, CROATS, AND SLOVENES**

Ethnic Group (Nation, Minority)	Language	Alphabet (Script)	Majority Religion
Croats	Croat (Croatian)	Latinic	Catholic
Macedonians	Macedonian	Cyrilic	Orthodox
Montenegrins	Serbian	Cyrilic/Latinic	Orthodox
Muslims (Bosnians)	Serbo-Croatian (Serbian, Croat)	Latinic	Islam
Serbs	Serb (Serbian)	Cyrilic	Orthodox
Slovenes	Slovene (Slovene)	Latinic	Catholic
Albanians	Albanian	Latinic	Islam/ Catholic
Hungarians	Hungarian	Latinic	Catholic
Germans	German	Latinic	Catholic/ Evangelic
Roma (Gypsies)	Roma languages/dialects	Latinic	Mostly Christian
Turks	Turkish	Latinic	Islam

Europe. Small and mid-sized farms, established in the nineteenth century and often unable to sustain large families, prevailed in this agrarian society. Unemployment was high, and the nation's slowly developing industry and mining activities could not sufficiently absorb the surplus unemployed population from the farms. This poor economy was also an important issue in interethnic relations.

As a consequence of the existing society being agricultural, peasants were the main electorates of all political parties, while the political leaders were from the bourgeoisie. Most political parties also had their own national (ethnic) provenience. The strongest Serb party was the National Radical Party or, simply, the Radicals (Narodna radikalna stranka, NRS), led by the experienced politician Nikola Pašić. Until Pašić's death in 1926, the party retained its leading role as a government party. The Yugoslav Democratic Party, or Democrats (Jugoslovenska demokratska stranka, JDS), was the second most important party. In addition to Serb liberals from Serbia proper, its voters were liberally oriented Serbs in Croatia, Bosnia and Herzegovina, and Vojvodina, but also those who had previously supported Slovene liberals (members and voters of the Slovene National Progressive Party—Slovenska narodna napredna stranka, SNNS). Both the NRS and JDS advocated a centralized state and the unification of all Yugoslav (ethnic) nations into a new Yugoslav nation. The most important party in Croatia was the Croat Republican Peasant Party (Hrvatska republikanska seljačka stranka, HRSS), under the leadership of Stjepan Radić, the "uncrowned Croat king." Demanding at least as many rights in the new kingdom as the Croat nation had had under Austria-Hungary, the HRSS wanted Croatia's own parliament (*sabor*) and head of state (*ban*). The strongest party of the Slovene bourgeoisie was the Slovene People's Party (Slovenska ljudska stranka, SLS), led by Anton Korošec, a Catholic priest. This party demanded autonomy for the Slovene nation and opposed intensified centralization. Similar demands were made by the Yugoslav Muslim Organization (Jugoslavenska muslimanska organizacija, JMO), under the leadership of Mehmed Spaho, which represented Serbo-Croatian-speaking Muslims, the majority of whom lived in Bosnia and Herzegovina. There were also the left-wing, all-Yugoslav communists—the Communist Party of Yugoslavia (Komunistička Partija Jugoslavije, KPJ). KPJ was the only important political party that was not ethnically based.

The strong (ethnic) national foundations of these parties to a large extent determined the political life in the new country from its very beginning. Regarding the future development and organization of the state, two opposing blocs—centralists and federalists/decentralists—were formed. Although the centralized and unitary concept prevailed very soon, the ideas of democratization, decentralization, and federalization of the Yugoslav state persisted.

The Serb bourgeoisie advocated a highly centralized and unitary state under the Karadjordjević dynasty that would guarantee Serb domination. Having control of the state apparatus, government, and army, they were able to force their will and establish the Kingdom of Serbs, Croats, and Slovenes as a centralized and unitary state ruled by the Karadjordjević dynasty. This centralized and unitary concept was also supported by the Entente powers (Belgium, France, Great Britain, Russia), which saw this state and the Karadjordjević dynasty, related to the Romanov dynasty of Russia's Tsars, as barriers to the quick spread of socialist ideas after the October 1917 revolution in Russia. Additionally, this Entente standpoint enabled the Yugoslav state to gain some territories from Hungary, where the Yugoslav (Serb) army had helped crush the revolutionaries of Bela Khun (who, influenced by the Russian October revolution, started a socialist revolution in Hungary). Fearing that a violent revolutionary workers' movement and a series of strikes during 1918–1921 might endanger their privileged social position, the bourgeoisie and most politicians from the territories of the former Austria-Hungary were willing to accept the centralized and unitary arrangements. This centralized concept got its constitutional confirmation in the Constitution of the Kingdom of Serbs, Croats, and Slovenes of 1921 and later in the Constitution of the Kingdom of Yugoslavia of 1931.

The first foreign policy goal of the new state and its temporary government was to solve the questions of boundaries. They had to determine almost 3,000 miles of borders that needed to be newly drawn in the midst of ethnically mixed historic lands, a process that provoked many conflicts and caused (at least some) pain to all involved nations. Continuing the foreign policy of the former Kingdom of Serbia, the Kingdom of Serbs, Croats, and Slovenes kept its alliances with England and France, which did not help much in determining its new borders. A plebiscite was called for at the peace conference in Paris to determine the fate of southern Carinthia (an area of 818.6 square miles). The plebiscite question was whether the area should belong to the Kingdom of Serbs, Croats, and Slovenes or to the Republic of Austria. In the 1920 plebiscite a majority of the population in the territory voted for Austria, which meant that this region, although it was historically settled by Slovenes, was given to Austria. With the Treaty of Rapallo, the new state had to agree to a border that had already been determined in the London Pact, giving to Italy the Slovene coastland, Istria, some islands, and the city of Zadar (3,190 square miles) for its role and active participation in World War I.

Neither the new kingdom's monarchy nor its neighbors were satisfied with the new borders. Also, the aspirations of Italy to become a regional superpower and the Hungarians' desire to renew their kingdom under the (previously removed) king Karl of the Habsburgs were perceived to be great threats. With the exception of Romania and Greece, the Kingdom of Serbs, Croats, and Slovenes did not have friendly relations with any of its neighbors.

Ethnic Structure of the Population in the New Kingdom

The population of the new monarchy after World War I represented a colorful mosaic of different nationalities. The newly established country was one of the most ethnically diverse countries of Europe. Additionally, the

Creation of Yugoslavia, 1918–1920

The circumstances after World War I enabled the Yugoslav Idea to be realized. On 1 December 1918, the Kingdom of the Serbs, Croats, and Slovenes was created on the ruins of Austria-Hungary and out of the inheritance of Serbia and Montenegro. The new state had to settle on about 1,850 miles of frontier with neighboring countries. There were many disputes over the boundaries, especially with Italy and Austria.

TABLE 4.2   YUGOSLAVIA'S NATIONAL STRUCTURE, 1921

Group	Population	Percent of Total Population
Serbs	4,665,851	38.83
Croats	2,856,551	23.77
Slovenes	1,024,761	8.53
Bosnian Muslims	727,650	6.05
Macedonians or Bulgarians	585,558	4.87
Germans	513,472	4.27
Hungarians	472,409	3.93
Albanians	441,740	3.68
Romanians, Vlachs, and Cincars	229,398	1.91
Other Slavic	174,466	1.45
Turks	168,404	1.40
Jews	64,159	0.53
Italians	12,825	0.11
Others	80,079	0.67
Total	12,017,323	100.00

SOURCE: Banac, Ivo. *The National Question in Yugoslavia: Origins, History, Politics.* (1984; reprint, Ithaca, NY: Cornell University Press, 1993), 65.

new borders determined after World War I left significant segments of the area's main South Slavic groups (Yugoslav ethno-nations) outside the country, thus creating sizable Yugoslav (especially Slovene and Macedonian, but also Croat) minorities in the neighboring countries (Italy, Austria, Hungary, Albania, Bulgaria, Greece).

According to Ivo Banac (1984, 49–58), the first census taken in 1921 in what became Yugoslavia reveals a good deal about the official ideology, but it is not particularly helpful as a demographic guide to the actual sizes of individual ethnic groups at that time. As nationality was not a census rubric, mother tongue and religion of the population were the only possible guides to nationality. On the basis of data about religion and language (as stated by the population), professor Ivo Banac of Yale University interpreted the ethnic structure of the population as presented in table 4.2.

However, the official census included only three linguistic possibilities: (1) Serb or Croat, (2) Slovene, or (3) other Slavic. Considering the language, the second category makes it relatively simple to conclude that there were 1,024,761 Slovenes in the new kingdom, 39,606 of them outside the lands historically considered part of Slovenia (i.e., outside the new kingdom's portions of the former Austrian provinces of Carniola, Styria, and Carinthia, and outside the former Hungarian part of Slovene ethnic territory, Prekmurje). The third category ("other Slavic") refers to several groups, mainly to the Czechs around Daruvar (in Slavonia), the Slovaks (mainly in Bačka and the Banat), and the Ukrainians (also called Ruthenians, in Bačka and Bosnia), but also to the handful of Poles and Russians. Except for Russians, who were mostly postrevolutionary émigrés, the "other Slavic" speakers were the remnants of various Habsburg colonizing efforts in the past. The first category—"Serb or Croat"—is the most misleading. In addition to Serbs and Croats, it included Montenegrins and Bosnian Muslims (Bosnians) as well as a large Macedonian and/or Bulgarian population in the southeastern parts of the country, who were officially considered South Serbs (although only a small portion of them in northern Macedonia declared themselves Serbs). Thus, the census "Serbianized" perhaps as many as 585,000 people. The main problem, however, is that this category did not determine the actual size of the Serb and Croat populations. Instead, it combined both groups into one category.

The misleading linguistic information must, therefore, be augmented with data on the size of religious communities. The number of Orthodox Christians is one of the keys to the Serb census. If one excludes the approximate number of Macedonians and/or Bulgarians (585,000), and the other non-Serb Orthodox groups, notably the Romanians, Vlachs, and Cincars (229,398), taking into account also linguistic criteria, the Serbs emerge as a community of 4,665,851 people. This community can be divided into five basic groups (see table 4.3).

It is much easier to examine the kingdom's Muslim community. This community numbered 1,337,687, and more than half of them (727,650 persons) were ethnic Bosnian Muslims.

In addition to the Bosnian Muslims, the Yugoslav Muslim community consisted of the Muslim Albanians, Slavic Macedonian Muslims, Turks, and Muslim Roma (descendants of the Turkish Roma—Xoraxané, Roma who spoke Turkish and were adherents of Islam) (see table 4.4).

Considering the census data on the religion and language of the population in the country, one can conclude that there were some 2.8–2.9 million Croats who were Catholic. They represented the largest group among the new kingdom's 4,735,154 Catholics. In addition to Croats, other large, predominantly Catholic groups were Slovenes (1,024,761) and members of German (513,472), Hungarian (472,409), and Italian (12,825) minorities. There was also a small Albanian Catholic community (25,543).

TABLE 4.3 POPULATIONS OF THE BASIC GROUPS OF THE SERB COMMUNITY, 1921

Group	Population
Serbs of the pre-1912 Kingdom of Serbia	2,259,746
Serbs of Vojvodina (401,386), Bosnia-Herzegovina (827,829), Dalmatia (105,460), and Croatia-Slavonia (658,242)	1,992,917
Montenegrins of the pre-1912 Kingdom of Montenegro, only a small fraction of whom considered themselves distinctively Montenegrin, rather than Serb	168,392
Serbs of the Sandžak of Novi Pazar (98,868), Metohia (15,213) and Kosovo (78,506)	192,587
Fraction of the Macedonian population that may have considered itself Serb	52,209
Total Serb Community	4,665,851

SOURCE: Banac, Ivo. *The National Question in Yugoslavia: Origins, History, Politics.* (1984; reprint, Ithaca, NY: Cornell University Press, 1993), 65.

TABLE 4.4 POPULATIONS OF THE GROUPS OF THE BOSNIAN MUSLIM COMMUNITY, 1921

Group	Population
Bosnian Muslims who lived in Bosnia-Herzegovina	588,247
Bosnian Muslim diaspora in pre-1912 Serbia	11,981
Bosnian Muslim diaspora in the former Habsburg territories	5,497
Slavic Muslims of Montenegro	13,370
Slavic Muslims of the Sandžak of Novi Pazar (90,302), Metohia (955), and Kosovo (17,298)	108,555
Total Bosnian Muslim Community	727,650

SOURCE: Banac, Ivo. *The National Question in Yugoslavia: Origins, History, Politics.* (1984; reprint, Ithaca, NY: Cornell University Press, 1993), 65.

Other religious communities in the new monarchy included Protestants (including 54,000 Slovak Lutherans), Greek Catholics (Uniates), and Jews.

A map of the kingdom's religious communities of the time would have revealed some interesting features, important also to ethnic relations in the country. For example, there was a Serb-Orthodox "island" in the old

Croat lands, encompassing portions of northern Dalmatia, Lika, Kordun, Banija, northwestern Bosnia, and, less compactly, western Slavonia (the counties of Požega and Virovitica). Clutching this "island" from the southeast and the northeast were the two compact Croat Catholic "claws" (enclaves) in western Herzegovina and central Bosnia. The compact Muslim communities of eastern Bosnia separated the mentioned "island" from Serbia. And within the "island" there was a solid Muslim lagoon around Cazin and Bihać, sometimes referred to as the Turkish Croatia. In the southeast, Serbs of Montenegro and eastern Herzegovina were separated from Serbia proper by a Bosnian Muslim "channel" in the Sandžak, which was connected with the predominantly Muslim Albanian community of Kosovo and western Macedonia and with the Turks further east.

The 1921 census provided only partial information about Yugoslavia's minorities. Language was the principal indicator for the size of the German minority. The Germans (513,472) had significant contingents in Slavonia, Bačka, and Baranja, the Banat, and parts of Slovenia (notably Kočevje/Gotschee and Maribor). These Germans (except the Gotschee Germans who came in the thirteenth century) were the descendants of German colonists, whom the Habsburgs had imported from southern Germany (chiefly from Swabia) in the eighteenth century and settled in the recently liberated and depopulated Danube basin. Their area of settlement was to a large extent identical to that of the 472,409-strong Hungarian minority, except that the Hungarians predominated in northern Bačka and had their smaller colonies in Prekmurje. The Hungarians, too, were largely eighteenth-century settlers, although considerable portions of the urban Hungarians were Magyarized Slavs. The Ashkenazic Jews of what became northern Yugoslavia were, on the whole, also of German or Hungarian culture. The somewhat smaller Sephardic Jewish community lived in the former Ottoman possessions and Dalmatia and had been largely integrated into the urban society. Its members usually spoke Ladino (Judeo-Spanish) as their first language. The two Jewish communities together numbered 64,159 people.

The other non-Slavic minorities also included 12,825 Italians, mainly Italianized Croats of Dalmatia and the Croat seashore, and 229,398 Romanians, Vlachs, and Cincars of the Banat, eastern Serbia, and Macedonia. There were also 441,740 Albanians in Kosovo, Metohia, western Macedonia, and southeastern Montenegro. Their symbiosis with the Turks in the urban centers presents a difficult task for those who would want to determine the exact Turkish contingent of that time. There is no doubt that a sizable portion of the urban, upper-class population in these areas consisted of Turkized Albanians. The situation is somewhat clearer in eastern Macedonia, where the Turks lived in compact colonies after the Ottoman conquest. However, one can estimate that the new kingdom's Turkish community numbered some 168,404 people in 1921.

The ethnic structure of the kingdom indicates that no national or religious group represented an absolute majority in the monarchy. However, the ruling regime did not want to officially recognize the existing ethnic diversity and made no serious attempt to resolve the "national question" (i.e., about relations among the nations and national minorities) in the new monarchy. To govern a country as if a Serb majority existed, as the ruling regime actually did, could only have brought problems and escalated ethnic conflict.

The first, bigger changes in the ethnic structure of the population in the territory occurred immediately after the establishment of the Kingdom of the Serbs, Croats, and Slovenes, when most German- and Hungarian-speaking bureaucrats of the former Austro-Hungarian Empire left. In Slovenia, for example, this meant that two-thirds of the German-speaking population left, mostly high- and mid-ranking bureaucrats and officials. They were replaced largely by Serbo-Croatian-speaking bureaucrats and officials, which naturally resulted in an increase in Serbo-Croatian-speaking population. Similar changes occurred also in Croatia, where Austrian officials emigrated out of Dalmatia and Hungarian officials emigrated out of the rest of Croatia. A relatively small number of German bureaucrats left Bosnia and Herzegovina. Significant changes happened in Vojvodina. After the war, more than 50,000 ethnic Hungarians emigrated from Vojvodina to Hungary until 1921, decreasing the region's percentage of ethnic Hungarians by almost 4 percent. The number of Croats increased fourfold; their percentage of the whole population of Vojvodina increased to more than 8 percent. Alterations in census methodology also changed results: Although the 1910 census asked people for their language of communication, the 1921 census asked for their mother tongue. Additional changes in the ethnic structure of the population were also occurring in the next decade, that is, from 1921 till 1931.

Between 1919 and 1922, around 30,000 U.S. prewar immigrants of Croat, Serb, and Slovene ancestry visited the kingdom. Although many had intended to remain, most of them decided to return to the United States due to unfavorable economic and political conditions in the new kingdom.

In addition to differing birth and mortality rates among ethnic groups and in different parts of the country, the heavy economic and political

TABLE 4.5   POPULATION ACCORDING TO LANGUAGE OF COMMUNICATION OR MOTHER TONGUE, 1910–1931

Mother Tongue	Year	Bosnia and Herzegovina Population*	%	Dalmatia Population	%	Croatia and Slavonia Population	%	Slovenia Population	%
Serbo-	1910	1,854	96.0	327	98.1	2,385	87.3	0	0.0
Croatian	1921	1,826	96.6	612	98.6	2,445	89.2	11	1.0
	1931	2,250	97.2	659	98.7	2,724	89.3	24	2.1
Slovenian	1910	4	0.2	0	0.0	16	0.6	917	86.2
	1921	5	0.3	1	0.2	22	0.8	985	93.3
	1931	4	0.2	1	0.2	35	1.1	1,079	94.3
Hungarian	1910	6	0.3	0	0.0	112	4.1	21	2.0
	1921	3	0.1	0	0.0	71	2.6	15	1.4
	1931	3	0.1	0	0.0	66	2.2	8	0.7
German	1910	23	1.2	1	0.4	134	4.9	106	10.0
	1921	16	0.9	1	0.2	123	4.5	40	3.8
	1931	15	0.6	1	0.1	128	4.2	29	2.5
Other	1910	45	2.3	5	1.5	85	3.1	20	1.9
	1921	40	2.1	7	1.1	79	2.9	5	0.5
	1931	44	1.9	7	1.0	99	3.2	4	0.4
Total	1910	1,932	100.0	333	100.0	2,732	100.0	1,064	100.0
	1921	1,890	100.0	621	100.0	2,740	100.0	1,056	100.0
	1931	2,316	100.0	668	100.0	3,052	100.0	1,144	100.0

*All populations given in thousands

Note: A number of 0 indicates less than 500; for Bosnia and Herzegovina, Dalmatia, and Slovenia (without its most northeastern part), language of communication was determined in 1910.

SOURCES: Winkler, 1931: 212–213; *Recensement de la population dans le Royaume des Serbs, Croates et Slovénes du 31 janier 1921*, 1924: 2–3; Stanovnistvo predratne Jugoslavije po veroispovesti i materinjem jeziku po popisu od 31.3.1931, 1945.

crises in the 1920s and the 1930s intensified emigration, which also resulted in a somewhat changed ethnic structure of the population during this period. However, no major changes in the ethnic structure occurred after this until the beginning of World War II.

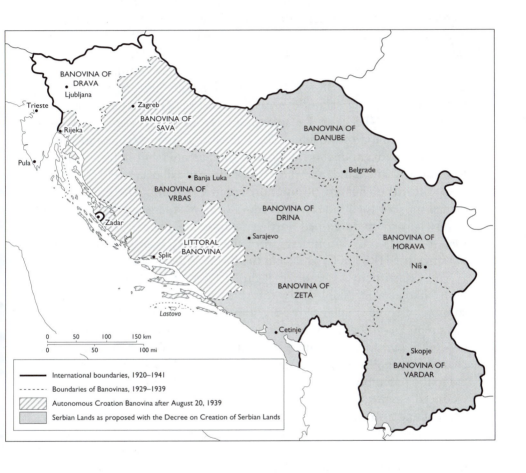

Kingdom of Yugoslavia, 1929–1941. Official politics of the Kingdom of Yugoslavia recognized only Serbs, Croats, and Slovenes as constitutive tribes of the nation of Yugoslavia, giving all other groups minority status. Because minorities were victims of forced assimilation, interethnic conflicts were common during the interwar period. Only the German minority, which was well organized and economically strong, had a major influence on Yugoslav politics.

Constitutional and Political Development in the Kingdom of Serbs, Croats, and Slovenes and the Kingdom of Yugoslavia

When the temporary government had signed the pacts concerning its borders and had succeeded in pacifying internal unrest during 1919 and 1920, it called elections for the new Constituent Assembly. On 28 November 1920, the elections were held. The strongest parties were the NRS with 91 seats in the Assembly, the JDS with 92 seats, the Communist Party of Yugoslavia (KPJ) with 58 seats, and the HRSS with 50 seats. The distribution of votes was very significant, as the votes were distributed along ethnic lines. The NRS gained seats only in Serbia, but it was virtually unknown in Croatia or Slovenia. The JDS won seats in Serbia and Bosnia and Herzegovina and some in Croatia and Slovenia, but it also won seats from Kosovo and Sandžak, where, out of fear of Nikola Pašić's Great Serbia policy, the Muslim population voted for them. The communists gained most of their votes in Macedonia and Montenegro and not in the industrially more developed northern part of the country. All other parties won seats only in one region of the country each (e.g., the SLS in Slovenia, the HRSS in Croatia, and the JMO in Bosnia and Herzegovina).

The Constituent Assembly met on 12 December 1920. The leader of NRS, Nikola Pašić, established a government of the NRS and JDS with the support of some smaller parties. Without consultations with the Assembly, on 30 December 1920 his government issued a decree (*Proclamation* or—*Obznana*) that prohibited the political work of the KPJ. This decree changed the political space. On 5 January 1921, the government submitted to the Assembly its plan for the Constitution (*Nacrt ustava*), which introduced a centralized unitary parliamentary monarchy with a weak parliament and a strong monarch.

This constitution, passed on the anniversary of the battle of Kosovo, was known as the Vidovdan (St. Vitus Day's) Constitution (Vidovdanski ustav/Vidovdanska ustava). The constitution defined the Kingdom of Serbs, Croats, and Slovenes as a hereditary, parliamentary monarchy. It introduced a highly centralized unitary political system dominated by a monarch with strong prerogatives.

Observed from the perspective of ethnic relations, unitarism was the main determining factor in the formulation of the ethnic policy that ignored the "national question." Unitarism was reflected in the constitutional concept of "one nation of three names" (*troimeni narod,* or "three-name nation"), historically divided into three "tribes"—Serbs, Croats, and

Slovenes. This concept, based on Serb expansionist tendencies, denied the very existence of Macedonians, Montenegrins, and Bosnian Muslims (Bosniaks) as distinct ethnic groups that would also be part of this "three-name nation." The constitution recognized only one official "Serbo-Croatian-Slovene language" (Article 3), which had never existed in practice. The "Serb-Croat-Slovene" nationality of an individual was required for the exercise of certain political rights, such as the right to be elected to public offices (Article 72) or to be employed as a higher public servant (Article 19). As to other citizens, they had to comply with certain additional demands, such as a ten-year permanent residence following the acquisition of citizenship, to be able to exercise these rights (Articles 19, 72). The Constitution did not establish any special protection or linguistic rights for the numerous ethnic minorities with the exception that Paragraph 13 of Article 16 provided that minorities of other "race and religion" had the right to elementary education classes in their mother tongue under the conditions determined by law.

Also, the territorial organization and divisions of the new kingdom were determined by centralism and by unitarism. There was no ethnic or regional autonomy, for the intention was to divide all distinct ethnic communities into several administrative units to decrease their internal ethnic coherence. According to Article 95, the largest administrative units were districts (*oblast*), with up to 800,000 inhabitants. Other, smaller administrative units were departments (*okrug/okrožje*), counties (*srez/okraj*), and communes (*opština/občine*).

Immediately after its adoption, the revision of the Vidovdan Constitution was already being widely discussed. Combined with other unresolved political issues, this topic provoked constant political tensions resulting in numerous governmental crises and occasional early elections. The elections of 18 March 1923—held under the electoral law of 21 June 1922, which discriminated against smaller political parties and established smaller districts in Serbia than in other parts of the country—determined a new political balance. Of 34 parties or groups running in the elections for 312 seats, 15 elected one or more deputies to the parliament. The victorious NRS won 108 seats, but the JDS suffered a substantial loss and elected only 51 deputies. The HRSS strengthened substantially and won 70 seats. Because of the unresolved "national question," its support increased substantially in comparison with 1920. The result of this new political arrangement was constant political instability, reflected also by seven different governmental cabinets, all led by Pašić and NRS, in the next two years. In 1923, in response to overtures from Zagreb, Pašić's representatives held talks with Stjepan Radić and his associates about Serb-Croat relations, but these were unsuccessful. The elections of 8 February 1925 witnessed a large turnout. Nearly 77 percent of registered voters cast ballots. Forty-five parties and/or groups presented lists of candidates, but 32 of them failed to elect even a single deputy. The Radicals (NRS) increased the number of their seats to 123, but with their allies they managed to secure 160 seats—a majority in the parliament. Despite harsh government actions against Radić's party, the HRSS remained the strongest opposition party. Although it polled more votes in 1925 than it had in 1923 when it had been able to campaign freely, it still won fewer seats in 1925, namely 67. The opposition (the HRSS, SLS, JMO, etc.) was still fragmented, but it started to organize—which in view of the government's weak majority led to several governmental crises.

The imprisonment of Stjepan Radić for his "anti-Yugoslav conduct" was the harshest action of Pašić's government against the HRSS. (See also below, in the section on Croats.) Later, however, Radić and Pašić came to an agreement—made possible by King Aleksandar, who authorized his confidant Mita Dimitrijević, an admirer of Radić, to talk with Radić in prison. In their talks Radić indicated his readiness for an accord. Subsequently, after Radić was amnestied and later given a post in the cabinet, the widespread public view was that King Aleksandar had succeeded in "buying off" Radić. Although characterized by some as a "Croat capitulation," the agreement between Radić and Pašić was an important gain for Radić, his party, and its other leaders. It increased their political influence substantially. This agreement was also a gain for the palace, but it reduced the prestige of the Radicals because it was a defeat of the NRS's harsh policy against the HRSS. The Agrarian Party leader, Dragoljub Jovanović, reported that Radić, as early as August–September

Formal portrait of King Aleksandar of Yugoslavia wearing a military uniform (Underwood and Underwood/Corbis)

1924, had said, "Good . . . I will recognize the monarchy. But, for God's sake, give me time to turn my automobile around. For five years I have been talking to these people about a peaceful and neutral republic. I cannot change all of my politics at once. Let them give me time, or else . . . everything will go to hell." (Dragnich, 1983, 37)

Radić himself, in a letter from jail dictated in April 1925 but published later, said: "We did not become monarchists out of fear, or in order to get out of prison, but because we entered, as a party, into the constructive period of our work" (Dimitrijević, 1939, 186).

However, the first public indication of the changing HRSS and Croat position on the existing political system was a statement in the parliament on 12 March 1925, by Radić's nephew, Pavle Radić:

"We view the unity of the state as beyond doubt . . . We recognize the total political situation as it is today under the Vidovdan Constitution with the Karadjordjević dynasty at the head . . ." (Dragnich, 1983, 37).

Consequently, the party changed its name to the Croat Peasant Party (Hrvatska seljačka stranka, HSS) thereby dropping the word *Republican* from the party's official name. After weeks of negotiations between representatives of the King, HSS, and NRS a formal agreement was reached in mid-July 1925. The agreement opened the way for a Pašić-Radić cabinet, which was formed on 18 July 1925.

After Nikola Pašić died in December 1926, the NRS started to fall apart. However, it still remained the strongest party after the new elections held in autumn 1927 and succeeded in creating a coalition government with the Slovene People's Party (SLS). Great political opponents until then, Stjepan Radić and Svetozar Pribičević became the leaders of a new opposition. The existing government was supported in the eastern and western parts of the kingdom (Serbia and Slovenia), and the opposition had the absolute majority in Croatia and Bosnia and Herzegovina. Although the opposition, now united in the so-called Peasant Democratic Coalition (Kmečko demokratska koalicija, KDK), was not very numerous, it was very active and critical in parliamentary debates. Quarrels in the parliament reached their peak on 25 June 1928, when Puniša Račić, a member of the NRS, killed two Croat deputies with a pistol. Stjepan Radić and two other deputies were seriously hurt in this fight, and Radić died as a result of it. The existing government gave up power soon after these events.

King Aleksandar offered the post of prime minister to numerous politicians. Initially no one wanted it, but at the end of July 1928 the president of the SLS, Rev. Dr. Anton Korošec, took the job. For the first time, the government of the Kingdom of Serbs, Croats, and Slovenes was not led by a Serb. Several politicians claimed that Korošec, a Catholic priest, was an agent of the Vatican, which deepened political crises and forced Korošec—whose government was unable to stop violent unrest in Croatia following the death of Stjepan Radić in August 1928—to resign at the end of December 1928. After the resignation of Korošec, King Aleksandar concluded that the only way to retain the monarchy was to create a personal dictatorship of the king. On 6 January 1929, he annulled the Vidovdan Constitution of 1921, dissolved the parliament, consolidated the supreme royal rule, and actually took the government into his own hands. This marked the beginning of the "January Sixth Dictatorship" and ended a period of constant political instability (1921–1929), during which twenty-five different governments had reigned. A package of (special) laws and decrees proclaimed by the king further limited the people's right to association and other political rights, including the freedom of speech. He forbade the activities of all religious and tribal political parties and other national ethnic religious organizations and trade unions. All criticisms of the existing system or initiatives to change the existing system were declared criminal activities and were to be prosecuted. Centralization and unitarism were further strengthened. On the same day, the king also put up a new government. The king named General Petar Živković the prime minister.

In October 1929 the "Law on the Name and Division of the Monarchy into Administrative Regions" was passed. It introduced the new official name of the monarchy as "The Kingdom of Yugoslavia," thereby embodying the concept of the unitary one-nation-state of one "Yugoslav nation" (*jugoslovenska nacija*). "Tribal names," ethnic life, religion, and political parties were now forbidden. This law also determined a new territorial organization and division, introduced in order to strengthen the authority and supervision of the central government and to promote the formation of a uniform nation. The new, largest administrative–territorial units, replacing districts, became provinces, called *banovinas* (*pl. banovine*). Eight banovinas were named after major rivers (Drava, Sava, Zeta, Vrbas, Drina, Danube, Morava, and Vardar), and one was called Littoral Banovina. Banovinas were established to reduce formerly existing administrative atomization and increase the authority of the central government. Their borders were conceived in such a way as to break up historically formed lands and ethnic communities and divide them between two or more different banovinas. Wherever possible, banovinas were designed in such a way as to strengthen the share of the Serb population in their total populations. With this administrative division the king hoped to weaken and suppress national (ethnic) feelings and rebellions of the people in certain regions against the centralized government. Banovinas and their governors, bans, appointed by the king himself, had far less autonomy than the old historical lands had had in Austria-Hungary. Banovinas were divided into smaller administrative units, namely counties and communes, that were also units of local government (Žagar, 2000, 76–77).

The government, denying the very existence of ethnic diversity, kept trying to establish a unified "Yugoslav nation," which provoked even more unrest in the state. To try somehow to solve the difficult situation, the king issued a new constitution on 3 September 1931, the Constitution of the Kingdom of Yugoslavia, also called the Granted Constitution (oktroirani ustav/oktroirana ustava). Although, at first sight, this constitution seemed very similar to the Vidovdan Constitution, it no longer defined the country as a constitutional parliamentary monarchy but only as a constitutional monarchy—thereby manifesting the King's main intent. This constitution consolidated the "national unitarism" together with the "Yugoslav (national) ideology" based upon it. The constitution increased the power of the monarch again, and the power of the parliament, the National Assembly (narodna skupština), was further reduced. The constitution forbade every kind of political association on a "religious, tribal (ethnic) or regional" basis (Para. 1, Article 13), thereby substantially restricting political rights such as rights to association, gathering, freedom of speech, etc. The only trace of linguistic or ethnic pluralism in the new constitution was the definition of an official "Serb-Croat-Slovene" language (Article 3), based on the recognition of the actual existence of at least three different languages.

This constitution defined Yugoslavia as the hereditary constitutional monarchy with a bicameral parliament. The monarch, who had all the power, was not responsible to anyone. The constitution did not give immunity to the members of the House and Senate. These were dependent on the king, who named half of the Senate. The other half of the Senate was elected by the councils of banovinas and communes.

The constitution (Articles 82–86) did not change the administrative/territorial organization of the state determined by the law of 1929, which was still used to control the state from the center. There were still nine banovinas, divided into counties and communes, and the capital city, Belgrade, was still designated a special region. Again, smaller administrative/territorial units were defined as units of local government.

However, there were quite a few changes in the electoral system, introduced by a new electoral law (zakon o izborima) issued on 9 September

1931. It gave two-thirds of the seats in the Parliament to the party or coalition of parties that won a majority. Another law, issued a week later, prohibited all political gatherings and parties based on religious, ethnic, or regional adherence. This law requested that every political party had to nominate and elect their candidates from the whole territory of Yugoslavia. In practice this meant that no pre-1929 political party could participate in the elections, as these parties had been strongly regionally based.

In November 1931 only one state list appeared on the ballot. In accordance with the new constitution only a state list, which had candidates in all electoral districts of the country, could appear on the ballot. According to governmental data the turnout of the voters was around 65 percent, which the king and General Živković proclaimed to be a great success and a show of support by a majority of the population of Yugoslavia for their policies. The opposition, however, was critical of the results, as were foreign governments. In May 1932, General Živković established a new party, the Yugoslav Radical Peasant Democracy (Jugoslovenska radikalna kmečka demokracija), which was renamed the Yugoslav National Party (Jugoslovenska nacionalna partija, JNP) in 1933. This weakened and diminished the influence of old political parties in Serbia (especially the NRS, which was no longer a ruling party), while most old (bourgeois) political parties in other parts of the country were renewed and started their political activities anew. Some of them issued plans for the reconstruction of Yugoslavia—*punktacije*. The *Zagrebačke punktacije* called for the restoration of the situation before 1 December 1918 and the abolition of Serb hegemony, which would enable nations to decide freely on their destinies. The Slovene People's Party (SLS), Yugoslav Muslim Organization (JMO), and Ljuba Davidović (a leader of a faction of the divided Democratic Party and one of the more important leaders of the opposition) issued similar plans that again showed differences between the desires of Serbia and the other Yugoslav lands. The government of General Živković took action against those who were issuing these punktacije and arrested several important politicians, especially in Croatia and Slovenia—among them Vladko Maček and Anton Korošec. They also continued their repression against the outlawed communists, who continued with their secret activities. The king's authoritarian policy and police surveillance on opponents of the regime provoked discontent and even some armed actions. This gave an opportunity to Croat and Macedonian nationalists to develop their respective organizations—the Croat Ustaša and the Inner Macedonian Revolutionary Organization (VMRO)—which now conspired against the regime. The conspiracy culminated with the assassination of King Aleksandar during his unofficial visit to Marseilles, France, in 1934. A member of VMRO, Vlada Georgijev, killed the king on the order of the leader of the Croat Ustaša, Ante Pavelić.

Because Aleksandar's eldest son, Petar, was only eleven, royal powers were assumed by a regency of three men, as provided for in the king's will. The first regent was Prince Pavle Karadjordjević, Aleksandar's first cousin. The other regents, Radenko Stanković, senator and minister of education, and Ivo Perović, governor of the Sava banovina, were eminent but little-known men. It was soon evident that the important person in this triumvirate, and the one who would in effect be the regent, was Prince Pavle. Prince Pavle tried to normalize the political situation in the country and pardoned Maček and Korošec. However, the incompetence of the government of Boguljub Jevtić—who had taken office as prime minister on 20 December 1934—resulted in student unrest, which forced Jevtić to dismiss the parliament in February 1935. New elections were called for 5 May 1935. The list of candidates put forward by the regime won 60 percent of the popular vote, and the opposition list gathered 37.5 percent. According to the existing electoral law the victorious group got two-thirds of the seats in the parliament, which angered the opposition. Vladko Maček, who succeeded the deceased Stjepan Radić as the leader of the opposition, declared that his deputies would not enter the parliament.

When Jevtić had to resign, Prince Pavle named a new prime minister, Milan Stojadinović, a Serb politician and economist. On 24 June 1935, Stojadinović introduced a new government that included politicians who had been oppressed during King Aleksandar's dictatorship. Among the ministers were Anton Korošec, a leading Slovene politician, and Mehmed Spaho, a Bosnian Muslim leader. The Croats, however, did not want to enter the government because they did not recognize the constitution of 1931. Stojadinović articulated the aims of his government in a speech to his party's congress in the summer of 1936:

> Serbs, Croats, and Slovenes, in an atmosphere of confidence, should build the internal organization of their own house in unity . . . There have been plenty of mistakes from many sides. Until now we have suffered most from "integral" patriots who proclaim themselves the sole guardians of Yugoslavia . . . carrying out a policy of full equality of all citizens of this country, holding onto the principle of equality of all clans (nationalities) and religions, highly respecting everyone's feelings—I believe that we will create in our country an atmosphere of mutual confidence in which it will be

easier to solve the Croat question, which today looks so difficult . . . In our program the principle of wide self-government is emphasized. That is our political ideal. We shall work for its realization. For eighteen years already there has existed in our political life a huge misunderstanding . . . (Dragnich, 1983, 104–105).

Because the parliament was still dominated by the JNP, Stojadinović decided to dissolve this party and established a new state party, the Yugoslav Radical Union (Jugoslovenska radikalna zajednica, JRZ), with an almost identical agenda. The only difference was regarding ethnic relations; the new party suggested that Slovenes, Croats, and Serbs should have been given more autonomy than they had before. However, Vladko Maček demanded the establishment of a Croat autonomous unit and a division of the country into six or seven autonomous (ethnic) units, which was not acceptable for Stojadinović. Simultaneously, Serb nationalists accused Stojadinović of being too indulgent to Croats. The opposition against the government increased, and in March 1936 one of the Radicals tried to shoot Stojadinović in the parliament. Although the unsuccessful attempt on his life had initially strengthened Stojadinović's government, this soon changed. The opposition resented the government's cooperation with Italian Fascists after the treaty on political and economic cooperation with Italy was signed in March 1937, but especially resented was the government's attempt to ratify the Concordat with the Vatican Holy See, which had been signed by Bogoljub Jevtić in July 1935. Protests of the Orthodox hierarchy against this Concordat stimulated the united opposition to prepare mass protests in Belgrade. Stojadinović's popularity in Yugoslavia sank even more when he established economic and political contacts with Nazi Germany at the beginning of 1938.

At the National Assembly elections on 11 December 1938, Stojadinović's party did worse than expected. His Radical Union won 54.1 percent of votes; the United Opposition, headed by Maček and strengthened by the National Bloc Agreement (between the Peasant Democratic Coalition under the leadership of Vladko Maček and the Serb opposition parties, among which the largest was Davidović's fraction of the Democratic Party) of October 1937, received 44.9 percent of the votes. However, under the electoral law Stojadinović got 306 deputies, and the United Opposition got only 67 deputies. These threatened that they would not take their seats in parliament. When Stojadinović reported to Prince Pavle that his party had won by 300,000 votes, Pavle told him that he wished the margin had been greater. Considering the fact that this party was the ruling party in a semidemocratic system, Stojadinović could not have been pleased with the outcome.

Prince Pavle, ready to get rid of Stojadinović, provoked a cabinet crisis in February 1939 and then asked for and received the resignations of the whole cabinet. The new prime minister became Dragiša Cvetković, one of five ministers who had resigned at the prince's order to provoke the cabinet crisis.

The existing ethnic tensions in the country, tense international relations, the rise of Fascism and Nazism in Europe, and the pressure from the British government to get ready to resist any possible attacks planned by the Nazis forced Cvetković and his government to address the "Croat question" immediately. They tried to find a compromise with the Croat politicians. These endeavors resulted in the Cvetković-Maček Agreement (Sporazum Cvetković-Maček), which was signed by the Prime Minister Dragiša Cvetković and Vladko Maček (the leader of HSS and the Peasant Democratic Opposition), on 23 August 1939.

This compromise agreement was possible because the Croat and Serb elites came to recognize that ethnic differences would not disappear and that existing national identities could not be transformed into a new Yugoslav national identity. The agreement anticipated the formation of the ethnically defined Banovina of Croatia (Croat Banovina—Banovina Hrvatska), which was to get wide autonomy with elements of statehood. The agreement emphasized the equality of Serbs, Croats, and Slovenes in the common state as the foundation for resolving the national question in Yugoslavia. As a result of the compromise, the Croat Banovina was formed by a special decree, issued by the regency under the constitutional provisions for what to do in a state of emergency. This new banovina included all counties with a majority Croat population. The Banovina of Croatia got its parliament (Sabor) again. The Sabor was given a substantial autonomy and many functions. The king appointed the banovina's governor (ban) upon the recommendation of the Sabor. In a way, the creation of the Banovina of Croatia meant decentralization of the existing political system and marked a turning point in the Yugoslav political development, which had been previously characterized by centralism and unitarism. It could be considered the beginning of the process of democratization, decentralization, and federalization. On the one hand, claims for similar autonomy, decentralization, and federalization were to be expected also from other nations in Yugoslavia. This would have been an opportunity for democratization and for the official recognition and democratic regulation of the existing ethnic pluralism in Yugoslavia. On

Vladko Maček, Croatian leader in the period between
World War I and World War II (Darko Stuparić, ed.
Tko je tko u NDH, Hrvatska 1941–1945.
Zagreb, Croatia: Minerva, 1997)

the other hand, this agreement could have been just a political bargain between the two largest national elites to ensure their future domination.
The democratic nature of this agreement could also be questioned because of the way the decree for the establishment of the Banovina of
Croatia was issued. The decree issued under the constitutional provisions
for a state of emergency should have been confirmed later by the parliament, but this never happened. Instead, the order under the state of emergency dissolved the parliament, and the elections for the new parliament
did not take place at all because a week later World War II began.

On 1 September 1939, Germany attacked Poland on the pretext that it
had to defend the interests of Germans in Poland, and World War II began in Europe. The Yugoslav government proclaimed its neutrality. In
spite of that, Adolph Hitler asked the Yugoslav government to join the Tripartite Pact (Germany-Italy-Japan) at the beginning of 1941. At first, the
Yugoslav government resisted the signing of the Pact, because Great
Britain had asked Yugoslavia not to break its traditional friendship with
the western democracies. Additionally, influenced by the communists,

there were also demands to intensify the cooperation with the Soviet Union. However, when Bulgaria, Hungary, and Romania signed the Tripartite Pact, the Yugoslav government, now encircled only by Tripartite Pact member states, also had to give in. It signed the Tripartite Pact in Vienna on 25 March 1941. This provoked mass demonstrations and a coup d'etat by the army under the leadership of General Bora Mirković, aided by the British SOE (Special Operations Executive). The main internal reason for the coup d'etat was the intention to liquidate the Cvetković-Maček agreement. Resenting and fearing Fascism and Nazism, the people and army did not want to be part of the Tripartite Pact. Although the new prime minister, General Dušan Simović, did not cancel the signature of the Tripartite Pact, Germany, Italy, and their allies nevertheless attacked Yugoslavia on 6 April 1941.

The Yugoslav state and its army disintegrated within days following the attack. This proved the fragility of the existing political system that, still very centralized and unitary, had been unable to resolve the "national question." The ruling regime had not yet started with democratization and reform of the Yugoslav political system, which lacked the cohesion necessary to mobilize people for its defense. The territory of Yugoslavia was occupied and divided among the aggressors.

Ethnic Relations and the Unresolved "National Question(s)"

With the exception of most Serbs and some Montenegrins, all other ethno-nations and ethnic groups were unhappy about the Serb hegemony and domination in the Yugoslav monarchy between World Wars I and II. Croat and Slovene intellectuals felt especially betrayed by the way the Yugoslav idea was realized in a new centralized unitary state. All those who hoped for democracy were disappointed because of the lack of democracy in the new country. The introduction of the king's dictatorship further increased this dissatisfaction. The official policy that ignored the very existence of ethnic diversity was unable to address problems in ethnic relations and to ensure ethnic equality in the country. Furthermore, the continuation of Serb domination and the inability of the regime to resolve the "national question(s)" aggravated ethnic relations and even stimulated ethnic tensions.

Serb domination existed in the government and administration, including the military and bureaucracy. For example, although Croats represented more than one-fifth of the total population, only 4 percent of all

government ministers in the interwar period were Croats. Serbs dominated the army and diplomatic service. Of eighteen ministers heading
legations (there were no embassies at that time), fifteen were Serbs and
only three were Croats. In 1934, of 127 secretaries and counselors, 106
were Serbs, 18 Croats, and 3 Slovenes. Similar proportions existed in the
judicial appointments. The non-Serb population also criticized the distribution of governmental assistance to the clergy. The Croats complained
that, proportionally, the Orthodox clergy got much more help from the
government than did the Catholic clergy. The Serbs were quick to explain:
the Catholic clergy did not marry, but the Orthodox priests had families
to support. The same types of arguments were used in discussions about
governmental support for universities. The government claimed that Serb
universities received more support because they were bigger (Dragnich,
1983, 140–141).

A specific example of the Serb domination was the new Yugoslav army,
which was actually the somehow transformed Serb army and which played
an important role in the process of formation of the new state and in the
consolidation of its regime. This army was seen as the only viable deter-
rence and defense against possible aggression. Regent Aleksandar (who
later became king) and other Serb political leaders used it as a powerful
political weapon in the negotiations about the new kingdom. After the
unification, the former Serb army included some thirty-five hundred officers of the former Austro-Hungarian army and a few hundred officers of
the former Montenegrin army. However, the commanding Serb generals
and higher officers were especially devoted to the Karadjordjevićs' throne.

Besides political and cultural issues, poor economic conditions were
also an important issue in interethnic relations, especially in Serb-Croat
relations in the kingdom. A member of the Croat Peasant Party, Rudolf
Bičanić, published a relatively brief book entitled *The Economic Foundations of the Croatian Question* in 1938 that had an enormous political impact among Serbs as well as Croats. This book sought to show that Croatia was unfairly treated economically and was even exploited to the
advantage of the Serb areas. On the other hand, the booklet *The Croatian
Question and Numbers* published by Bogdan Prica (1937) was practically
unnoticed. Its statistical tables and text tried to demonstrate that the
Croat areas were neither neglected nor exploited. However, in 1939, the
newspaper *Srpski glas* began publishing a series of articles, mainly by
economists, which discussed different economic issues, especially taxes
and expenditures. Each of the authors tried to prove that his "national"
areas were receiving much less from the Yugoslav budget than they paid

in. The same claims were made about the issues of currency and debts. In 1918 when the Yugoslav state was established there were five currencies circulating in its territory. Croat authors, on the one hand, tried to prove that the currency reform—in which Austro-Hungarian areas got only one dinar (unit of Yugoslav currency) for four Austro-Hungarian crowns—favored the Serb areas; Serb authors, on the other hand, tried to prove that the reform was correct. These articles were collected and published in a book entitled *The Truth about the Economic Foundation of the Croatian Question,* edited by Slobodan M. Drašković (1940).

When discussing the issues of transportation and public works, Croat authors tried to calculate what each region brought into the common state, contending that some 2,000 locomotives and 50,000 railroad cars that Yugoslavia got from Austria-Hungary were in reality Croatia's contribution. Moreover, they maintained that the new railroad construction in the period 1920–1935 was mainly in Serbia. They admitted that Serb railroads had previously been badly destroyed but suggested that areas outside Serbia should not be expected to contribute to the new construction effort. All of these issues placed a burden on ethnic relations and were keys to resolving the "national question(s)" in the new Yugoslav monarchy. However, the regime failed to recognize their importance or could not find adequate answers to these questions. This contributed to the frailty of the existing regime, for the kingdom later lacked the necessary internal cohesion to mobilize people for the defense of the country at the beginning of World War II.

Interwar Histories of the Yugoslav Nations

Slovenes

At first Slovenes happily accepted the unification of the Kingdom of Serbs, Croats, and Slovenes. They could hardly wait for the unification, as they were afraid of German and Italian aspirations to Slovene lands during the process of drawing new borders. They were also naïvely convinced that a bright future was awaiting them in the new Yugoslav state. However, their happiness disappeared soon after unification, when they realized that the Serb bourgeoisie would dominate the new state.

The life of the Slovene people in the first years after World War I was marked by numerous protests and fights based on class differences. There were several protests by the peasant population, which fought for a just

solution to the agrarian question in Prekmurje, Dolenjska, and Bela krajina. Because of the hard conditions of life there were also strikes in mining and industrial centers (Trbovlje, Novo mesto, Maribor). These
protests were influenced by the spread of the ideas of the October Revolution and the impact of revolutionary movements in neighboring countries (Italy, Hungary, etc.).

The most important political parties that influenced the political life of
the Slovenes were the Slovene People's Party (SLS), the Liberal Party
(Liberalna stranka, LS) and the Social-Democratic Party (Socialno-
demokratska stranka, SDS). These were already active among Slovenes
during the Habsburg period. During the first months following the end of
World War I, in spite of old political animosities, these parties shared
power in the autonomous provincial government for Slovenia. Also, later
they had to work together because of the danger of the socialist revolution
and the unsolved question of the frontiers with Italy, Austria, and Hungary.

At the Paris Peace Conference, Italy wanted to acquire all territories
(the Slovene coastland, Istria, Dalmatia) that Britain had promised to it
with the London Pact of 1915, when Italy had entered the war on the side
of the Entente powers. The Italian army started its occupation of Slovene
territories on the western side of the country soon after the truce was
signed. The Italian army even crossed the border assigned to it by the
London Pact, but it had to withdraw to a demarcation line. It took the
government of Italy and the Kingdom of the Serbs, Croats, and Slovenes
two years to sign a peace agreement, in Rapallo in November 1920. With
this agreement one-quarter of the Slovene ethnic territory (the coastland
and a part of Notranjska), with more than 300,000 inhabitants, came under the Italian rule.

The Yugoslav-Austrian border in Styria (Štajerska/Steiermark)—a former Austrian province with a predominantly German population in the
north and a predominantly Slovene population in the south—was decided by the military actions of Major Rudolph Maister, who in November 1918 captured Maribor and the Drava Valley with his volunteer
Slovene army. Maister was promoted to general to have greater authority
in negotiations with Austrians. At the end of November 1918, he negotiated an agreement on the frontier in Styria that almost followed the ethnic border. This border, with some smaller changes, later became the new
state border between the Republic of Austria and the Kingdom of Serbs,
Croats, and Slovenes. A much more complicated situation existed in
southern Carinthia (Koroška/Kärnten, an ethnically mixed Austrian
province, in what is today southern Austria), where military fights occurred after the government of the land of Carinthia declared the inclu-

sion of the entire land of Carinthia in the Republic of Austria. The Slovene military forces were too weak to stop the more numerous and better equipped German "Heimwehr" (an armed Austrian militia) and had to withdraw. It took the Slovene political leadership until May 1919 to convince the government in Belgrade to order the intervention of the Serb army, which occupied the whole of southern Carinthia as an Entente army. The Paris Peace Conference then decided to solve the Carinthian question with a plebiscite. The great powers divided the territory of south Carinthia into two zones, where the population would decide by a popular ballot which country a respective zone would join. Since Austrian propaganda convinced the population to vote according to their political persuasions (the Kingdom of Serbs, Croats, and Slovenes was a backward kingdom; Austria was a republic), a majority of the population voted for Austria. Some 10,000 ethnic Slovenes were among those who voted for Austria. The outcome of the plebiscite in zone B (22,025 votes for Austria and 15,279 for the Kingdom of Serbs, Croats, and Slovenes) meant that the border between Austria and the new kingdom was finally drawn and that the new kingdom lost most of southern Carinthia.

The new kingdom was, however, able to annex Prekmurje, which before had belonged to the Hungarian part of the Austro-Hungarian monarchy. The Yugoslav army was able to occupy Prekmurje because the Yugoslav army helped to crush the communist revolution of Bela Khun, which broke out in Hungary in 1919. The international powers at the Peace Conference in Paris allowed the Yugoslav army to occupy and keep Prekmurje. Several thousand Slovenes were left in Hungary (in Porabje, with the seat in Szentgotthárd/Monošter), and several thousands of Hungarians lived on the Slovene side of the border.

The peace agreements after World War I divided the Slovene ethnic population among four states: the Kingdom of Serbs, Croats and Slovenes (ca. 1.05 million), Italy (290,000), Austria (ca. 70,000), and Hungary (8,000). Slovenes in Austria, Italy, and Hungary were oppressed, and their cultural life became increasingly hard. These states did not keep their promises written in the peace agreements to ensure the protection and development of ethnic minorities in their territories. They even denied the existence of Slovene minorities and tried to assimilate them. Therefore, Slovenes in these countries had to fight for their very existence. As they fought for their identity, Slovenes had the financial support of the government and of nongovernmental organizations from Slovenia and what became Yugoslavia. The question of Slovene minorities in Italy, Austria, and Hungary remains an important issue even today.

Slovenia was the most developed part of the newly established Yugoslav state. As such, this unification helped Slovenia's economy. Slovene enterprises easily sold their products to the Yugoslav markets. It is interesting to note that, in spite of the political centralism of the Yugoslav authorities, the Slovene language, culture, and education flourished in Yugoslavia during that period (e.g., the University in Ljubljana was founded in 1919; the Academy of Sciences was created in 1939; the National Museum was established in 1921, etc.).

The SLS and the Liberal Party had different views on political and ideological questions. The SLS demanded Slovene national individuality and the autonomy of Slovenia, and the Liberal Party advocated centralism in the new kingdom. The SLS, which, because of its autonomist program, was in opposition to the government of the Kingdom of Serbs, Croats, and Slovenes during the first years after World War I, slowly started to adapt and to abandon its hard autonomist demands. Consequently, in February 1927 the SLS entered the new kingdom's government. Its leader, the Catholic priest Rev. Anton Korošec, even became the first non-Serb Prime Minister after the July 1928 shooting in the parliament and the killing of Stjepan Radić. However, the political crises deepened, and Korošec had to resign in December 1928.

On 6 January 1929, King Aleksandar dissolved parliament and proclaimed his personal rule. His dictatorship provoked even greater resistance. The SLS fought against it although they still cooperated in the government until 1931. In December 1932, the SLS issued the Slovene Declaration. They demanded not only autonomy for Slovenes in Slovenia but also the unification of the Slovene ethnic territory that was divided among Yugoslavia, Italy, Austria, and Hungary. They demanded their own flag, financial independence, political, and cultural freedom, and the democratization of Yugoslavia, which they said should be divided into several autonomous units—including Slovenia.

Also, Slovene intellectuals from the Liberal Party, who in the beginning supported Yugoslav political unification, later started to fight against Yugoslav centralism. They opposed cultural unification because they did not want to give up their Slovene cultural heritage, which in the period before World War I represented the main weapon against Germanization. Again, they began to consider the Slovene national consciousness more important than the Yugoslav state consciousness.

The dictatorship slowly weakened after the death of King Aleksandar in 1934. Political parties revived. In 1935 the SLS again joined the government. From the mid-1930s, the communists also became more and more important, especially after the establishment of the Communist Party of

Slovenia (April 1937). They were still illegal, but they attracted many followers because they propagated and organized a movement for national defense against the growing Fascism and Nazism.

In the years just before World War II, the SLS, the most powerful party, became more and more intolerant toward the others. The Catholic Action (a movement of Catholic intellectuals within the SLS), especially, fought not only against leftists and bolshevism but also against everything liberal, democratic, and parliamentary. This policy resulted in hostility with all democratic forces of the left and with liberals, which became evident especially during World War II.

Croats

The unification of the South Slavic lands into the Kingdom of Serbs, Croats, and Slovenes provoked different reactions in Croat political circles. The majority of the leaders of Croat political parties supported the unification. On the other hand, the leader of the HRSS/HSS, Stjepan Radić, warned that the unification was happening too fast. Above all, Radić warned against the hegemony of the Serbs and against centralist unitarism. However, he supported the idea of a federation of equal nations (Serbs, Croats, and Slovenes).

A rebellion of former Austro-Hungarian soldiers in Zagreb took place on 5 December 1918. Antimonarchist demonstrations took place in other Croat towns and villages also. These events demonstrated how correct Radić was when he warned against fast unification. At the beginning of the year, Radić even gathered signatures for a petition in which he impugned the right of the National Council of the State of Slovenes, Croats, and Serbs to make a decision on annexation to the Serb Kingdom of lands that were represented by the National Council. He went so far as to send a petition to the Peace Conference in Paris, thus causing problems for the Yugoslav delegation, which at that time was fighting for international recognition of the new state.

Resistance against the authorities in Belgrade strengthened also because of the bad economic policy. Poor peasants were unhappy because the agrarian reform did not take place. During the years 1918 and 1919, the peasants rebelled and tried to wrest ownership of the land away from large estate owners through violence. To stop further rebellion, at the beginning of 1919 the authorities promised agrarian reform in favor of poor peasants, which they later failed to carry out.

Ineffective and unethical internal politics of the unstable government also hindered success in solving border questions. The government of the Kingdom of Serbs, Croats, and Slovenes was forced to sign a peace treaty with the Kingdom of Italy in Rapallo in November 1920. According to this treaty, 160,000 Croats remained in Italian territory. The Italian authorities treated them as former citizens of Austria-Hungary and, as such, enemies of the state. Italy gave them and the Slovenes very limited minority rights. After Mussolini's Fascists took over the government in Italy, the discrimination against the Croat and Slovene minorities in Italy intensified. The Italian Fascists forbade the use of Croat and Slovene languages in public and even in churches; also, the publishing of books and newspapers and the functioning of all Croat and Slovene societies in the Slovene language were prohibited. Italian authorities even Italianized the names of places and individuals (both their last and first names). On the other hand, Italian authorities demanded minority rights for members of the Italian minority, especially in Dalmatia. Members of Italian minorities could choose whether they would live in Italy or the new kingdom. According to the Conventions of Nettuno, the Italians also had the right to use the Italian language in their communications with authorities in Dalmatia.

Most Croats supported the policy of the HSS, which as its main aim demanded a republic for Croats. In December 1920 the party was officially renamed the Croat Republican Peasant Party (HRSS). The party also demanded social justice and freedom for all national (ethnic) groups. The HRSS soon became the largest and most influential political party in Croatia. In the first election in 1920, this party gained an absolute majority in Croatia and Slavonia; in the elections of 1923 it also gained popularity in Dalmatia and in Bosnia and Herzegovina.

Croat politicians even wanted to internationalize the Croat question. In July 1924, Stjepan Radić traveled to Paris and London to forward the Croat nationalist cause. However, the politicians of France and the United Kingdom did not care much about the Croat question. They wanted to maintain the Kingdom of Serbs, Croats, and Slovenes at any price to preserve the balance of power in the Balkans and in the eastern Mediterranean area. Similarly unsuccessful was Radić's trip to Moscow. Nevertheless, he wanted to show politicians in Europe how far the Croats were ready to go to reach their goals.

The shootings in the Yugoslav parliament in June 1928 were the climax of the Yugoslav political drama. After the king's dictatorship was proclaimed on 6 January 1929, other political groups in Croatia also joined the HSS (which was renamed from the HRSS under political pressure in

1925) in the fight against Serb hegemony. Some Croats even started to deny that they were South Slavs. These came under the influence of Fascism and Nazism and in their agendas started to glorify all the factors that divided Croats from Serbs (religion, alphabet, etc.).

Among these ideologies and movements we must mention especially the extremist and nationalist Ustaša movement under the leadership of Ante Pavelić, former deputy of the Croat Party of the Right, which demanded an independent Croatia. Pavelić's attitude toward the Serbs was especially supported by the Fascists in Hungary and Italy. In 1931 the authorities of both states allowed him to organize military camps for his supporters, drawn from unemployed Croat workers who lived as emigrants in Europe and the United States. From the beginning it was a relatively small group, which, nevertheless, committed quite a few acts of sabotage and quite a few killings during the early 1930s. In 1934 this group also cooperated in the assassination of King Aleksandar in Marseilles. Later, the influence of the Ustaša movement strengthened, reaching its peak during World War II in the so-called Independent State of Croatia.

Probably the most important factor for the fate of the Yugoslav monarchy was that there was no solution in sight to the troubled Croat-Serb relations. In the summer 1922 a group of Serb and Croat intellectuals met in Ilidja, near Sarajevo. Most of them were former members of the Yugoslav Committee. They demanded changes to the Vidovdan Constitution that would allow for a just solution to the Croat-Serb dispute. These questions were also discussed at a meeting of public officials in the fall of 1922 in Zagreb. This meeting was attended by the leader of the Yugoslav Democratic Party (JDS), Ljuba Davidović, and by the president of the parliament, Ivan Ribar. However, the new kingdom's government rejected all proposals by the opposition to change the Vidovdan Constitution, among them a proposal from the HRSS in May 1921. According to this plan, the state would have been reorganized into free national states: Croatia, Serbia, and Slovenia would have become neutral republics. Montenegro, Macedonia, and Bosnia and Herzegovina, which were characterized as half-tribal and half-historical homelands, would have had to decide with plebiscites about their positions in a common state and to which national state they should be annexed.

Although many Croat politicians hoped that the introduction of a king's dictatorship and the abolition of the Vidovdan Constitution on 6 January 1929 would make a compromise agreement possible, the "Croat (national) question" remained unsolved. An attempt to solve the troubles in the Croat-Serb relationship was made with the agreement between

Cvetković and Maček of 1939. However, in spite of this agreement, Serb-Croat relations did not improve, and even deteriorated, during World War II.

Bosniaks

As it was during the periods of the Turkish Ottoman Empire (1463–1878) and Austria-Hungary (1878–1918), after the end of World War I the territory of Bosnia and Herzegovina was again a part of an ethnically plural state, this time the Kingdom of Serbs, Croats, and Slovenes. Again, the Serb-dominated centralist and unitaristic policy making did not help in the development of a Bosniak identity.

During the interwar period, Bosnia and Herzegovina was one of the most underdeveloped regions in the Kingdom of Serbs, Croats, and Slovenes. Almost 88 percent of the population made their living from farming, development of which was hindered by the continued feudal system, unjust ownership, and agrarian overpopulation. The major landowners and the free peasants were mostly Muslims; the majority of Orthodox Serbs or the Catholic Croats living in Bosnia and Herzegovina were landless or even serfs. Political parties in Bosnia and Herzegovina engaged in disputes regarding the agrarian question, connected closely with other economic-social, religious-national, and political problems. There were many fights on national as well as on social grounds. In the 1920s many rebellions broke out because poor peasants and serfs (mostly Serbs and Croats living in Bosnia and Herzegovina) wanted ownership in the lands of the big estate owners (mostly Muslims).

The Bosnian Muslim population (the Bosniaks) started to organize themselves, provoked by the government of the Kingdom of Serbs, Croats, and Slovenes in Bosnia and Herzegovina who in 1918 and 1919 gave most leading administrative positions to Serbs coming from Serbia. These new Serb officials often took violent actions against the Muslims in an attempt to get revenge for the hundreds of years of Muslim supremacy during the Turkish rule. The government in Belgrade and the local Serb bourgeoisie who in this way acquired power over the land stimulated social, national, and religious tensions and fights. "Approximately 1000 killed, 76 burned women, 270 robbed and deserted villages: this is for us Muslims the happy coming into being of that Yugoslavia which we were ready to serve with all our hearts," said the religious leader of the Bosniaks, Mehmed Djemaludin Efendi Čaušević, in a 1919 interview with a French newspaper (Balić, 1992, 5).

Belgrade authorities, in an attempt to control everything, even tried to get the Muslim religious community under control. However, the attempt to move the center of the supreme religious representative of the Muslims (reis-ul-ulem) to Belgrade did not succeed because of very firm opposition from the Bosniaks. They preserved their cultural and religious center in Sarajevo and, in answer to political pressure in February 1919, established the Yugoslav Muslim Organization (JMO). Its political leader was Dr. Mehmed Spaho. This organization, based on religious principles and led by Muslim landowners, was supported by the majority of the Bosnian Muslims from Sandžak regardless of their class. Although the JMO supported the new monarchy, it also demanded autonomy and the geographic integrity of Bosnia and Herzegovina in its historic boundaries. In fact, the JMO listed the geographic integrity of Bosnia and Herzegovina in its borders of pre-1878 as its condition for voting for the Vidovdan Constitution. Therefore, Article 135 of the Constitution determined that Bosnia and Herzegovina would remain in its historic borders and that its administrative units would remain intact. The JMO continued as the political representative of the Muslims of Bosnia and Herzegovina.

Most Serbs of Bosnia and Herzegovina supported the politics of the National Radical Party (NRS), although some were supporters of the Democratic Party (JDS) and other parties. Croats from the beginning supported Hrvatska težačka stranka (the Croat Labor Party) and Hrvatska pučka stranka (the Croat People's Party). After the parliamentary elections of 1923, the HRSS/HSS began to gain Croat voters. On the basis of its program, which demanded federalism, it came to represent most Croats in Bosnia and Herzegovina.

After 6 January 1929, all of the abovementioned political parties were forbidden in the new kingdom. The territory of Bosnia and Herzegovina was divided among the Banovina of Vrbas, Banovina of Zeta, Banovina of Sava, and Littoral Banovina. These banovinas also included wide regions outside of the historical boundaries of Bosnia and Herzegovina. The Muslims did not have the majority in any of them; the territorial integrity of Bosnia and Herzegovina was broken. Kingdom authorities strengthened centralism and unitarism and negated the national individuality of the Bosnian Muslims as well as of the other Yugoslav nationalities. They offered two possibilities to Bosniaks: to become either Serbs or Croats. Only a small number of Muslims, especially intellectuals, Croatized and identified themselves as Croats of Muslim religion. Even fewer were the Bosniaks who identified as Serbs. This is the period in which, declining to identify with the Croats or Serbs, the Bosnian Muslims strengthened their national identity.

When party politics was restored, the JMO immediately demanded that Bosnia and Herzegovina remain one entity as it was before World War I. The leadership of the JMO formulated this demand again in the "Sarajevske punktacije" of 1933, which demanded the territorial and administrative reorganization of the Yugoslav state on the basis of the historic political units and the autonomy of Bosnia and Herzegovina in Yugoslavia. In spite of their policy demanding autonomy, the JMO entered the government of the Yugoslav Radical Union and supported the unitaristic policy of the government of Milan Stojadinović. In return, Stojadinović had to yield to JMO demands on some questions, which provoked protests from the Serbs of Bosnia and Herzegovina.

After the Cvetković-Maček agreement was signed on 26 August 1939, the boundaries of Bosnia and Herzegovina were changed again. Many territories came under the Banovina of Croatia, which provoked unrest among the Muslim and Serb population. The fights among the political leaders of the Serbs, Croats, and Muslims sharpened. Some Muslim politicians even organized a movement for the autonomy of Bosnia and Herzegovina. Opting for national autonomy as the only possible solution to the national question in Bosnia and Herzegovina were also more and more influential Bosnian-Herzegovian communists, who said, " . . . such a solution would be in the common interest of Muslim, Serb and Croat workers and peasants . . ." (*Opča enciklopedija . . .*, 1977, 627).

The abovementioned developments made ethnic relations in Bosnia and Herzegovina worse and strengthened the hostility among Bosnian Muslims, Serbs, and Croats, which became especially evident during World War II.

Serbs

World War I left catastrophic consequences and much devastation in Serbia. More than one-quarter of the whole population, 1.25 million people, lost their lives. Material damage amounted to around one-half of the gross national product (GNP) of Serbia. Serb politicians were convinced that because of the enormous price Serbia paid for the victory, it had the right to decide on the destiny of the new common state.

In spite of the fact that Serbia ceased to exist as a separate entity and lost its own constitution after the unification with other South Slavic peoples on 1 December 1918, Serb politicians were determined in their hegemonic policy. The newly established Kingdom of Serbs, Croats, and Slovenes became a centralized monarchy based on a unitary ideology. All Serb political parties supported this ideology and the introduction of a centralized system, because it insured their interests and a Serb majority in all state institutions—including diplomacy, the army, the customs services, state control, etc.

Such a centralistic and unitaristic policy provoked revolt from other ethnic groups. Ethnic unrest was especially significant in Kosovo, which became part of Serbia during the Balkan Wars (1912–1913). Although the Serbs came as "saviors" to liberate Kosovo, which had been the cradle of the Serb state during the Middle Ages, (inter)ethnic and religious relations there deteriorated. The Albanians, who settled there after the Battle of Kosovo polje (in 1389), fought the idea of a Serb, and later a Yugoslav, state and especially its attempts to Serbianize them. The Belgrade authorities did not spare any attempts to change the ethnic structure of Kosovo and so "make good for the injustices done to the Serbs during the centuries of Turkish rule." Violent military occupation and pacification followed a planned and forced policy of Serbianization, carried out especially by not allowing the use of the Albanian language in schools and administration and by settlement of Serb and Montenegrin colonists.

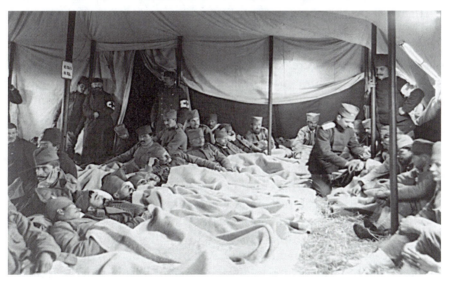

Medical personnel tend to wounded soldiers in a Serbian ambulance tent near Adrianople (in present-day Turkey) during the Balkan Wars. (Library of Congress)

Among them were many war veterans from Serbia to whom the Serb authorities gave the land in Kosovo. According to some data, the authorities moved 60,000 Serb peasants from Bosnia and Herzegovina, Lika, and Montenegro to Kosovo. Albanians, who were organized in old clans (large families), answered the Serb measures with armed rebellions led by the Committee for the National Protection of Kosovo. This committee had the support of Italy, which financially supported the movement. The Belgrade regime started quite a few military operations in Kosovo. Although Yugoslav authorities were obliged by international treaties to respect their national minorities, they saw in Albanians a population that should be assimilated as soon as possible.

Relations between the people and the new Serb authorities were also strained in fertile Vojvodina, which was a part of Austria-Hungary before World War I. In this annexed land, where, in addition to the Serbs (33.8 percent), there were Hungarians (28.1 percent), Germans (21.4 percent), and other ethnic groups, autonomist tendencies soon started to appear. They were first shown in attempts by the peasants to prevent the export of food to Serbia and Bosnia and Herzegovina. As in other regions of Yugoslavia, in Vojvodina unrest arose because of the unsolved national and social questions. These popular uprisings were organized under the slogans of the October Revolution and under the leadership of the communists.

In Serbia problems in food supplies came about because of the technologically obsolete farming methods. An increase in production was also hindered by overpopulation of the rural areas. Small farms with obsolete farming technology were hardly able to feed numerous families and were not able to produce for market. Poor economic conditions in the countryside forced people into massive economic emigration, which substantially reduced the available work force. Consequently, the scarce work force even further decreased the production of food. Industry in Serbia had been completely devastated during World War I, but it developed quickly afterward because of war reparations given to Serbia at the peace conference. In spite of this, Serbia could not compete with the better-developed industries in Croatia, Slovenia, and Vojvodina.

One attempt to improve ethnic relations in the Yugoslav monarchy by solving the "Croat national question" was the previously described Cvetković-Maček agreement of 1939. As a reaction of Serb nationalist circles to this compromise agreement, a Serb cultural club under the leadership of well-known lawyer and Belgrade University history professor Slobodan Jovanović organized propaganda activities that were openly chauvinist. These activities took place in the Serb cultural club that—

based on Serb cultural heritage—gathered mostly Serb intelligentsia. The club was very successful in spreading hatred against the Croats, which existed "hidden" among the Serbs. Again, the depth of this hatred was especially shown during World War II.

Montenegrins

At the beginning of November 1918, Montenegro was freed from Austro-Hungarian occupation. At the same time the agitation for the unconditional unification of Montenegro and Serbia progressed. The unification was proclaimed by the People's Parliament (skupština) in Podgorica on 26 November 1918. It took three days of arguments before this proclamation, which in reality meant the annexation of Montenegro to Serbia, passed. Simultaneously, the Montenegrin deputies deposed the Montenegrin Petrović-Njegoš dynasty.

It is interesting to note that the leaders of the Montenegrin movement for the unification of Montenegro with Serbia did not question the future position of Montenegro in the united state, even though political conditions favored Montenegro. Montenegro was a part of the victorious alliance in World War I. Because the inner political conditions in Yugoslav lands were strained and the Italian army was stationed on the Yugoslav coastland, it would have been possible for Montenegrins to demand at least an equal if not an autonomous position in the new state.

Most Montenegrins awaited the unification of Montenegro with the other Yugoslav lands as the realization of the Yugoslav alliance and as a way out of political and economic crises. However, not all Montenegrins actually favored the unification. Especially against it were the so-called *zelenaši* (greens), who proclaimed their fidelity to their deposed King Nikola, while another group, the *belaši* (whites), supported the Karadjordjević dynasty. The groups vigorously fought each other. Approximately one-half of the people of Montenegro were in favor of the unification with Serbia, whereas the other half were in favor of the continuation of Montenegro as an independent state.

Until the first constitution of the Yugoslav monarchy was adopted, all the old laws of the Kingdom of Montenegro were in effect in Montenegro. The parliament (*skupština*) in Podgorica elected five members to the Executive National Council, which governed Montenegro. The Council operated mainly to restore public order. Among its other duties were reinstatement of judicial police and army authorities, organization of educational and health institutions, supplying the population with food, and rebuilding the war-devastated country. However, the outbreak of a bloody civil war—the so-called Christmas uprising—between the belaši and the zelenaši on the Orthodox Christmas in January 1919 prevented the implementation of this program. Because of the ties between the Italian royal dynasty of Savoia and the Petrović dynasty (Jelena, the daughter of the Montenegrin King Nikola, was the wife of Vittorio Emanuele, the king of Italy) and because of its own political interest, Italy financially supported the zelenaši and helped them to fight until May 1924.

The Executive National Council elected by the skupština in Podgorica administered Montenegro until 20 April 1919. After that, Montenegro was administered by the Commissary of the Kingdom of the Serbs, Croats, and Slovenes, later replaced by an Inspector of the Ministry of Internal Affairs of the Kingdom. This situation remained until April 1922, when the Kingdom was divided into thirty-three territorial units, including the Zetska oblast, which encompassed most of today's Montenegro—without Sandžak (north of the Tara River)—and western Metohija with the towns of Peć and Djakovica. With that, the geographical name of Montenegro was also abolished and replaced by Zeta.

Political life in Montenegro was very tense, especially during the first two years after the unification. By 1920, sharp political and party polarization had occurred. The first political party established in Montenegro after the unification of Yugoslav lands (at the end of 1918) was the Communist Party of Yugoslavia. The approaching election for the Constituent Assembly (28 November 1920) also stimulated the establishment of the other parties in Montenegro. With the exception of the Montenegrin Federalist Party, all the other parties were only branches of Serb or Yugoslav parties (NRS, JDS, etc.). In contrast to these, the Montenegrin Federalist Party, which appeared at the end of 1922, wanted Montenegro to be an equal part of the federated Yugoslav state. But this party did not fight a real political fight; it was ready for compromise with other parties. It never was a strong organization, and it did not have many followers.

A solution to the nationalist question was one of the goals of the Communist Party. Starting in 1926, it aligned with all those political groups that opposed unitarism and centralism. The communists, with their populist slogans, started to become beloved among Montenegrins. The growth of their influence was stopped after 6 January 1929, when the dictatorship forbade political activities of all parties. The dictatorship also introduced a new administrative division of the country. The Zetska oblast became the Banovina of Zeta on the basis of the law on administra-

tive division of the Kingdom (Zakon o nazivu i podjeli Kraljevine Jugoslavije na banovine) of 3 October 1929. The new banovina annexed
Boka kotorska, Dubrovnik, Herzegovina up to the Neretva River,
Sandžak, and Metohija with Djakovica, Kosovska Mitrovica, and Peć
townships. This administrative division (with the exception of Dubrovnik, which in 1939 became part of the Banovina of Croatia) was kept until World War II. The capital of Zetska Banovina was Cetinje.

In the years following the introduction of King Aleksandar's dictatorship, the opposition movement strengthened under the leadership of the
Montenegrin communists. During that period the Montenegrin Front for
National Freedom was established, to fight against the remains of the January Sixth Dictatorship and for democratic freedoms and national equality. After 1937 communists started to operate in the countryside and
helped develop movements among high school and university students.
The Communist Party became the most influential political party in
Montenegro, which was later confirmed by events during World War II.

Macedonians

Although several borders in Europe were changed after World War I, the
borders in the region of settlement of ethnic Macedonians determined after the Balkan wars remained in most cases unchanged (with the exception of the Bulgarian-Yugoslav border near Strumica). Ethnic Macedonians continued to live in three states: Bulgaria (Pirin Macedonia, 2,700
square miles), Greece (Aegean Macedonia, 13,350 square miles), and the
new state, the Kingdom of Serbs, Croats, and Slovenes (Vardar Macedonia, 9,925 square miles).

Although the borders remained unchanged, the air was still filled with
demands for new borders in these territories. Especially loud were political representatives of the Kingdom of Bulgaria. Even before the peace
agreement between Bulgaria and the Kingdom of Serbs, Croats, and
Slovenes was signed, some Bulgarian armed troops that supported an organized fight for an "autonomous Macedonia" illegally invaded Vardar
Macedonia. With this military action, led by Todor Aleksandrov, Bulgarian authorities tried to create the impression with the European diplomats that because of the unsolved Macedonian question new frontiers
needed to be drawn in this region. The situation somehow quieted after a
peace agreement with Bulgaria was signed in 1919, which resulted in the
movement of some of the population. Most of the Greek population

emigrated from Vardar Macedonia to Greece, and some of the Slavic population moved from Aegean Macedonia to Bulgaria and to the newly established Kingdom of Serbs, Croats, and Slovenes.

After conditions settled down, the Yugoslav (Serb) authorities started to enforce their laws in this most southern Yugoslav region—which was, before World War I, under the influence of Bulgaria and Greece, although it was formally annexed to Serbia after the second Balkan War (1913). Yugoslav authorities first closed all Bulgarian schools that remained from the period before World War I. At the same time they started to colonize Macedonia with Serb peasants and to establish centralist, unitarist rule. After this, numerous new problems arose, especially national and social ones.

Even though the Kingdom of Serbs, Croats, and Slovenes signed an international treaty in St. Germain in September 1919 under which it was obliged to respect the rights of national minorities and their cultural individuality, it violated this agreement many times during the next years. This was true especially with regard to the Macedonians, whose very existence was denied by the Yugoslav authorities. They counted Macedonians as (South) Serbs because of existing linguistic similarities. As a result of such policies, Macedonians mounted numerous rebellions, against which the central government used considerable force.

Because of the unsolved national question and a difficult and complicated social and economic situation that in particular affected all classes of the non-Serb population, members of the other ethnic minorities in the area also felt dissatisfied. Most rebellions and armed actions came from the Albanians, who had settled in western Macedonia at the end of the eighteenth century. (They settled this territory after the so-called Karpoš rebellion, when the Serb and Macedonian populations of the regions rebelled against Turks and escaped to Hungary together with the Austrian Army out of fear of Turkish revenge.)

During the whole interwar period, Macedonians were also an important factor in Yugoslav-Bulgarian relations. Because of the policy of non-recognition from the Belgrade regime, the Inner Macedonian Revolutionary Organization (Vnatrešna makedonskata revoljucionarna organizacija —VMRO), supported by the Bulgarians, worsened Bulgarian-Yugoslav relations through terrorist actions. Because of many attacks by the Bulgarians on Serb officials and police, the Belgrade government was even forced to close its borders with Bulgaria. This did not prevent a Macedonian terrorist from killing the leader of the Yugoslav secret services on 13 July 1928. The British and French governments, which in the past had tried to negotiate better relations between Bulgaria and Yugoslavia, advised Bulgarians to outlaw the VMRO and settle their differences with the Serbs. Representatives of the Italian government, which financially supported the VMRO, also were invited to cease their support. However, Mussolini did not accept the invitation.

Until World War II, the Yugoslav authorities tried to strengthen their influence in Macedonia, while Macedonians, Turks, Albanians, and members of other ethnic minorities labored to solve their national and social questions.

Cultural Developments during the Period of Karadjordjević's Yugoslavia, 1918–1941

World War I only deepened the antagonisms between rich and poor in the Yugoslav monarchy, which became even more evident during the interwar period. Once the Kingdom of Serbs, Croats, and Slovenes was established, new avenues opened for cultural development and connections among Yugoslav peoples—as well as between the peoples of Yugoslavia and other European nations and the world. Also, several important cultural, scholarly, and scientific institutions of all nations were established in this period. Culture in Yugoslavia, more precisely the cultures of Yugoslav nations, and their achievements became comparable with that of other contemporary European nations.

Slovenes

With the establishment of the Kingdom of Serbs, Croats, and Slovenes, the Slovene language developed very quickly. Slovene art also developed very quickly and by World War II had reached the level of the rest of Europe. In addition to the already established writers and poets (i.e., Oton Župančič, Anton Gradnik, Ivan Pregelj, etc.), Slovene art developed primarily in Expressionism, evident most in the plastic arts (France and Tone Kralj, Veno Pilon, Ivan Čargo) and less in literature (Slavko Grum). In addition to Expressionism, avant-garde artistic movements were also present, especially Futurism (poet Anton Podbevšek) and Constructivism (painter August Černigoj, poet Srečko Kosovel, art director Ferdo Delak).

At the end of the 1920s and in the 1930s, New Reality (an artistic trend in the second half of the 1920s, directed against objectivity and a clear, defined relation toward everyday life) and Social Realism (an artistic trend of the 1930s that emphasized the misery of the life of the poor because of capitalism) prevailed. In prose, the emphasis was on the plight of the poor because of the inequalities of capitalism (Mile Klopčič, Prežihov Voranc, Miško Kranjec); in drama, historical or contemporary bourgeois and peasant motifs were popular (Bratko Kreft, Ferdo Kozak, Ivan Potrč). In poetry and prose, in addition to Social Realism, Existentialism (a trend in philosophy that deals primarily with questions about the existence of human beings) was also influential (Edvard Kocbek). In music, Marij Kogoj, composer of the opera *Črne maske* (*Black Masks,* 1929), and Slavko Osterc made significant contributions. Osterc, who taught at the Conservatorium in Ljubljana, especially influenced new composers in the 1930s (Matija Bravničar, Lucijan Marija Škerjanc, etc.).

Architecture developed quickly. The most important architect was Jože Plečnik, a founder of Slovene (and also European) modern architecture, who looked for harmony between buildings and their environment. Other notable architects of the interwar period were Vladimir Šubic, who built a Ljubljana skyscraper, and Vladimir Mušič, who followed Functionalism (an artistic trend that emerged in the 1920s and prevailed through the 1970s).

An important development was the establishment of new Slovene scholarly, scientific, and cultural institutions. The most important was the University of the Kingdom of Serbs, Croats, and Slovenes, established in Ljubljana in 1919. Although some demanded that instruction be in the Serbo-Croatian language, instruction in the Slovene language was introduced here. In 1929, when the dictatorship of 6 January was introduced, the Belgrade authorities wanted to close the university. The reaction of the rector, Milan Vidmar (a well-known mathematician and world-renowned chess player), was to ask King Aleksandar to become the patron of the celebration of the tenth anniversary of the university, which was then renamed the University of King Aleksandar. In addition to the university, other important institutions established in the interwar period were the National Gallery of Arts (1918), National and University Library (1941), and the Academy of Arts and Sciences (1938).

Croats

Croat culture, especially literature, developed very quickly after World War I. The most important author was the writer Miroslav Krleža, with his dramas and novels. During the period of Expressionism and Modernism, lyrical poetry also reached a high esthetic level (Antun Branko Šimić, Tin Ujević, etc.), as did the drama of Milan Begović and the novels of August Cesarec.

The Zagreb Academy of Plastic Arts was established in 1922, and the famous sculptor Ivan Meštrović became its first rector. His sculptures represented motifs from people's poetry and legends, the Bible, and symbolism. He created large, impressive monuments. His creativity influenced many younger Yugoslav sculptors (e.g., the Croat Antun Augustinčić).

Painters who tended to follow the movements of Expressionism (an artistic trend at the beginning of the twentieth century that emphasized spiritual and sentimental expression in the plastic arts) and Cubism (an artistic trend in painting in the beginning of the twentieth century that restricted the human body and other figures to basic geometrical figures, such as cube, cylinder, and sphere) were prominent (e.g., Marin Tartaglia, Zlatko Šulentić). Later, some graduates of the Zagreb Academy (Marijan Detoni, Franjo Šimunović, etc.) were also important. The group Zemlja (Earth), which represented the "left" of the Croat plastic art movement, also had a major impact in Croatia. The initiator of the group was the painter, graphic artist, and illustrator Krsto Hegedušić, who, in 1930 in the village of Hlebine, established a school of Naïve painting whose main representative was Ivan Generalić. (Naïve was a Croat school of nonacademic painters who painted mostly motifs from nature.)

After World War I Croat music was resurrected. The main ideologues of the national music were Anton Dobronić and Jakov Gotovac, the father of Croat comic operas like *Ero s onoga svijeta (The Ero from the Other World)*, 1935.

Bosniaks

Although Bosnian Muslims were not recognized as a separate "tribe," there were quite a few writers from this group who established themselves at that time (e.g., Šemsudin Sarajlić). This was the period of social literature, when Hamza Humo, a poet, dramatist, and writer of short novels, wrote about the Muslim people's movements provoked by the conflicts between the East and West. In lyrical poetry, Husnija Čengić and Hamid Dizdar established themselves, and Rasim Filipović contributed in the field of drama. In the 1930s a generation of socially engaged writers, who reached their peak during World War II or in the years after it, started to publish (e.g., Skender Kulenović).

As was the case with literature, renewal in plastic arts was slow. At first these arts developed under the influence of the schools of Munich and Prague. A younger generation of artists established themselves, especially Omer Mujadžić. In building, the Prague school of architecture prevailed, with elements of Constructivism and Functionalism.

Music also started to develop in this period. To foster better conditions, the Ministry of Education of the Kingdom of Serbs, Croats, and Slovenes established a regional school of music in Sarajevo in 1920, in which established musicians from other parts of Yugoslavia taught. In 1923 the Philharmonic Society of Regional Music School (Filharmonično udruženje Oblasne muzičke škole) was established. The Sarajevo Philharmonic was created in the same year. However, the first professional instrumental group in Bosnia and Herzegovina was the orchestra of the National Theatre in Sarajevo established in1921.

Serbs

In literature, a picturesque and antagonistic vision of Modernism prevailed, which put under question all the social and national values of the old bourgeois. In the 1920s, Serb poetry in the style of the Modern Avantgarde (e.g., Oskar Davičo) deserves to be mentioned. During the same period, some novel writers also became famous (e.g., Miloš Crnjanski). During the interwar period, the writer Branislav Nušić reached the peak of his creativity. He continued to describe the old Serb patriarchal petit bourgeois society through satire and humor. Other novelists of this period described life in Serb towns and villages (e.g., Branko Ćopić). The poetry of Desanka Maksimović and other poets who wrote about the homeland, political freedom, and nature also deserves to be mentioned.

In visual arts volume and space prevailed over colors and lines. However, colors prevailed again in the works of Colorist Expressionists (Petar Lubarda, Marko Čelebonović, etc.). The first Serb sculptors to achieve prominence were Djordje Jovanović and Simeon Roksandić. Some artists devoted themselves to graphics. The most famous of these was Dragan Lubarda.

After World War I, the needs of Belgrade as capital of the new state represented a challenge for architects. Mainly unsuccessfully, Momir Korunović and Milica Krstić tried to create a new national style on the basis of the Serb architecture of the Middle Ages.

During the period 1911–1941, ten films were shot. The first, *Karadjordje,* was created in 1911. The best film of the period was *S verom u boga*

(*With Faith in God*) by Mihailo Popović. Popović is also the author of the historical spectacle *Kosovski boj* (*The Battle of Kosovo*, 1939). In September 1939, TV was demonstrated at the Belgrade Fair, but it took until the mid-1950s before it was introduced for wide public use.

Creativity in the field of music also bore fruit. Mihailo Vukodragović and others composed in a national and expressionist spirit. Some Serb composers who studied abroad (e.g., Milan Ristić) temporarily accepted dodecaphony and other contemporary musical trends.

Montenegrins

The interwar period in Montenegrin culture was marked especially by some literary almanacs that enabled Montenegrin artists to publish, and the people to read, artistic works. The first was the scholarly-literary oriented *Lovćenski odjek* (*The Echo of Lovćen*). The first issue was published in 1925. It ceased publication after fifteen issues. The first five issues were devoted exclusively to Njegoš and were the first scholarly works on his work and life. Later literary journals included *Zapisi* (*Notes,* 1927–1933 and from 1935 on), *Razvršja* (1932), *Granit* (*Granite,* 1934–1935), and others. As there were no schools of higher education in Montenegro at the time, students had to study in other places, mostly in Belgrade. On the one hand, this led to a weak literary life in Montenegro; on the other hand it made it easier for writers to overcome Montenegrin traditionalism and to include Montenegrin literature in common currents of European social literature.

Montenegrin writers wrote social literature influenced by their own bad living conditions. So, for example, in 1928 Janko Djonović wrote a poem *Crnci i Crnogorci* (*Blacks and Montenegrins*) in which he compared the bad living conditions of the Montenegrins and the blacks. During and after World War I most Montenegrin painters continued to work outside Montenegro (e.g., Mihajlo Vukotić). Musical creativity was connected with the cities of Podgorica and Cetinje, where Aleksa Ivanović and Jovan Milošević worked. After 1920 Antun Homen, who worked in Kotor, and Ivan Brkanović, who worked in Zagreb, joined them.

Macedonians

The new kingdom's official policy of nonrecognition of the Macedonian national individuality, language, and culture hindered the cultural development of the Macedonians. The first Macedonian men of literature showed up as late as the beginning of the 1930s. Most of them were playwrights (Vasil Iljoski, Anton Panov, and Risto Krle) and poets (Kočo Solev-Racin, Venko Markovski, and Kole Nedelkovski). The most important was a poet named Kosta Racin, who published the first collection of poems in the Macedonian language in Yugoslavia, *Beli Murgi.* This collection was published in Samobor, Croatia, in 1939. Markovski and Nedelkovski were forced to emigrate to Bulgaria, where they published their poems in Macedonian émigré papers and in special collections. The young Macedonian poet Mite Bogoevski also wrote his first works during this period.

Other branches of the arts also developed relatively late in Macedonia. Modern plastic art started to develop after 1926, when the first exhibit of watercolors and oil paintings of the university-educated painter Dimitar Avramovski Pandilov opened.

Music was at first limited to singing societies. The Serb singing society Mokranjac Stevo—which organized different types of musical activities—played an important role as the initiator of the first school of music in Macedonia. The school was established in Skopje in 1934. The first Macedonian composers (Todor Skalevski, Petre Bogdanov-Kočko), who found inspiration for their works in Macedonian folk music, became known during the pre–World War II period and reached their peak in the postwar years.

The Unresolved "National Question(s)"

Although the creation of the Kingdom of Serbs, Croats, and Slovenes was considered a positive development that contributed to the ethnic and cultural development of most ethnic groups, everybody but Serbs and, to a large extent, Montenegrins was unhappy with the actual Yugoslav state. They disliked the centralized and unitary political system dominated by Serb bourgeoisie, which often denied the very existence of ethnic diversity or at least was unable to manage it in a democratic way by ensuring equality to all ethnic communities. The official unitaristic ethnic policy of "one Yugoslav nation" of three names defined only Serbs, Croats, and Slovenes as its constituent tribes and did not recognize Macedonians, Montenegrins, or Muslim Bosniaks as specific and equal nations. Additionally, it did not establish adequate protection of the existing national (ethnic) minorities. It failed to fulfill the high expectations of a population that had hoped for a democratic, decentralized multinational federation that would recognize and respect the individuality and rights of every ethnic community.

The previously described ethnic policy, the denial of the existence of ethnic diversity, the absence of democracy, the constant political crises, the problems in the functioning of democratic institutions of the highly centralized and ineffective political system, the economic and social problems, and the crises resulting from the underdeveloped economy of this agrarian country were some factors that influenced ethnic relations and contributed to growing ethnic tensions in the Yugoslav state in the period between World Wars I and II. Almost everybody felt exploited and cheated. For these reasons, all attempts to reach acceptable compromises and to resolve social, nationalistic, and other questions failed. The existing regime was unable to ensure the necessary political cohesion, which proved a fatal defect when the country was attacked and occupied in 1941.

Timeline

1 November 1918	Rudolph Maister captured Maribor and the Drava Valley with his voluntary army
25 November 1918	General Maister negotiated an agreement on the frontier in Styria that actually followed the ethnic border
1 December 1918	Proclamation of the Kingdom of Serbs, Croats, and Slovenes
20 April 1919–April 1922	Montenegro administered by the Commissary of the Kingdom of Serbs, Croats, and Slovenes
12 August 1919	Yugoslav army occupied Prekmurje
3 September 1920	Provisional parliament enacted an electoral law for the Constituent Assembly
10 September 1919	Kingdom of Serbs, Croats, and Slovenes signed an international Treaty in St. Germain
autumn 1919	Aleksandar University of the Kingdom of Serbs, Croats, and Slovenes established in Ljubljana
20 October 1920	Carinthian Plebiscite
12 November 1920	Treaty of Rapallo
28 November 1920	Elections for the Constituent Assembly

12 December 1920	First meeting of the Constituent Assembly of the Kingdom of the Serbs, Croats, and Slovenes
30 December 1920	New kingdom's government issued a decree that prohibited the political work of the Communist Party.
28 June 1921	Constituent Assembly adopts Vidovdan (St. Vitus Day's) Constitution
2 July 1921	Constituent Assembly renamed National Assembly (Narodna skupština)
21 June 1922	National Assembly enacted new electoral law
18 March 1923	Elections for the National Assembly
8 February 1925	Elections for the National Assembly
mid-July 1925	Agreement between the Radical Party and the Croat Peasant Party opened the way for Pašić-Radić cabinet
18 July 1925	Pašić-Radić cabinet was formed
10 December 1926	Death of Nikola Pašić
11 September 1927	Elections for the National Assembly
20 June 1928	Shootings in the Assembly: Puniša Račić killed two Croat deputies with a pistol; Stjepan Radić and two other deputies were seriously hurt
27 July 1928	Slovene People's Party leader Anton Korošec formed new government
8 August 1928	Death of Stjepan Radić
2 January 1929	Resignation of Prime Minister Anton Korošec
6 January 1929	King Aleksandar suspends Vidovdan Constitution; the beginning of the January Sixth Dictatorship
3 October 1929	Law on the Name and Division of the Monarchy into Administrative Regions introduced the new official name of the monarchy, the Kingdom of Yugoslavia
3 September 1931	The king issued the so-called Granted Constitution (oktroirani ustav/oktroirana ustava)
8 November 1931	Elections for the National Assembly
7 November 1932	"Zagrebačke punktacije" (Zagreb Declaration) signaled the strengthening opposition to dictatorship
31 December 1932	SLS issued the Ljubljanske punktacije (Slovene Ljubljana Declaration)
January 1933	Yugoslav Muslim Organization issued the so-called Sarajevske punktacije (Sarajevo Declaration)

9 October 1934	King Aleksandar assassinated in Marseilles; Prince Pavle becomes regent
20 December 1934	Bogoljub Jevtić formed a new government
February 1935	Student unrests forced Jevtić to dismiss the parliament
5 May 1935	Elections for the National Assembly
24 June 1935	Jevtić's resignation; Prince Pavle appointed a new Prime Minister, Milan Stojadinović
25 July 1935	Stojadinović signed the Concordat with the Vatican
6 March 1936	An unsuccessful attempt on Stojadinović's life in the National Assembly
11 August 1938	Academy of Sciences and Arts established in Ljubljana
11 December 1938	Elections for the National Assembly
3 February 1939	Prince Pavle forced Stojadinović to resign and named Dragiša Cvetković as Prime Minister

Significant People, Places, and Events

ALEKSANDAR I KARADJORDJEVIĆ (1888–1934), king of the Serbs, Croats, and Slovenes (1921–1929) and king of Yugoslavia 1929–1934. Aleksandar received his education in Geneva, St. Petersburg, and Belgrade. In 1909 he became crown prince, and in 1914, regent of Serbia. During World War I he was supreme commander of the Serb Army. From 1 December 1918, he was the regent of the Kingdom of Serbs, Croats, and Slovenes, and on 17 August 1921, he became the king of the Serbs, Croats, and Slovenes. To express how sensitive he was regarding the equality of the "tribes" that constituted his state, he gave his sons Serb (Djuradj), Croat (Petar), and Slovene (Pavle) names. He tried to establish good relations between the new kingdom and the western European democratic states; in internal Yugoslav politics he was a staunch defender of a centralist regime, fighting against democracy and national autonomy within the kingdom. In foreign policy he sought help from France for the preservation of the independence and territorial unity of Yugoslavia, and he was assassinated by Croat and Macedonian nationalists during a state visit to Marseilles in 1934.

ANDRIĆ, IVO (1892–1975) A writer and poet, Nobel laureate. Andrić studied in Zagreb, Vienna, Krakow, and Graz. Because of his engagement in Mlada Bosna, he was imprisoned by the Austrian authorities from 1914 to 1917. He served as a diplomat between the world wars. He wrote *Travnička hronika* (*Chronicle of Travnik*), *Gospodjica* (*Miss*), and *Na Drini ćuprija* (*Bridge on Drina*), for which he received the Nobel prize for literature.

KOSOVEL, SREČKO (1904–1926) Slovene poet. Srečko Kosovel's poetry was connected with his home region (Karst). He wrote expressionist lyrics on the life of the individual, death, the decay of European civilization, the necessity of changing the world, and the new ethos. His lyrics became widely known only after his death, when his poems were published in *Pesmi* (*Poems*, 1927) and *Izbrane pesmi* (*Selected Poems*, 1931). He also wrote essays, poetry for children, and literary criticism.

KRLEŽA, MIROSLAV (1893–1981) Croat writer. Krleža wrote about Croat history, human destiny in the wars, and the destitution of consciousness and morale in bourgeois society. His most important works were *Hrvatski bog Mars* (*The Croatian God Mars*, 1922), *Gospoda Glembajevi* (*Lords of Glembaj*, 1928), and *Povratak Filipa Latinovicza* (*Return of Filip Latinovicz*, 1932).

PAŠIĆ, NIKOLA (1846–1926) Serb statesman and cofounder and leader of the Radical Party. At first Pašić was a defender of the socialist and radical democratic ideology of Svetozar Marković. Because of his participation in the rebellion of Timok he was sentenced to death in 1883, but he succeeded in escaping from Serbia. He received amnesty and returned to Serbia in 1889. During the period 1891–1914 he was president of the Serb government many times. During this period he fought against the pro-Austrian policy of the Obrenovićs and defended Great Serbian ideals. During 1912–1924 and 1924–1926 he was president of the government of the Kingdom of Serbs, Croats, and Slovenes and until his death a defender and promoter of a centralist and monarchist Yugoslav state.

RADIĆ, STJEPAN (1871–1928) Croat politician. Because of his activities in opposing and demonstrating against the authorities, Radić was imprisoned twice when he was still a student. From 1902 he was secretary of the Croat united opposition. In 1904, together with his brother Ante, he established the Croat Peasant Party, which in 1910 sent deputies to the Croat parliament (Sabor). In spring 1918 when Austria-Hungary felt apart, Radić opposed monarchist rule and unconditional unification with Serbia. In 1919 the Croat Peasant Party got fifty seats in the parliament and became the largest party in Croatia, in spite of the fact that Radić himself was imprisoned for his political activities. Radić served as Minister of Education in the government of

Nikola Pašić during 1925–1926. After 1927 he again become an oppositionist politician, and from 1928 until his death he was leader of the opposition.

SPAHO, MEHMED (1883–1939) lawyer and Bosniak politician. Spaho was president of the Yugoslav Muslim Organization from 1921–1939. He fought for autonomy and, above all, for the territorial integrity of Bosnia and Herzegovina in its historic borders. With the support of the Muslim population of Bosnia and with some very successful tactics, he was a minister in different Yugoslav governments (1918–1919, 1921–1922, 1925, 1927–1929, and from 1935 onwards). Together with Milan Stojadinović and Anton Korošec he founded the Yugoslav Radical Union, which was a proregime political party.

Bibliography

Allcock, John B. "Macedonia." In Turnock, David, and Carter, Francis W. (eds.). *The States of Eastern Europe*, Vol. 2, *South-Eastern Europe*. (Aldershot, U.K.: Ashgate, 1999): 141–166.

Allcock, John B. "Montenegro." In Turnock, David, and Carter, Francis W. (eds.). *The States of Eastern Europe*, Vol. 2, *South-Eastern Europe*. (Aldershot, U.K.: Ashgate, 1999): 167–194.

Balić, Smail. *Das unbekannte Bosnien. Europas Brücke zur islamischen Welt.* [*The unknown Bosnia: Europe's bridge to the Islamic world*]. (Köln, Germany: Böhlau Verlag, 1992).

Banac, Ivo. *The National Question in Yugoslavia: Origins, History, Politics.* (1984; reprint, Ithaca, NY: Cornell University Press, 1993).

Dimitrijević, Mita. *Mi i Hrvati. Hrvatsko pitanje (1914–1939): Sporazum sa Hrvatima* [*We and the Croats: The Croat question (1914–1939): Agreement with the Croats*]. (Belgrade, Serbia-Montenegro: Živ. D. Blagojević, 1939).

Dragnich, Alex N. *The First Yugoslavia: Search for a Viable Political System.* (Stanford, CA: Hoover Institution Press, 1983).

Hoptner, Jacob B. *Yugoslavia in Crisis, 1934–1941.* (New York: Columbia University Press, 1962).

Lampe, John R. *Yugoslavia as History: Twice there Was a Country.* (Cambridge, U.K.: Cambridge University Press, 1996).

Lederer, Ivo. *Yugoslavia at the Paris Peace Conference.* (New Haven, CT: Yale University Press, 1963).

Opća enciklopedija Jugoslavenskog leksikografskog zavoda [*General encyclopedia of Yugoslav Lexicographic Institute*], 1: *A-Bzu,* Bosna i Hercegovina—povijest [Bosnia and Herzegovina—History]. (Zagreb, Croatia: Jugoslavenski leksikografski zavod, 1977): 624–628.

Prunk, Janko. *A Brief History of Slovenia: Historical Background of the Republic of Slovenia.* (Ljubljana, Slovenia: Mihelač, 1994).

Vodopivec, Peter. "Seven Decades of Unconfronted Incongruities: The Slovenes and Yugoslavia." In Benderly, Jill, and Kraft, Evan (eds.): *Independent Slovenia: Origins, Movements, Prospects.* (New York: St. Martin's Press, 1994): 23–46.

Žagar, Mitja. "Yugoslavia: What Went Wrong? Constitutional Aspects of the Yugoslav Crisis from the Perspective of Ethnic Conflict." In Spencer, Metta (ed.). *The Lessons of Yugoslavia* (Research on Russia and Eastern Europe, vol. 3.). (Amsterdam: An Imprint of Elsevier Science JAI, 2000): 65–96.

CHAPTER FIVE

Yugoslav Nations during World War II (1941–1945)

T HE BEGINNING OF WORLD WAR II marked the end of the Kingdom of Yugoslavia. The fact that it failed to solve the national
question contributed to its collapse. The communist-led resistance
united national liberation movements in the country on the principle of
"equality, brotherhood, and unity of (Yugoslav ethno-)nations" and successfully liberated the territory of Yugoslavia from the occupiers in 1945.
The communists then hoped to solve the national question by the introduction of federalism. However, their desire to wield the power and absolute control in the country was incompatible with political pluralism
(the multiparty political system) and led to the establishment of a centralized Soviet-type federation after World War II.

The Occupation and Division of Yugoslavia

After the coup in Yugoslavia in 1941, the new prime minister, General
Dušan Simović, did not invalidate his predecessor's signature to Yugoslavia's accord with the Tripartite Agreement. However, on 27 March
1941, Hitler ordered a plan to attack and divide Yugoslavia anyway, because he was angry about the reaction of the people of Yugoslavia to the
signature of the Tripartite Agreement. The attack began on 6 April 1941.
Eighty-five German, Italian, Hungarian, and Bulgarian divisions (around
870,000 soldiers) attacked Yugoslavia and, in a *blitzkrieg*, defeated the
Yugoslav army after less than a fortnight (200,000 Yugoslav soldiers and
12,000 officers became prisoners of war). Yugoslav Foreign Minister Aleksandar Cincar-Marković and General Danilo Kalafatović signed an unconditional capitulation of the armed forces on 17 April 1941; by then
King Petar and most of the members of the Yugoslav government had

already fled Belgrade and flown to Cairo, which was controlled by the British.

Yugoslavia, unprepared for the war, fell apart in days. The Yugoslav army and its old military doctrine, based on the experiences of the Balkan Wars and World War I, proved inadequate. Also, people were not willing to defend the country. They were dissatisfied with centralist and unitary Yugoslavia, which, ruled by the Karadjordjević dynasty and dominated by Serbs, had failed to resolve any important national, social, and/or economic problems. The prewar regime had used its repressive apparatus to stop any expression of dissatisfaction or unrest; the ruling classes and political leaders of different ethno-nations were united only in fighting revolutionary movements. Such a practice deepened differences among the ethno-nations and contributed to a climate of ethnic intolerance.

After the capitulation, the occupation forces divided Yugoslavia in accordance with their wishes and their respective levels of political and military power. Germany annexed northern Slovenia; and a great part of Serbia (with Belgrade) were also under its military occupation or direct administration. Italy annexed southern Slovenia, most of northern and middle Dalmatia, and Boka Kotorska. Montenegro was under a special Italian occupational administration. Kosovo and western Macedonia were annexed to Greater Albania (under Italian surveillance). Hungary occupied Prekmurje, Medjimurje, Bačka, and Baranja; Bulgaria occupied most of former Yugoslav Macedonia and southeastern Serbia.

The Independent State of Croatia (NDH—Nezavisna država Hrvatska) was established in the territory of Croatia (excluding Dalmatia between Zadar and Split and Medjimurje and Baranja), Bosnia and Herzegovina, and Srem. This state, dependent on occupiers and ruled by the Ustaša government of Ante Pavelić, was independent only in name. Its government wanted to create an ethnically cleansed Croatia with the help of German and Italian occupational forces. Serbs, Jews, Gypsies (Roma), and Muslims, as well as any Croats who opposed the new political order, were persecuted and murdered. Mass murders, especially of the Serb population, took place in eastern Herzegovina, Lika, Kordun, Banija, and some regions of Bosnia. Concentration camps were also established. Around this time, 2 million Serbs in NDH started to organize their own defense.

A similar strategy of terror as in the NDH was exercised by the occupational administrations in other occupied territories (see above). The territories' governors forced Germanization, Italianization, Hungarization, etc., and emigration with the intent of ethnic cleansing. The occupying forces also took advantage of the area's bad interethnic relations. The

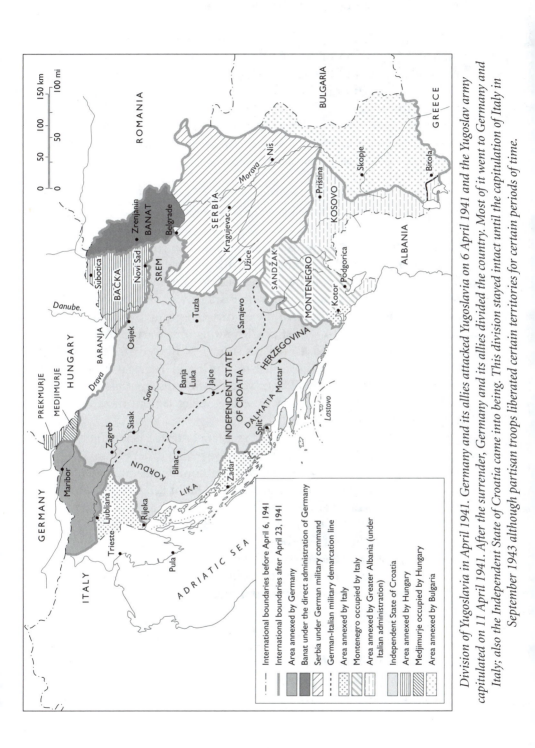

Division of Yugoslavia in April 1941. Germany and its allies attacked Yugoslavia on 6 April 1941 and the Yugoslav army capitulated on 11 April 1941. After the surrender, Germany and its allies divided the country. Most of it went to Germany and Italy; also the Independent State of Croatia came into being. This division stayed intact until the capitulation of Italy in September 1943 although partisan troops liberated certain territories for certain periods of time.

occupation of Yugoslav territories by different armies brought about a different organization of the administrations in different parts. The administrative leaders of the occupation gave good jobs to members of pro-Fascist or pro-Nazi organizations, especially to members of the Kulturbund (Cultural Union), which was, from 1939 on, the front organization of Germans in Yugoslavia. Several members of the former Yugoslav elite, bureaucracy, and police were also given important posts and participated in the occupational administration.

The Beginnings of the Armed Resistance

Occupying forces and administrations, assisted by some local ethnic political leaders, started their occupation with political terror and a policy of ethnic cleansing that forced numerous people from their homes. Many of those who were displaced fled into the woods and tried to organize an armed rebellion. In addition to these scattered groups, the Communist Party of Yugoslavia (Komunistička/Komunistična partija Jugoslavije—KPJ) began an organized armed resistance. However, its leader, Josip Broz-Tito, also fomented a socialist revolution in Yugoslavia in spite of different orders from Stalin. These were the first disagreements between the KPJ and the Communist Party of the Soviet Union; these disagreements reached their peak in 1948.

The KPJ's preparations for armed resistance started immediately after the Axis powers' attack on Yugoslavia. However, on orders from Moscow, the decision to fight the occupiers was postponed and implemented on the day of the German attack on the Soviet Union (22 June 1941). By 27 June 1941, the KPJ had already established the Main Staff (military command) of its partisan National Liberation Movement, or NLM, (Narodnooslobodilački pokret [Serbo-Croatian]—NOP and Narodnoosvobodilno gibanje [Slovene]—NOG) under Tito's leadership. At the same time, some of the members of the Central Committee of the KPJ went from Belgrade to different regions and organized armed resistance there. On 4 July the KPJ ordered the start of the resistance, which began almost simultaneously in all parts of Yugoslavia except Macedonia, where it began in October 1941, due to complicated interethnic relations in Macedonia (see the section on Macedonians in this chapter), Serbia, Montenegro, and—especially because of the repression of the NDH against the Serb population—Bosnia and Herzegovina saw the most rapid development of

A group of Yugoslav partisans, nearing a German garrison at the Litija Bridge in occupied Slovenia, deploy on both sides of a road to watch for signs of the enemy. (Hulton-Deutsch Collection/Corbis)

the armed resistance. Partisan units were created in Slovenia and Vojvodina. The armed rebellion commenced in Croatia; however, it included mostly Serbs, as initially the Croats, influenced by Vladko Maček's policy of waiting, did not begin fighting.

The first fights brought relatively great successes to the partisan movement. By August 1941, the partisans liberated the first territories in western Serbia, Kordun, Lika and Banija (in Croatia), Montenegro, and western Bosnia. When the partisans took control of these territories, the problem arose of how to administer them, because the communists that led the NLM insisted on a social revolution. This revolution went on under the slogan "The old ways should never be repeated." The old Yugoslav administrative authorities, which the Axis forces had left untouched, were abolished and the NLM started to create new local authorities, National Liberation Committees, which were the nucleus of a new revolutionary administration.

The Reaction of the Yugoslav Government-in-Exile to the National Liberation Movement

The former Yugoslav political parties and their leaders did not know what to do after the capitulation and occupation in April 1941. The KPJ was the only political party that had a political strategy, and it started to organize the NLM. The other political parties and most politicians pursued a strategy of waiting. They waited for decisions of the king and the Yugoslav Government-in-Exile, who, from July 1941 on, were in London. Although the king and the Government-in-Exile declared that the war against the Axis should continue, they asked their subjects not to attack the occupiers but to hold off until they received further instructions. They planned to establish illegal organizations and start military actions just before World War II would be reaching its end. They then hoped to reconstruct the monarchy with the help of the Western Allies.

The parliamentary parties and the Yugoslav Government-in-Exile were surprised by the successful beginning of an uprising under the leadership of the KPJ. Fearing the initial successes of that NLM, led by the supranational Communist Party, the Government-in-Exile supported the movement of the Chetniks, or the King's Army in the Homeland. Based on the agenda of a Greater Serbia, this movement presented itself as a savior of threatened Serbdom and as a resistance movement that would attack the occupiers at the "right moment."

The first groups of Chetniks started to gather in southern Serbia, Kosovo, and northern Montenegro in April 1941. These were groups of officers of the king's army that succeeded in escaping and had not become prisoners of war after the Yugoslav army had capitulated to Hitler's initial attack. Under the leadership of Kosta Pećanac, a World War I hero and staunch Serb nationalist, they fought first against the Albanians of Kosovo. In spite of the fact that some of these Chetniks wanted to fight the occupying forces—in accordance with traditions of anti-Turkish resistance—by August 1941 they had sided with the German occupiers out of fear of the NLM.

A second group of Chetniks gathered in May 1941 under the leadership of Colonel Dragoljub-Draža Mihailović in Ravna gora (Suvabor planina) in western Serbia. Their intention was to preserve at least a spark of the Serb independence. Out of this nucleus an uncontrolled army developed, loyal to the monarchy and the myths of Serb history, which left deep traces in the midst of occupied Yugoslavia. Its members thought themselves to be called by God to revenge the crimes of the Ustaša army against the Serbs. They also fought to implement a program of ethnic cleansing in Serb-controlled regions. They fought against the Croat and Muslim populations in Bosnia and Herzegovina, Sandžak, Dalmatinska Zagora, and other regions. In the name of Greater Serbia and in revenge for Ustaša crimes, they killed thousands of Muslims and Croats and terrorized any members of the Serb and Montenegrin population who supported the partisan movement.

The Chetniks enjoyed the support of the Yugoslav Government-in-Exile. Draža Mihailović became its minister of war in January 1942. The Western Allies initially recognized the Chetniks as the legal army of the Yugoslav government, which put a stop to any official recognition of the NLM led by the communists. This pro-Chetnik sentiment was influenced by the traditional British sympathy towards the monarchy and the plans of Western anticommunist leaders for Yugoslavia's social and legal order after the war. The Soviet Union accepted this policy, fearing that its support for the partisan movement would complicate its relations with the Western Allies. However, realizing the Chetniks' actual collaboration with the occupiers from 1943 on, the British government changed its policy because of its own war interests. In 1944 the Allies stopped their support of the Government-in-Exile and the Chetniks. They increased their aid to the NLM, recognizing the partisans as the only military units that were fighting against the Nazis and Fascists in the territory of Yugoslavia. This provided the basis for their recognition of the new political realities in Yugoslavia after World War II.

During the occupation, the Axis forces also helped create other ethnically based collaborationist military or semimilitary units in the occupied territories. In Serbia proper there were military units led by leaders of the puppet governments of Serbia, Dimitrije Ljotić and Milan Nedić. The Italians in Slovenia supported the formations of the Domobranci (village defenders), groups of young men formed to help Italians defend Slovene villages from the partisans. After the capitulation of Italy to the Allies in 1943 the Domobranci came under the German command. On 20 April 1944, they even received the blessings of the Catholic bishop of Ljubljana, Dr. Gregorij Rožman. A few units of the King's Army in the Homeland subordinated to the Chetniks, the so-called blue guard, were also organized in Slovenia. However, these units were destroyed during the period of Italian capitulation in 1943 by the partisans. In Kosovo the Italians supported collaborationist groups of armed ethnic Albanians, the so-called Balists.

The National Liberation and Civil War, 1941–1945

Although a few Chetnik units had engaged in some small skirmishes with Germans in the very beginning of the war before they started their collaboration with the occupiers, the partisan NLM was the only group that led a fight for the liberation of Yugoslavia throughout World War II. Its program had many facets. The movement fought against the occupiers and their domestic collaborators, such as the Ustaša and Chetniks. The NLM was also a part of a global anti-Fascist coalition. Its slogan called for fraternity and unity of the peoples of Yugoslavia. On ethnically mixed territories it fought against the genocide carried out by the occupying authorities and their domestic collaborationists. Its vision was a Yugoslav federation of equal nations.

However, the communist-led partisan NLM also pursued a socialist revolution as its goal. In addition to social justice and equality, the declared revolutionary goals included fair and good interethnic relations and ethnic equality, decentralization, and social and political reforms that had not been carried out in the Yugoslav monarchy ruled by the Karadjordjević dynasty.

The vision of the NLM that called for liberation, social justice, and unity-in-diversity proved to be the only all-Yugoslav vision capable of uniting all Yugoslav nations and the majority of the population. This program, elaborated upon first in Slovenia with the creation of the Liberation Front of the Slovene Nation (OF—Osvobodilna fronta slovenskega naroda) in April 1941, also attracted some democratic activists of bourgeois parties and their left-wing democratic factions, thereby creating a wide base of support for the resistance. Afterward, such programs were adopted and carried out elsewhere in Yugoslavia. The NLM experienced its ups and downs, but it was constantly growing and strengthening. Regardless of its growth and the inclusion of many patriots of diverse political orientations, however, the KPJ's leading role in the movement was never endangered.

After Tito, a supreme commander of partisan units, moved from Belgrade to a liberated territory in western Serbia in September 1941, he met twice with Draža Mihailović to talk the Chetniks into cooperating with the NLM. However, the Chetniks, who considered the revolutionary communists the main threat to their Greater Serbia ideas and their plans to restore the old Yugoslav monarchy, rejected cooperation with the partisans. Instead, the Chetniks had by autumn 1941 entered into secret negotiations with the occupying authorities. In spring 1942 the collaboration between the Chetniks and the occupying forces became open, especially in territories under the Italian occupation. Under the circumstances, the NLM started to fight against the Chetniks as well as the occupiers. Of the many battles, the most important one was the Battle of Neretva River in March and April 1943, when the Chetniks, with the help of the Italians, tried to destroy the command and core of partisan units, who were encircled by the Germans and Ustaša. However, the partisans, evacuating their wounded, succeeded in breaking through the Chetnik front. The Chetniks were defeated and did not recover from this defeat.

The military successes of the partisan units resulted in liberation of some territories, which survived for varying periods of time in spite of the superior strength of the occupying forces. Some liberated territories, for example, in Lika, Bosanska Krajina, and Kordun, existed throughout the war. The partisan movement established National Liberation Committees as new local authorities in these territories, but the partisan movement also operated on half-liberated and on occupied territories.

On Tito's initiative, in liberated Bihać, the AVNOJ (Anti-Fascist Council of National Liberation of Yugoslavia) was formed on 26–27 November 1942 as the supreme political authority of the NLM. At its second meeting, on 29–30 November in Jajce, the AVNOJ also declared itself the supreme political representative of the Yugoslav nations. It proclaimed the equality of all Yugoslav nations and the creation of a Yugoslav federation. The AVNOJ established its (pro tempore) government, the National Committee of Liberation of Yugoslavia, and elected Tito, who was declared a Marshal of Yugoslavia, for its president. The return of King Peter and the Government-in-Exile to the country was prohibited until the people had decided on their destiny after the war.

When the Western Allies actually recognized the political situation in Yugoslavia in 1944, they insisted on a compromise between the National Committee of Liberation of Yugoslavia and those politicians and parts of political parties that had not collaborated with the enemies during the war. This was the essence of an agreement made between Tito, on behalf of the National Committee of Liberation of Yugoslavia, and Ivan Šubašić, president of the Government-in-Exile, signed on the island of Vis on 16 June 1944.

By the end of World War II in Europe, the partisan liberation army had freed the whole territory of the former Kingdom of Yugoslavia and large parts of the historic Croat and Slovene territories that had been ceded to

Josip Broz-Tito addresses a session of the Provisional Parliament in Belgrade just prior to the November 1945 elections. (Bettman/Corbis)

Italy after World War I. These territories included Istria, the Slovene coastland, the city of Trieste, Zadar, and the islands of Cres, Lošinj, and Lastovo, which the AVNOJ had formally annexed to Yugoslavia in September 1943. This established the conditions for the negotiation of Yugoslavia's post–World War II borders.

Although the armed fight by partisans against the domestic collaborators of the occupying forces could be considered also a civil war, it was above all an anti-Fascist and anti-Nazi fight within the global anti-Fascist coalition. This was recognized by the Allies, especially at the end of World War II. However, a bloody civil war, characterized by ethnic atrocities and genocide, also broke out in Yugoslavia, especially in territories controlled by the Ustaša and the Chetniks. These practices started from the very beginning of World War II, and their main protagonists were these same Ustaša and Chetniks who tried to destroy or convert the local populations from other ethnic origins and religions (i.e., the Ustaša wanted to exterminate or convert local Serbs to Catholicism, and the Chetniks wanted to convert local Croats to the Eastern Orthodox religion or exterminate them). They also wanted to exterminate their political opponents who were of the same ethnicity. As an element of this civil war, there were also occasional fights among different collaborationist military formations.

Americans from Yugoslavia and the Events in the Old Homeland during World War II

Initially, and until the end of 1942, emigrants from Yugoslavia supported the Yugoslav peoples' fight against the Axis through correspondence with important world leaders, members of the Yugoslav regime, and later its representatives in exile (e.g., Louis Adamic, an American writer, ethnic activist, and political organizer, the winner of the 1932 Guggenheim Prize, corresponded in March and April 1941 with Vladko Maček and General Simović, encouraging them to fight against the Nazis).

On 19 April 1941, representatives of Slovene fraternal organizations gathered in Chicago and, as the leaders of the Slovene ethnic group in the United States, founded the Yugoslav Relief Committee, Slovene Section, in order to raise financial support for their suffering homeland. This movement developed rapidly among Slovene Americans, and by the end of 1943 they had already collected eighty thousand dollars.

In 1941 and 1942 Adamic corresponded with President Franklin D. Roosevelt on the issues of the different guerillas fighting the Axis in Yugoslavia. He also wrote a letter in February 1942 in which he recommended the founding of an American Foreign Legion, which could be called the Legion of Freedom, with bases in northeastern Africa and/or the Middle East:

> This Legion might consist of small and extremely mobile units of Yugoslav, Greek, anti-Fascist soldiers now not functioning as warriors, and would be under the Stars and Stripes, commanded by the American field officers. Such a Legion would develop commandos for raids on the occupied countries, establish contact with anti-Nazi leaders there, serve as a factor in psychological warfare, and prepare the eventual invasion (Adamic to Roosevelt, 3 February 1942, Franklin D. Roosevelt Memorial Library).

In September 1942 Americans from Yugoslavia were engaged in two political issues of significance. One involved a split between Serbian Americans and Croatian Americans; the other involved President Roosevelt's use of the word *Serbia* instead of *Yugoslavia* in a speech. Great Serbian propaganda coordinated by Konstantin Fotić, the Yugoslav ambassador to the United States, and by other Serb and Croat nationalists in the first half of 1942 led to great splits among the Serbian Americans and the Croatian Americans, who rejected Great Serbian ideas. To mend the splits, the director of the Office of Strategic Services, Elmer Davis, called a meeting of representatives of Yugoslav immigrants in the United States for 18 September 1942. The meeting was led by Allan Cranston, chief of the Foreign Language Division at the Office of Strategic Services, and by the Assistant Secretary of State, Adolf Augustus Barle Jr. At this meeting sixteen representatives of Yugoslav American groups signed a resolution pledging the unity of all groups in the war for freedom and opposing any effort to set one group of Yugoslav Americans against another.

From December 1942 until April 1943, the leaders of Slovene, Croat, and Serb Americans called their respective congresses, in which they called for unity of all Yugoslav Americans in the war effort and also accepted resolutions in which they tried to find solutions for their national questions in a federated Yugoslavia. On 19 June 1943, Etbin Kristan (for Slovenes), Zlatko Baloković (for Croats), and Žarko Bunčić (for Serbs) organized the United Committee of the American Serbs, Croats, and Slovenians under Adamic's leadership. After Bulgarian and Macedonian Americans established the Bulgarian-Macedonian American National Congress in July 1943, it joined the United Committee, which was then renamed the United Committee of South Slavic Americans.

Yugoslav Americans directed their activities after 1944 to gather relief for Yugoslavia, and they established a special organization for that purpose. After 1944 the so-called Yugoslav Relief Committee, which changed its name frequently, gathered about 20 million dollars for Yugoslavia's relief.

At the end of 1944 and in the first half of 1945 the leaders of groups of Americans from Yugoslavia directed their activities toward favorable solutions of territorial claims in Yugoslavia regarding Trieste, the coastland, and Carinthia. They continued their work in this field after World War II. They succeeded in drawing the state legislatures' and the Congress's attention to the Trieste question through members of Congress who were friends of Louis Adamic and Zlatko Baloković. Moreover, Adamic wrote many articles on these issues, and he also gathered information on Trieste for his journalist friends so that they could write about these issues and publicize them.

Changes in the Ethnic Structure of the Population during World War II

The brutal consequences of the unsolved "national question" in the Kingdom of Yugoslavia under the Karadjordjević dynasty were felt during World War II, when forced deportations and numerous murders on the basis of ethnicity by foreign occupiers and their domestic aides caused substantial changes in the ethnic structure. According to official data, among the 1.7 million people in Yugoslavia who lost their lives during World War II were 410,000 soldiers and 1.3 million civilians. The scholars already in the former Yugoslavia, however, agreed that the number of casualties could be reduced to one million (Žeravić, 1993, 120; Kočović, 1990, 190). Most of the civilians were victims of interethnic fights and ideological battles. The Nazi-Fascist Ustaša regime of the Independent State of Croatia murdered around 200 thousand civilians of Serb ethnicity in Croatia and Bosnia and Herzegovina to ethnically cleanse these regions, and the Serb Chetnicks committed murders and brutality against the non-Serb (mostly Croat) population in the territories under their control. These atrocities could be considered early forms of ethnic cleansing.

The consequences of forced migrations in the interest of ethnic cleansing were felt in Slovenia. When Adolph Hitler came to Maribor, a city in northeastern Slovenia, he ordered his subordinates, "Make this land German again." On the basis of this order, the German occupying authorities, who planned to deport one-quarter million of the Slovenes, immediately started forced deportations from Slovene Styria to Nazi concentration camps in Germany and to Serbia. The most numerous deportations took place in autumn 1941 and the winter of 1941–1942, from the region of Spodnje Posavje between the Sava and Sotla rivers. The German authorities forcibly deported around 37,000 Slovenes from this area; their homes were settled mostly by the Kočevje (Gottschee) Germans.

After the Kočevje/Gottschee region was annexed to Italy in April 1941, during the period from 15 November 1941 to 22 January 1942, some 97 percent of the ethnic Germans from this region were resettled in other territories of the Third Reich. Those Kočevje/Gottschee Germans who had been resettled in the homes of Slovene deportees and refugees near Brežice and Krško were forced to leave their new homes after the end of World War II, when Slovene families came back. They fled to Austrian Carinthia and later dispersed all over Germany and Austria. Many of them found new homes in the United States. One could say that the tragic destiny of Kočevje/Gottschee Germans was caused by their blind trust in the policies of German Nazi ideology. They shared that destiny with other German-speaking populations of Yugoslavia. Because of the fear of persecution by the communist regime that took over in Yugoslavia, and also on the basis of decrees of the president of the Anti-Fascist Council of National Liberation of Yugoslavia (AVNOJ) of 11 November 1944, all those who sympathized with the Nazi policy of the negation of Yugoslavia as a state or who collaborated with the Nazi occupying forces were forced to leave Yugoslavia, and their property was confiscated. As a result, the ethnic structure changed in some Slovene cities (e.g., in Ptuj, Maribor, Celje, and Ljubljana) and even more so in parts of Croatia and in Vojvodina. According to some German estimates, 650,000 Germans lived in Yugoslavia in 1940; the census of 1951 showed that only 35,000 Germans remained.

Histories of the Individual Yugoslav Nations

Slovenes

The occupation of Slovenia was welcomed by no one except the members of the German ethnic minority in Styria, the Meža Valley, and Kočevje/Gotschee, and the Hungarian ethnic minority in Prekmurje. Most of the Slovene population was not in favor of the occupation. Therefore, at the beginning there were no political groups or movements that would cooperate with the occupiers. In spite of that, there was also no unified concept on how to fight the occupiers. Part of the Slovene political leadership that stayed in the homeland had, on 6 April 1941, created the National Council in Ljubljana under the leadership of Dr. Marko Natlačen, the former ban (governor) of Dravska Banovina. The National Council started to cooperate with the Italian occupiers on the grounds that this would reduce the number of Slovenes who were persecuted. Simultaneously, though, the Council advocated a "wait and see" policy: Slovenes should wait for the outcome of the war, which would be decided by the Great Powers.

In spite of this position, there were many Slovenes ready to resist because of the occupiers' violence and assimilation policy. The illegal Komunistična partija Slovenije, KPS (Communist Party of Slovenia) realized this and initiated a resistance organization with some Slovene Christian Socialists, Liberals in the Sokol (Falcon) sports association, and artists (independent cultural workers—men of arts and letters). This organization, established in Ljubljana as early as 26 April 1941, was initially called the Anti-Imperialist Front but was soon (after the German attack on the Soviet Union) renamed the Liberation Front of the Slovene Nation (OF). Later twenty organizations, societies, and movements joined the OF.

The resistance movement in Slovenia arose first in the cities and from there spread to the countryside, while in other regions of Yugoslavia it developed mostly in the countryside. In the fall of 1941 the OF was the first among all the groups in the territory of Yugoslavia to establish Slovene National Liberation Councils as new local authorities with military, judicial, and political functions in the liberated territories. The NLM followed the Slovene example in other parts of Yugoslavia.

An unbridgeable gap grew between the OF and followers of pre–World War II political parties with a part of the Slovene clergy under the leadership of Gregorij Rožman, the Bishop of Ljubljana. When the false expectations of the communist leaders to end the war quickly had not materialized, by spring 1942 the communists started to kill the collaborators of the occupiers and the communists' political opponents, such as Dr. Marko Natlačen. As a consequence, this strengthened the beliefs of the Catholic leaders that the communists posed a greater danger than the occupiers. They demanded that the occupying authorities, especially the Italians, fight against the partisan liberation movement and offered occupiers the cooperation of their own military units, the so-called Village Guardians.

In Slovenia there were units of the Chetniks, later known as the Plava garda (Blue Guard), and the vaška straža (Village Guardians), later called the Bela garda (White Guard). The Chetniks accused the OF of supporting the secession of Slovenia from Yugoslavia, and the Village Guardians justified their fight against the communists and the OF by declaring them enemies of the Catholic Church and of religion.

In autumn 1942 came Tito's first attempt to control the Slovene resistance movement, which until then had developed completely independently from the resistance movement in other regions of Yugoslavia. Arsa Jovanović, a leading Yugoslav communist who was sent from Tito's Supreme Command of Yugoslav partisan resistance, ended his mission to establish central control over the Slovene partisans unsuccessfully in April 1943. This led to some conflicts between the OF and the Yugoslav Supreme Command. Edvard Kardelj, a Slovene communist leader, tried to resolve this conflict by strengthening the role of the KPS and KPJ—as was the case in other parts of Yugoslavia. In the Dolomitska izjava (Dolomits' Declaration) of February 1943 the Christian Socialists and Liberal Sokols recognized the KPS's leading role in the OF and ceased their own political activities and organizations. This document indicated that the Communist Party projected a soviet-type system after the war.

The capitulation of Italy in September 1943 made it possible for the partisan movement to grow quickly in Slovenia because the Slovene partisans liberated territories previously held by the Italians and siezed their military equipment. At the same time, it made possible the development of lawmaking bodies in the liberated territories. The Slovene National Liberation Council was established as the first Slovene parliament. By that time, Slovene partisan units had destroyed most Slovene collaborationist military formations. The Germans, however, saved a part of the Village Guardians and organized them into the Slovensko domobranstvo (Slovene Home Guard)—auxiliary police units. In the presence of Bishop Gregorij Rožman they swore a solemn oath to Hitler on his birthday in 1946, declaring that they would fight against the communists and their allies on behalf of the German army.

When Slovene émigré politicians (especially Dr. Miha Krek and other Slovene members of the Yugoslav Government-in-Exile) realized by autumn 1944 that the war would end soon, they unsuccessfully started to ask leaders of the Slovene Home Guard to stop their collaboration with the occupiers. In the last months of 1944 the leaders of the Catholic and Liberal parties in Slovenia also started to prepare for the end of the war. In December 1944 some of their leaders signed the so-called Narodna izjava (National Declaration), in which they demanded a united Slovenia as part of the new federated kingdom of Yugoslavia. They also demanded the establishment of a National Committee for Slovenia as the supreme national authority in Slovenia. They tried to establish a new Slovene National Army from the Slovene Home Guard units. However, they did not succeed because of resistance from the leaders of those units.

During the last months of the war many troops and armies operated in the Slovene territory: In addition to Slovene partisan units and the Yugoslav (partisan) army, there were some Soviet troops and several units of the German Army, the Chetniks, Ustaša, and some other collaborationist military units. The war in Slovenia lasted until 15 May 1945, one week after the formal capitulation of Germany, at which time the last German, Chetnik, Ustaša, and other units capitulated.

Some members of the Slovene Home Guard and Ustaša units successfully escaped to southern Austria, where they surrendered to the Anglo-American Allies. However, the Allies returned many of them to Yugoslav authorities, and the Yugoslav army and police killed many of these prisoners, up to 12,000 Slovene Home Guards alone, without due process of law. This sad event in the Slovene history is commemorated in June every year by the Slovene political émigré community all over the world and is still today very much discussed in Slovene public life.

On 5 May 1945, Slovene partisans inaugurated the Slovene Government in Ajdovščina and, on 18 May 1945, they abolished the Supreme Command of the Yugoslav Army in Slovenia, which meant that the Slovene partisan army was now included in the unified Yugoslav Army. At this time, it was no longer possible to restore the old centralized Yugoslav monarchy; Slovenia was a federal unit in a new federation.

Croats

After the occupation of Croatia, the leader of the Croat Peasant Party, Vladko Maček, did not flee abroad as did most of the important Yugoslav politicians; he returned to Zagreb instead. On 10 April 1941, he, together with the Ustaša, declared the Nezavisna država Hrvatska, NDH (Independent State of Croatia). Maček issued a proclamation in which he asked Croats to cooperate with the new authorities. Although formally independent, in reality the state was divided by Germany and Italy into occupation zones. Germany had a decisive influence on the internal and external policies of Ante Pavelić's Ustaša government.

In their political propaganda, the Ustaša described themselves as the "liberators" of the Croat nation from "the Serb Belgrade dictatorship" and as guardians of "a thousand years of Croat statehood." After they proclaimed their state they also started a "racial revolution" against Jews, Gypsies (Roma), and—above all—Serbs, who comprised 30 percent of the population of the new state. Pavelić held Bosnian Muslims to be "brothers of the purest Croat blood." As for the Serbs, he planned to exterminate one-third, force one-third to emigrate, and force the other third to become Catholics. The number of Serbs killed during Pavelić's regime was estimated at between 30,000 and one million. According to the latest scholarly research, the number is about 330,000 (Žerjavić, 1993, 120).

Not only Serbs, Gypsies (Roma), and Jews, whose lives were threatened, were unhappy because of the killings, but also Croats and Bosnian Muslims, who soon recognized that the NDH was not the state that had been promised. Some people in the NDH were ready to fight the Ustaša regime and the occupation army.

The resistance to the occupation in Croatia experienced problems. Croat communist leaders were convinced that the Soviet Red Army would invade Croatia in some weeks; therefore they could not decide whether or not to start preparations for an armed resistance. However, on the day of the German attack on the Soviet Union, the Komunistička partija Hrvatske, KPH (Communist Party of Croatia) issued a proclamation in which it asked Croats to start the armed resistance. The level of resistance differed from region to region. In cities such as Zagreb, Karlovac, and Sisak, people were ready to fight; partisan units were organized in such areas in and around industrial cities. The armed resistance developed slowly in the countryside, where it was stopped primarily by the leaders of the Croat Peasant Party who, in accordance with instructions from the Yugoslav Government-in-Exile, demanded a policy of neutrality and waiting.

At the same time this party still cooperated with the Ustaša. In 1941 the resistance developed widely in the regions settled with Serb populations (Lika, Kordun, and Banija) and in occupied territories in Gorski kotar, the Croat coastland, and Dalmatia.

The Italian authorities in the occupied part of Croatia found themselves in a difficult situation in the second half of 1941. On the one hand, they were surprised by the uprising. On the other, they did not want to cooperate with the Ustaša regime, which was more and more dependent on the Germans. Italians had strained relations with the Ustaša. To strengthen their position, the Italians started to take advantage of the fights between the Croats and Serbs. They were convinced that the main reason for the partisan uprising lay in the numerous massacres perpetrated by the Ustaša against the Orthodox Serb population, and they started to support the Serb Chetniks. The Ustaša government signed an agreement (the so-called Rome Agreement of May 1941) with the Italian Fascist government to give part of Dalmatia to Italy. On 22 August 1941, Italian premier Benito Mussolini ordered his troops to occupy ethnically mixed regions of the NDH territories that were settled by Serbs (Dalmatia, Herzegovina, Lika, and Kordun). This angered the Croat Ustaša leadership in Zagreb. At the same time it also deepened the gap between most of the Croats and Pavelić, who was not able to ensure Croat territorial integrity. According to one British report, the Croat Ustaša regime was supported by only 10 percent of the Croats. However, the unwillingness of the Croat Peasant Party to cooperate with the communists prevented much faster growth of the resistance against the Ustaša regime.

The resistance movement became widespread at the beginning of 1942. This process was hastened also by the liberation of Bosanska krajina, when a majority of the partisan units with Tito moved to this region in the middle of the NDH. With the liberation of the territory of Bosanska krajina and the establishment of the so-called Bihaška republika (Republic of Bihać), the partisans were able to undercut the myth of the "mighty NDH." They also shook the confidence in the Ustaša with the Germans. With the equal treatment of people regardless of their national origin, the resistance movement started to gain respect among the people. Simultaneously the Croat Peasant Party, which was still against armed resistance, started to lose its followers.

With the development of the liberation movement and the widening of liberated territories, a new political administration was also developed. In April 1943 the resistance established the Zemaljsko antifašističko vijeće narodnog oslobodjenja Hrvatske, ZAVNOH (Anti-Fascist Council of National Liberation of Croatia), which, on 14 June 1943, declared itself the supreme political body of Croatia. The ZAVNOH presented itself as a coalition of different political groups of Croats, Serbs, and other ethnic groups in Croatia. However, it was completely in the hands of the communists. Inside the ZAVNOH there were differences originating from the personal ambitions of individual leaders and from local patriotism. It is interesting to note that Tito was not happy when, on 20 September 1943, the ZAVNOH declared the annexation of Istria, Rijeka, and Zadar to Croatia. Tito thought that with this decision, the Croat communists (their leader was Andrija Hebrang) had usurped powers that should have been solely in the hands of Yugoslavia as a common state. The nationalism of the Croat leader was, according to the majority of members of the Central Committee of the KPJ, so dangerous that they replaced Hebrang in October 1944 with the more flexible and less powerful Dr. Vladimir Bakarić.

In September 1944 some Ustaša leaders and Anglophile circles of the Croat army, in expectation of Allied invasion at the Adriatic, tried to collaborate with representatives of the Croat Peasant Party in the hope of saving themselves from being accused of collaboration with the Nazis. They wanted to organize a coup d'etat in order to save Croat statehood. In this coup, the Ustaša would appear to be dissolved, and members of the Croat Army would appear to ally with the Chetniks to stop the communist threat in western Yugoslavia. The leadership of the Croats would appear to be in the hands of Vladko Maček. The Archbishop of Zagreb, Alojzije Stepinac, also played a part in the game, as he supported the coup. Pavelić did not want to play a part in organizing the coup, and he asked the Gestapo for help. The main leaders of the coup were arrested on 30 August 1944.

When Tito declared an amnesty for all who had collaborated with the occupiers but who were not involved in war crimes, the Croat Domobranci (regular army) deserted in masses. They realized that the Allies were winning the war and no longer wanted to collaborate with the Nazis. All this led to the end of the NDH and to the communist takeover of Croatia.

Bosniaks

When Yugoslavia was occupied in 1941, some politicians from Bosnia who had fought for its autonomy during the Yugoslav state period after World War I launched the idea that Bosnian Muslims were of Gothic, non-Slavic origin. In connection with this they started to fight for a Bosnian state within the German Reich, outside the NDH. Hitler reacted negatively and instead supported the more powerful Ustaša of the NDH; thus Bosnia and Herzegovina remained part of the NDH.

With the inclusion of Bosnia and Herzegovina in the NDH, another theory—that the Muslims of Bosnia and Herzegovina were "brothers of the purest Croat blood"—started to prevail in Croat circles. This theory had been promulgated by Croat nationalists since the early 1930s. The result of this ideology was that the Bosnian Muslims were supportive of the NDH for some time. Some Muslims adapted to the new circumstances as they saw an opportunity for Bosnian autonomy, but most of them did not lean to either side.

The Ustaša planned the extermination of the Bosnian Serbs in order to create an ethnically cleansed, pure Croat "Lebensraum" (life-space). Already in 1941 in the name of this ideology, the Ustaša had murdered 20,000 Serbs in the vicinity of Bihać and Cazin alone. This "ethnic policy" of the NDH soon provoked uprisings by the threatened Serb peasant population. These uprisings developed into revenge against the Croat and Muslim peasants. Because of the Ustaša terror, many Bosnian Serbs joined the Chetnik movement.

The KPJ soon intervened in the ethnic fights among the Serbs, Croats, and Bosniaks, trying to unify them into a liberation movement to fight with the KPJ against all types of Nazism-Fascism. The KPJ succeeded in transforming the uprisings of Serb peasants into a partisan movement and, by the end of August 1941, into a partisan uprising. Because the Serb ethnic group prevailed in the partisan movement in Bosnia, Bosniaks did not join en masse—despite the fact that by the end of 1941 a majority of the partisan units in Yugoslavia, together with the leadership of the movement, had moved to the region of Bosnia and Herzegovina. This area became one of the bloodiest battlefields of the war. On this territory, in addition to the concurrent national liberation and socialist revolutions, an ethnic and religious civil war was also taking place in which the Chetniks and Ustaša were especially involved. The battles, both military and political, decisively influenced the destiny of Yugoslavia (e.g., attempts to destroy partisan units by the occupiers, the meetings of the first and second AVNOJ, the decisive defeat of the Chetnik movement in April 1943, etc.).

Under the slogan "Brotherhood and Unity," the partisan movement succeeded in including Bosniaks, especially after the capitulation of Italy in September 1943. Some groups of Bosniaks, though, still fought on the side of occupiers. After a special Muslim SS Division (Handžar) was established in 1943, the idea of creating a Bosnian state within and loyal to the German Reich was revived. It was supported by a circle of politicians who, at the beginning of the war, had spread the idea of Bosniaks as being *Übermenschen* (above normal human beings). Later the autonomist concept for solving the Muslim question (which the Bosnian Muslims saw as autonomy of Bosnia and Herzegovina in the interwar Yugoslavia) showed up only on the local level. In Cazinska krajina, for example, Huskin's Army (or Huskin's Militia) fought for local autonomy. It was named after Huska Miljković, who, before he organized this unit, was a communist activist and partisan officer. Similar units were organized in eastern Bosnia also.

After the end of World War II, the "new" Bosnia and Herzegovina in the "new" Yugoslavia was created. However, this could not prevent the later events of the 1990s, when all the problems of ethnic relations in Bosnia and Herzegovina surfaced again.

Serbs

After the occupation and division of Yugoslavia in April 1941, the Serb population came under different occupational regimes that successfully used the unsolved national question from prewar Yugoslavia and provoked further animosities and hatreds of non-Serbs toward the Serbs. This policy of national hatred and revenge surfaced especially in the NDH, Bačka, Banat, and Kosovo.

A polarization among the Serbs became very obvious. Some Serbs started to cooperate with the occupiers. Among them were the old structures of administration led by Milan Aćimović, the fascist movement Zbor under the leadership of Dimitrije Ljotić, and General Milan Nedić, who became the president of the new civil government of Serbia. The communists and, initially, Chetniks advocated resistance to the occupation, but they were unable to unite.

The resistance was almost completely controlled by the KPJ and developed differently in different regions. As mentioned in the previous sections of this chapter, the Serb population in the NDH—because of the Ustaša terror—first fought in revenge against the Croats and Bosniaks and later, under the leadership of the KPJ, was organized into a partisan NLM. A strong resistance movement arose in Vojvodina also. It lasted only until autumn of 1941, however, because the partisan ways of fighting the war (guerilla tactics) were not suitable for Vojvodina's flat land. The uprising was very successful in the so-called narrower Serbia (i.e., Serbia without Kosovo and Vojvodina), however. In autumn 1941 partisan units in Serbia under the leadership of the KPJ succeeded in liberating a wide region, named Užička republika (the Republic of Užice). In this liberated territory the first "people's" authorities were created, ushering in the beginnings of the socialist revolution in Yugoslavia.

The partisan resistance movement, determined to fight the occupiers, forced the Chetniks to reveal their plans. The Chetniks said that they were against fighting the occupiers because "the time had not come yet to fight." They claimed that Serb blood should be spared and they should "save the biological substance of the (Serb) nation." In spite of this fundamental difference between the two groups, the partisans and Chetniks did not fight each other at first; they even coordinated common actions against the Wehrmacht, the regular German army. These actions did not have much effect, but the Chetniks took part in them because they did not want to leave all initiatives to the partisans.

The Chetniks then attacked partisan units in Užiška republic on the night of 1 November 1941. It signaled not only the end of cooperation but also the beginning of civil war in Serbia. The reasons for this could be found in the Yugoslav Government-in-Exile's support of Mihailović as the supreme commander of the uprising in Yugoslavia and in the German repression of Serbs and in ideological differences between the Chetniks (who were defending the monarchy) and the partisans (who from the very beginning wanted to introduce the communist order). On 10 October 1941, the leadership of the Wehrmacht ordered that for each slain German their soldiers should kill 100 Serbs; for each wounded German they should kill 50 Serbs. In Kragujevac, for example, German troops murdered 2,300 hostages. Among those killed were teachers and students from Kragujevac's high school. These German actions influenced Serb public opinion, and some Serbs started to distance themselves from the partisans because they feared revenge from the Germans; they even reported the actions of the partisans to Nedić's Government in Serbia.

In mid-November 1941, the Germans launched an offensive against the troops of both Tito and Mihailović. Although Mihailović offered a cooperation plan to the Germans on 11 November the Germans ignored that offer. Mihailović's and Tito's troops fled to Sandžak, where the conditions under the Italian occupation were easier for them. However, a common destiny did not force Tito and Mihailović to cooperate; by December they began to fight each other and continued to do so until after the end of the war.

In Serbia, even when peace prevailed, the partisan movement could not recuperate for a long time. In accordance with a secret agreement, most of Mihailović's Chetniks became members of Nedić's police force. Partisans labeled the Chetniks as traitors to Serbia and the anti-Fascist movement because of this. Their role is still discussed in Western historiography, especially because the Serb Chetniks retained contacts with the Allies and saved the lives of hundreds of Allied pilots by allowing them to bail out of their planes over Mihailović-controlled territories. This situation prevailed in Serbia until the beginning of 1944, when, according to some data, only a few thousand partisans still fought in Serbia. Mihailović, who returned from exile to Serbia after Italy capitulated, had 20,000 men at his disposal and 45,000 men in reserve (in addition to the forces under Nedić's and Ljotić's leadership). The Chetniks tried to prevail in Serbia and called the Svetosavski kongres (Svetosavski Congress) on 25-28 January 1944 in Ravna Gora (Suvabor planina). The participants in the congress, among them some representatives of the former (bourgeois) political parties, demanded the renewal of the prewar political system in Yugoslavia; they also expressed their opposition to the decisions of the Jajce meeting of the AVNOJ. For propaganda purposes, to be better accepted in other parts of Yugoslavia they declared themselves to be in favor of a federated kingdom of Yugoslavia.

Only five months after the Svetosavski Congress strong partisan units started to gather in eastern Bosnia. In August 1944 they started an invasion of Serbia to fight the Wehrmacht and the Chetniks, who still controlled the Serb countryside. In September 1944, after the capitulation of Bulgaria and Romania, Soviet troops also invaded Serbia (on the basis of an agreement between Tito and Stalin). In this new situation, Mihailović tried to cooperate with Soviet field commanders, who accepted his cooperation in some cases. Soon after the fights were finished, however, the Soviets arrested the Chetniks and turned them over to Tito or deported them to the Soviet Union. In this situation Mihailović could do nothing but leave Serbia to the partisans. He fled to Sandžak and Bosnia and was captured by Tito's army in 1946.

With the help of the Soviets, Tito's partisans liberated most of eastern, northern, and mid-Serbia by the end of October 1944. After the liberation of Belgrade (20 October 1944), a majority of the Red Army troops went to Hungary to fight against the Germans and Hungarians there, leaving Tito's partisans to end their fight against Nazi–Fascist forces in the territory of Yugoslavia and to liberate the rest of country.

Montenegrins

After the Italians occupied Montenegro, they tried to reinstall the Montenegrin dynasty of Petrović-Njegoš, which was related to the Italian dynasty of Savoi. They did not succeed in this because Prince Mihailo Petrović-Njegoš did not want to cooperate with the Fascists. Montenegro therefore stayed under the Italian occupation and under the civil administration of an Italian high commissioner.

The mass uprising of the Montenegrins against the Italians of 13 July 1941 was a great success in Montenegro due to the influence of the KPJ, which had mass support among the peasant population. The success of this uprising could also be explained by the rich warrior tradition of the Montenegrins as well as by their pro-Russian feelings. It could be explained also by the lax Italian occupation. In a very short period of time almost all the territory of Montenegro (with the exception of some important cities) fell into the hands of the communists. But the communists made a mistake by starting to fight their "class enemy" (i.e., members of the Montenegrin bourgeoisie) which made them weaker. The Italians resumed their attacks and, by mid-August 1941, had again enforced their control in Montenegro—with the help of the Albanians and Muslims. The KPJ persisted with the NLM while representatives of the old bourgeois parties launched a campaign against the communists and started to call their policy dangerous. Leaders of the old parties even started to cooperate with the Italian occupiers. At this point the communists tried to convince the Montenegrins to fight the occupiers by force. Out of fear of the "red-terror," a significant percentage of Montenegrins started to cooperate with the Chetniks, who started to attack the partisans. The result was a strong criticism of Tito, addressed to the Montenegrin communists, who changed their practices. The partisan movement strengthened again in the late autumn, but the Italians launched a great offensive at the end of spring 1942, and most of the partisan units had to leave Montenegro (only 700 partisans stayed). A Chetnik reign of terror then started, to subjugate the people of Montenegro in revenge for their uprisings.

The situation remained unchanged until February 1943, when Montenegro Chetniks under the leadership of Pavle Djurišić and Baja Stanišić left for Bosnia, where they fought the partisans in the so-called fourth offensive. As soon as the Chetniks left, the partisan movement spread again. In Montenegro, partisans and Chetniks continued to fight each other until the capitulation of Italy.

After the capitulation of Italy, new partisan units were established, the liberated territory was enlarged, and the Germans later took only the coastland, Cetinje, Nikšić, Podgorica, and the main traffic routes. The partisans fought the Germans and the Chetniks to liberate the occupied territory until October 1944, when the final operations for the liberation of Montenegro started, and Montenegro was liberated in two months. After that 36,000 Montenegrin partisans participated in the liberation of the rest of Yugoslavia.

Macedonians

After the occupation of Yugoslavia, most of Yugoslav Macedonia was annexed to Bulgaria. The Bulgarian Fascist government proclaimed the Macedonians to be Bulgarians and tried to incorporate Macedonia fully into its state. To strengthen the Bulgarian administrative political system, the government sent a large number of Bulgarian officials and police to Macedonia. It also put in place a wide net of Bulgarian elementary and middle schools and tried to assimilate Macedonians as quickly as possible. For these reasons, the Macedonians did not see the new Bulgarian authorities as liberators but rather as occupiers. They did not accept the Bulgarian propaganda slogan of "Daughter Macedonia" being freed from "the Serb abductors" and returned into "mother Bulgaria's" lap.

The western part of Macedonia, inhabited by an ethnically mixed Macedonian and Albanian population, was annexed to so-called Great Albania, where the Italian Fascists governed in cooperation with Albanian nationalists. The Italians encouraged national hatred among the Albanians, Macedonians, and Serbs. They introduced the Albanian language into schools and administration and forced peasants to pay tribute (a practice that dated from the old Turkish feudal order) to Albanian nationalists who administered the western part of Macedonia.

When the Germans' Axis partner, Italy, dropped out of the war in the summer of 1943 and left western Macedonia unguarded, Tito's partisans were able to set up a bridgehead in Macedonia. In western Macedonia the partisans met with the support of a rapidly growing noncommunist partisan force that was aiming primarily at the "reunification" of all of Macedonia (i.e., with Pirin Macedonia in Bulgaria and Aegean Macedonia in Greece) and the founding of a Macedonian state, preferably linked to one or several western powers. To make its new military position in Macedonia politically safe, the KPJ reiterated a decision on the future status of Macedonia that had been taken back in 1937. According to this decision, a future communist Yugoslavia should grant Macedonia the status of "sixth republic," and its inhabitants should be regarded as ethnic Macedonians (and no longer the southern or "Mountain Serbs").

In spite of the terror from the Bulgarian occupiers and the call of the KPJ, the uprising of Macedonians did not develop in the beginning of the war as successfully as it did in other regions of Yugoslavia. It was hindered by the Bulgarian-oriented leader of the Macedonian communists, Metodije Šatorov-Šarlo. He decided not to follow the Yugoslav party line but rather the Bulgarian party line, because the "Macedonian nation was finally united with its Bulgarian brothers." He followed a passive policy of waiting that was completely different from the decisions of other Yugoslav communists. The leadership of the KPJ put into power a new leader for the Macedonian communists, Lazar Koliševski. After these problems were solved, the uprising in Macedonia started in October 1941.

Even though new partisan units were established, armed resistance in Macedonia could not develop fully. The Bulgarian communists tried to separate the liberation fight of Macedonians from the liberation fights of other Yugoslav ethno-nations. As a consequence, the Macedonian communists tried to start a resistance movement on an ethnic and nationalistic basis, which was not acceptable to the KPJ. For these reasons, attempts of the KPJ to organize an uprising against the Bulgarians did not succeed at the end of 1941 or the first half of 1942.

The Macedonian uprising started to develop fully in February 1943 when Tito sent Svetozar Vukmanović-Tempo to Macedonia. The next month Tempo created the Central Committee of the Communist Party of Macedonia. The party organization in Macedonia became an independent organization and was not under the Serbs, as those who opposed the armed resistance were saying. The liberation movement started to develop; once the first liberated territories were created, it meant the end of the propaganda of "Bulgarian liberators of the Macedonian nation."

Many new partisan units developed in Macedonia after the capitulation of Italy. At the same time the partisans developed a large liberated territory in western Macedonia. In 1944 the liberation struggle also spread into mid- and eastern Macedonia, especially after a manifesto was issued by the supreme partisan command of Macedonia that promised the sovereignty and equality of the Macedonian nation in the future Yugoslav community of nations. In August 1944 the Antifašističko sobranie na narodnoto osvobodjuvanje na Makedonija, ASNOM (Anti-Fascist Council of National Liberation of Macedonia) was created, which laid the cornerstone for the modern statehood of the Macedonian nation. In November 1944 partisan units liberated Macedonia.

In 1943–1944, the leadership of the KPJ had at least four good reasons for its decision to make Macedonia the sixth republic of the new federal Yugoslavia and for simultaneously encouraging the process of building a separate nation there. First, this considerably helped the KPJ and national liberation leadership to establish and maintain control over this territory and its geographically and strategically exposed southern border. Second, by this decision Vardar Macedonia was tightly tied to Yugoslavia, and Bulgarian aspirations toward this region and its population were effectively warded off. Third, it gave Yugoslavia the opportunity to gain a certain degree of support in (still Bulgarian-ruled) Pirin Macedonia and thus provided an efficient tool to interfere directly into Bulgarian politics. Fourth, the ambiguous idea of a Macedonian nation supplied the Yugoslav leadership with an equally effective tool to operate in Greece, considering its Slavic minority in Aegean Macedonia. The condition sine qua non of the KPJ's Macedonian policy was, of course, the close affiliation and integration of the new republic and its nation-in-progress into the Yugoslav federation based on its peoples' "brotherhood and unity."

The decision on the foundation of a Macedonian republic was proclaimed on 29 November 1943, by the AVNOJ at Jajce. However, it took more than seven months before the Macedonian partisans and communists formed ASNOM, their AVNOJ-like republican parliamentary representation. This happened on 2 August 1944—St. Elias's Day (an important day in Macedonian history—see chapter 2). In the ASNOM presidium all key positions were held by those representatives of the partisan movement who supported Macedonian unification, but the communists had no particular influence. At the end of November 1944, when Vardar Macedonia was finally cleared of German and Bulgarian troops, the ASNOM presidium represented the highest political authority in this new Yugoslav republic. In late December 1944, however, things began rapidly to change. The communists took over some key positions inside ASNOM and then transferred almost all executive powers onto their new government. By mid-April 1945, when ASNOM was transformed into a parliament, this body had lost its political weight. Now the prime minister and key cabinet ministers, all members of the Central Committee of the Communist Party of Macedonia, were in charge. This communist conquest of all formal and informal power in Macedonia was carefully planned and directed by the "major party," the local Macedonian party functionaries being no more than tools of the KPJ and its inner circle around Tito.

Culture during World War II, 1941–1945

Wars in general do not provide the best environment for artistic creation. However, no other period in the history of humankind produced as many artistic creations in as short a period of time as World War II. Culture and art were as badly needed as bread and weapons; they helped people either to survive or to die with dignity. Art flourished everywhere—in prisons, during the marches on liberated territories, in concentration camps, and even in death chambers. People created with the tools available. They created either out of momentary personal inspiration or as part of a magnificent propaganda machinery of individual states. In addition to the established artists, so-called common people were also creative in the arts. Cultural creativity helped them survive; it was a search for relief from despair, and it gave them courage. Common people became poets and painters; already established writers were able to produce important artistic creations based on the reports of the war. Artists developed thousands of ways to express the horrors of war.

A tragic consequence of the war in the whole territory of the former Yugoslavia was the damage to and destruction of several works of art, including important historic, cultural, and artistic monuments; several important works of art were also stolen or lost.

Slovenes

The importance of culture and language for the historic formation and survival of the Slovene nation were reconfirmed during World War II, when the occupational authorities limited or even forbade cultural creativity in the Slovene language. Negative reactions of people to this occupational policy helped the OF (Liberation Front) in their policy of cultural silence, that is, their boycott of all performances that were connected with the occupation. Symbolically, the cultural silence was announced at a choral concert in the Union Auditorium in Ljubljana, when the popular song *Lipa zelenela je* (*Linden Tree Became Greener*), which describes the rebirth of the linden tree in the spring after the winter, was sung as the last song. The meaning of the song was symbolic: The winter—the Italian occupation, during which the Slovenes should not be culturally active—would be over soon, and the spring—freedom—would come. At the same time, the OF called all artists and "cultural workers" to join the Slovene partisan movement, initially with a limited success. Only after the capitulation of Italy (September 1943) did the cultural silence mean a complete stop to any cultural activity outside that of the OF. However, in 1944—under the pretext of a charitable activity, but also as an opposition to the cultural silence—110 different anticommunist writers who did not join the partisan movement published an almanac, *Zimska pomoč* (*Help in the Winter*).

Often having ideological content, culture and cultural creativity were important elements of the Slovene rebellion against Fascism and Nazism. The NLM published around 1,100 titles (novels, poetry, and other books and brochures) and hundreds of issues of different periodicals during the war. The most important authors were poets Karel Destovnik-Kajuh, Matej Bor, and Igo Gruden, writer Ciril Kosmač, and writer/poet Edvard Kocbek, who reached his peak in literary creativity (espousing the beliefs of Christian values) after World War II. Composers wrote more than 300 compositions, mostly original songs for choruses, aimed at mobilizing the masses in the fight against occupiers. Among many brass bands and choruses organized in partisan military units, the most famous was the Partisan Chorus, consisting of wounded and handicapped partisans. Additionally, numerous cultural groups (theater, folklore, and dance groups; puppet theaters, schools of classical ballet, etc.) were established. Also during the war, so-called Partisan graphics and paintings, and even some sculptures, were created. The most important painter was Božidar Jakac. Slovene partisan brigades were named after poets and writers during this period as well.

In the liberated territory the NLM established the Scientific Institute, which was to prepare a scholarly foundation for the postwar fights for and negotiations on Yugoslav borders. It is a unique example of a (resistance) research institute in occupied Europe.

During, and especially after, World War II, Slovene artists and cultural workers who violated the cultural silence became "nonpersons." Some, who opted for the anticommunist side during World War II, were also convicted—as national traitors—in trials at courts of national honor; especially vilified were those who joined military formations that had collaborated with the occupiers. Victims of the Domobranci massacre (see the next chapter) after the war were poets France Balantič and Ivan Hribovšek, who had created modern Symbolistic and Expressionistic poetry and reached their creative peak during the war.

Croats

During World War II many Croat writers joined the partisan movement (from the older writers, such as Nazor—who at first supported the idea of Croat independence—to the younger ones, such as Kaštelan). Especially famous was the poet Ivan Goran Kovačić, whose poem *Jama* (*The Cave*) is considered one of the best literary creations in the former Yugoslavia during World War II. The poem speaks of the victims of the Ustaša slaughter during the war. Music also played an important role in mobilization for the NLM, especially chorus songs.

Painters and sculptors created in the newly liberated territory. Especially important were the drawings and watercolors of such artists as Marijan Detoni; the linocut map *Mi pamtimo* (*We Remember,* 1943) of Vanja Draguš, a member of the prewar group Zemlja; and the work of the sculptor Antun Auguštinčić.

The state administration of the NDH (Independent State of Croatia) also tried to support its country's official Croat literature and culture in general. However, creations of artists funded by the NDH did not have any significant artistic value.

Bosniaks

During World War II quite a few men of culture from the Muslim community joined the Partisan movement. In literature, mostly authors from the younger, socially engaged generation warrant mention here. The most important among them was Skender Kulenović, who wrote poems in which he described the destruction and death during World War II. Some important works in the field of plastic arts were also created. Music and musical creativity were often in the service of the NLM as well as other movements (Chetniks, Ustaša, etc.).

Serbs

Word War II and the NLM provoked the development of emotional lyrics and helped to foster authentic and patriotically engaged, but sometimes also nationalistic, poetry. In addition to established authors, quite a few young writers and poets started to write (e.g., Skender Kulenović). Many painters and sculptors joined in the NLM (e.g., Branko Šotra, etc.). During this period most paintings depicted scenes from the war or from victorious days. Dušan Vlaić's pictures, painted in a German concentration camp, were quite important.

Montenegrins

Among Montenegrin authors, the most important was Mirko Banjević, who wrote heroic poetry about the partisan national hero of World War

II, commandant Sava Kovačević. Also known were Banjević's poems on the events of World War II, like the poem *Sutjeska* about the famous battle with the same name. Janko Djonović, another prominent poet, wrote his poetry in a concentration camp.

Macedonians

World War II represented a turning point in Macedonian history. It meant the beginning of the independent development of the Macedonian culture and language, which finally brought recognition of a separate national identity of Macedonians in the "new" Yugoslavia. Many credits for this go to men of literature, who took part in the NLM and spread the Macedonian language through numerous publications and periodicals (*Dedo Ivan, Mlad borec, Makedonija, Ilindenski pat,* etc.). In addition to authors who had already written during the interwar period, several new artists, such as Slavko Janeski, started to write during the war. They wrote about events from the history of the Macedonian people (e.g., the Ilinden Uprising and the everyday fights of the NLM). During the NLM some men of literature lost their lives. The most important among them was Mite Bogoevski, author of a collection of poems, *Sproti Ilinden,* which was published after the war in 1959. The activities of the NLM were also the themes of plays performed by numerous drama groups within the Macedonian partisan units.

A wealth of creativity developed in the field of music, especially after 1943. The musicians from previous periods continued to create. World War II was the period when many choruses and other musical groups were created in Macedonia. Some of them continued their work as professional groups after the war.

The End and a New Beginning

The beginning of World War II in this territory in April 1941 marked the end of the Yugoslav monarchy, which collapsed like a house of cards. The Yugoslav territory was occupied and divided by Axis forces. Their occupational authorities were helped by domestic collaborators and their military formations, the most notorious ones being the Ustaša and Chetniks and the puppet regimes. The Ustaša-led NDH (Independent State of Croatia)—independent only in its official name, but actually a puppet regime controlled by the Germans and Italians—was also established.

However, very soon after the occupation the communist-led NLM (National Liberation Movement) was established in the former Yugoslavia and started its armed resistance against all occupiers and their domestic collaborators. Although the NLM experienced a very different path of development in every part of the country, it represented a common front of all freedom-loving patriots, Yugoslav nations, and "nationalities" (national minorities) in the national liberation war. Founded on the principles of equality of all nations and of brotherhood and unity, the NLM laid foundations for a new federation of equal nations when it established the Democratic Federative Yugoslavia (DFJ). However, the ideal of the "socialist revolution" pursued by the communists led to the introduction of a rather centralized Soviet-type federation and political system after World War II. This political system, although after the split with the Soviets in 1948 substantially reformed and evolved in the postwar period, also failed to resolve the "national question" in the former Yugoslavia—which became especially obvious in the 1990s.

The issues of the civil war that took place in Yugoslavia during World War II became a burning political issue at the end of the twentieth century. Discussions held during the transition period of the 1990s focused on two dimensions of the civil war: the fighting of communist partisans against the military and political formations of domestic collaborators of the occupiers on the one side, and the atrocities of domestic collaborators and fascist regimes against the population on the other. However, this issue should be observed from the global perspective: The partisans as a constituent part of the global, victorious anti-Fascist/anti-Nazi coalition were fighting against the quisling military formations of domestic collaborators that fought on the side of the Axis forces. So, rather than a civil war, the fighting of partisans against the domestic quisling military formations was an anti-Fascist/anti-Nazi national liberation war. The actual proponents of the civil war in Yugoslavia during World War II were the Ustaša and Chetniks, two military formations of occupiers' collaborators, who carried out their ethnically based politics of "ethnic cleansing" and genocide against the civilian population in the territory under their control; the victims of the Ustaša policy were especially Serbs and other non-Croats, and the Chetniks committed the most war crimes against Croat civilians.

Timeline

6 April 1941   Eighty-five German, Italian, Hungarian, and
               Bulgarian divisions (around 870,000 soldiers)

	attacked Yugoslavia; part of the Slovene political leadership that stayed in the homeland had created a National Council in Ljubljana under the leadership of Dr. Marko Natlačen
10 April 1941	The Croat Ustaša, under the leadership of Ante Pavelić, rushed to proclaim the Independent State of Croatia (Nezavisna država Hrvatska, NDH)
17 April 1941	Yugoslav Foreign Minister Aleksandar Cincar-Marković and General Danilo Kalafatović signed an unconditional surrender and capitulation of the Yugoslav army
Mid-April 1941	The first groups of Chetniks under the leadership of Kosta Pećanac started to gather in southern Serbia, in Kosovo, and in northern Montenegro
26–27 April 1941	Creation of the Anti-Imperialist Front, which, after the German attack on the Soviet Union, was renamed the Liberation Front of the Slovene Nation (Osvobodilna fronta, OF)
4 May 1941	A second group of Chetniks gathered under the leadership of Colonel Dragoljub-Draža Mihailović in Ravna gora (Suvabor planina) in western Serbia
27 June 1941	The KPJ established the Main Staff (military command) of its partisan National Liberation Movement under Tito's leadership
4 July 1941	The KPJ ordered the start of the resistance
7 July 1941	Uprising in Serbia (near Bela Crkva in western Serbia)
13 July 1941	Mass uprising in Montenegro under the leadership of the KPJ
27 July 1941	Uprising in Bosnia and Herzegovina (in Drvar region)
August 1941	Partisans liberated the first territories in western Serbia, Kordun, Lika, and Banija (in Croatia), Montenegro, and western Bosnia
22 August 1941	Mussolini ordered his troops to occupy ethnically mixed regions of the NDH that were settled by the Serbs (Dalmatia, Herzegovina, Lika, and Kordun)
September–November 1941	Partisan units liberated a wide region and organized the Užiška republika (the Republic of Užice), in south Serbia
10 October 1941	The leadership of the Wehrmacht ordered that for each slain German, their soldiers should kill 100 Serbs
11 October 1941	Uprising in Macedonia (in Prilep region) started

21 October 1941	German troops murdered 2,300 hostages in Kragujevac
1 November 1941	Chetniks attacked partisan units in Užiška republika
26–27 November 1942	First meeting of the Anti-Fascist Council of National Liberation of Yugoslavia—AVNOJ
January–April 1943	Fourth Offensive; the battle on the Neretva River in mid-February early March 1943; Tito sent Svetozar Vukmanović-Tempo to Macedonia; mass uprising started to develop there
28 February 1943	The Dolomits' Declaration (Dolomitska izjava); the Christian Socialists and Liberal Sokols recognized the CPS's leading role in the OF
14 July 1943	The establishment of the Anti-Fascist Council of National Liberation of Croatia (Zemaljsko antifašističko vijeće narodnog oslobodjenja Hrvatske, ZAVNOH), which declared itself the supreme political board of Croatia
8 September 1943	Capitulation of Italy
20 September 1943	Slovene National Liberation Council established as the first Slovene parliament; ZAVNOH declared the annexation of Istria, Rijeka, and Zadar to Croatia
29–30 November 1943	AVNOJ proclaims itself the supreme power in Yugoslavia
20 April 1944	Swearing-in of Slovene home defenders that they will fight together with German army
16 June 1944	Tito–Šubašić agreement
2 August 1944	Anti-Fascist Council of National Liberation of Macedonia (Antifašističko sobranie na narodnoto osvoboduvanje na Makedonija, ASNOM) was created
September 1944	After the capitulation of Bulgaria and Romania, Soviet troops also invaded Serbia (on the basis of an agreement between Tito and Stalin)
20 October 1944	Liberation of Belgrade
November 1944	Partisan units liberated Macedonia
December 1944	Leaders of the Catholic and Liberal Parties in Slovenia signed a so-called National Declaration (Narodna izjava; dated 29 October 1944, the anniversary of the founding of the State of the

Slovenes, Croats, and Serbs) in which they demanded a united Slovenia as part of the federated kingdom of Yugoslavia

7 March 1945	Tito established the first temporary government of Democratic Federative Yugoslavia
mid-April 1945	ASNOM was transformed into a Macedonian parliament
5 May 1945	Slovene partisans inaugurated the first Slovene government in Ajdovščina
8 May 1945	Capitulation of Germany
8–15 May 1945	Fights of the German soldiers together with different groups of anticommunist forces from Yugoslavia continued until capitulation of General Alexander von Löhr to the Yugoslav Army
18 May 1945	The dissolution of Main Staff of Yugoslav Army for Slovenia by the direct order of Josip Broz-Tito, which meant that the Slovene partisan army was included in the unified Yugoslav Army

Significant People, Places, and Events

BAKARIĆ, VLADIMIR (1912–1983) Lawyer, Croat politician. During World War II, Vladimir Bakarić served as the secretary of the Central Committee of the Communist Party of Croatia. After the war he was the president of the Croat government, a member of the presidency (collective leadership) of Yugoslavia, and the vice president of Yugoslavia. He was also a theoretician of the Socialist state, dealing with the economic development of Socialist society, the development of democracy, and self-management in Yugoslavia.

BALISTS (Balli kombëtar) Balists were a volunteer Albanian militia organized in 1943 by the National Front of Albania. Led by rich landowners, this organization was organized supposedly to fight the occupiers. In reality its primary goal was to prevent ethnic Albanians from being included in the NLM. The organization even signed an agreement with the supreme Italian command to fight the NLM in Kosovo, Western Macedonia, and Albania.

BLUE GUARD (plava garda) Unlike the Home Guard, the Slovene Chetniks were not supported by the Italians. Chetnik units, which the Partisans called plava garda (Blue Guard), were organized in April 1942. At its peak it numbered 350 armed men in the woods. As their commander, Major Karel Novak, did not recognize the supreme Chetnik command, the movement eventually split up. After the Italian capitulation in September 1943, the partisans trapped the main Blue Guard group at Grčarice and completely destroyed it.

CHETNIKS During World War II, Chetniks were members of the Yugoslav king's army in the homeland, under the leadership of Dragoljub Draža Mihailović. They fought against the Partisans and cooperated with the Italian occupiers as units of the Milizia volontaria anticomunista (MVAC). Most of the Chetniks operated in the south of Croatia and in Bosnia. In Slovenia they were also called the Blue Guard.

COMMUNIST PARTY OF YUGOSLAVIA (Komunistička partija Jugoslavije—KPJ) The KPJ was established in Belgrade initially as the Socialist Workers' Party of Yugoslavia (Socialistička radnička partija Jugoslavije) in April 1919, and it changed its name to KPJ in 1920.

In the 1920s, the underground party largely restricted itself to intellectual debates. In 1923 the party had a major debate on the national question and adopted a resolution allowing nations the right to self-determination and secession; nevertheless it should be noted that, in a lively debate, the centralist position had also been strongly supported by important party elements.

By the mid-1930s, with fascism menacing Europe, the KPJ accepted the idea of the Popular Front (1935), and the party began reorganizing into a federation of national units—separate Communist Parties of Slovenia and Croatia emerged during this time. The newly federated KPJ moved its headquarters to Zagreb, and Tito became its General Secretary. Although the Axis invasion of Yugoslavia began on 6 April 1941, the KPJ declared opposition to it only after the German Reich invaded the Soviet Union (22 June). The KPJ, with Tito as military commander, then organized the Yugoslav Partisan resistance (National Liberation Movement—NLM; Narodnooslobodilački pokret [Serbo-Croatian]—NOP; Narodnoosvobodilno gibanje [Slovene], NOG; and Narodnoosvobodilniot pokret [Macedonian], NOP) and started a "socialist" revolution. The party, which in the late 1930s had about 4,500 members, grew with the resistance successes, drawing support from various parts of the country. By the end of the war there were 141,000 regular KPJ members, and 150,000 belonged to the youth organization (Savez komunističke omladine Jugoslavije, SKOJ).

As the strongest and, later, the only political party, it came to power in the country after WW II.

Djilas, Milovan (1911–1995) Montenegrin politician and writer. Milovan Djilas was one of the leaders of the partisan movement during World War II, vice president of the Yugoslav government, and president of the federal Assembly of Yugoslavia. In 1954 he criticized the policy of KPJ and was relieved of all political duties in Yugoslavia. He became a leading critic of the communist regime who fought for the multiparty system in Yugoslavia and was twice sentenced to long imprisonments. His books, *The New Class* and *Conversation with Stalin,* were banned in Yugoslavia and were published there only after 1988.

Hebrang, Andrija (1899–1949) Croat politician and statesman. Hebrang was one of the most influential Croat communists, and as such he stood for Croat interests. His colleagues in the KPJ reproached him that he did not fight enough for Yugoslavism. During the split with Stalin in 1948 he was expelled from the KPJ and later arrested, because of a suspicion that he worked against the interests of the NLM and that he later sabotaged post–World War II Yugoslav economic policies. He was murdered in prison in 1949.

Home Guard (domobranci) In September 1943 in Ljubljana, the Slovene Home Guard was established to fight against the Liberation Front. It was organized with German approval and assistance by Leon Rupnik, a former Yugoslav army general, who had been appointed president of the formerly Italian Province of Ljubljana, then occupied by the Germans. At the end of the war, the Home Guard numbered between 15,000 and 20,000 men, and most of them retreated together with family members to Austria, where they were met by the British and disarmed as German collaborators. In June 1945, the British returned several thousand Home Guard members to Slovenia, where many were brutally murdered at several locations (Kočevski Rog, Škofja Loka, Teharje, and elsewhere). Estimates of the number of executed Home Guards vary from 7,000 to 11,000.

Kardelj, Edvard (1910–1979) Slovene politician and publicist. Edvard Kardelj was one of the leading members of the KPJ and cooperated with Tito when the Yugoslav communist organization was reestablished in the late 1930s. He published a book, *Razvoj slovenskega narodnega vprašanja* (*Development of the Slovene National Question*), in the 1930s. During World War II he was one of the leaders of the Liberation Front and a member of the "Supreme Staff" of Yugoslav Partisan units. After World War II he served as the foreign minister, member of the presidency of the Communist Party of Yugoslavia, member of the presidency of Yugoslavia, etc.

LJOTIĆ, DIMITRIJE (1891–19??) Serb politician. Dimitrije Ljotić started in politics as an activist in a peasant cooperative movement soon after World War I. In 1935 he established Jugoslavenski narodni pokret Zbor (the Yugoslav National Movement Zbor), which propagated fascist ideas of a corporate state in which the economy and political order were based on corporations (it was banned in 1940). His followers played an important role in a Fifth Column (i.e., pro-Fascist groups) in the years before Hitler's attack on Yugoslavia. After the occupation he organized a special armed group to fight partisans and openly cooperated with the Germans.

MIHAILOVIĆ, DRAGOLJUB (DRAŽA) (1893–1946) Yugoslav general and leader of the Chetniks. During World War II Dragoljub Mihailović organized military resistance under the auspices of the Royal Yugoslav Government-in-Exile, which named him minister of war in 1942. Because of his fights against the partisan movement and cooperation with occupation forces, the Allied forces no longer supported him after the Conference in Teheran (December 1943). Because of his cooperation with the occupation forces he was condemned to death and executed by the communist Yugoslav authorities in 1946.

NAZOR, VLADIMIR (1876–1949) Croat poet, novelist, and interpreter. Nazor was one of the most important Croat poets of the first half of the twentieth century. He showed his pride in being a Croat as early as first book, *Slavenske legende* (*Slavic Legends,* 1900). His other important works are the novel *Veli Jože* (1909), the book of poems *Lirika* (*Lyric,* 1910) and *Intima* (1915), and the 1945 work *S partizanima 1943–1945* (*With the Partisans* 1943–1945). During World War II Nazor served as a member of the Presidency of AVNOJ and as president of ZAVNOH. After the war he served as the president of the Croat parliament.

NEDIĆ, MILAN (1877–1946) Serb general and politician. Milan Nedić was the chief of the general staff of the Yugoslav Army and minister of war in the Royal Yugoslav Government and, from August 1941, the president of the quisling Serb government. After the war Yugoslav communist authorities imprisoned him. In prison he committed suicide in 1946.

PAVELIĆ, ANTE (1889–1959) Lawyer, Croat politician, and president of NDH. Pavelić served in the Yugoslav parliament as deputy of the Croat Party of Law (1927–1929). After King Aleksandar proclaimed a dictatorship, Pavelić left for Italy and organized the Ustaša movement. After the collapse of Yugoslavia in April 1941, Pavelić became the president (*poglavnik*) of the NDH (Independent State of Croatia) with the help of Italy's Fascist leader, Mussolini. In 1945 he left for Austria. Because he was sentenced to death in the homeland for crimes of the Ustaša against humanity, he left Austria for Italy and went from there to Argentina, to Paraguay, and to Franco's Spain, where he died in 1959.

PIJADE, Moša (1890–1957) Montenegrin politician, publicist, and painter. During World War II, Moša Pijade was one of the principal organizers of the uprising in Montenegro. Later, as a member of the supreme staff of the NLM, he dealt primarily with the problems of organization of a "people's administration." He authored the first written regulations on the organization and duties of the National Liberation Committees (Fočanski predpisi). He organized TANJUG, the Yugoslav press agency; he also served as a member of the Yugoslav delegation at the peace conference in Paris after World War II. Pijade translated Karl Marx's *Das Kapital* and *Communist Manifesto.* In addition he painted more than 120 pictures, of which more than two-thirds were eventually lost.

RANKOVIĆ, ALEKSANDAR (1909–1983) Serb politician. Aleksandar Ranković was a leading member of the KPJ beginning in 1927. During World War II he was the organizing secretary of the Central Committee of the Communist Party of Yugoslavia, responsible for security services. From 1946 until 1963, he was Yugoslav minister of the interior and the vice president of the Yugoslav government; during 1963–1966 he served as the vice president of Yugoslavia. In 1966 he was relieved of all functions because of the interference of the security forces he led in the functions of the state.

REPUBLIC OF UŽICE (Užička republika) The short-lived Republic of Užice (in western Serbia), the first large liberated territory in Yugoslavia and the largest liberated territory in the occupied Europe (with a population of one million), was captured by the partisans in autumn 1941. On this territory the first stirrings of people's authorities (National Liberation Committees) were established, thereby creating the framework for the building of a socialist regime in Yugoslavia. The republic ended in November 1941, after the Partisans had to withdraw their forces to Sandžak.

ROŽMAN, GREGORIJ (1883–1959) Slovene, Catholic priest and Bishop of Ljubljana. After he finished his studies by earning a doctorate from a school in Vienna (1912), Gregorij Rožman became professor of moral theology and canon law at Celovec/Klagenfurt School of Theology. In 1919 he became professor of canon law at the University of Ljubljana, and he became bishop of Ljubljana in 1929. In May 1945, he left for Austria; in August 1946 the Military Court in Ljubljana sentenced him

to eighteen years in prison because of his cooperation with the occupiers. In 1948 he left for Switzerland and then the United States. From
his residence at Cleveland's St. Lawrence Church he visited many
Slovene emigrant settlements in the United States, South America, and
Western Europe.

RUPNIK, LEON (1880–1946) Slovene general and politician. Leon Rupnik
established himself as a fighter against the communists and Liberation
Front. From June 1942 to August 1943 he served as the mayor of Ljubljana. After the Germans took over from the Italians as occupiers, he
served as the president of the Province of Ljubljana. In September 1944
he became the inspector general of the Slovene *domobranstvo* (home
defenders). After the war he escaped to Carinthia, but the Western Allies extradited him to the Yugoslav authorities, who sentenced him to
death for cooperation with the occupiers. A firing squad executed him
in 1946.

STEPINAC, ALOJZIJE (1898–1960) Croat cardinal and Archbishop of Zagreb. After earning a doctorate in philosophy and theology in Rome he
became the Archbishop of Zagreb in 1937. Although he welcomed the
establishment of the Independent State of Croatia, already in May 1941
he protested against persecution of Croat citizens only because they
were adherents of different, non-Catholic faiths, nationalities ideologies, or political persuasions. After World War II Stepinac protested
against the brutal persecution by the winners of the war against those
who lost the war, and Yugoslav authorities arrested him in September
1946. In October 1946 he was sentenced to sixteen years in prison. Because of the numerous protests that came from all over the world, the
Yugoslav authorities let Stepinac out of prison and interned him in a
parish manor-house in Krašić, where he lived out the remainder of his
life.

ŠUBAŠIĆ, IVAN (1892–1955) Lawyer and Croat politician. After the
Cvetković-Maček Agreement and establishment of Banovina Croatia
(26 August 1939), Ivan Šubašić was named the Croat ban (governor).
After the occupation of Yugoslavia in 1941 he emigrated to the United
States, and from there in 1944 to England. He was named the president
of the Yugoslav Royal Government. He signed the agreement with the
Yugoslav communist leader Tito in June 1944 in Vis. In March 1945 he
became the foreign minister in the Tito-Šubašić government but resigned in September 1945.

VUKMANOVIĆ, SVETOZAR-TEMPO (1912–) Montenegrin, statesman, and
politician. Svetozar Vukmanović organized an uprising of partisans

against the occupiers in Bosnia and Herzegovina during World War II and later (from November 1942 onward) also in Macedonia. In 1944 he returned to Belgrade, where, after the war, he served especially in the state-led trade unions. He wrote some books, including one on economic problems, another on the workers' movement, and a book of memoirs.

WHITE GUARD (bela garda) The White Guard, a name used for counterrevolutionaries during Russia's Bolshevik revolution, was appropriated by the Slovene Partisans and applied to the Village Guard and the Legion of Death. Later, the general term *belogardizem* (White Guardism) was used for the entire anticommunist movement organized by the conservative forces in Slovenia during World War II. Slovene anticommunists regard it as a derogatory term.

Bibliography

Benson, Leslie. *Yugoslavia: A Concise History.* (New York: Palgrave, 2001).

Harriman, Helga H. *Slovenia under Nazi Occupation, 1941–1945.* (New York: Studia Slovenica, 1977).

Irvine, Jill A. *The Croat Question: Partisan Politics in the Formation of the Yugoslav Socialist State.* (Boulder, CO: Westview Press, 1993).

Kočović , Bogoljub. *Žrtve drugog svetskog rata u Jugoslaviji.* (Sarajevo, Bosnia and Herzegovina: Svjetlost, 1990).

Lampe, John R. *Yugoslavia as History. Twice there Was a Country.* (Cambridge, U.K.: Cambridge University Press, 1996).

Malcolm, Noel. *Bosnia: A Short History.* (New York: New York University Press, 1994).

Poulton, Hough. *Who Are the Macedonians?* (London: C. Hurst, 1995).

Roberts, Walter R. *Tito, Mihailović, and the Allies, 1941–1945.* (New Brunswick, NJ: Rutgers University Press, 1973).

Singleton, Fred. *Twentieth Century Yugoslavia.* (New York: Columbia University Press, 1976).

Tomasevich, Jozo. *The Chetniks.* (Palo Alto, CA: Stanford University Press, 1975).

Vodopivec, Peter. "Seven Decades of Unconfronted Incongruities: The Slovenes and Yugoslavia." In Benderly, Jill, and Kraft, Evan (eds.). *Independent Slovenia: Origins, Movements, Prospects.* (New York: St. Martin's Press, 1994), 23–46.

Žerjavić, Vladimir. *Yugoslavia: Manipulations with the Number of Second World War Victims.* (Zagreb, Croatia: Croat Information Centre, 1993).

CHAPTER SIX

The Yugoslav Federation, 1945–1991

The History of the "New" Yugoslavia

THE PERIOD OF THE YUGOSLAV FEDERATION presented in this chapter is in many ways crucial for the understanding of recent historic events in the former Yugoslavia. Although initially, immediately after World War II it might have seemed that the National Liberation Movement (NLM) had managed to resolve ethnic problems and tensions in Yugoslavia by the introduction of federalism based on the principles of equality and the brotherhood and unity of Yugoslav nations, ethnic problems and tensions resurfaced together with many other problems later. Obviously the existing political system and ruling regime were unable to address these issues successfully, which resulted in the tragic collapse of the Yugoslav federation in the beginning of the 1990s. Due to the complexity of this period and its events, this chapter discusses only a few events from this period that the authors consider especially important for the country's story.

The Communist Party of Yugoslavia Takes Control

Four years of occupation and civil wars during the 1940s hit Yugoslavia very hard. The material damage was assessed to be 47 billion U.S. dollars (according to the value of the dollar in 1939); casualties were approximately 1.05 to 1.7 million. Although some of the most important industrial centers in Slovenia and Croatia were not bombed during the war, the GNP of Yugoslavia in 1945 did not reach one-half of what it was in 1941. This meant that the reconstruction of the country was a major and difficult task and responsibility—especially for the Communist Party of Yugoslavia (KPJ), which emerged as the main—if not the only—political force in the so-called second or new Yugoslavia after World War II.

Yugoslavian president Josip Broz-Tito opens the eighth Yugoslavian Communist Party Congress. In his speech Tito praised Nikita Khrushchev and accused the Chinese communists of Stalinist methods in trying to take over world communism. (Bettman/CORBIS)

Because of its role in the NLM during World War II, the KPJ could count on the wide support of the people of Yugoslavia, which soon became evident. However, in many ways the situation was very uncertain and rather difficult in the time immediately after the war (e.g., because of peace conferences and negotiations about the borders, reconstruction of the destroyed country, hardships in economically backward countries that badly needed economic development, etc.). The communist leaders who were trying to consolidate their position and the new regime were ready to use all means available to ensure their complete control of the country. Soon after the end of World War II the allied forces (Great Britain and the United States) returned to Yugoslavia many Ustaša, Slovene Home Defenders, and Serb Chetniks who had fled to Austria and Italy and surrendered there, and more than thirty thousand of them were killed without due process. The terror continued when the new regime tried to destroy the remaining dispersed Chetniks, Ustaša, Domobrans (Croat army), and

Home Defenders (Slovene Domobrans) units in different parts of the country, and also when they fought against speculators, war profiteers, and (real and invented) opponents of the regime, who were often put into criminal camps while their property was confiscated. Even before the nationalization took place, many mines, banks, insurance companies, railroads, factories, and other important companies that had belonged to collaborators of the occupiers during World War II were confiscated or "patriotically nationalized" by the communist authorities.

In the beginning the new authorities were more lenient toward the peasants, as the leaders were aware of the decisive importance of agrarian production for sustaining the population and the country as a whole. For this reason, the first measure enacted by the Temporary People's Assembly was the Law on Agrarian Reform, which was adopted on 23 August 1945. Under the slogan "Land Belongs to the Person Who Works on It," without compensation the authorities took the land away from the great estate owners, the Catholic and Orthodox churches, monasteries, and other religious institutions. Together with the land of those ethnic Germans who were accused of collaborating with the occupiers during World War II, there were around 3.71 million acres nationalized. In accordance with a 1946 law that followed the Soviet example, one-half of the nationalized land was united in cooperative societies, intended to be the cornerstone for future socialist farming.

The communists wanted to have complete control over intellectual life also. They established literacy for the people as their aim. The level of literacy increased from 50.5 percent in the year 1921 to 81.0 percent in 1961 and grew even more later on.

The third Conference of the AVNOJ in August 1945 renamed itself the Contemporary People's Assembly. In accordance with the Tito-Šubašić Agreement (signed on the Island of Vis in 1944), it also included thirty-six members of the Yugoslav parliament of 1938, sixty-nine representatives of political parties from the interwar period, and thirteen independent personalities who had not collaborated with the occupiers during World War II. The Contemporary People's Assembly adopted ten basic laws that reshaped the country and legalized the supremacy of the KPJ. The law on "activities against the people and state" provided for harsh punishment for any ethno-nationalist propaganda and/or agitation. This law also hindered or even forbade open discussion on interethnic relations and tensions; as a result it was impossible to find solutions to these problems.

As provided by the Tito-Šubašić Agreement, "free elections in which all participating parties would have an equal chance to win" were called. This was the condition for the Western powers to recognize the new authority in the country. For these elections the KPJ and its allies united into the People's Front of Yugoslavia (Narodni front Jugoslavije) and chose Tito as their leader. In these elections the communists that controlled the police, judiciary, and media had an important advantage. For this reason the opposition did not want to participate in the elections. Consequently, candidates from the People's Front got almost 90.5 percent of votes in the elections of 11 November 1945. Although in Slovenia and Vojvodina almost one-quarter of the populace abstained or voted against the People's Front of Yugoslavia, the party still won the elections convincingly, which confirmed the legitimacy of the "new Yugoslavia" abroad.

The Constituent Assembly, controlled by the communists, deprived the Karadjordjević's dynasty of all its rights on 29 November 1945 and proclaimed the Federal People's Republic of Yugoslavia or FPRY (Federativna Narodna od republika Jugoslavija/Federativna ljudska republika Jugoslavija, FNRJ/FLRJ/FNRJ). The federal republic consisted of six People's Republics: Serbia (with the autonomous province of Vojvodina and the autonomous authority, or oblast, of Kosmet), Macedonia, Montenegro, Bosnia and Herzegovina, Croatia, and Slovenia. On 31 January 1946, the Constituent Assembly passed a new constitution, which introduced a Soviet-type political system and federation in Yugoslavia. Following the Soviet example, the centrally planned (directed) economy—based on requiring the "social ownership of the majority of the means of production, transportation and communication," which in reality was state property—was introduced. The constitution proclaimed "mines and other wealth of the land, water resources, natural power, railways, air transport, mail, telegraph, telephone and radio . . ." to be the people's property.

Consequently, the legislation of 1946 and 1948 nationalized—with the exception of farming—more than 90 percent of the country's private property. In accordance with the five-year economic plan (*petletka*), which was an instrument of the new economic system, the more developed republics of Yugoslavia were to progress more slowly and wait for the less developed republics to catch up.

Industrialization and electrification were declared to be central economic goals. As a result an accelerated urbanization took place; some 1.2 million people migrated from the countryside into the industrial centers, which also influenced the ethnic structure of several areas.

Politically this period was one of continuing turmoil and conflict with opponents and enemies of the new regime. In March 1946 the authorities caught the Chetniks' leader Draža Mihailović, who was sentenced to death on 16 July 1946. A few weeks later in Ljubljana, a judicial process started against General Leon Rupnik, leader of the Slovene Home Defenders, and, in absentia, also against the bishop of Ljubljana, Dr. Gregorij Rožman, and the leader of the Slovene People's Party, Dr. Miha Krek. The proceedings against Rožman and Krek were regarded, first of all, as processes against the Catholic church, which was condemned for having cooperated with the forces of the occupation during World War II. Processes against priests, the Catholic church, and the Vatican followed. Among the accused was also the archbishop of Zagreb, Alojzije Stepinac. The authorities accused him of collaboration with the Ustaša. They arrested him in September 1946 and sentenced him to sixteen years in prison. Simultaneously, prosecutions against the Ustaša, Chetniks, Macedonian nationalists, profiteers, and bribed functionaries continued. In this period of so-called mature Stalinism, proceedings against spies also took place. The accused were mostly personalities from the intellectual and bourgeois circles, who had cooperated with the NLM in the past but were, in the new circumstances, considered a possible bourgeois opposition (e.g., trials against Črtomir Nagode in Ljubljana, against Tom Janicković and other respected members of the Croat Peasant Party in Zagreb, and against Dragoljub Jovanović in Belgrade).

The Fight for Borders

In spite of the fact that World War II was not yet over, at the peace conference in Paris it was very apparent that there were numerous differences among the Allies, especially between the United States and the Soviet Union. The Iron Curtain, about which Winston Churchill had already spoken in his famous speech in Fulton, Missouri, in March 1946, became a real frontier between Eastern and Western Europe.

Under pressure from the Western Allies, the Yugoslav Partisan army had to leave Trieste, Gorizia, and the regions of so-called Venetian Slovenia in the northwest of Friuli-Venezia Guilia. The question of the Yugoslav-Italian border was to be solved by a council of foreign ministers of the four major powers (the United States, the Soviet Union, Great Britain, and France). Due to the complicated state of East-West relations and the complicated ethnic situation (the region in question was an ethnically mixed area in which Italians, Croats, and Slovenes lived), an agreement was not reached about the border until May 1946. French Foreign Minister Georges Bidault suggested the establishment of the Free Territory of

Trieste as a compromise. This territory would represent a buffer zone between Italy and Yugoslavia, or between East and West, and would be governed together by Anglo-American (Zone A) and Yugoslav (Zone B) military authorities. In spite of the fact that the governments of Italy and Yugoslavia finally signed the peace treaty on 10 February 1947, fights around the Free Territory of Trieste did not cease. In 1953 there was even the danger that this would escalate into a military duel, and Italy and Yugoslavia again negotiated through the Anglo-American intermediaries. Under new circumstances of improved relations between Yugoslavia and the West, it was now possible to reach an agreement. Yugoslavia was no longer a Soviet satellite (see this chapter's following segment). The result of the negotiations was the London "Memorandum Between the Governments of Italy, the United Kingdom, the United States and Yugoslavia Regarding The Free Territory of Trieste" of October 1954, according to which most of Zone A with the city of Trieste/Trst remained in Italy, and Zone B and a smaller part of Zone A became part of Yugoslavia.

During the war, the Yugoslav authorities also counted on changes of the border with Austria in southern Carinthia; however, the annexation of the Slovene coastland, Istria, Zadar, and some islands in the Adriatic Sea was the only correction of the Yugoslav borders after World War II. The Macedonian ethnic minorities in Greece and Bulgaria also remained outside of Yugoslavia. The Yugoslav authorities counted on the communists' being welcomed to power in these states; they hoped that the authorities would give all the rights of ethnic minorities to the South Slavic populations in Greece, Bulgaria, etc.—which did not occur in practice.

Tito's Split with Stalin and the Cominform (Inform-Bureau)

As far as foreign policy after World War II is concerned, Yugoslavia became an ally of the Soviet Union and its satellites in Eastern Europe. Although the Yugoslav Army was the fourth mightiest military power in Europe inside the anti-Hitler coalition, the Yugoslav communists felt threatened. Aggressive Yugoslav foreign policy can be explained by Tito's desire to make Belgrade the international center of the people's democracies, but possibly also an ideological competitor of Moscow. Until 1948 Yugoslavia hoped for a federation with Bulgaria and tried to establish control over Albania. It also made a net of bilateral agreements with Poland, Czechoslovakia, Hungary, and Romania. Tito did not hide the fact that his vision of socialism was different from Stalin's. Instead of the monolithic structure of an International Workers' Movement under

Stalin's control, Tito's idea later was an open and dynamic socialist society. It is interesting to note that to the United States, Yugoslavia remained one of the Kremlin's "satellite police states," assisting the Soviets in their "drive toward world conquest." The U.S. administration also held Tito himself in little regard. As President Truman told a group of business and trade newspaper editors in April 1948: "I am told that Tito murdered more than four hundred thousand of the opposition in Yugoslavia before he got himself firmly established there as a dictator" (Lees, 1997, 46–47). Within this context, no one appreciated the signs of trouble that surfaced in Yugoslavia during the first months of 1948.

In January 1948, a Yugoslav delegation that included Milovan Djilas journeyed to the USSR for discussions on military and political assistance, but little came of the talks. (Djilas, a Montenegrin communist and a member of the Yugoslav Communist Party's highest executive body, became a dissident and leading critic of the Yugoslav regime in the 1950s and was the author of many books. For this reason, he was imprisoned by the Tito regime many times.) In February, while the Yugoslavs languished in Moscow, Stalin suddenly summoned the leadership of both Bulgaria and Yugoslavia to the Kremlin to discuss the Balkan federation. Tito, claiming ill health, refused to attend; Kardelj and Vladimir Bakarić joined Djilas to represent Yugoslavia in his stead. Before their meeting with Stalin, Djilas warned his fellows that Stalin would attempt "to force Yugoslavia down to the level of the occupied East European countries." When he met with the Yugoslavs and the Bulgarians, Stalin criticized the independent behavior of both countries and called for the formation of a Yugoslav-Bulgarian federation. Although he had previously promised Yugoslavia that it could absorb Albania, he now declared that that could occur only after the creation of a federation. Stalin also demanded an end to the civil war in northern Greece between the Greek communists and the British forces after World War II. This civil war, fought in an ethnically mixed area where the ethnic Macedonians lived, was supposed to end on the grounds that Great Britain and the United States, the latter pictured by him as the most powerful state in the world, would never permit the communists "to break their line of communication in the Mediterranean." In addition, the Soviet leader later insisted that the Yugoslavs sign an agreement with the USSR calling for Soviet consultation on foreign policy issues. Kardelj, who later recalled that his "blood boiled" at this insult, signed the document in the middle of the night and only at Vjačeslav Mihajlovič Molotov's insistence. Molotov was at the time the foreign minister of the Soviet Union.

By the first of March, the Yugoslavs had decided to resist Stalin's demands. Within a few weeks, the Soviets notified Tito that they intended to withdraw all military and civilian advisers and technicians from his country in response to their unfriendly treatment. The two countries' Communist Party Central Committees then exchanged letters in which the Soviets charged the Yugoslavs with various ideological errors and anti-Soviet actions and the Yugoslavs proclaimed their innocence. This exchange culminated in the expulsion of Yugoslavia from the Cominform (see the end of this chapter) on 28 June 1948, and Stalin's call on the people of Yugoslavia to overthrow Tito. At the same time the fifth congress (Convention) of the KPJ, a supreme body that was supposed to meet every four years and elect officers of the party, took place. The Cominform also gradually imposed a blockade on trade with Yugoslavia to deprive it of the goods vital to its reconstruction and economic development.

The Yugoslavs had refused a Soviet suggestion that the argument between them be settled by the Cominform, and they did not attend the June meeting that denounced them for their "departure from Marxism-Leninism" at home and abroad. The Yugoslav party rejected the Cominform's action and called on its members to "close ranks" with the masses and "work even more persistently on the building of our Socialist homeland," as only such actions would demonstrate the falsity of the Cominform's charge (Lees, 1997, 51).

Dedijer later wrote that until spring 1948 "conflict between the new Yugoslavia and the Soviet Union had seemed impossible to me." (Dedijer, 1970, 36). Veteran Yugoslav diplomat Leo Mates also recalled the "shock" felt by the Yugoslavs, as well as "the suspicion that the old fox has some designs" on his country. The letters exchanged in secret between the two countries' communist organizations and leaders throughout the spring reflected this Yugoslav sense of unease as Tito and the party stressed their conviction that the Soviets had been misinformed and that a meeting between the two parties would clear the air. The Yugoslavs continually asserted their loyalty to Marxism, the Soviet Union, and their own country, noting their wish to be the Soviets' "most faithful friend and ally." As the correspondence proceeded, the Soviets charged the Yugoslavs with reverting to capitalism; the Yugoslavs labeled such ideas insulting. Tito also leveled charges of his own, asserting that the Soviets had wronged Yugoslavia by providing only meager aid and by recruiting spies from within the party and government.

Because the KPJ was not ready to subordinate its activities to Stalin's vision of the ("real") Socialism, it was expelled from the Cominform in

June 1948. Most Yugoslav communists accepted and supported the policy of their leaders. However, after the first enthusiasm diminished, doubts about the justifiability of Tito's insurgence and Yugoslavia's capabilities to survive without Soviet support appeared. Several supporters and sympathizers of the Cominform and its resolution against Yugoslav communist leadership (mostly officers of the Yugoslav Army and state security services of Serb and Montenegrin nationality), but also some suspected to be the sympathizers, were arrested and sent to be reeducated in special concentration camps. The best known was the camp on Goli otok, a stony karstic island in the Adriatic, where, from July 1949 on, around 16,000 people were "reeducated" under this most cruel regime.

The U.S. administration's response to the rift between Tito and Stalin, formulated by George Kennan and the policy planning staff he headed, was a cautious one. The split between Tito and Stalin had occurred without the knowledge of the West. In Kennan's words, an "entirely new problem" was how to fashion a policy toward "a communist state resting on the basis of Soviet organization principles and for the most part on Soviet ideology, and yet independent of Moscow" (Less, 1997, 53).

It is interesting to note that a congressman of Slovene descent, John Blatnik from the Minnesota Iron Range in northern Minnesota, first informed President Truman that the split between Tito's Yugoslavia and the Soviet Union was genuine and real. He warned that the position taken by the United States could help determine whether any of the Soviet satellites would follow Tito's example, and whether Tito himself could remain in power. If the West was "too cold toward Tito," the Soviets would use this to demonstrate that the communist states had no choice but to remain within the bloc; however, a Western move to embrace Tito could undermine his position among his followers in Yugoslavia as well as arouse "strong and justifiable criticism in this country." The policy adopted by the administration was that it "would welcome a genuine emergence of Yugoslavia as a political personality in its own right," hoping for a "normal development of economic relations" between Yugoslavia and the West, provided that the former was "willing to adopt a loyal and cooperative attitude in its international relationships."

Yugoslavia's Own Way to Socialism: Self-Management and the "Third Way"

During the period 1949–1952, Yugoslav political leadership started to reform all spheres of the society. In May 1949 Edvard Kardelj, Slovene politician and the leading Yugoslav ideologue, introduced to the Yugoslav parliament the Law on People's Committees (Zakon o ljudskih odborih), which again gave autonomy to the local authorities at the expense of the federal authorities. Reforms continued in other fields—including economics—and replaced the previous Soviet model of state socialism with a new self-management socialist system. Its main slogan was "Factories to Workers." These reforms introduced a model of "social property" that replaced "state property" and gave the administration of industrial enterprises to the workers' committees (elected after 1950). They also mitigated political pressure toward noncommunists, gave up forced collectivization in farming, and let loose commerce with farm products. Because the KPJ was afraid that this would mean capitalist-style domination by large enterprises and large farmers in the countryside, a second agrarian reform was introduced in May 1953, limiting the size of farms to almost 25 acres of arable land. In the name of socialist democracy, party leaders decentralized even the KPJ and renamed it the League of Communists of Yugoslavia or LCY (Savez komunista Jugoslavije, SKJ/Zveza komunistov Jugoslavije, ZKJ/Sojuz na komunistite na Jugoslavije, SKJ). Officially, the party gave up direct administration of the state; the party was only to give directions. The life of the state was to be in the hands of communes—basic units of local government. The republics and the state were to only be coordinators. However, these reforms and formal changes did not abolish the political monopoly of the LCY, which still had all power in its hands. Tito remained the indisputable and untouchable Yugoslav leader. Other important political leaders were Edvard Kardelj, Milovan Djilas, and Aleksandar Ranković.

Closer economic and political relations with the West after the split with Stalin in 1948 enabled Yugoslavia to survive the political and economic isolation imposed upon it by the Soviet Union and its bloc. Yugoslavia's foreign policy from the 1950s on was that of equidistance from both the West and the East. Its allies were primarily among the so-called developing countries of the Third World. This developed the cornerstones of the movement of nonaligned countries, which proclaimed the equidistance from two main military treaty organizations (pacts), NATO and the Warsaw Treaty Organization. The nonaligned movement began with the Conference of twenty-nine mostly Asian and African countries in Bandung, Indonesia, on 18–24 April 1955. The movement was institutionalized at a conference in Belgrade, Yugoslavia, on 1–6 June 1961. Yugoslavia played a leading role in this movement until the state's dissolution in the 1990s.

After Stalin's death in 1953, relations with the Soviet Union and other Eastern European countries were normalized. Consequently the role of the party and state control increased, and as the first victim of this movement, the ideas of Milovan Djilas, who criticized the privileges of the LCY and its politicians and demanded freedom of speech, were defeated. This meant the end of the first attempt at reforming the socialist system in Yugoslavia. However, there was only a limited consensus regarding the future development of the country. Although Slovene Edvard Kardelj emphasized the need for reforms of the system, Aleksandar Ranković, a Serb politician and the head of the secret police, demanded an increased role and control by the LCY.

In spite of limitations and divisions, the ongoing social and political reforms contributed to a faster development of the country again in the 1950s. Yugoslavia's economic growth during 1952–1962 was one of the fastest in the world. The standard of living and the level of literacy and education increased rapidly, which was also true for some freedoms of citizens. This was a period of rapid development in culture, humanities, and science. However, the state economy and socialism were still the main hallmarks of the one-party system dominated by the LCY. The federation remained rather centralized, and the republics, dependent on federal funds, still had no or rather limited say in the politics of the state. This led to continuous conflicts between the republics and the center, but also to conflict between the more and less developed parts of Yugoslavia. Less developed southern republics condemned Slovenia's and Croatia's "policy of colonial thinking" and reproached Slovenia and Croatia with accusations of getting rich.

By the end of the 1950s ethnic tensions intensified again. Some politicians from the southern republics thought that with stronger communes and the federal state the republics had become unnecessary. The conservative communist circles demanded strengthening of the federal state and unification in the fields of politics, economics, and culture. The north, and especially Slovenia, criticized and rejected this position and such initiatives for territorial and political redefinition of Yugoslavia. Additionally, the Slovenes and Macedonians were angry because of the lack of respect shown in the regime for their languages and cultures. They were not able to use their languages in the army or in dealing with the federal authorities and with embassies and consulates abroad.

Rejected suggestions to dissolve the republics, consequently, strengthened their desires for autonomy and, in many cases, also their respective nationalist leanings. Tendencies toward cultural integration caused unexpected resistance in Croatia and Macedonia, and especially among Slovenians, who started to fight against unitarist and centralist tendencies and engendered polemics—which again opened the nationalist question in

Yugoslavia. However, the idea of cultural unification in Yugoslavia influenced the placement of a special category for "Yugoslavs" among the ethnic categories in the census of 1961.

At the end of the 1950s the conflicts between defenders of centralism and proponents of decentralized socialist self-management spread to the Yugoslav communist leadership. None questioned the leading role of the LCY and socialism; however, the defenders of decentralized self-management asked for more "national" and other rights for the republics and also for economic reforms that would enable them to maintain a more stable economic policy, taking into account the specific situation in every republic. They also demanded that the various enterprises be able to freely decide what to do with their profits. In a way this conflict was seen as an ethnic conflict: Kardelj as the leader of the self-management section was perceived as the defender of Slovenia's interests, and Ranković as a main proponent of the centralist model was believed to defend Serb interests. Kardelj was convinced that the future of Slovenia lay in the community of Yugoslav nations and that self-management, which was his invention, enabled the system to adapt to specific interests of the republics. He believed that this was a necessity. Ranković defended centralization, expressing the Serb fear that with the decentralization the "Catholic North" would get too much at the expense of the "Orthodox South."

Also disputed was the concept of the economic plan for 1962, with which the federal administration tried again to get a decisive role and control in the economy. Slovene and Croat enterprise managers especially resisted, as they tried to inject some elements of a market economy into the socialist economy. When tensions were exceptionally high, Tito even threatened resignation. This encouraged Aleksandar Ranković, who wanted the position of secretary general of the LCY, under the pretext that it was necessary to unburden Tito. Edvard Kardelj opposed Ranković and threatened that Slovenia would secede from Yugoslavia if Tito resigned (Pirjevec, 1995, 249). According to the Croat politician Vladimir Bakarić, it was not easy to convince Tito not to resign, but Tito did not like Ranković's demand. Tito thought for quite a long time before deciding between the two concepts for the future development of Yugoslavia. At the beginning he was in favor of centralism as propagated by Aleksandar Ranković; therefore, Kardelj was in disgrace. Later, however, he supported Kardelj, and Ranković had to withdraw from politics in Yugoslavia.

In the 1960s, the disputes on the future of Yugoslavia in politics and economics and the question of future interethnic relations were also influenced by social unrest. The Yugoslav authorities reacted to this unrest with the introduction of economic reforms and started preparations for a new constitution, which was to be a compromise that would, on the one hand, stress socialism in Yugoslav society and, on the other, attempt to democratize Yugoslav society and its power structures.

Based on the concept of self-management, the constitutional reform of 1963 introduced a new official name—the Socialist Federal Republic of Yugoslavia—and made the position of the republics even stronger. Cultural autonomy also increased in Yugoslavia. In 1967 Macedonians got their desired independent Macedonian Orthodox Church, which had until then been subordinated to the Serb Orthodox Church. Beginning in 1968 Muslims were acknowledged as a distinctive nation (*narod*), and Kosovo and Vojvodina gained more autonomy. Old Serb politicians were against this, as they saw in these changes the neglect of Serb interests.

The importance of individual federal units also grew with the reorganization of the army, at which time, in addition to the Yugoslav People's Army, territorial defenses (National Guard-type military units of individual republics) were established. The idea of organizing republic-level military units was best used by the Territorial Defense Force of Slovenia (a predecessor of today's Slovene Army), which bought part of its weapons from foreign countries. However, the federal authorities were unhappy with the fact that Slovenia was able to buy military equipment from foreigners without their mediation.

With economic reforms the federal state again lost some authority. The role of the banks in monetary matters was strengthened at the cost of the state. Profits did not go to the state anymore, but were retained by individual enterprises. Because the taxes on imports were lowered, new items (washing machines, TV sets, small kitchen appliances such as mixers, etc.) came to market, which contributed to a rise in the standard of living. In 1967 the Yugoslav authorities opened state borders with Italy and Austria, and Yugoslav citizens were given an opportunity to travel to the West, as the authorities were now issuing passports. Open borders enabled faster development of tourism, especially along the Adriatic coast and in spas. Yugoslavia also achieved great success with social issues, as it extended social, health, and pension benefits to most of its people. Every citizen could now afford to be treated by the health system. The pension system was so effective that people did not have to worry about their well being in old age.

These reforms enabled the Yugoslav economy to better integrate into the world economy. For the "socialist enterprises," which were accustomed to a redundant privileged position in home markets protected by customs barriers, competing with highly developed economies was a real shock. Because of the opening of the economy to free enterprise economics, numerous enterprises—especially those in the less developed southern republics—were forced to lay off workers, a practice unknown in socialism thus far. Because unemployment was on the rise in the country, people started to look for employment in the West. From the southern republics of Yugoslavia mostly unskilled workers left; from Slovenia many skilled and educated people also emigrated. This new economically inspired emigration became an important factor in the development of Yugoslav economy.

With the opening of the borders, Western values also came to Yugoslavia, especially human rights and political pluralism. These values became part of the value systems of younger members of the LCY, who took over important posts in the Yugoslav economy, politics, and culture at the beginning of the 1960s. The older generation of communists accused them of accepting Western capitalist values and named them liberals. Because the older communists were afraid that party liberals' ideas would bring a restoration of the multiparty system to the country in the long run, they decided to get rid of the political newcomers. In defending a political monopoly by the communist party, Edvard Kardelj joined the opponents of party liberalism.

In the second half of the 1960s and the beginning of the 1970s, the older generation of communists, whose leader was Tito, succeeded in getting rid of the liberal leadership of the republics. At first, they succeeded in getting rid of Croat liberals, who had even demanded Croat independence. Subsequently, party liberals were also expelled from the party leadership in Slovenia and Croatia. This meant the final defeat of defenders of economic and political reforms in the framework of a one-party socialist system.

After 1971, purges were a fact of life, not only in politics but also in other arenas. Instead of professionals, politically correct people, whether they did or did not have the proper education, came into leadership. The state again started to direct the economy, and the role of the army in society was strengthened. Anyone who criticized the state could be called before the court of justice. Yugoslavia returned to the path it had left at the end of the 1950s. Once again the defenders of centralism, who saw the future of Yugoslavia and its republics in a special type of "association of free producers," came to power.

This marked the beginning of the period of so-called late Titoism (1974–1980). Although the ideas of "democratic centralists" dominated the federal constitution of 1974, the constitution also embraced a few reformist ideas. Additionally, this constitution did not only preserve the autonomy of the republics and autonomous provinces, but it further increased it. However, it also preserved the political monopoly of the LCY.

The Constitution of 1974 also established a collective head of state—the federal presidency. Tito, who was at the same time president of the LCY and president of Yugoslavia, was elected president of Yugoslavia for life. After his death in 1980 the principle of rotation was used, as provided for in the Constitution of 1974. This principle meant that the one-year term of the president and the vice president of the Socialist Federal Republic of Yugoslavia (SFRY) rotated among members of this collective body on the predetermined order, so that the vice president became the president the following year. Although the federal presidency had rather limited powers formally, it was very influential. In practice, most powers were concentrated in the hands of a small number of leaders, who were at the same time the leaders of the communist party and the Yugoslav state. Additionally, high army officers were more and more present in political life. The army was expected to fight for law and order within the state after Tito's death.

The most important piece of legislation during this period was the Law of Associated Labor. Adopted in November 1976, it enforced self-management of the republics and introduced the principle of discussion and arrangement into the economy. All relatively independent economic units became the (Basic) Organizations of Associated Labor, in which the workers, in accordance with self-management principles, decided what and how much they would produce and how the earned money would be spent. These principles meant that workers and employees should have managed and controlled the economy, the same way all the people—organized in the Socialist Alliance of Working People—were supposed to manage the society. The system of self-management in economy should have supplemented the principles of the market economy in determining the price of the final product.

Republics and communes that became responsible for their own development were forced into extensive investments, which were often mainly in the interest of groups of local magnates. This system stimulated production of products that were work intensive and technologically less demanding to produce, which encouraged the employment of workers with minimal education. This practice provided for full employment, which meant that everybody was employed, but the economic results of the system were bad. Because of the old technology, bad quality of products, and bad economic performance, the system was destined to fail. The catastrophe that then threatened the Yugoslav economy was postponed by international loans. Yugoslavia became one of the most indebted countries in the world. This borrowed money was spent mostly on housing and for infrastructure, as well as for investments in the underdeveloped regions (Kosovo, Bosnia and Herzegovina, Macedonia, Montenegro), which did not generate sufficient incomes to pay for these loans. A strategy to focus on production investments that would yield the money to pay for the loans was not developed and implemented.

In spite of all this, people were happy because of the rise in the standard of living (both private and social); there were also no problems with employment. This situation lasted until the end of the 1970s, when, because of the world energy crisis, the inflow of foreign capital stopped. The situation in Yugoslavia was catastrophic. The external debt owed by the state was 20 billion U.S. dollars. Inflation and unemployment were on the rise, while at the same time, productivity and the standard of living of the population declined. In the shops there were fewer and fewer articles for general consumption. Tito's death in 1980 meant the beginning of the end of Yugoslavia.

The Constitutional Development of the Yugoslav Federation, 1945–1980

The new federation "of equal and brotherly" nations was actually already formed during World War II in 1943. The formation of the Democratic Federal Yugoslavia (DFY) at the Second Conference of AVNOJ in November 1943 and the decision on cooperation between the partisan movement and the king's Yugoslav Government-in-Exile started the process and initiated this new period in the country's historic development. This act was seen as the consensual decision of Yugoslav nations for a common life in the future and the realization of their right to self-determination. Observed from the ethnic perspective, the formation of the federation, despite all limitations and internal contradictions, meant a step toward decentralization and democratization.

The Constitution of the Federal People's Republic of Yugoslavia (FPRY) of 1946 introduced the slightly adapted Soviet model of the federation. The communist ideology dominated all spheres of life, including ethnic relations. Following its prewar orientation, the KPJ insisted on ethnic equality and the protection of minorities. However, the monopoly of power of the KPJ reduced the constitutionally provided autonomy of ethno-nations and federal units (People's Republics). Considering the official ideology that the national liberation war and "socialist revolution" resolved all ethnic conflicts, the constitution provided no formal mechanism for the management of ethnic relations and conflicts, which was also a common characteristic of all subsequent federal Yugoslav constitutions. The official ideology and those who espoused it did not want to admit that ethnic conflicts were normal phenomena in a country as ethnically and culturally diverse as Yugoslavia. However, this deficiency of Yugoslav constitutions was replaced by informal mechanisms for the management and resolution of (ethnic) conflicts. Namely, until the 1980s, Tito, as the undisputed Yugoslav leader, and the KPJ intervened informally and were successful in the management and/or resolution of (occasional) ethnic conflicts when they escalated. All the tragic consequences of the previously mentioned deficiency of Yugoslav constitutions became obvious in the 1990s, when both abovementioned informal mechanisms that had intervened successfully in the past ceased to exist.

The Constitutional Law of 1953, the new federal constitution (Constitution of the Socialist Federal Republic of Yugoslavia) of 1963, and constitutional amendments (1967, 1968, 1971), as well as the simultaneous changes of the individual republics' constitutions, were results of dynamic political and constitutional reforms in Yugoslavia after the introduction of self-management. The initial idea of self-management was that workers themselves, through workers' councils in factories, should manage their own factories. However, self-management soon spread to all spheres of social and political life and became a universal social and political ideology and system—called the political system of socialist self-management. To underline differences between the Soviet system and socialist self-management, the name Federal People's Republic of Yugoslavia was officially changed to the Socialist Federal Republic of Yugoslavia (SFRY) in 1963.

The ideology of self-management also necessitated a new role of the KPJ, which renamed itself the League of Communists of Yugoslavia (LCY) at its seventh congress in Ljubljana in 1958. The published *Program of the LCY* included a special chapter, "Federation and Relations between the Nations of Yugoslavia." It stressed the importance of the principle of the self-determination of ethno-nations, which had been emphasized by the national liberation struggle as the basis for the creation of the Yugoslav federation. Underlining the importance of the principles of equality and "brotherhood and unity of the Yugoslav nations" as well as the protection of national minorities, the program ascertained that for the implementation of the actual equality of ethno-nations, economic equality was essential. The program criticized nationalism, defined as "the remains of the bourgeois nationalism" incompatible with self-management and democratic socialism, and warned against its destructive potential. A utopian projection presented in the Program was that the newly developed self-management would resolve all conflicts, including ethnic conflicts, thereby rising above the conflicted class society. Very soon, however, developments showed a different reality of aggravating ethnic relations in the 1960s.

Constitutional amendments in the late 1960s strengthened decentralization and democratization by increasing the autonomy and independence of federal units (Socialist Republics, or SRs, and Socialist Autonomous Provinces, or SAPs) and by stressing the importance of ethnic pluralism. The constitution defined SRs as nation-states "based on the sovereignty of the people and the power of and self-management by the working class and working people." As such, they were "socialist, self-managing communities of the working people and citizens and of nations and nationalities having equal rights" (Article 3). Both SAPs within the SR of Serbia, were not defined as states, but only as "autonomous, socialist, self-managing democratic socio-political communities," which were to provide for the ethnic equality and preservation of ethnic plurality of these multiethnic communities" (Article 4). However, the important role of the federal center of government was preserved throughout the period. Despite frequent changes, the constitutional and normative regulation had not succeeded in introducing mechanisms for the management of ethnic relations and conflicts that would ensure the functioning of the system in times of aggravated social and ethnic relations, which was, in turn, proved by the subsequent course of events.

Considering the regulation of ethnic relations, the Constitution of the SFRY of 1974 followed the trends started by the constitutional amendments in the 1960s and early 1970s. The constitution emphasized ethnic, but also social, pluralism and (to a certain degree) enabled its manifestations in the political system. It further decentralized the federal system and increased the autonomy and independence of federal units, SRs and SAPs. The constitution defined SRs as nation-states—"states based on the sovereignty of the people and the power of and self-management by the working class and working people." As such, they were "socialist, self-managing communities of the working people and citizens and of nations and nationalities having equal rights" (Article 3). Both Socialist Autonomous Provinces (Kosovo and Vojvodina) within the Socialist Republic of

Serbia were not defined as states but only as "autonomous, socialist, self-managing democratic socio-political communities," which were to provide for the ethnic equality and preservation of ethnic plurality of these multiethnic communities (Article 4).

Both chambers of the Assembly of the SFRY, the Federal Chamber and the Chamber of Republics and Provinces, reflected a federal structure on the basis of parity. Each republic, irrespective of its size, elected thirty delegates into the Federal Chamber, and each SAP elected twenty delegates (Article 291). The Chamber of Republics and Provinces was composed of delegations of the assemblies of SRs and SAPs, and those delegates retained their tenure in their respective republics or province assemblies (Article 292). These solutions were introduced to ensure the equality of the republics (as nation-states) as well as of all the nations and nationalities (national minorities) in both chambers of the assembly of the SFRY. The constitution defined which matters were to be decided by the consensus of the assemblies of all SRs and SAPs. A form of the minority veto was given to the SRs and SAPs to ensure their equality (Articles 289, 295–296, 298–304).

In order to ensure equality of federal units, nations, and nationalities, the parity structure was also introduced in the presidency of the SFRY, which was the collective head of the state. Additionally, the principle was adopted that the federal and ethnic structure of Yugoslavia should be considered in the formation of the Federal Executive Council, which was the federal government (Article 348 and Amendment XLIII, 1988).

The territory of the Yugoslav federation was composed of the territories of the SRs. The borders and territory of a certain SR could only be changed with the consent of the respective republic (Article 5), thereby giving these borders a special status similar to the status of international borders.

The fact that the federal constitution of 1974 defined SRs as nation-states based on the sovereignty of the people and nations with their own nationalities was especially important for their future development. The republics were given practically all the attributes of statehood, from entirely symbolic ones (a national anthem, a coat of arms, a flag, etc.) to the entire structure of state authority bodies, which were sovereign within their own spheres. The rights, duties, and powers of republics were determined and regulated by the republics' constitutions, whose only requirement was that they were not to be in contradiction with the federal constitution.

Although formally decentralized even with the introduction of certain confederate solutions, the former Yugoslavia was more centralized than anticipated by those who instituted the constitutional system. President Tito and the League of Communists of Yugoslavia (LCY), as the transformed Communist Party of Yugoslavia (KPJ), were the main integrative factors and played the central role in political processes. Their functioning was mostly informal, as the constitution did not determine precisely their roles and ways of exercising their influence. The constitution did not create any formal institutions of the political system that could have assumed the informal roles and functions of President Tito and the LCY in the management of conflicts and in ensuring the necessary cohesion within the system. This deficit became especially obvious in the 1980s and in the beginning of the 1990s, following the death of President Tito and the dismantling of the LCY.

Yugoslavia: Prelude to Dissolution, 1980–1989

After the death of President Tito, the Yugoslav communist leadership tried, under the slogan "Also after Tito—Tito," to continue the internal and external policies of Tito's regime. Retaining the old system in Yugoslavia was no longer possible, however, because the state had no leader who could, with Tito's charisma, paper over the regional differences in the state and in interethnic relations. The old-style Marxist politicians were not even aware of Yugoslavia's problems and condition, least of all the 20 billion-dollar external debt of the country. In autumn of 1981 the country found itself near bankruptcy, and the communist leadership established a commission of 300 politicians and scholars to write a plan for a way out of the deep crisis. This commission did not do any good, as its members just wrote long texts. The plans had no common sense; the commission did not change the cornerstones of the economic system. The economic agony of the state continued and also grew into a political crisis.

The leadership of the LCY did not like the demands of the intellectuals, who asked for more rights, especially the repeal of Article 133 of the Penal Code of Yugoslavia, which put the brakes on freedom of speech and press. At this time of deep economic crises, Slovene writers published some books on forbidden themes, such as the extermination of approximately 12,000 members of Slovene military formations (Domobranci) that had collaborated with the occupiers right after World War II, the "Stalinist" judicial processes, Goli otok (Goli Island) and other communist resocialization camps where those who supported Stalin against Tito were confined, the men and women of culture who were turned into nonpersons because of their opposition to the communist regime, etc. The West, for its strategic interests after the split with Stalin, had supported an independent and stable Yugoslavia, tolerating such repression against the opposition to the regime.

In March 1981 ethnic unrest began in Kosovo, the least developed region in Yugoslavia, which experienced especially high unemployment and difficult economic conditions. Increasingly, Serbs and Albanians, the majority population in the region, believed that they could not live together in a common homeland. The unrest of the Albanian population was seen by the state as "antisocialist" and "nationalist," and the state's reaction was to handle it the way totalitarian states handled the unrest of their populations: using militia, army, and tanks. Such ruthless repression was also used with Slovenes and Croats (on a smaller scale), whose demands for greater democracy and a higher level of independence were not liked in Belgrade.

The federal government (Federal Executive Council), led from May 1982 on by Milka Planinc (a Croat female politician who came to power in Croatia after the purges against liberals at the beginning of the 1970s), tried to solve the country's economic problems with the so-called program of economic stabilization, which attempted to promote a more active role for the Yugoslav economy in the international economy. Her government had to put in place many unpopular measures in the course of trying to pay off the external debt; that meant a blow to the "normal" consumer society developed after the past three decades (i.e., some products, such as a very popular brand of coffee, were in short supply.) These measures included the unpopular rationing of gasoline and the institution of exit taxes ("temporary down-payments" that were later returned) for each border crossing, introduced to discourage citizens from going and buying consumer goods in Italy, Austria, and Greece. People disliked these measures for inflicting damage, especially to Slovenia's policy toward its national minorities in neighboring countries. Slovenia wanted to protect these people's ethnic identity by strengthening ties through cultural exchanges and economic cooperation, and Planinc's new measures made that difficult.

Although these measures led to a surplus of 300 million U.S. dollars in the balance of (foreign) trade, they did not reform the so-called "agreement" economy, which was not adjusted to international markets. Following the principles of self-management, the "agreement" economy, in determining economic policy and conditions, used agreements between different kinds of organizations of associated labor, SRs, SAPs, and local communities. The system and conditions in the country did not change at

all. State institutions, especially the army, did not join the austerity measures that affected the people, whose lives—as did that of the state—depended on credit. The country was, in 1982, able to pay only the interest
on 20 billion U.S. dollars loaned by foreign creditors. Galloping inflation
caused social unrest. There were more and more strikes, and one million
people were unemployed. In such a situation, every republic tried to protect its own interests in spite of the fact that the republics all loudly
proclaimed their adherence to "self-management and basic principles of
revolution."

Due to measures of Planinc's government, the country was able to pay
off the interest and part of the principal on the foreign debt. However, the
Yugoslav leadership decided that a change was necessary. The new government of Branko Mikulić, a Bosnian Serb who became a federal prime
minister in 1986, achieved no successes—especially with the economy.
Parts of the country were brought to the verge of economic collapse, because certain giant firms failed. Politics and politicians were still reigning
over the economy, which curtailed any serious economic reform.

During Mikulić's government, federal centralism was on the rise, as
was the political interference of the Yugoslav army, which even got financing outside the budget with a special tax. During 1986 two traditional options for the future of Yugoslavia reemerged: The authoritarian and centralist approach, demanding an even stronger monopoly of the federal
communist leadership, was advocated by new Serb leader Slobodan
Milošević, and the other option, which argued for democratization and
decentralization, initially just for the increased autonomy of the republics
and later for confederalization, was championed by Milan Kučan, a
Slovene politician. When tensions intensified between advocates of these
opposing options, there was no room for compromise. Soon these conflicts grew into conflicts between republics and became perceived as ethnic conflicts. Republican leaderships, especially the Serb one, used their
respective nationalisms for the mobilization of political support.

The new prime minister, Ante Marković, a Croat appointed in 1989,
tried to reform Yugoslavia with help of the West. He wanted to introduce
a market economy and a multiparty political system; his major success
was the introduction of a "convertible currency." This meant that the
country officially declared convertibility of its currency, the dinar, not
only within a country, but also abroad. It became possible to sell and buy
dinars at a determined official exchange rate in banks and exchange offices. However, there was no political and social consensus, which was
necessary for the success of the proposed economic and political reforms.

The economic, social, and political crisis was aggravated throughout the 1980s, and, consequently, differences, quarrels, and nationalism(s) in Yugoslavia continued to escalate.

In such a situation, the ruling regime, initially unwilling to acknowledge the existence of this crisis, was unable to undertake the necessary reforms of the existing political system. Although changes were urgently needed, it was impossible to secure the consent of all the federal units, which was necessary for the adoption of constitutional amendments. As previously mentioned, there were two conflicting concepts abut the future development of Yugoslavia. The centralization concept urged for a stronger federation, reduced autonomy and/or the independence of federal units, a (re)centralized political system, and also a stronger role (monopoly) for the LCY. The decentralization option saw a solution in the further decentralization of the federation, increased autonomy and independence of federal units, reduction (and, ultimately, abolition) of the political monopoly of the LCY, introduction of political (party) pluralism, and further democratization of the existing political system. Finally, a compromise solution was adopted that did not solve any of the major problems. These Amendments of 1988, however, enabled the beginning of democratization and the necessary economic and political reforms. In this context, these amendments introduced certain elements of centralization at the level of the federation, such as the provision for special stable financing of the federal Yugoslav People's Army, slightly changed spheres of operation and functioning of federal bodies, etc. (Amendments XXXVII–XLI). Although the level of centralization was much smaller than that advocated by centralists, these amendments did not include any proposals of decentralists.

The subsequent attempts and proposals to amend the federal constitution and reform the political system (in the years 1989–1991) all failed due to a lack of political consensus. Differences and conflicts between the two opposing political camps were constantly growing, until finally these differences completely paralyzed the existing political system. Differences among SRs and SAPs, which became especially evident in the different level of democratization in every federal unit in the late 1980s, actually led to the existence of a somehow different (political) system in every federal unit.

Long before the actual disintegration happened, the process of disintegration of Yugoslavia had already started. In reality the constitutional reforms in republics that were to harmonize the republic constitutions with the federal constitution, as amended in 1988, led to substantial changes exceeding the initially defined aim. The adoption of the new constitutions of the republics of Serbia and Croatia, and almost 100 amendments to the constitution of Slovenia, changed relations in the federation and changed the federation itself substantially in the beginning of the 1990s, although there were no new formal changes to the federal constitution.

Changes in Ethnic Structure of the Population after World War II

The consequences of the emigration of the Germans immediately after World War II were seen the most in Vojvodina, where South Slavs started to immigrate to and settle the farms where Germans had lived before. In the process of the organized colonization of Vojvodina, 250,000 persons came here from war-devastated parts of Yugoslavia, where soil was not as suitable for farming as in Vojvodina. New colonists, mostly Serbs and Montenegrins from Montenegro and Bosnia and Herzegovina, often did not know how to farm on the fertile plains of Vojvodina. The authorities did not care that the colonists had problems adjusting to the lifestyle in the new area of settlement; they achieved their goal to change by changing the ethnic situation in favor of the Serbs in Vojvodina, as the colonists between 1945 and 1948 represented 13.6 percent of its total population.

Other significant changes in ethnic structure occurred in regions that had belonged to Italy prior to World War II. Following the Paris Peace Conference of 1947 the border between Italy and Yugoslavia was drawn in 1954 by the London Memorandum of Understanding, which in its Special Statute also determined the rights of national minorities. (However, it was not until 1975 that the Agreements of Osimo finally determined the borderline between Yugoslavia and Italy.) On this territory—which encompasses today's Western Slovenia (the regions of so-called Primorska) and Istria with Reka, the city of Zadar, and the islands of Cres, Krk, Lastovo, and Palagruža in Croatia—changes had already occurred during the period between the two world wars because of the ethnic policy of fascist Italy. Between 1947 and 1954, 300,000 persons emigrated from the frontier area to Italy and overseas, especially to Australia. Among them were 200,000 Italians and 100,000 Slovenes and Croats who opposed the communist regime in Yugoslavia. These numerous emigrants caused a very strong reduction in the population as a whole (in the commune of Izola/Isola alone, for example, by more then 40 percent). From the county of Koper alone, the number of emigrants reached more than 25,000 (among them 21,200 Italians, 3,700 Slovenes, and more than 100 Croats).

In their place, Slovenes and emigrants from the other republics of Yugo-slavia settled. Between the years 1955–1959, a full 19,700 people immi-grated to the area, 13,600 from other parts of Slovenia and 6,100 from the other republics of Yugoslavia.

Soon after World War II ended, mass emigration of ethnic Turks from the cities in Macedonia, Kosovo, and Sandžak occurred. On the basis of a special agreement between the governments of Yugoslavia and Turkey that allowed for emigration of Turks to Turkey, between 230,000 and 300,000 Turks, Albanians, and Serbo-Croat-speaking Muslims, who were considered ethnic Turks by the authorities, emigrated to Turkey until 1971. However, there are no official data regarding how many of these emigrations were stimulated by the Yugoslav authorities. After World War II some emigrations affected all ethnic groups in Yugoslavia, and a few groups were reduced substantially. However, Yugoslavia remained a multinational state in which no ethnic nation had a majority. (This was different from the Soviet Union or Czechoslovakia, where one ethnic na-tion represented a majority of the population.) In Kosovo, for example, the Albanian minority was a local majority. Nevertheless, a comparison of data of the pre- and post–World War II censuses shows that these forced, semiforced, and semivoluntary migrations and emigrations substantially changed the ethnic structure of some regions—as well as Yugoslavia as a whole.

There was an increased share of the Yugoslav nationalities and Gypsies (Roma), and the percentages of some ethnic minorities (e.g., Germans, Romanians, Vlachs, Jews, etc.) decreased. A relatively large German mi-nority almost disappeared. The number and percentage of Slovenes and Croats increased also, due to the inclusion of a territory that before World War II had belonged to Italy.

After World War II, when the migrations ended by the mid 1950s, there seemed to be no significant ethnic conflict in Yugoslavia—with the excep-tion of ones in Kosovo and a part of Macedonia. However, even these struggles in Kosovo and Macedonia had more of the character of strug-gles among political elites. It looked as though the actual situation was in agreement with the official political ideology that all ethnic conflict had been resolved in the national liberation war. Other views might be that prewar and interwar ethnic conflicts entered their dormant stage. Simul-taneously, internal migrations and colonization resulted in certain con-flicts between the autochthonous population and immigrants of different linguistic, ethnic, or religious backgrounds; these might be observed as ethnic conflicts. Although occasionally ethnic conflicts and nationalism in

Yugoslavia escalated, to most observers the ethnic situation seemed rather good until the 1980s, when the situation worsened rapidly.

This, however, does not mean that the ethnic structure had not changed in Yugoslavia. The bureaucrats, who invented new ethnic categories in censuses, contributed to these changes. An example was the introduction of the category "Yugoslav" (by ethnicity) in the census of 1971 as a result of the "victory" of "unitarists" at the time. In the census of 1971, the categories based on the census directions also included: "did not declare themselves on the basis of Article 170 of the Constitution of the Socialist Federal Republic of Yugoslavia" and "declared themselves according to the Region where they lived." The introduction of these census categories caused reactions, especially among Croats, Muslims, and some minority ethnic groups, who were convinced that this categorization made their positions worse while bettering the Serbs' status and their unitarist aspirations in Yugoslavia.

The majority of the population who identified with one of the above newly created categories lived in the territories where unitaristic and centralistic visions for the future of Yugoslavia were supported by the populace, especially the Serbs. This was true particularly in parts of Croatia, Bosnia and Herzegovina, and Vojvodina as well as in other Serbo-Croatian speaking territories with a large percentage of Serbs. In Slovenia, Macedonia, and Kosovo, where the majority of the population opposed the policy of centralism in Yugoslavia, there were also fewer people who identified with these new categories.

Until the beginning of the 1980s, the changes in ethnic structure of certain regions of Yugoslavia were based predominantly on a large natural increase of population (e.g., in Kosovo), on economic emigration to Western Europe and overseas (eastern Serbia and Macedonia), and on internal migrations within Yugoslavia, especially from the economically less developed southern republics and Kosovo to Slovenia, northern Croatia, and the capital, Belgrade.

The intensity of emigration to Western Europe and overseas was influenced after 1960 by many factors, such as the lack of natural and economic potential, the density of population, and the level of economic development of individual regions. This economic emigration from Yugoslavia, which was partially temporary and partially permanent, did not affect all regions in the same way. At the beginning of the 1960s, most migrants came from economically less developed regions of Croatia. Later, this process encompassed other regions of Croatia and, later still, other Yugoslav republics and autonomous regions. These were migrants whose intention was to earn "bread with butter," as they were qualified workers and peasants from well-developed agrarian, but also industrial, regions. Unlike other communist regimes in Eastern Europe, the Yugoslav regime supported these emigration movements, as it hoped that they would make it easier for the regime to deal with economic problems and especially unemployment at home. These expectations were fulfilled only partially because the economic crisis in the 1970s caused the Western European countries to close their doors to economic immigration.

The number of temporary workers moving abroad from Yugoslavia reached its peak in 1973 (1.4 million); after 1973 their number started to fall. Because of immigration laws that restricted employment of immigrant workers in some Western European countries, around 400,000 of them returned to Yugoslavia. However, according to the Census of 1981 there were still 875,000 temporary workers abroad (including family members). Most were from Croatia (24 percent), followed by Serbia proper—without the autonomous regions of Kosovo and Vojvodina (23.2 percent)—and Bosnia and Herzegovina (20.9 percent). The smallest contingents of temporary workers abroad were contributed by Slovenia (6.1 percent) and Montenegro (2.2 percent). Most temporary workers from Yugoslavia lived in the Federal Republic of Germany, in Austria, and in France, but they could be found in every Western European country.

Even larger were the internal (economic) migrations within Yugoslavia. In these migrations almost 2 million people, or 9 percent of the Yugoslav population, participated. These migrations, which were until the beginning of the 1980s economically motivated, greatly influenced the ethnic map of Yugoslavia. For example, the data from 1981 show that living in other parts of Yugoslavia were 400,000 people who were born in Bosnia and Herzegovina and that there were 60,000 people in parts of Yugoslavia outside Montenegro who had been born in Montenegro.

These internal migrations were key to changes in the ethnic map of many regions; some regions were marked by emigration, while others by immigration. Different stages of economic development of the regions were the primary reasons for different migration patterns. There were also other specific motivations. Migrants moved primarily toward the regions where there were better employment opportunities. Ethnic identities of prospective migrants also played a role in deciding the region of immigration. A part of the migration flow was toward republics' urban centers in the context of accelerated urbanization. Important also were the migrations of army officers, (federal) bureaucrats, and their families—throughout the country and especially to Belgrade—directed by the Yugoslav leadership in the name of "brotherhood and unity."

Census data show that all regions of Yugoslavia were ethnically mixed—at least to a certain extent—throughout its existence. Ethnically more homogenous regions, where 90 percent and more of the population belonged to one ethnic group, could be found only in Slovenia, Croat Zagorje, Herzegovina, the central part of Serbia, western and central Montenegro, a part of Metohija, and western Macedonia.

Histories of Individual Yugoslav Nations

Slovenes

Although the partisan army liberated most of the Slovene ethnic territories by the end of World War II, the borders with Austria and Hungary remained unchanged. Yugoslavia gained only some territory (the Slovene coastland and Istria) in the west that had belonged to Italy in the period between World War I and World War II. However, the city of Trieste remained Italian when the Free Territory of Trieste established by the peace treaty with Italy was divided between Yugoslavia and Italy by the "Memorandum of Understanding Between the Governments of Italy, the United Kingdom, the United States and Yugoslavia Regarding The Free Territory of Trieste" in 1954. However, it took more than twenty years to finally determine the border between Italy and Yugoslavia (this was accomplished by the Treaty of Osimo in 1975). All together, more than 200,000 ethnic Slovenes remained outside the borders of Yugoslavia after World War II as minorities in Austria, Hungary, and Italy. The protection of Slovene national minorities by the neighboring countries was always an important issue for Slovenia, which tried to put pressure upon the Yugoslav foreign policy for the improvement of the situation and protection of Slovene minorities abroad.

The peace treaty "Memorandum" and some bilateral treaties between Italy and Yugoslavia also included provisions about the protection of the Slovene minority. However, these provisions were never fully implemented. After years of requests, the special law on the protection of the Slovene national minority in Italy was adopted as late as 2001. Deriving from the constitutional arrangements in Austria-Hungary (1867) and from peace treaties after World War I, the international and constitutional protection of the Slovene minority in Austria was provided for by the Austrian State Treaty of 1955, especially by its Article 7. However, even the Austrian constitutional court has established a few times that Austria failed to realize these provisions fully. For these reasons it is not surprising

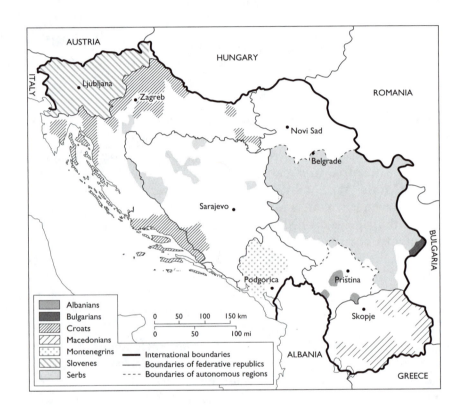

Ethnic Structure of Yugoslavia in 1961

Because of the emigration of population from Yugoslavia and mass internal migrations, the number of homogeneous territories (where one ethno-nation constituted more than 90 percent of the population) reduced very quickly.

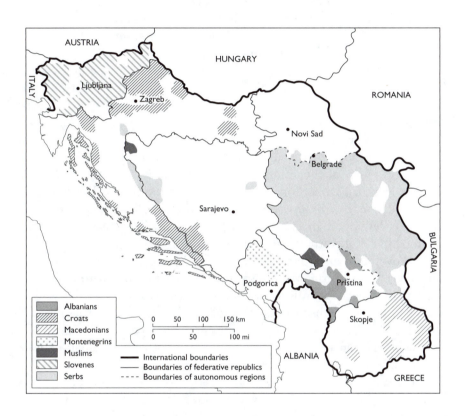

Ethnic Structure of Yugoslavia in 1981

At the beginning of the 1990s only one-third of the former Yugoslavia consisted of homogeneous territories.

that the Slovene minorities in Italy and Austria constantly demanded that their minority rights be fully implemented and protected. Nevertheless, during the Cold War the situation of the Slovene national minority living in an underdeveloped part of Hungary behind the Iron Curtain was much worse than that of the Slovenes in Italy and Austria. The situation of this Slovene minority had started to become better with the gradual liberalization in Hungary in the 1980s, and it improved substantially in the 1990s when a bilateral agreement on the protection of national minorities was signed between Slovenia and Hungary.

However, the Slovenes in Yugoslavia also found themselves in a contradictory position after World War II. On the basis of the constitution of 1946 they gained the status of a constitutive part of the Yugoslav federation. Formally, Slovenes gained their own state; their independence was, however, only an illusion. By the end of World War II the Slovene partisan units were already integrated into the Yugoslav Army. Later, Slovenia had to give up much of the autonomy and independence established by the Slovene National Liberation Movement during World War II, when independent Slovene economic, social, and cultural policies and institutions had been developed. In accordance with the federal constitution, Slovenia retained its self-governance only in education, culture, and health care.

In Slovenia as elsewhere in Yugoslavia, the communists took over all the powers after World War II. First they settled accounts with their political opponents. As mentioned previously, up to 12,000 members of the so-called home defense forces (Domobranci) returned to Yugoslavia by the Allied forces in the spring of 1945 were killed without due process of law. This was seen as a necessary precondition for the consolidation of the new regime.

The reconstruction of the war-torn country started immediately upon its liberation. Great troubles soon developed, as Slovenia had to help with the reconstruction of less developed parts of Yugoslavia by giving materials, money, and professionals. The philosophy was to equalize the level of economic development of the whole country (i.e., the better-developed parts of the country should wait for the rest of the country to develop to the same level of economic development). When, by the mid-1950s, the development of Slovenia in some sectors of the economy already started to lag behind the development in other parts of Yugoslavia, intolerance toward "Byzantine" Belgrade showed up again among Slovenes (and also Croats). Slovenes demanded that the available resources should be divided and administered in a better way. When a Slovene member of the parliament asked where the money for an undeveloped region in Yugoslavia was spent, the answer was: "It is your duty to give; it is up to us to spend the way we know!" (Tripalo, 1990, 42).

The conflict soon became real when in Slovenia, which gave 10 percent of its GNP to the federal government, the first strike after the war broke out in the coal mines of Trbovlje, Zagorje, and Hrastnik in the early 1950s. With their decision to strike, the miners surprised the political elite, who had to try to answer the question of why it was possible for the strike to occur in a country where the so-called people's democracy reigned.

As always during their history, the Slovenes were unhappy with the fact that the Slovene language was not seen as an official language in the federal army and in other federal institutions. When, in the mid-1950s, the intention of the federal authorities to create a unified cultural community with only one Serbo-Croatian language became apparent, this upset the Slovene political elite, intellectuals, and, above all, writers. Writers—who, during 1956–1957 got into polemics with their Serb colleagues—stressed that a search for "general Yugoslav criteria" in culture and "a unified socialist culture" had forgotten about the fact that there were different nations living in Yugoslavia who spoke different languages and who had, because of different and divided historical development, different cultural traditions. So, as many times before in history, the cultural questions and language became symbols in the defense of the independence of Slovenia and the Slovene nation.

In the 1960s the Slovenes started to demand the introduction of a market economy that would be directed toward exports, a lesser role for the federal authorities, and more responsibilities for the republics. In Yugoslavia, Slovenia was the most economically advanced among the republics. Productivity in Slovenia was four to five times the productivity of the most backward parts of the country. Slovenia had been providing 30 percent of the convertible exports of Yugoslavia, and wages in Slovenia were up to three times higher than in the least developed parts of the country, which provoked some dissatisfaction among others in Yugoslavia.

Slovene politicians tried diplomatically to hide their reservations about federal policy and about Tito, so that this would not hinder them in building a society as independent from the Federation as possible. The younger generation of Slovene communists, who tried to introduce more order and "European behavior" in public life, were especially serving this goal. These were the so-called party liberals. The ideals about a more independent role for the republics, the necessity of reforms in the economy, and a greater plurality of society were by the end of 1960s demanded the most forcefully by the then-president of the Slovene government, Stane Kavčič. While defending Slovene interests he soon came into conflict with federal authorities, especially during the period of the so-called road scandal, when the federal authority did not give Slovenia the money promised for building a freeway from Nova Gorica to Šentilj, spending it instead for less important road projects in Serbia and Bosnia. Slovenes developed a slogan, "Avtocesta Šentilj-Nova Gorica, naša je pravica!" ("It is our right to build a freeway from Šentilj to Nova Gorica!") (Ramet, 1992, 9). Later Kavčič wrote: "a road scandal was the first great uprising of those in Slovenia who wanted more real and less formal democracy and wanted to weaken centralism in the federation and strengthen independence of republics" (Kavčič, 1988, 430). Because of this scandal, Kavčič and his collaborators had to resign. The old-style communist politicians, dependable followers of the federal authorities such as Franc Popit, came to power again in Slovenia and marked the "leaden" 1970s.

Soon after the death of Josip Broz–Tito in 1980, discussions developed among the Slovene communists on how to combine freedom and socialism. Dr. Joža Vilfan started the polemics, and Stane Dolanc suggested an open discussion about democratic socialism. Even more vigorous discussions started within the youth organization—the Union of Socialist Youth of Slovenia—that initiated the creation of "new social (peace, ecological, feminist, etc.) movements." Discussions on democratization became popular, especially among intellectuals but also among (more liberal) politicians. In 1987 intellectual and political debates were also stirred up by issue no. 57 of the literary journal *Nova Revija*, which published a Slovene National Program demanding democracy and independence. A few youth-oriented newspapers (weeklies) such as *Tribuna, Katedra,* and *Mladina* criticized even more aggressively the Yugoslav People's Army, which spent 62 percent of the federal budget.

An already excited segment of the population in Slovenia became even more agitated when the federal authorities proposed a reform of the educational system, according to which the teaching of subjects such as literature, history, and geography was to be standardized in all schools in Yugoslavia. Those suggestions were initially hidden from the Slovene public, but when the Slovene cultural leaders learned about them, they rebelled and demanded that the Slovene authorities fight strongly against those ideas, which did not have anything in common with a very-much-propagated principle of national equality in Yugoslavia. These discussions showed that the League of Communists of Slovenia had no say on national policy in Yugoslavia in this regard. The federal authorities fought against democratization of Slovene society with sharp protests, which were addressed toward all Slovenes. The sharpest critique was from the Yugoslav People's Army, which in each Slovene complaint imagined an attack on the communist system and the Yugoslav federation. In May 1988 it started a process against the "counterrevolution" in Slovenia, with a trial against the "gang of four" (three civilians, Janez Janša, David Tasić, and Franci Zavrl, and a junior army officer, Ivan Borštner). They were accused of high treason for revealing a military secret. The trial was conducted in the Serbo-Croatian language before the military court in Ljubljana.

This process provoked mass revolt in Slovenia, and the public started to ask why Slovenia should stay in such a Yugoslavia. Also, Slovene communists under the leadership of the liberal Milan Kučan reacted, and in January 1989 the League of Communists of Slovenia, as the first then reigning communist party in eastern Europe, gave up their political monopoly in favor of political pluralism and democratization. The opposition, so far organized within the official umbrella (sociopolitical) organization—the Socialist Alliance of Working People of Slovenia—reacted immediately by establishing new independent political parties.

The first result of the emerging political pluralism in Slovenia was the so-called Majniška deklaracija (May Declaration) of 8 May 1989. With this declaration the representatives of the Slovene Society of Writers and some opposition parties (the Slovene Democratic Union, the Slovene Christian-Social Movement, the Social-Democratic Union of Slovenia) demanded a sovereign Slovene state that would be able to decide independently about its links with Yugoslavia and other nations in a renewed Europe. The less radical Temeljna listina Slovenije (Charter of Slovenia), issued by the communist authorities, still emphasized a reformed Yugoslavia as the best solution for the Slovene national question. As a result of the pressures from Belgrade authorities and the Yugoslav Army, the Slovene opposition and the League of Communists of Slovenia became more united in their fight against the policies of the federal authorities. Amendments to the constitution of Slovenia of 27 September 1989 gave even more political independence to Slovenia and stressed the unequivocal right of Slovenia to self-determination and secession. Three months later the communist-controlled Slovene Assembly voted for a law on political parties and elections that legalized a multiparty political system in Slovenia. The opposition then formed new parties, and, by the end of November 1989, united into the Democratic Opposition of Slovenia (DEMOS), with the intent of winning the elections against the ruling League of Communists of Slovenia.

Because the League of Communists of Yugoslavia, which was completely under the influence of Serb policy, did not tolerate radical political changes, the Slovene communists left the Fourteenth (Extraordinary) Congress of the LCY, which was the highest party organ, on 20 January 1990. This meant the end of the LCY, which started to disintegrate after Croat delegates also left the Congress. The disintegration of the LCY cut the most important political link between Slovenia and the federated Yugoslavia. In January 1990 the first multiparty elections since World War II were scheduled for April 1990. This showed that Slovenia wanted to (re)gain a place in the family of democratic states.

Croats

Yugoslav communist authorities tried to solve the national question in Yugoslavia by copying the Soviet federal model. They wanted to draw the frontiers among six federal units—republics—in a way that would satisfy the national aspirations of all Yugoslav nations. However, the existing ethnically mixed population made this goal impossible. Therefore, new frontiers among the republics divided anew the areas of settlement of some Yugoslav nations, among them the area of settlement of Croats. In addition to the People's Republic of Croatia, Croats also lived in Bosnia and Herzegovina (Posavina and south Herzegovina), Montenegro (Boka Kotorska), and Vojvodina (Srem and Bačka). At the same time the areas of continuos Serb autochthonous settlement (Kninska krajina, western Slavonia, and Baranja) became parts of Croatia. The federal authorities did not consider these arrangements a problem, believing that ethnic conflicts were second-rate "bourgeois" problems. However, history proved them wrong, and Serb-Croat relations remained central issues (and problems) in post–World War II Yugoslavia until its dissolution in the beginning of the 1990s.

Most of the Croats did not like the measures of the federal authorities that interfered with all forms of (social) life. Bad feelings were even stronger after the arrest of the archbishop of Zagreb, Alojzije Stepinac, in 1946 and his being sentenced to sixteen years in prison. The proceedings against Stepinac, in addition to numerous condemnations of the Vatican and the West in general, also had another consequence: the Catholic church became a symbol of Croat nationalism. Even more important was the fact that Croat-Serb relations were strained. In an interview for the

Belgrade newspaper *Politika* at the beginning of 1950s, even the leading Croat communist politician, Vladimir Bakarić, confessed: "Croat-Serb antipathy . . . was very much present . . ." This was confirmed by demonstrations in Zagreb after Zagreb's soccer team, Dinamo, won a soccer match against Belgrade's Crvena zvezda. A Slovene writer, Edvard Kocbek, commented prophetically: "In Belgrade the hatred towards Croats, in Zagreb towards Serbs reigned, that they would in the beginning of the war or state disorder . . . shoot at each other, slaughter . . . and torment . . . as they had never (done) in history . . . We are all sleeping on the volcano, which could erupt with the smallest shake . . ." (Kocbek, 1986, 47).

The conditions became even more complicated when economic troubles developed in Yugoslavia. The Croats were (like the Slovenes) disturbed by their required expensive contributions to a federal budget in which they had no control. Although Yugoslavia saw the economic reforms of the mid-1960s as a partial success, in Croatia the results of these economic reforms were disappointing. The Croats found their expectations often unfulfilled, and, in some cases, their economic position actually deteriorated. Leading Croat economists claimed, further, that economic resources and credits were more concentrated in Belgrade after the reform (specifically in 1967) than before (Djodan, 1968, 306). It was impossible to divorce economics from politics because it seemed clear to an increasing number of Croats that not only were they being exploited, but they were also being exploited as the Croats as a specific ethnic group. At the same time, discussions began on the harm done as a result of federal policies favoring the accelerated development of the underdeveloped areas in Yugoslavia, fostering the domination of Yugoslavia by Belgrade, and creating the economic and demographic impoverishment of Croatia. According to Croat nationalists, the Serb threat to Croatia was thought to take three forms: (1) the demographic displacement of Croats by Serbs, (2) catering to Dalmatian sentiment (as a specific regional identity that should weaken the identification of the Dalmatian Croats with Croatia) in order to split Croatia in two, and (3) the Serbization of the Croat language. This was seen as a threat not only by Croat nationalists but also by a majority of Croats.

The large emigration of Croat workers to Western Europe, which had formerly been construed as economic opportunity, was suddenly viewed as a Serb plot to move able-bodied Croats out of their homeland. According to the 1981 census, the number of Croats living in Croatia decreased from 3.51 million in 1971 to 3.45 million in 1981. Simultaneously, the number of the Serbs in the region was increasing due to immigration of

Serbs into Croatia. These Serb immigrants were believed to be taking the places relinquished by the Croat migrants in Western Europe.

Croat nationalists also believed that Dalmatian autonomism was reviving in the late 1960s and that Serb interference was tangibly present. To be sure, the Dalmatians viewed themselves as distinct from other Croats, as they continue to do today—but in most cases this feeling is as harmless as a Texan's pride in being Texan. The Central Committee of the Croat League of Communists took pains to make it absolutely clear that in its view no province in Croatia had any ethnic or historical basis for seeking autonomous status, nor had it the right to do so. It is interesting to note that the same attitude existed toward Istria and Istrian autonomist claims in the 1990s.

Croat grievances were spelled out in 1969 in an article by Petar Šegedin, the president of the Croat Literary Society, for *Kolo* (a bimonthly journal). His chief complaints were: (1) the Croats were treated as illegal residents in their own country; (2) Croat interests were subordinate to the interests of Serbia; (3) to feel Croat under current circumstances was to be worthy of pity; (4) to lose one's language was to lose one's (separate) ethnic identity; (5) the Croat nation had, by various nefarious means, been portrayed as criminal; (6) Croatia was still being equated with the Ustaša; (7) Belgrade was attempting to assimilate the Croats (i.e., to Serbize Croatia); (8) Croatia had become a no-man's land, (i.e., a land that other groups were also claiming as their home); (9) Croatia had lost everything essential to the preservation of its culture (its native Croat intelligentsia had been exterminated, and Croatia was becoming a "scienceless" land of ignorant peasants); and (10) the Serbs had a definite program designed to assimilate the Croat youth and to cause the Croat nation to disappear without a trace (Šuvar, 1974, 222). Stipe Šuvar, a leading Croat communist, said at the time what proved to be right in the 1990s also. Croat nationalism, he said, was characterized by the conviction that all of Croatia's misfortunes were due to the activities of other Yugoslav nations (especially the Serbs); by dependence on, and willingness to serve, various foreign imperialist forces, thus betraying the indigenous peoples; by a mystic belief in the superiority of the Croat nation; and by the tenet that Croat nationalism, like Macedonian, Slovenian, and even Serb (!) nationalism, could only blossom with the carving up of Yugoslavia (Šuvar, 1974, 332–334).

Serb nationalism was a particular problem among the Serbs of Croatia. It escalated in response to the wave of Croat nationalism, partly as an adjunct of the persistent Great Serb chauvinism centered in the Serb republic, and partly as a reflection of the traditional, religiously derived distrust that Croatia's Serbs have long felt toward their Croat cousins. Prosvjeta, the Serb cultural society in Croatia that was created in 1944, started to change its character around 1969 and became a stronghold for Serb nationalists and a forum for former Chetniks. Exploiting this institutional base, Croatia's Serb nationalists sought in the 1970s to create a Serb autonomous province within Croatia and demanded the establishment of a separate network of special Serb schools. Those further to the right even broached the idea of seceding from the Socialist Republic (SR) of Croatia and attaching themselves to the SR of Serbia (Remington, 1977, 209). In one of its last meetings in 1971, the executive committee of Prosvjeta demanded (1) that Croatian and Serb both be recognized as official languages of the SR of Croatia and that the republic's legislative acts be published both in Croatian and in Serb (in the Cyrillic alphabet); (2) that a Chamber for Interethnic Relations be formed within the Croat Sabor (Assembly), with the delegates from each national group chosen exclusively by the members of that group; and (3) that this chamber play a deciding role in all questions relevant to the equality of nationalities and that its decisions require the assent of all delegations (Savez Komunista Hrvatske, 1972, 235–236).

In 1971 Croat nationalism took a dangerous turn, however, riveting its attention on ethnically mixed Bosnia to the south. In the gathering storm, it was inevitable that Croat eyes should turn to Bosnia—a territory that many Croats continued to believe was rightfully theirs. This territory had been a part of Croatia during the heyday of Ustaša in Croatia, and some 20 percent of its population consisted of ethnic Croats. By then it had been openly admitted that, under Aleksandar Ranković, a Serb and for a long time the Yugoslav minister of the interior, the state security apparatus had systematically persecuted the Croats in Bosnia. *Matica Hrvatska*, a central Croat cultural society and important publishing company, claimed that the Croats were still being denied their rights in Bosnia and other republics and, therefore, sought to establish its own branches in Bosnia and Vojvodina to cater to the needs of Croats in those areas.

In 1971 and 1972 the Yugoslav authorities started to counter the nationalist movement in Croatia. At first, Tito considered sending troops into Croatia; eventually he decided to simply decapitate the Croat party. On 1 December 1971 Tito convened a joint meeting of the party presidiums of the League of Communists of Yugoslavia and League of Communists of Croatia at Karadjordjevo. Latinka Perović, Serbia's spokesperson at the session, declared that Yugoslavia would emerge from this crisis only if nationalism was wiped out in every constituent national group. The Croat party's leadership finally resigned. In the aftermath of the crisis tens of thousands of League of Communists of Croatia members were expelled from the League of Communists and 3,000 persons were imprisoned for political reasons, among them the future president of Croatia, Franjo Tudjman.

After the liberal communists were taken out of power in the League of Communists of Croatia, the regime of the "iron hand" reigned and Croatia became for two decades a "republic of silence." Agents of the State Security and Army Intelligence Services, fearing new eruptions of nationalism, interrogated everyone suspected of having ties with the Croat political émigré community and those in favor of renewal of the NDH (Independent State of Croatia). In spring 1974 they arrested a group of Serb "Neo-Stalinists" from Croatia. In October 1975 some members of the Croat Revolutionary Liberation Army (students, professors, and workers) were also arrested, and other members who succeeded in fleeing to the West were saying that the name of the organization had been made up by the State Security Services. They believed that through such actions against the Croats the State Security Services sought to retaliate for Croat repression against the Serbs and sought to persuade the public that no Croat opposition could exist without having ties with Ustaša or terrorists. All these measures strengthened the conviction of the Croats that the authorities would use all possible means to defend the existing regime. Also, on 22 December 1978—the celebration of Army Day—Tito admonished nationalists, the followers of Cominform as well as passive ideological opponents: "that regime will not tolerate those who were silent to retain position and reputation among the people but in reality worked against our system . . ."

The independence of Croatia was still a prohibited theme during this period because the LCY equated it with an attempt to rehabilitate the Ustaša and their NDH. Every arrest was meant also as a warning that Yugoslavia would not tolerate any expressions of Croat nationalism. The government punished people with imprisonment for even singing nationalist songs or carrying the traditional Croat coats of arms, (a chessboard in red and white), which had also been a coat of arms of the NDH during World War II.

After Tito's death, different ideas for changes in Yugoslavia developed among Croat intellectuals. The Croat poet Vlado Gotovac and historian Franjo Tudjman, already imprisoned once at the beginning of the 1970s, were among the first to be condemned and imprisoned for this "enemy propaganda." In September 1981 the authorities also imprisoned Marko Veselica, who in an interview said that Croatia was politically and economically exploited. In May 1981 the authorities also imprisoned Dobroslav Paraga, who gathered signatures on a petition demanding an amnesty for political prisoners.

However, among Croat intellectuals during that period a conviction grew that Croatia should secede from the eastern "Byzantine" parts of the state. They did not like the fact that most of the powerful positions in the state (not only in Yugoslavia but also in Croatia) were in the hands of ethnic Serbs. Among the Croats an interest in the Catholic Church and Catholicism also grew. For many Croats this was more a show of their identity—to differ from their Serb Orthodox co-citizens—than it was a sincere religious conversion. In spite of these facts the Croats, including Croat nationalists, remained silent even when communism fell in Eastern Europe in 1989.

The Croat communist regime and Croat nationalists also remained silent when Slobodan Milošević started to use Serb nationalism as a vehicle to win power in Serbia (see the section on Serbs in this chapter). At a time when mass demonstrations of the Serbs with their Serb national iconography were organized openly and broadcast on the state TV stations every day, Croat demonstrations were hidden. However, the Croat Democratic Union (Hrvatska Demokratska Zajednica, HDZ)—the main Croat opposition party, ideologically based on Croat nationalism—held its first demonstration on 28 February 1989 and soon got the mass support of Croats. The party was not legalized until December 1989, when Croat communists, following the Slovene example, decided to call for multiparty elections. During the preelection battle the Croat communists were hampered by the fight among the LC (League of Communists) factions (i.e., the reform wing and the wing of "defenders of the old ways"). On the other hand, Tudjman's HDZ gave the Croat people what they wanted—Croat nationalism as a weapon against Serb nationalism and pressures from Belgrade. Tudjman also gained support from the Croats abroad who supported him financially. Simultaneously the economic and political situation and crisis in Yugoslavia were deteriorating rapidly. Although they were internally divided, the Croat communists left the fourteenth LCY Congress in January 1990. Consequently, in May 1990 the HDZ overwhelmingly won the Croat elections. It looked as though Croat independence was within reach. However, the Croat Serbs (in rural areas) were against the independence, and they started an uprising against the new Croat leadership, which is described in the following chapter.

Bosniaks (Bosnian Muslims)

After World War II Bosnia and Herzegovina, as a constituent part of the new Yugoslav federation, became a people's republic within its historic boundaries. As no ethnic group represented an absolute majority in its complex ethnic structure, Bosnia and Herzegovina was defined as a "state" made up of all ethnic groups that lived in its territory. This made it different from Slovenia, Croatia, Serbia, Montenegro, and Macedonia, which were all defined as republics of respective (ethnic) nations.

Considering the existing ethnic diversity in Bosnia and Herzegovina, the third meeting of Zemaljsko antifašističko vjeće narodnog oslobodjenja Bosne i Hercegovine, ZAVNOBIH (Anti-Fascist Council of National Liberation of Bosnia and Herzegovina) issued a special decree in 1945 that declared this republic to be simultaneously Croat, Serb, and Bosniak (Bosnian Muslim). The majority of people believed in this, and interethnic relations among peoples and inhabitants of Bosnia and Herzegovina in the decades after World War II were stable and good. This was especially true among those who were born after World War II. The proof of this was the high rate of interethnic marriages. However, in spite of a traditionally high degree of tolerance in Bosnia among persons belonging to different ethnic groups, the developments in the beginning of the 1990s showed that the "national question" in Bosnia and Herzegovina continued to exist.

Attempts—at the federal and republic levels—to solve the Muslim national question existed throughout the existence of the Yugoslav federation. Although formally the authorities declared national equality for Bosnian Muslims (as Bosniaks were called then), they were not given the status of a constituent nation (*narod*) immediately after World War II. The first post–World War II censuses included the categories "Muslim—Croats" or "Muslim—Serbs" or "Muslim—ethnically undefined." However, when the census data were calculated, those who defined themselves as "Muslim—Croats" were included in the category "Croats," and those declared as "Muslim—Serbs" were included in the category "Serbs." It is interesting to note that the Muslim intelligentsia did not react to the census results or to their interpretation. There were hardly any protests in response to the omission of the Muslim nation in the official census results.

In January 1946, Husein Čišić, a deputy from Mostar to the federal assembly, tried in the Yugoslav parliament to explain the existence of Slavic Muslims who defined themselves as ethnic Muslims. He demanded the introduction of a sixth torch in the Yugoslav coat of arms to represent this group. Čišić was "rewarded" with a compulsory retirement. At that time recognizing Muslims as a constituent nation of Yugoslavia was not demanded even by the first Muslim communist men of distinction, Osman Karabegović and Avdo Humo.

The unsolved Muslim question, however, meant that there remained the danger of reviving the old national hegemonic appetites of Serbs and Croats in Bosnia and Herzegovina. Because the federal authorities had been aware of this problem when nationalism and ethnic conflicts started to escalate in Yugoslavia in the 1960s, in 1968 they finally declared Muslims of Bosnia and Herzegovina to officially be a "nation." Yet, the communist authorities did not allow the use of the name *Bosniaks,* which ethnic Muslims themselves usually used in Bosnia and Herzegovina. The authorities claimed that this would make the Serbs and Croats of Bosnia and Herzegovina into second-rate citizens. Thus, a category of ethnic Muslims, rather than Bosniaks, was introduced and was also used in censuses. The authorities hoped that this decision would mean the end of the Serb and Croat appetites in Bosnia and Herzegovina, which consequently would become ethnically and politically the most stable part of Yugoslavia.

When the Muslims were recognized officially as a nation, ethnic relations in Yugoslavia underwent an important change. Once the Muslims became one of a group of equal nations, the equilibrium among Yugoslav nations changed. This administrative political solution, based on the actual ethnic feelings of the Muslim population, opened the question of the national status of the Muslims of Slavic origin in Sandžak, other parts of Serbia, and some parts of Montenegro and Macedonia. Namely, the Muslim Slavs of Sandžak and Montenegro had traditionally defined themselves as Bosniaks and had considered Bosnia and Herzegovina their kin-republic.

The Serbs and Croats in Bosnia and Herzegovina who knew the actual ethnic situation there immediately accepted and recognized the national identity of Muslims. In turn, this recognition accelerated the process of self-identification of the Serbs and Croats in Bosnia and Herzegovina. Although those processes also resulted in "national homogenization" of all ethnic communities in Bosnia and Herzegovina, the 1960s and the 1970s brought a stable "ethnic equilibrium" there. It looked as if the Muslims, Serbs, and Croats in Bosnia and Herzegovina thought more about the socioeconomic system of self-management and other economic and social problems than about national problems, which were almost forgotten at the time. Also, the practice of distributing political positions proportionally according to nationality at every level of politics, culture, and economics helped foster brotherhood and unity in Bosnia and Herzegovina.

Bosnia and Herzegovina remained peaceful and in the strong hands of the communists during the period of "liberalism" in the early 1970s. Some conflicts occurred when the results of the 1971 census, in which the Muslims were for the first time counted separately, were published. The results showed that the Muslim nation in Bosnia and Herzegovina had a relative majority and that they were the third largest nation in Yugoslavia, after the Serbs and Croats. The Serbs, especially, did not like the results of the census, because they were convinced that they themselves were the largest group in Bosnia and Herzegovina. A communist strongman, Branko Mikulić, who was a Bosnian Croat, used this complexity of national composition in Bosnia and Herzegovina to say that this republic, in which three nations lived peacefully with one another, should be an example of tolerance for the whole of Yugoslavia. The authoritarian policy that (objectively) best served the Muslims was used to preserve the existing "ethnic equilibrium." For this reason a politician from Serbia reproached Mikulić, saying that he had changed Bosnia and Herzegovina into a "dark vilajet" (administrative unit during the Turkish rule), and that the authorities had used the Austro-Hungarian tactics of the period before World War I and tried to create a false Bosniak national consciousness in order to loosen the historic ties of Bosnia with Serbia.

After Tito's death in 1980, national conflicts became more and more frequent. Conflict took place between the communist regime and the Muslim community during the Islamic Revolution of Ayatollah Homeini in Iran. In March 1983, a pan-Muslim organization was established in Sarajevo. In the press this was used as a proof of damaging interference from abroad. Hamdija Pozderac, a communist politician who was a candidate for the presidency of the SFRY, was suspected of protecting the main Bosnian Islamic ideologists from persecution by authorities.

The ruling regime had to accuse a group of Bosnian Muslims of being nationalists in order to calm down the Serbs in Bosnia and Herzegovina and in Yugoslavia as a whole. In a political process, they convicted fifteen people for supporting the Islamic Declaration, published in 1973. This declaration demanded the creation of an Islamic entity independent from Yugoslavia. The author of the declaration, the future president of Bosnia and Herzegovina, Alija Izetbegović, tried to convince the court that the Islamic Declaration was only a scholarly work, intended to provoke discussion among the Muslims on their situation in society. Alija Izetbegović was sentenced to fourteen years of imprisonment.

In 1985 Vojislav Šešelj, an assistant professor at Sarajevo University, was condemned for writing an article in which he suggested changes in the internal borders of Yugoslavia and the creation of a Greater Serbia, including Vojvodina, Kosovo, Montenegro, and parts of Bosnia and Herzegovina. He "gave" the other part of Bosnia and Herzegovina to the Croats. In his vision, the Muslims as a nation were to be divided between the Serbs and Croats. For these ideas, which he wrote in an unpublished text, Šešelj was sentenced to 22 months' imprisonment. Such proceedings became a way of life in Bosnia and Herzegovina, so that when a Muslim was convicted in a political process, a trial against Serbs or Croats would follow, all with the intention of keeping the ethnic equilibrium and the communists in power in Bosnia and Herzegovina.

Political and economic crises in Yugoslavia and processes of democratization in Slovenia and Croatia also influenced political life in Bosnia and Herzegovina. The formal introduction of political pluralism further complicated the situation. Lacking democratic, multiparty political traditions and adequate democratic political culture, politicians instead used ethnicity and ethnic solidarity to mobilize their followers. As a result, ethnic political parties were established, and the political space in Bosnia and Herzegovina was divided along ethnic lines. The new (ethnic) political parties were Stranka demokratske akcije, SDA (Muslim Party of Democratic Action), under the leadership of Alija Izetbegović; Srbska demokratska stranka, SDS (Serb Democratic Party), under the leadership of Radovan Karadžić; and the Bosnian branch of Hrvatska demokratska zajednica, HDZ (Croat Democratic Union).

In September 1990, Alija Izetbegović declared that the SDA was against the principle of ethnic/national parity and that the next government of Bosnia and Herzegovina should be constituted on the basis of the political majority. According to the census, the Muslims comprised 44 percent of Bosnia and Herzegovina's population in 1991. The principle advocated by Izetbegović was in many ways similar to Milošević's perception of Yugoslavia at the time. As Milošević believed that a relative majority of Serbs in Yugoslavia would ensure his power, so Izetbegović thought that the Muslims would gain power in Bosnia and Herzegovina.

The communists in Bosnia and Herzegovina tried to convince the Muslim, Serb, and Croat leaders that the policy of (ethnic) fear among the population of Bosnia and Herzegovina—each ethnic community's fear of the possible hostile actions of others—was not a proper solution to the problem. However, the policy of ethnic fear continued for a year. During this period all national leaders proved incapable of reaching a workable compromise and preventing the bloodbath that eventually followed.

Serbs

The People's Republic (PR) of Serbia was a national unit of the Serbs in the new federation. However, many Serbs—traditionally settled in other parts of Yugoslavia—remained outside its borders. The Serbs represented a sizable part of the population in all Yugoslav republics, except in Slovenia. Initially, some Serb communist politicians hoped that in exchange for the recognition of the status of Montenegro and Macedonia as republics, Serbia would incorporate (at least) Bosnia and Herzegovina. However, these hopes did not materialize. Furthermore, the PR of Serbia was divided internally, as Vojvodina and Kosmet (Kosovo, Metohija)—where sizable national minorities lived (the largest being Hungarians in Vojvodina and Albanians in Kosovo)—were granted autonomy to enhance the rights of these minorities. Simultaneously, the Serbs in Bosnia and Herzegovina, Macedonia, Montenegro, and Croatia did not even request any cultural autonomy. Serb politicians could not even imagine that the Serbs would need minority protection and cultural autonomy in a country built on the slogan "Brotherhood and Unity."

The Serb and Montenegrin communist politicians continued to have a decisive impact on Yugoslav politics; additionally, the nation's capital being Belgrade, most employees of the federal administration were of Serb ethnic background. Although the number of employees from other ethnic origins increased substantially in comparison with the situation in pre–World War II Yugoslavia, other ethnic groups were still underrepresented in the federal institutions. The actual power and command in the army, secret services, and diplomatic corps especially remained, to a large extent, in Serb hands. For this reason, Serb politicians usually advocated the centralization of Yugoslavia. Their spokesman was Aleksandar Ranković, an "old guard" in the bolshevist tradition in KPJ/ZKJ, who was in charge of the state security apparatus until 1968. Serb politicians also fought the program of reforms prepared by Slovene politician Boris Kraigher in the mid 1960s, aimed at reforming the country's economy and politics by introducing decentralization and elements of a market-oriented economy. However, the victim of this ideological strife was Aleksandar Ranković, especially after rumors started to spread about the possibility of an army coup d'etat (he even bugged Tito's bedroom). The Serb nationalistic circles accepted Ranković's dismissal as a national tragedy, but one about which it was not suitable to talk at the moment. Only the Serb writer Dobrica Ćosić, in a letter to Tito, spoke of Ranković's dismissal as a great catastrophe for the party.

After the fall of Ranković, the—more or less—reformed communist leadership (Milentije Popović, Dobivoje Radosavljević, Miljenko Todorović, Petar Stambolić, and others) wanted to introduce reforms in Serbia also. In September 1966 the Central Committee of the League of Communists of Serbia acknowledged that the Albanians of Kosovo had been discriminated against by Serbs. Believing in equality of all Yugoslav nations, they suggested that the Serbs should give up the myth that all Serb (national) interests should automatically become Yugoslav interests also.

Influenced by the student unrest in Paris and Western Europe, the students in Belgrade started to protest against the difficult situation of young people in Yugoslavia in June 1968. One of their fears was that the reform of the federal institutions would mean fewer jobs, which would especially hurt the Serb intelligentsia. In November 1968 the Albanian population of Kosovo also started to demonstrate to demand more autonomy for Kosovo. Although they did not give up the idea of building a modern Serbia, the new Serb communist leadership, headed by Marko Nikezić and Latinka Perović, decided to stop the uprising of the Albanians by force. This intervention provoked even more violence.

The amendments to the Yugoslav constitution of 1971 provoked even more unhappiness among the Serbs. In their eyes, Yugoslavia became only a geographic term. "Serbia without its provinces (Vojvodina and Kosovo) is like Nedić's Serbia [during World war II] . . .," proclaimed the Serb Society of Writers. "In Kosovo, Croatia and Macedonia, the Serb nation has become a minority. What Nedić did not succeed in doing, the amendments [of 1971] did . . ." (Pirjevec, 1995, 300).

Believing that they contributed to the crisis in Yugoslavia, the ZKJ leadership and Tito decided to settle accounts with the "liberals." Marko Nikezić and Latinka Perović had to resign in October 1972. The defeat of the "liberals" in Serbia brought to power the communist leaders, who supported centralization and a strong central government in Yugoslavia but were unable to undertake the necessary reforms and modernization.

However, many Serbs thought that the new Serb communist leadership also failed to protect Serb national interests when the new constitution of the SFRY was adopted in 1974. They believed that the increased autonomy and independence of the republics further aggravated the position of Serbia in Yugoslavia. Serb nationalists were especially unhappy about the new federal constitutional arrangement for both SAPs—previously just the constituent units of the SR of Serbia—to also become constituent members of the federation. They believed that this reduced the control of Serbia over Kosovo and Vojvodina. (On the other hand, the political leaders of other republics feared that the new status in the federation of both SAPs—controlled by Serbia—would increase the domination of Serbia at the federal level, which actually was the intent of some Serb communist politicians.)

The Constitution of 1974 established a new unit, "narrower" Serbia (or as some called it, "Serbia proper"), which counted some 6 million inhabitants and, as such, became more manageable. However, Serb nationalists, upset especially by the fact that the Albanians actually came to power in Kosovo, opposed the new federal constitution and started to demand constitutional changes that would (re)introduce a strong central government. They believed that a strong federal government that everybody in Yugoslavia should respect would be able to run the country. However, until the death of Tito, there was no possibility of changing the Yugoslav constitution because of his objection to changes.

In autumn 1981 the demonstrations of the Albanians in Kosovo demanding republic status of the republic for this province provoked fierce reactions by the federal police and the Yugoslav People's Army, which brought tanks to the streets of Priština. The Central Committee of the LCY started a critical debate on the existing constitutional order, the results of which were "basic political points" to solve the problems of Kosovo. They envisaged an unconditional fight against "counterrevolutionary forces" in Kosovo and measures to prevent emigration of the Serbs and Montenegrins from the province. In accordance with Marxist doctrine, they explained the outbreak of Albanian nationalism with unsolved socioeconomic problems in Kosovo and demanded the stabilization of its economy. However, these basic points did not produce the expected results.

Simultaneously with the repression against the Albanians in Kosovo that continued throughout the 1980s, the Albanians tried everything possible to convince the Serbs and Montenegrins of Kosovo to emigrate. Mostly for economic reasons, the Serbs and Montenegrins, but also the Albanians, continued to emigrate from Kosovo in great numbers. (It is interesting to note that many Albanians who had to emigrate because of economic reasons became well-known owners of pastry shops all over Yugoslavia and abroad, but also cleaners of New York City skyscrapers.) Consequently, the number of Serbs and Montenegrins in the province was constantly decreasing. News about the Albanian terror against the Serbs, including profanation of Serb churches, monasteries, and cemeteries, continued to appear in the Belgrade media. The Serb Orthodox Church also dramatized the events of Kosovo and stepped forward to protect the Serb nation and its holy places. The Orthodox Church in its statement declared: "Kosovo is our memory, our heart and the center of our being" (Ramet, 1995, 111). The political consequence of the Serb "national problems" was also the fall of the federal government of Milka Planinc in mid-1986. After the Thirteenth Congress of the LCY, Slobodan Milošević became the leader of the Serb communists.

In this political situation, the Belgrade daily *Večernje novosti* published excerpts from a Memorandum of the Serb Academy of Arts and Sciences in September 1986. This draft was written by sixteen members of the Serb Academy, the spiritual leader being the writer Dobrica Ćosić. The Memorandum declared the situation of the Serb nation to be catastrophic: the Serbs were scattered and divided into "seven" republics and autonomous provinces, economically subjugated by Slovenia and Croatia, and, because of the old hatred of the communists, the Serb nation was robbed of its spiritual, cultural, and state identity. According to the Memorandum, the Serb nation was threatened even in the "narrower" Serbia, but especially in other republics and in both autonomous provinces where the Serbs were in the minority. In their view the situation was especially critical in Kosovo and Croatia. Therefore, according to the Memorandum, the federal constitution of 1974 needed to be changed to protect the Serb nation and enforce its complete national and cultural unity regardless of the republic or province in which Serb people lived (Čović, 1991, 256–300).

The Memorandum of the Serb Academy provoked negative reactions in other parts of Yugoslavia. The only communist leader who did not attack the Memorandum was Slobodan Milošević; furthermore, he soon became the spokesman for the new militant Serb nationalism. Already during his official visit to Kosovo in November 1986, he had proclaimed himself a protector of the Serbs and Montenegrins of Kosovo. In the city of Kosovo Polje he protested against those police, composed mainly of Albanians, who tried forcefully to disperse the Serb demonstrators, and he said to those Serb demonstrators, "Nobody has the right to beat you!" Milošević successfully used the "national" frustrations of the Serbs to further his aims. Milošević soon became a Serb national and political leader, and he gained more followers every day. Only a few recognized, however, that his ideas about "Serbia, which will be great, or will not exist" were taken from the Memorandum of the Serb Academy (Ramet, 1992, 227).

The "Special Committee for the Protection of Kosovo Serbs and Montenegrins" established at the end of 1986 soon discovered a new weapon—mass demonstrations. Milošević also recognized the power of mass demonstrations and started to use them. Claiming that the Serbs and Montenegrins in Kosovo were subjected to Albanian nationalism, these demonstrations, called rallies or mass demonstrations of truth, were at first organized to express the solidarity of the people of Serbia with the Serbs and Montenegrins of Kosovo. Soon, however, they became the main expression for support of Milošević and his policies. The outbreaks of chauvinism, the personal cult of Slobodan Milošević, demands for the hegemony of Serbs in Yugoslavia, and accusations against political opponents of Slobodan Milošević (whom participants of rallies often declared to be traitors to socialism, counterrevolutionaries, or even fascists) were the main characteristics of these mass demonstrations. They put pressure on political life and increased political tensions in Yugoslavia, which helped Slobodan Milošević to consolidate his power. With this tactic Milošević succeeded in removing Fadil Hodža, the most important (Albanian) communist leader in Kosovo. During the fights for political power in Kosovo, Milošević and the Yugoslav People's Army became allies. In December 1987 Milošević succeeded in deposing the president of Serbia, Ivan Stambolić, who represented the moderate faction in the League of Communists of Serbia. Once he took absolute power over Serbia, Milošević started to use his power to try to negotiate new arrangements in Yugoslavia.

Using the tactic of "mass demonstrations of truth" Milošević managed to provoke the resignations of the autonomy-oriented communist leaders of Vojvodina (in autumn 1988) and Montenegro (in January 1989). However, when he tried to dismiss the leadership of the Kosovo communists, headed by Kaçuša Jašari, and take away Kosovo's autonomy, miners from the Trepća zinc mine demonstrated. They walked 35 miles to Priština and demonstrated for five days in front of the provincial League of Communists headquarters against the removal of their party leaders. The Serb leaders answered with mass demonstrations at Ušće (where the Sava River runs into the Danube); one million people gathered on 19 November 1988. Demonstrators asked for a new Federal Constitution, the abolishment of Kosovo's autonomy, and weapons to fight their main enemies: the Albanians and Slovenes. Consequently, in January 1989, Milošević was able to replace the communist leadership in Kosovo with Rahman Morina, an Albanian who was loyal to him. This provoked new unrest and strikes, especially after miners in Stari trg, near Titova Mitrovica, started to strike at the end of February 1989 and demanded the resignation of the new provincial leadership. Milošević characterized these protests as a "counterrevolution."

Fearing that the same strategy could be used in Slovenia, the Slovenes supported the Albanian miners and organized a mass manifestation "for

Serbian leader Slobodan Milošević in Belgrade, February 1988. Milošević was handed over to officials of the United Nations war crimes tribunal on 28 June 2001. (AFP PHOTO/Corbis)

peace and coexistence" (*Za mir in sožitje!*) in the cultural center, "Cankar Hall" in Ljubljana, which worsened already bad relations between Serbia and Slovenia. The Serbs answered with demonstrations in Belgrade in which they accused the Slovenes of nationalism and demanded the arrest of Azem Vllasi, an Albanian political leader from Kosovo who was supposed to be guilty of organizing the events. The Serb authorities soon introduced an economic embargo on Slovenia (the Republic of Serbia prohibited the import of Slovene goods into Serbia). They started to threaten to bring mass demonstrators into Ljubljana in order to tell the Slovenes the truth about Kosovo, but also to change the Slovene communist leadership.

When Morina—whom the miners from Stari trg called upon to resign—offered his resignation, the miners in Stari trg ended their strike on 27 February 1989. At the same time the federal government proclaimed martial law in Kosovo. On 28 March 1989, the Parliament of the Republic of Serbia proclaimed a new Serb Constitution, which almost abolished the autonomy of Kosovo and Vojvodina. Kosovo Albanians protested. Even the official Serb data claimed that twenty-two Albanians were killed in the ensuing fight; however, it is believed that actually 140 protesters were killed.

After the successful overthrow of the independent republics and provincial political leaders of Montenegro, Vojvodina, and Kosovo, Milošević controlled one-half of the votes in the Yugoslav presidency. On 28 June 1989, the Serbs celebrated the 600th anniversary of the Battle of

Kosovo, for which one million people gathered at Gazimestan. The Albanians were hiding in their homes, and Milošević for the first time spoke about the possibility of armed fights for the defense of the interests of the Serb nation, fights that could occur in the near future.

Montenegrins

After World War II Montenegro became the smallest Yugoslav republic (5,333 square miles; 377,000 inhabitants) and gained its autonomy. As did other republics, it got its own national institutions—including its central bank and Academy of Sciences and Arts.

Despite the modernization in their republic, Montenegrins remained divided into thirty-five tribes, and even today they still know to which tribe each of them belongs. Historically, one-third to one-half of them consider themselves Serbs (*belaši*) and another one-half to two-thirds could be considered Montenegrin nationalists (*zelenaši*) (Ramet, 1992, 211–212). Because of their relatively large representation among employees in the federal institutions, but especially because of the economic aid that Montenegro received as one of the most economically underdeveloped regions of the former Yugoslavia, the Montenegrins traditionally advocated a strong and centralized federal government. In this, they were traditional allies of the Serbs.

During the period of prosperity after World War II, tensions between zelenaši and belaši diminished in Montenegro; the principle of "Brotherhood and Unity" upon which the Yugoslav federation was built contributed to that. However, these divisions sharpened again after Tito's death. The belaši especially helped Serb leader Slobodan Milošević when he exported his ideas to Montenegro. Milošević, whose ancestors came from Montenegro, knew that the idea of Serb nationalism would work in Montenegro, especially when Montenegro's economy was completely blocked because of numerous strikes.

On 20 August 1988, Milošević's followers seized the opportunity to exploit the divisions caused by these strikes; his action committee organized a protest involving 30,000 people in the Montenegrin capital of Titograd. Further protests followed on 18 September (50,000 persons, in Nikšić) and 7 October 1988, when demonstrators gathered in huge numbers in the center of Titograd. When the police tried to stop a demonstration of railroad workers, seven people were wounded. The next day the Montenegrin leadership was condemned by the Belgrade media for prohibiting the people from expressing themselves. Strikes developed into political demonstrations, with demands being made to replace the political leadership in Montenegro and in Kosovo. Although these demands were not successful initially, these events brought Branko Kostić to political prominence. He was then a vice president of the Montenegrin parliament, but three years later he became president of the Federal Republic of Yugoslavia consisting of Serbia and Montenegro, one of the successor states of the SFRY. (This country was also called rump Yugoslavia, although Milošević initially used this name to describe all territories where the Serbs lived in the former Yugoslavia east of the Virovitica-Karlovac-Karlobag line.) Three months after the initial demonstrations a group of young Montenegrin communists under the leadership of Momir Bulatović openly attacked the Montenegrin leadership again. Bulatović, who knew all too well that his criticism of the republic leadership would remain unpunished because of Milošević's support, became a leader of the Montenegrin communists in January 1989. He was only thirty-four years old then.

Milošević was now using a metaphor that Hitler had used after the *Anschluß* (the German annexation) of Austria in 1938, that Serbia and Montenegro were "inseparable, like eyes in the same head." At the crossroads of the 1990s a theory on ethnic unity of the Serbs and Montenegrins was revived. This ideology was advocated and spread especially during the time of Karadjordjević's Yugoslavia but was dismissed after 1945. The alliance and cooperation of Serbia and Montenegro seemed strong and useful in the late 1980s and during the 1990s. However, the situation would change by the end of the 1990s.

Macedonians

The creation of the Yugoslav federation and the establishment of the People's Republic (PR) of Macedonia immediately after World War II were very important historic developments for the Macedonians. It was the first time in history that their nation and its statehood were officially recognized. However, the complexity of the "Macedonian national question" was still very important. There were at least two important topics on the Macedonian national agenda: (1) the internal organization and status of the new Macedonian republic within Yugoslavia had to be established, and (2) the issues of Macedonian national unity and ethnic minorities in Greece and Bulgaria had to be addressed. Macedonian nationalists, but also some other Macedonian politicians, did not give up the idea of Macedonian national unity and wanted to complete their nation-building by the creation of a Macedonian state that would unite Vardar, Aegean, and Pyrin Macedonia. The realization of this idea would result in a major international conflict in the region. Up to early 1945 the Yugoslav communists managed to avoid such conflict and succeeded in making the nationalists in the Macedonian NLM pledge allegiance to the Yugoslav federation.

Already during World War II, in the summer of 1944, the popular partisan leader Metodi Andonov, called Čento, succeeded in becoming the president of ASNOM (Anti-Fascist National Liberation Council of Macedonia). Up until the formation of the first Macedonian government, a bitter power struggle took place between the Central Committee of the Communist Party of Macedonia (KPM) and Čento. Čento, a Macedonian nationalist, opposed the communist policy in almost all vital aspects. In particular, he was strictly against sending troops to the north to fight the Germans, fervently arguing instead for the partisans to mount a campaign toward the Aegean port of Salonika (Thessaloniki), which in his eyes was the true historical capital of Macedonia and should therefore be taken under Macedonian control.

In the spring of 1945 he suggested founding a separate Macedonian Orthodox Church in the Vardar region instead of resurrecting the Serb Church organization, which had been abolished in the Vardar region by the Bulgarian occupiers and brought under Bulgarian control. He was also against the return of those Serbs that the Bulgarian occupiers had deported in 1942 from Macedonia to Serbia. Additionally, Čento did not agree to the stationing of Yugoslav troops from Serbia in Macedonia. He also proposed building Macedonia's own telegraph agency (TAM). When the anti-Serb and Greater-Macedonian sentiments of Čento and his followers took forms that were considered politically alarming, for example, the riot of the Macedonian partisan brigade in late November 1944, the Skopje communists were advised to take action. The Yugoslav communists took action and installed a pro-Yugoslav Macedonian communist, Lazar Koliševski, as Čento's first deputy in the ASNOM Presidency in December 1944. In January 1945, a special working body was created that was led by Koliševski and that functioned as the de facto government.

Finally, when the temporary wartime parliament was transformed into a republican parliament (Narodno sobranie) and a new official government in Macedonia headed by Koliševski was installed, Čento became a powerless president of the Macedonian parliament and was deposed from his post in March 1946. After Čento was deposed, he announced in a public speech in Prilep that he would leave the country in order to present the cause to the United Nations for an independent and united Macedonia. He was arrested immediately after the speech, tried at the end of 1946, and sentenced to eleven years of forced labor. As Čento was very popular among Macedonians, demonstrations followed throughout Macedonia; there is evidence that during a protest demonstration in the Macedonian town of Resen near the Greek border, thirty-seven pro-Čento demonstrators were killed. These events were followed in 1946 by a wide-ranging purge of Macedonian nationalists.

At the same time, the building of the Macedonian nation was actually taking place. The authorities had codified the Macedonian language by 2 August 1944 (previously the literature had been written in different Macedonian dialects). The ASNOM decided that in the Macedonian state the (colloquial) Macedonian language would be introduced as the official language. The authorities set up a commission for the language and orthography consisting of philologists, writers, military persons, party functionaries, and educators. The result of the commission was a new Macedonian language. The commission proposed a new alphabet and the first regulations for spelling, which were officially proclaimed. The government's decision to adopt the new orthography was immediately popularized in a brochure entitled *Macedonian Orthography* and implemented in the first textbook dictionary with reading materials for the first grade (entitled *Bukvar so čitanka za prvo odelenie*). In January 1946, 16,000 copies of the first short grammar book of the new language were published. In 1946 the authorities of the People's Republic of Macedonia also established the University of Kiril i Metodij (Cyril and Methodius) in Skopje, with departments for South Slavic languages and a chair for the Macedonian language. In 1946 the Writers' Union of Macedonia was founded, and the first piece of fiction in the new language, a collection of short stories, was published. In April and May 1946, performances in the new Macedonian National Theater and Macedonian Opera took place. (It took until May 1954 for the first Macedonian opera to be written and performed, however.) On 2 May 1946, the first film with Macedonian subtitles was shown in Skopje. It is also interesting to note that at the time more than two-thirds of the Macedonian population could not read or write in any language. The authorities were able to teach the population to read and write very quickly, and in less then a decade the literacy situation changed completely.

In October 1946 a new daily newspaper in the Macedonian language was established. The most important medium to transmit the new Macedonian language and national identity was the educational system. A good indicator of the effectiveness of the school system in its national function was the fact that the first postwar emigrants from Macedonia expressed a clear-cut national consciousness. Emigrants to Australia defined themselves as ethnic Macedonians and immediately engaged in squabbles with Greek and Bulgaro-Macedonian emigrant groups. It worked that way because none of the ethnic Macedonians had opposed the policy of a special Macedonian language.

The Čento and Koliševski groups shared a single view in favor of the existence of a separate Macedonian nation. There were two groups, however, who fought against the idea. One group were Greater Bulgarian chauvinists, that is, people whose ethnic consciousness was clearly Bulgarian and whose political sympathies went in the direction of annexation of Vardar Macedonia to Bulgaria. The other group consisted of members of the former Macedonian Revolutionary Organization, led by the exiled Ivan Mihajlov, who defined themselves as Bulgarians in ethnic terms but were opting for a united, independent, and pro-Western Macedonia outside Yugoslavia. Both groups were persecuted by the Yugoslavian secret police until the mid-1950s.

After the fall of Ranković in the 1960s, the Macedonian Orthodox Church became an independent autonomous church. The independence of the Macedonian Orthodox Church was a further step in Macedonian nation building. Also, the process of consolidation of the Macedonian republic and its institutions continued.

During the 1970s and 1980s ethnic relations between the ethnic Macedonians and Albanians in Macedonia worsened. This trend also continued later. The proportion of Albanians in the population was constantly growing because of their high birth rate, and the ethnic Macedonians started to fear that they would become a minority in their own state. Based on their numerical strength, in the 1980s and 1990s the Albanians started to demand not only ethnic minority rights in the fields of culture, education, etc., but also more political rights. These ethnic and political tensions and its bad economic situation were the main reasons that Macedonia was the last of the Yugoslav republics to declare its independence from Yugoslavia.

Albanians

The previous segments focused only on Yugoslav nations and did not present ethnic histories of national minorities in the territory of the former Yugoslavia. However, for an understanding of the post–World War II historic development the Albanians must be discussed here as well. As the largest national minority during the post–World War II period, Albanians represented an important ethnic and political factor in Yugoslavia. Their percentage of the population increased substantially in this period. In the territory of their traditional settlement they became a local majority in Kosovo and substantial (national) minorities in Macedonia, "narrower" Serbia, and Montenegro. Additionally, as a consequence of economically inspired emigrations from Kosovo and other regions of their traditional settlement in the former Yugoslavia, they also moved to other parts of the country. Considering that Yugoslav Albanians were more numerous than some Yugoslav nations, it was not surprising when their demands arose to be given the status of a constituent Yugoslav nation. However, their demands for Kosovo to become a republic were unacceptable to the Serb and Yugoslav political leadership in the 1980s. This should be observed also in a historic perspective, especially from the perspective of Serb-Albanian relations. The Serbs, especially Serb nationalists, still consider Kosovo as the (historic) cradle of their culture and nation, while the Albanians consider this disputed territory to be their homeland. The "Albanian question" has always been a problem for Serb and Yugoslav governments, which they often tried to solve by force, and which then provoked new and even more radical demands from the Albanian side.

To understand recent historic developments, the history of Serb-Albanian relations should be studied carefully—especially the history since the seventeenth century. The turning point was 1690, when part of the Slavic Christian population left Serbia, Kosovo, and northern Macedonia in the so-called "Great Migration of Serbs." They fled their homes after the failure of the rebellion against the Turks, fearing an expected Turkish revenge. The Turkish authorities then gave their houses to groups of Muslim Albanians, which changed the ethnic structure in Kosovo substantially. After this, the numbers of Albanians steadily increased. By the end of World War II Albanians already represented three-quarters of the population in Kosovo. In some parts of western Macedonia and in eastern Montenegro, Albanians also became a sizable minority, or even the local majority in some communities such as Gostivar, Tetovo, and Ulcinj.

The Yugoslav communist authorities were aware of the dangers of ethnic, economic, and social tensions in the regions of Albanian settlement immediately after World War II. They were aware of the fact that the Albanians were still praying for the recreation of the Great Kingdom of Albania and were opposed to the Serb rule in the areas of the Albanian settlements. Although the Serb parliament issued a law to create the autonomous Kosovo-Metohian Authority (Kosovsko-metohijska oblast), which established autonomy in this territory under the rule of Serbia, the Albanians there remained unhappy. Most of the political power in Kosovo was still in the hands of ethnic Serbs and Montenegrins. The unhappiness of the Albanians grew because of their bad economic situation and because of Great Serb nationalism. Some Albanians saw the Great Albanian separatism as their best answer to these problems.

The Yugoslav, Serb, and Kosovo authorities often fought against Great Albanian separatism by the use of force (i.e., the armed forces) and police terror. The first peak of the Serb terror was in 1955 and 1956, when Ranković's agents of the Federal Ministry of the Interior decided to confiscate weapons that the Albanians had stored in their homes in accordance with their ethnic traditions. During this brutal action, which took a few hundred lives, they gathered 9,000 weapons. However, the Albanians did not give up their push for separatism, so the authorities started to threaten Albanian intellectuals. In July 1956, with no basis, the authorities organized a secret prosecution against a group of intellectuals in Prizren. Thousands of Kosovo Albanians were followed and controlled by the Serb secret police. For example, the secret police kept a record of the readership list of the completely legal daily in the Albanian language, *Rilindija.* The situation changed for the better at the beginning of the 1960s, and in 1963 Kosovo got its own constitution and the status of an autonomous province. However, only after the fall of Ranković did the situation really calm down. Among the first decisions that signaled a new situation was the introduction of the language reform, which codified the Albanian language so that the same language was spoken and written in Albania and Kosovo. This meant that the Yugoslav communists acknowledged the cultural unity of the Albanian nation, regardless of its political borders. The Central Committee of the LCY at this time freely discussed the "Albanian Question," and also other interethnic tensions in Yugoslavia—which was a new development, considering that ethnic tensions had previously been long hidden behind the slogan of "Brotherhood and Unity."

The discussion about the national questions in Yugoslavia and the autonomy of Kosovo (and Vojvodina) provoked the anger of those who were in favor of a strong federal state, especially the anger of Serb nationalists. In May 1968 Dobrica Ćosić spoke out against the "federalization" of Yugoslavia. Tito himself said, " . . . if such standpoints on Kosovo prevail, then it will be bad for Serbia and Yugoslavia . . ." (Smole, 1992, 12).

After the economic reforms in Yugoslavia failed (as outlined previously in this chapter), the Albanians began to demonstrate. The first anti-Serb demonstrations erupted in October 1968 in Prizren, Peć, and Suva Reka. On the eve of the Albanian national independence day and the Day of the Republic (the official celebration and anniversary of the Yugoslav federation established in 1943) on 28 November 1968, a wave of demonstrations erupted among the Albanians of Kosovo and also in Macedonia. This was the first time that demonstrators demanded that Kosovo be transformed into the seventh republic of Yugoslavia.

The federal constitution of 1974 again changed the situation of Serbia in the federation. The SAPs of Kosovo and Vojvodina became direct constituent elements of the Yugoslav federation. As already mentioned, advocates of centralism and Serb nationalists saw this as a formal reduction of the control of Serbia over these provinces and, in a way, as the loss of Kosovo—which they considered to be the cradle of the Serb nation, as Peć was the seat of the Serb Orthodox Church.

In the 1970s the Albanians of Kosovo held most of the important political positions there and actually ruled the province. One cannot deny that in this period the situation of the Albanians of Kosovo became substantially better. However, ethnic unrest began in Kosovo again at the end of 1974. Albanian students wanted to unite Kosovo with the regions in Montenegro and Macedonia where the Albanians lived, and some Albanian irredentist groups (e.g., Kosovo National Liberation Movement, Revolutionary Movement of United Albanians, Marxist-Leninist Communist Party of Albanians in Yugoslavia, etc.) with the same aim were organized in the mid 1970s. The Albanians in Yugoslavia, who were three times more numerous than the Montenegrins, wanted their own republic in the federation. However, on the grounds that the Albanians were not a constitutive Yugoslav nation but a national minority, the constitution of 1974 did not grant Kosovo such a status. In February 1976 the authorities arrested nineteen Albanians, including the writer Adem Demaçi. The court found them guilty of organizing an Albanian nationalist movement for the liberation of Kosovo, and they were sentenced to fifteen years of forced labor. In spring 1980 another group of Albanians was tried because they were considered "unfriendly" to the people and the state. Only one year after Tito's death, in 1981, an uprising of Albanians in Priština and other Kosovo towns also took place.

At the same time, the dissatisfaction of the Serb authorities and that of the Serbs and Montenegrins in Kosovo grew. Ethnic Albanians held most important positions in Kosovo, not only in the provincial administration but also in the secret police and the League of Communists. The reason for this was partially the official status of the Albanian language in Kosovo. Although all Albanians spoke Serb, only a few Serbs spoke Albanian.

Because they did not speak or write Albanian, many Serbs and Montene-grins lost their traditional privileges in the workplaces. Nevertheless, the economic and social situation of the Albanians was still bad—usually worse that those of the Serbs and Montenegrins. Out of every 1,000 Serbs and Montenegrins, 228 were employed in the public sector; at the same time, only 109 Albanians out of every 1,000 had such jobs. On the other hand, it must be emphasized that the percentage of Slavs in Kosovo dropped from 21 percent in 1971 to 14.9 percent in 1981. In 1981, accord-ing to the official census data, 1,230,000 (83.1 percent) people in Kosovo declared themselves Albanians. In addition to economically motivated emigration of the Slavic population from Kosovo, the main reason for the rapidly growing proportion of Albanians in the province was the demo-graphic explosion of the Albanian ethnic group, which grew at a rate of twenty-five per thousand—the highest birth rate in Europe. This meant that the Albanian population doubled in one generation. Those data es-pecially worried the Serbs.

However, the federal authorities were also aware of the anti-Serb and anti-Yugoslav feelings among the Albanian population of Kosovo. They tried to soften the situation by raising the standard of living of the people there. However, substantial financial investments in the province—mostly in mines, energy, and large automated industries—created only a few jobs and did not reduce unemployment, which should logically have been the first priority. As a consequence, unemployment remained high; the differ-ences between Kosovo and the rest of the Yugoslav state increased rather than decreased. The difference in GNP per capita between Slovenia and Kosovo was 5:1 in 1953 and 7:1 in 1981.

Regardless of all the problems in the post–World War II period, Kosovo saw substantial social, economic, political, and cultural development. The University of Priština, with its 61,000 students, became the third largest university in Yugoslavia. However, the quality of higher education in Kosovo was poor and not comparable to universities in other parts of Yugoslavia. The consequence of poor economic and social conditions and the poor quality of higher education in Kosovo was that quite a few grad-uates were unemployed, mostly Albanians, and among these graduates, Albanian nationalism grew. In these conditions of growing ethnic dis-tance between Albanians and non-Albanian populations, there was no possibility of meaningful dialogue between the ethnic groups.

The unrest, in which 10,000 to 20,000 young people participated from 11 March 1981 through early April, grew into a revolution. From Priština, demonstrations spread to other centers in Kosovo and even to the Albanian settlements in Macedonia and Montenegro. The slogan of demonstrators was "Kosovo-Republic!" After martial law was declared in the whole province of Kosovo, the army and federal police quickly intervened and the demonstrations stopped. According to the official data, eleven people were killed in the fights, but in Albanian circles, rumors circulated of more than 1,600 being dead. The federal authorities claimed that "internal and external enemies of Yugoslavia" provoked the "counterrevolution" in Kosovo. The provincial secret police were included among the internal enemies because they did not inform Belgrade of the upcoming events in time to prevent them. The Albanian political leadership, with Mahmut Bakalli, was also condemned as an enemy. Among the external enemies, the Albanian government in Tirana was openly mentioned, and the Soviet Union was mentioned secretly. The purges that followed against alleged separatists and chauvinists and within the League of Communists of Kosovo also provoked polemics by the Albanian government of Enver Hoxa.

In mid-November 1981 the federal authorities and LCY wrote a plan to solve the Kosovo problem that included fighting against groups of counterrevolutionaries, measures to stop the emigration of the Serbs and Montenegrins from the province, and stabilization of the economy. However, this plan did not change conditions in the province. The Albanians demanded more political rights (the most radical even demanded the independence of Kosovo), while the Serbs and Montenegrins protested against physical and other terrors implemented by the Albanian majority, which was attempting to "convince" the Slavic minority to emigrate. The Belgrade media wrote and talked about the Albanian terror in Kosovo, and the Serb Orthodox Church came to the defense "of the Serb nation and its holy places." As mentioned in the section in this chapter on the Serbs, future events were foreseen in the Memorandum of the Serb Academy, with the idea of "Serbia, which will be great or will not exist."

Slobodan Milošević soon started to implement the ideas of the Memorandum in Kosovo. His promises of changes within the federation (in favor of Serbia, of course) and the decision to intervene in Kosovo brought him unforeseen popularity in Serbia and among the Kosovo Serbs. Millions of Serbs went to the "meetings of truth" about Kosovo, convinced that Milošević would realize Serb national interests that had been almost forgotten in Yugoslavia after fifty years of life under the slogan "Brotherhood and Unity." The Albanian population of Kosovo did not feel good when the Serbs, using Chetniks' symbols and slogans at meetings, demanded the resignations and arrests of the Albanians' leaders. The

Albanians answered with mass demonstrations in Priština in November 1988, when they demonstrated in support of their attacked leaders, Kaçusha Jashari and Azem Vllasi, in front of the provincial League of Communists headquarters. In spite of mass protests by the Albanians, Milošević let everyone know that he was not going to give up on constitutional changes and that he would abolish the autonomy of Kosovo even if it were not lawful to do so. This provoked new unrest and strikes, which reached their peak in a strike of the miners in Stari Trg near Titova Mitrovica. On 27 January 1989 Serb politicians demanded that the Presidency of Yugoslavia declare martial law in Kosovo. On 3 March 1989 the Serb authorities arrested the Albanian politician Azem Vllasi, who was accused of being the leader of the "Albanian secessionists." On 28 March 1989 the Amendments to the Constitution of the SR of Serbia were adopted by the Serb parliament. With Milošević's mass meetings campaign, Serbia gained control over the provinces of Vojvodina and Kosovo. The Albanians protested again, and up to 140 people were killed (various accounts differ as to the exact number). The situation in Kosovo became extremely tense. Slobodan Milošević was aware of that and, on 28 June 1989, while celebrating the 600th anniversary of the Battle of Kosovo in front of more than one million people in Gazimestan (only a few miles from Priština), he said: "Six centuries later we are again in conflict and on the verge of fights. Those fights do not involve arms yet, although we can not exclude armed fights" (Silber and Little, 1997, 72). And the world did not have to wait long for the beginning of one of the bloodiest wars of the second half of the twentieth century.

The autonomy of Kosovo had been all but completely abolished by the adoption of the new Constitution of the Republic of Serbia in 1990. Serb repression of Albanians and others in Kosovo continued throughout the 1990s, until the international intervention took place (see the following chapter).

Culture in the "New Yugoslavia," 1945–1990

The diversity of Yugoslavia was reflected in the arts during this period. In spite of the fact that the Yugoslav communist party in the 1960s tried very much to create a common Yugoslav socialist culture, this policy could not create one Yugoslav nation, let alone a common Yugoslav culture. In spite of this, some Yugoslav projects in the field of culture were rather successful. One of them was the project to produce the *Enciklopedija Jugoslavije*

(Encyclopedia Yugoslavia) led by Miroslav Krleža; another was a history of the peoples of Yugoslavia (up to the eighteenth century), which was written and published in 1958. The Encyclopedia went from A to Z; it was printed only in the Serbo-Croatian language in the Latin alphabet. The project on the history of the peoples of Yugoslavia was stalled because of differences in interpretations of the history of the period from the mid-eighteenth century onward. In addition to the already established Serb, Croat, and Slovene cultures, the Macedonian and Montenegrin cultures were also recognized; once the Muslims were recognized as a special ethno-nation, the (Bosnian) Muslim culture was also recognized. National minorities or, as the constitution defined them, nationalities, had their minority rights (at least on paper) to their cultural activities and education; in reality, however, their equality and the furthering of their cultural development was not realized (with the exception of the policy of Slovenia toward its autochthonous Italian and Hungarian minorities) until the second half of the 1960s.

The Yugoslav authorities put large sums of money and huge efforts into education. The numbers of elementary, middle, and high schools increased rapidly. From 1952–1953 onward the authorities introduced a compulsory eight years' worth of education. In 1953 school attendance was 71 percent of children of ages 7–15; in 1987, it was 97 percent. However, there were huge regional differences in quality of education, and schools were also under ideological pressure and continuous reforms, which reached their peak in the 1970s.

In addition to three universities in the interwar period (Belgrade, Zagreb, Ljubljana), schools of higher education, other new universities, and other education centers were opened. The number of schools of higher education jumped from thirty-three after World War II to 340 in the mid-1980s. Many newly established higher education schools were brought together for political reasons or were established by the authorities to show their efforts for national equality. However, many schools did not have adequate faculty and equipment.

After World War II there were many changes in the field of culture. A higher standard of living and more free time enabled the masses to attend cultural performances and visit cultural institutions. Before World War II only the higher social classes had been able to do so. Amateur culture was significant at first. In 1946 there were 3,000 amateur drama groups and only forty-two professional theatres. Later came "professionalization" of drama and theatre; the actors and others working in professional theatres became state employees. Simultaneously, many amateur groups had to close, because they did not get adequate support and funding from the state to continue with their productions. The number of professional theatres increased, until there were sixty-eight in the mid-1980s.

During the years after World War II, the number of titles published also increased (from 3,413 in 1948 to 11,293 in 1975, when the number of titles reached its peak). Seventy percent of the titles were published in Serbo-Croat, 17 percent in Slovene, 5 percent in Macedonian, 3 percent in Albanian, and 3 percent in other languages. The number of newspapers increased from 457 in the 1950s to more than 3,000 in the 1980s. Half of them were organs of different factories or political organizations, controlled by the LCY. Until the 1990s no independent major newspapers were legally published. However, there were some clandestine newspapers.

Because of the Socialist system, the fields of culture did not have complete autonomy. The federalization of Yugoslavia brought new impulses to some Yugoslav republics for cultural development; however, the system often hindered broader artistic, scientific, and scholarly development. During the first years after World War II, culture (just as politics and the economy) was modeled after the Soviet communist example. Scientists and artists had to follow the directions of the authorities. Their creations had to be in line with the Marxist-Leninist ideology. The polemics of people of different world views (convictions) that at least partially existed in the interwar period were exchanged for the one-minded, controlled culture of the years right after World War II.

Only after the conflict with the Soviet Union in 1948 were people of culture able to search more freely and to make contacts with the contemporary cultural trends of Western Europe, a process that had been interrupted in 1941. Artists could again devote themselves to the common people and their intimate thoughts, as the collective ideas of great social breadth were not as important anymore. The world of dreams and disappointments returned to literature. In painting, clear and large figures gave way to abstractions. In music, partisan and workers' songs withdrew in favor of more entertaining music such as jazz. In film, partisan themes were exchanged for contemporary themes and comedy. Already at the end of the 1950s, existentialist thinking and interest in human intimacy concentrated on the individual, who was notably part of the wider society and subjugated to its needs—which in reality meant the departure from the previously proclaimed Social Realism (see chapter 4).

Although the process of liberalization went slowly in the field of politics, American films were shown in the movie theaters, and the works of until-then "questionable" Western writers were already translated by the

1950s. Already-established people of culture tried to connect with currents and traditions from pre–World War II, and the younger generations from the mid-1950s on wrote about actual problems (contemporary mistakes and the disappointments of the people, to whom the socialist regime had not given what it promised). This brought the younger generation into quarrels with the communist ideologues, who reproached them for falling under the "decadent" influences of the Western world. The program of the LCY in 1958 proclaimed the principle of freedom of creation, and the LCY (at least on paper) withdrew from judging art; however, often it did not follow its proclaimed line. Thus, in the 1950s and 1960s, in the art circles in Yugoslavia, sharp fights were fought between those who advocated the new ideas and the so-called realists and traditionalists.

At the end of the 1950s, literature of the peoples of Yugoslavia became known worldwide. In 1961, Ivo Andrić received the Nobel Prize in literature for his works, novels *Na Drini ćuprija* (*Bridge on the Drina*) and *Travniška kronika* (*Chronicle of Travnik*). In the 1960s many new literary and scholarly journals and reviews were published containing esthetic and philosophical polemics criticizing the authorities. Also, demands for cultural liberalization and against dogmas were published. Most artists were against "Yugoslavism," and as a result they got into sharp polemics on national cultural self-esteem. This resulted in creative pluralism that replaced previously uniform socialist realism and enabled development in cinematography that followed the Western trends. Authorities responded with a prohibition against the showing of such movies and of the publishing of certain books; they also abolished a few journals and confiscated some issues of newspapers or journals through judicial processes. In the 1970s the government changed tactics; it tried to direct cultural activities by channeling money so that cultural works would retain their socialist character. In this way the authorities tried to fight separatist nationalism in different environments. In spite of this, in all fields of culture the consequences of cultural openness toward the world were seen.

The circumstances in the mid-1960s were rather different in different republics. The Yugoslav films that had the most positive echoes in the world were attacked the most; these included Želimir Žilnik's *Zgodnja dela* (*Early Works*), Aleksandar Patrović's *Mojster in Margherita* (*Master and Margherite*), and Živojin Pavlović's *Zaseda* (*Ambush*). In 1974 *Praxis*, a philosophical journal, was abolished. A confrontation took place between the authorities and the nationalistic-minded intelligentsia, especially in Serbia and in Croatia, where well-known men of culture and cultural institutions protested in 1967 against unifying the Croatian and

Serbian languages into one language. (Although the languages had been codified into one language since the mid-nineteenth century and several political attempts had existed to unify the languages, writers and poets had continued to write in the Croatian or Serbian language.)

In 1978 the authorities tried to find a common language with the intelligentsia. However, the peace was very short. Politicians reacted to what they considered ideologically inadequate happenings in culture by organizing different meetings within political organizations, to which they invited cultural workers and artists. Defenders of free cultural creativity were able to act to some extent autonomously from the official ideology and in accordance with their artistic inspirations. Most artists defended the nationalist interests of individual Yugoslav nations against the existing unitaristic and centralistic tendencies. Artistic circles were many times misused for political purposes. The politicians used art and literary critique to establish their control; also, different commissions and organizations (e.g., the Society of Writers) took care of providing ideological controls and tried to perform ideological differentiation among artists. This meant that artists who did not want to join state-run artist organizations could not publish their works and/or had difficulties in ensuring the necessary funding for their artistic work; some of them were, unofficially, even turned into "nonpersons."

In the 1980s, when political tensions increased, two trends increased in the Yugoslav culture: (1) the defense of freedom of creativity (people of culture followed a policy of solidarity regardless of national group), and (2) with some, using culture to play a role in defense of national rights, which politics did not do. This period of politically confused conditions was also the most pluralistic period in the whole history of post–World War II Yugoslavia. During this period different alternative cultures were developed. Contemporary art thus became a tool to show conflicts among contemporary and conservative currents, as well as between generations.

Culture was the field in which the decay of the state and the failure of the forcibly implemented ideological model were most exposed. Simultaneously with its growing internal differences, Yugoslav cultural society almost vanished in the second half of the 1980s; conflicts between people of culture from different ethnic origins were on the table every day, especially between the Serbs, who advocated centralism and "Yugoslavism," and the Slovenes, who fought for autonomy, decentralization, distinct national identity, and individuality. In the second half of the 1980s, ideological fights became more numerous, and the judiciary system tried to intervene. From 1984 on, politicians tried to prevent nationalist and antisocialist movements with administrative and judicial interventions.

The Union of Writers of Yugoslavia, at its congress in Novi Sad in 1985, demanded complete freedom of artistic creativity. Similar demands had already existed before among reform-minded intellectuals, but also within the Union of Socialist Youth of Slovenia and in some other organizations and associations. In a way, these demands and activities can be considered the beginning of and a model for democratization in the former Yugoslavia that also influenced the official sociopolitical organizations, including the LCY, and the political establishment. Interestingly, the Union of Writers of Yugoslavia became the first federal institution that disintegrated, after it failed to find necessary compromises because of intolerance of its members for different ethnic origins.

Slovenes

Although there was a lot of ideology in Slovene culture, especially immediately after World War II, people eventually made contact again with contemporary European cultural trends. In addition to Social Realism, which prevailed in the first decade after World War II, Neoromanticism (a European literary trend that stressed opposition to positivism and an attempt to return to the imagination), Symbolism (a trend in literature and painting that emphasized imagination and spiritual forces in symbolic form), and Expressionism (see chapter 4) showed up again. Around 1960 one could follow a strong showing of Existentialism and Modernism (see chapter 4 for more information on both of these). At the beginning of the 1970s, Modernism intensified, connected with the new avant-garde (a movement that turned away from existing art and searched for new ways of expression). In the 1980s, the first signs of Postmodernism (a literary trend in which modernist experimentation is replaced by more traditional approaches) appeared.

In the field of literature many generations of poets and writers made themselves known. Among the older generation of poets, the best-known were Ciril Zlobec and Janez Menart; among the younger generations, Veno Taufer and Tomaž Šalamun were prominent. Among the other writers of the time, Rudi Šeligo and Drago Jančar are noteworthy. The most successful dramatists were Primož Kozak and Dane Zajc.

Among painters, Lojze Spacal and Emerik Bernard especially deserve mentioning. Graphic artist Adriana Maraž and artist Jože Tisnikar, as the main representatives of naïve painting (a trend similar to primitive art, which takes simplified motifs from nature and life) in Slovenia, were also successful. The development of publishing encouraged illustrators such as

Marlenka Stupica. Design, scene design (stage sets), and photography flourished. Also, caricaturists (Marjan Amalietti) and comic strip artists (Miki Muster) deserve to be mentioned here. In sculpture, Drago Tršar and Stojan Batič were prominent, and the best architects were Edo Ravnikar and Boris Podrecca.

After World War II, Slovene cinematography started to develop. Socialist Realism (a theory of art developed after 1932 based on Social Realism, which demanded that arts should contribute to the revolutionary development of the society) initially prevailed in cinematography. Although films depicted the misery in the lives of ordinary people during World War II and in the postwar period, the directors were not limited strictly by the rules of Socialist Realism. Even the first post–World War II film, *Na svoji zemlji* (*On Our Land*), showed this. It was directed by France Štiglic. In the 1960s, 1970s, and 1980s several films were produced that established some Slovene film directors and actors.

In addition to the music composers from the interwar period, Uroš Krek, Primož Ramovš, and Vinko Globokar were important during this period. At the same time, jazz and other popular music developed. Ideological objections to this "bourgeois" music disappeared in the 1960s. The first festivals of modern entertainment, as well as rock music, also developed during this period. Many newly established ensembles copied American and British rock. Alternative culture developed in the 1980s. It was built on visual effects and multimedia. Art was politically engaged; it created a history of its own. Artists who were embraced mostly by the younger generations also played important roles in the process of democratization and often managed to provoke furious reactions from the authorities, especially the federal authorities (e.g., the band Laibach; the consortium of painters, designers, and visual artists Neue Schlowenische Kunst; alternative theaters such as Sestre scipion nasice; etc.).

Croats

After 1945 Croat culture was to a great extent in the service of the communist ideology and the new socialist social order. It was expressed in the so-called *poezija obnove i lopatarskog pjesništva* (poetry of reconstruction and shovel poetry), which, based on the communist ideology and Social Realism, described the high-minded contribution of common people to the reconstruction of war-devastated Yugoslavia. Among the first who fought against such an approach was Vesna Parun. Jure Kaštelan and other poets started to write to lyrical works again. Also, literature "escaped" from the "reconstruction and shovel literature" to the metaphor. This was shown in the prose of Vladan Desnica and Ivan Aralica. Aralica, with his novels, especially marked literary creativity in the 1970s and 1980s and is considered the first Croat contemporary novelist.

In the field of art, Zagreb became the Croat national art center, where different styles (naïve art—mainly motives from nature; informal, conceptual art; postmodern retrospectives, etc.) met. Especially in the plastic arts, during the first years after the war, themes of the National Liberation Movement still prevailed, broadened with motifs of reconstruction and socialist building. In addition to that, painters continued to search individually for new ways of expression. Among representatives of the younger generation were Edo Murtić and Zlatko Prica. After World War II many possibilities opened to sculptors also, who created many representative monuments. Of special importance are the sculptures of Antun Augustinčič (the monument of Marshal Tito in Kumrovec and the monument in front of the UN building in New York). A new generation of architects were creators of numerous interesting projects that reflected the times and society.

Socialist Realism and themes of World War II prevailed in music during the first post–World War II years, when important musicians included members of the older generation as well as composers who started to create in the period after World War II (Natko Devčić). At the end of the 1950s, the generation of composers born between 1920 and 1940 started to integrate different avant-garde and experimental currents of modern music into their works. The main representatives of this style were Milko Kelemen and Dubravko Detoni. The generation of composers who grew up in the 1970s (e.g., Marko Ruždjak) wrote music that combined new electronic sounds with traditional instruments.

Scholarly work in the field of music also developed, particularly after the establishment of the Muzikološki zavod (Institute of Music) in 1969 and the Zavod za muzikološka istraživanja JAZU (Research Institute of Music at Yugoslav Academy of Sciences) in 1979. Dragan Plamenac's works on Croat musical history and Josip Andeis's writing on the general history of music and the history of Croat music also deserve mentioning.

Bosnian Muslims

In Bosnia and Herzegovina after World War II, with regard to the cultural creativity of the Muslims, changes occurred to such an extent that one could call it a completely new period. These changes were made in the context of the establishment of Bosnia and Herzegovina as an equal socialist republic and multiethnic federal unit within Yugoslavia. With that, the possibility for equal development of culture of the Muslims opened up, especially after 1968, when the Yugoslav authorities recognized the Muslims as one of the constitutional nations of Yugoslavia.

New possibilities in the cultural development of the Muslims opened in literature, which developed in all genres after World War II. During the first postwar period the themes of World War II and the reconstruction of the homeland prevailed. This period was marked by the poetry of Skender Kulenović, who had established himself already in the interwar period, and the poetry of Izet Sarajlić. In the 1950s the literature of the Bosnian Muslims again followed European trends. The first writer to come to prominence was poet Marko Dizdar; later, other younger poets and writers followed (Meša Selimović and Alija Isaković). Most of them reached their peak at the end of the 1960s, when a new generation established themselves (Irfan Horozović). For this period, the development of many genres is significant. Children's literature developed quickly; also drama (Isaković), travel writing (Tvrtko Kulenović), etc., gained readers. Scholarly writing in the fields of literature, criticism, aesthetics, and essays developed as well (Muhsin Rizvić).

Like literature, plastic art was also chained into the aesthetic norms of Socialist Realism until 1950. In the 1950s the development of the Udruženje likovnih umjetnika Bosne i Hercegovine (Society of Plastic Artists of Bosnia and Herzegovina) and the establishment of the Državne škole za slikarstvo i umjetničke zanate (State School for Painting and Art) were important. In the first half of the 1950s, plastic artists started to fight against the authorities for free artistic expression. In 1959 an art gallery was established in Sarajevo, signifying a new period in plastic artists. A new generation of young painters also brought plastic art to the country outside Sarajevo.

Other artistic forms developed as well, especially printing, illustration for publishing, and graphic and industrial design (for example, artistic creations of furniture). Architecture also developed, from Rationalism (a trend in architecture that tries to solve architectural problems by using simple solutions) to Modernism, and later to Postmodernism. Music began to follow the styles of the rest of Europe. The opera was established in 1946, numerous new music education programs were begun on the high school level, and, in 1955, the Academy of Music was established. Musical creativity, mostly patterned on modern European musical movements, was evident among composers of the younger and midgenerations (e.g.,

Avdo Smailović). Popular music also followed European trends, and especially known was Bosnian rock music of the 1970s and 1980s (e.g., the band Bijelo dugme [White Button]).

Radio came to the area in 1946, followed by TV in 1961, which helped to popularize culture. Cinema in Bosnia- Herzegovina reached an international level in the 1970s and 1980s, especially with the films of Emir Kusturica and Hajrudin Krvavac (*Valter brani Sarajevo* [*Walter Defends Sarajevo*]).

The culture of Bosnian Muslims after World War II became comparable with modern European culture. However, it continued to build on specific traditions and national motifs.

Serbs

Serb men and women of culture during the years after World War II also followed the general pattern; that is, initially they had to follow the contemporary sociopolitical lead. This meant that cultural creativity was derogated from the ideological-political centers and that artists were forced by the authorities into socialist realism, which often lessened the artistic value of their cultural creations. No imagination was allowed. This was especially seen in literature in so-called building-lyrics ("*graditeljska lirika*"—a Serb version of poetry based on the communist ideology and Social Realism, which described the high-minded contribution of common people to the reconstruction of war-devastated Yugoslavia). Its authors (Veles Perić, Antonije Marinković, etc.) had never reached any higher artistic value. In the mid-1950s in Serb literature, theme and psychological differentiation and emotional and intellectual depth again asserted themselves (without them, literature could not show a modern vision of the world), and literature again started to develop. During the period following the 1950s, poets who had asserted themselves already in previous periods included Miodrag Pavlović and Vasko Popa, who with their works were the first to distance themselves from the pathetic building-lyrics.

Even more differentiated than poetry was modern Serb prose, in which the novel prevailed. In this respect, the novels of Miloš Crnjanski (*Seobe—Migrations; Roman o Londonu—A Novel about London*) and Nobel Laureate Ivo Andrić were especially important. In addition to Crnjanski and Andrić, Danilo Kiš, Milorad Pavić, and Dobrica Ćosić deserve to be mentioned.

Also, creativity in the field of plastic arts was dynamic. It was not only marked by the philosophy of modern art and the nature of the creations themselves, but also by the parallel creativity of different generations with different historic experiences and philosophies. This is exactly what helped its richness and facilitated the assertion of different emotions at the same time. During the period 1945–1990, many painters asserted themselves (e.g., Marko Čelebonović and Branko Milijuš), successfully representing Serb plastic arts at home and abroad.

Additional great developments were seen in the field of sculpture, to which mainly Olga Jevrić and some younger artists from the school of Toma Rosandić contributed and which graphic art revived. This can be seen not only in the number of graphic artists but in their vision also (e.g., Mihail Petrov and Branko Šotra).

After World War II, the attitude toward architecture changed; the principles of modern urbanism gained support, and architecture started to adapt to the needs of contemporary spatial development. Architecture had to fight many battles, especially because of financial difficulties but also because of some politically dominated decisions, for example, the building of urban settlements in close proximity to factories and mines. One of the most important projects of this period was the building of Novi Beograd (a new part of Belgrade, built on the left bank of the Sava River). Later architecture followed modern European and world trends.

There were many difficulties to overcome before musicians were able to resume activities in the field of music, as most of the musical establishments had been destroyed during the war. After their rebuilding, the leading role in the field of music was put in the hands of the Belgrade Opera, in which numerous singers (such as Julijana Anastasijević) and musicians (such as Olga Jovanović) worked. A new opera came under the umbrella of the Serb National Theatre beginning in Novi Sad in 1947, and also in Subotica from 1945–1955. Many composers became prominent. It is interesting that the younger generation of composers rarely accepted the avant-garde extremes of European music trends.

The most helpful influences for the rapid development of culture were radio and television, which enabled a wide circle of people to follow cultural achievements. Radio programming was renewed soon after Belgrade was liberated, but it took Belgrade TV until August 1958 to start its broadcasts. Soon after the end of World War II, film started to develop; its achievements were aided by the material and financial support of the Serb republic. The first Serb film, *Slavica,* was shown by spring 1947. After that, about ten artistic films and thirty documentaries were made annually.

Many film directors became known worldwide (Veljko Bulajić, Živojin Pavlović, Emir Kusturica, etc.). Also contributing to the development of film were the building of a "film city" in Košutnjak (near Belgrade) in 1947 and the establishment of the Academy for Film, Radio, and Television.

Montenegrins

Cultural creativity for Montenegrins after World War II was marked particularly by the polycentric development of cultural institutions. The authorities established such institutions in places where, previously, there had very rarely been cultural performances. In spite of the fast development of all fields of culture, the leading role was still in the hands of the writers of literature. Especially during the years immediately after World War II, the cult of father and home-farm was intensified. Many had lost their fathers during the war, and many had to leave their homes during the war. Prominent writers included Mihailo Lalić and Miodrag Bulatović, who in 1980 became famous because he accused the Slovenes of having "Aryan aspirations" after they established a "language court" to protect the Slovene language. During the postwar years many writers and poets of younger generations who did not use the themes of the NLM as their predecessors had were able to enrich Montenegrin literature with new genres.

The liberation and renewal of the Montenegrin statehood (as one of the six Yugoslav republics) made it possible for the arts to develop. Among the painters, Petar Lubarda, with the dramatic Expressionism and originality of his works, brought something new. In addition, older-generation artists (such as Milo Milunović) and sculptor Risto Stijović were successful. Montenegrin sculptors built several monuments in wood and in bronze.

After World War II architecture came into being, especially when the new city of Titograd (Podgorica) was built, with many Modernist monumental buildings. At the same time development also intensified in the field of music, in spite of the fact that the Music Academy (in Titograd) was not established until as late as 1980. Many Montenegrins worked in the field of music in other places.

Radio Titograd was established in 1949. A symphony orchestra, mixed chorus, *tamburitza* (a custom-made string instrument with a pear-shaped body, somewhat similar to a mandolin) orchestra, etc. also operated under its auspices. Many music festivals were held. There were quite a few composers who worked in Montenegro. In addition to the older prewar generation, during the postwar period Cvjetko Ivanović, Branko Zenović, and others also became known.

Macedonians

The standardization of Macedonian language and the establishment of the University of Kiril i Metodij (Saints Cyril and Methodius) contributed to a fast development of Macedonian culture after World War II. Also, the Writers' Union of Macedonia was founded in 1946, and the first piece of fiction in the new language, a collection of short stories, was published. In April and May 1946, performances in the new Macedonian National Theater and Macedonian Opera took place. On 2 May 1946, the first film with Macedonian subtitles was shown in Skopje. In the next decades all fields of culture developed relatively quickly. Initially, Social Realism was the most influential artistic trend, but soon other styles were also embraced.

In October 1946 a new daily newspaper in the Macedonian language was established. However, the most important media for transmitting the new Macedonian language, culture, and national identity were the educational system and, later, radio and TV.

Conclusion: The Death of the Country

The Yugoslav communist leadership was aware of the potential destructive energy of nationalism and the danger of escalated ethnic conflicts in this multiethnic country. This is why the communists fiercely fought against nationalism in all ethnic groups in Yugoslavia. They wanted to resolve the "national question" by the establishment of the federation of equal nations (and, later, nationalities) after World War II. For this reason they officially recognized the existence of ethnic diversity in Yugoslavia (actually, in every republic and province) and proclaimed the principles of national equality and "brotherhood and unity" of Yugoslav nations (and nationalities). However, the regime failed to establish and develop adequate, formal mechanisms and institutions within the political system for the prevention, management, and resolution of ethnic and other escalated social conflicts. This proved to be one of the important factors that contributed to the failure of the Yugoslav federation. The Yugoslav federal system failed to provide ways to preserve the necessary cohesion in this multiethnic country. There was also no adequate mechanism that could replace the informal social and political roles of the late president Tito and the dismantled KPJ. Before, as informal forces and decisive factors, they had managed to provide the necessary cohesion and had been successful in the prevention, management, and resolution of escalated conflicts in the post–World War II era. After the death of the President Tito and the collapse of the KPJ in the late 1980s the process of the disintegration of the federation started and accelerated, and the paralyzed Yugoslav political system, which lacked the consensus necessary for reforms, was unable to stop it.

In spite of all criticism it should be acknowledged here that the post–World War II constitutional and political developments of the former Yugoslavia did pave the way for the creation of independent successor states. These nation-states of the former Yugoslav nations will be described in the following chapter.

Timeline

7–26 August 1945	Third convention of the AVNOJ (Anti-Fascist Council of Liberation of Yugoslavia)
23 August 1945	Contemporary People's Assembly adopted the Law on Agrarian Reform
11 November 1945	Elections for the National Assembly
29 November 1945	Federal People's Republic of Yugoslavia (FPRY) proclaimed
22 December 1945	United States and United Kingdom recognized the FPRY
January 1946	Husein Čišić, a deputy to the federal assembly from Mostar, tried in the Yugoslav parliament to explain the existence of Slavic Muslims
31 January 1946	Constituent Assembly passed the Constitution of the FPRY
11 June 1946	Seven-year compulsory education introduced
16 July 1946	Yugoslav authorities sentenced Chetnik leader Draža Mihailović to death
September 1946	Yugoslav authorities arrested archbishop of Zagreb, Alojzije Stepinac, and later sentenced him to sixteen years in prison
5 December 1946	National Assembly adopted the first law on nationalization

10 February 1947	Governments of Italy and Yugoslavia signed the peace treaty in Paris
28 April 1947	Five-Year Plan (*petletka*) was adopted
July 1947	Trial against Črtomir Nagode in Ljubljana
15 September 1947	Peace Treaty between Italy and Yugoslavia enforced; the Slovene Coastland was annexed to Yugoslavia; the Free Territory of Trieste/Trst was established
28 April 1948	The National Assembly adopted the second law on nationalization
19–23 June 1948	A proclamation about the expulsion of Yugoslavia was adopted by the members of Cominform at its meeting in Bucharest
28 June 1948	Fifth Congress of the KPJ learns of Yugoslavia's expulsion from the Cominform
29 May 1949	Edvard Kardelj introduced to the Yugoslav parliament the Law on People's Committees
June 1949	Eastern European countries ceased to respect all agreements with Yugoslavia
2–7 November 1952	Sixth Congress of the KPJ in Zagreb renamed the party as the League of Communists of Yugoslavia (LCY), and announced a program of reform
13 January 1953	Constitutional Law introduced the concept of workers' self-management; Milovan Djilas expelled from the communist party
4 October 1954	London Memorandum (Memorandum of Understanding between the Governments of Italy, the United Kingdom, the United States, and Yugoslavia Regarding the Free Territory of Trieste) introduced; Free Territory of Trieste divided between Italy and Yugoslavia
15 May 1955	Austrian State Treaty signed
4 December 1957	The Second Five-Year Plan adopted
13–15 January 1958	First mass strike after World War II in Trbovlje
22–26 April 1958	Seventh Congress of the LCY; the new program adopted
25 June 1958	General law on education adopted
1 October 1959	Eight-year compulsory education adopted in Slovenia
March 1961	Economic reform introduced

7 April 1963	New constitution introduced greater decentralization in the federation; the state was renamed the Socialist Federated Republic of Yugoslavia (SFRY)
7–13 December 1964	Eighth Congress of the LCY endorses markets reform
24 July 1965	Market reforms implemented
July 1966	The Brioni Plenum dismisses Aleksandar Ranković
18 July 1967	Macedonians implement their independent Macedonian Orthodox Church
January 1968	Yugoslav authorities acknowledged the Muslims as a nation (*narod*)
June 1968	Student demonstrations all over Yugoslavia
October–November 1968	First anti-Serb demonstrations of Kosovo Albanians in Prizren, Peć, and Suva Reka
Summer 1969	A scandal started in Slovenia regarding the building of roads
April–June 1971	Student demonstrations in Ljubljana
1971–1972	The Croat Spring and the rise and fall of the mass movement (*maspok*) in favor of greater independence for Croatia
October 1972	Serb liberalism collapsed
21 February 1974	New constitution of the SFRJ
10 November 1975	Treaty of Osimo between Italy and Yugoslavia
February 1976	Authorities arrested nineteen Albanians, including the writer Adem Demaçi
25 November 1976	Law of Associated Labor introduced the principle of discussion and arrangement into the economy
4 May 1980	President Josip Broz-Tito died
11 March 1981	In Kosovo, unrest of the Albanian population began; the Yugoslav People's Army sent tanks to Priština/Prishtin
May 1982	In Ljubljana, the first issue of the *Nova revija* (*New Journal*) was published
16 May 1982	Milka Planinc became president of the federal government (Federal Executive Council)

18 July–20 August 1983 Process against Alija Izetbegović and other members of pan-Islamic Muslim organization

19 August 1983 Death of Aleksandar Ranković

January–February 1986 Serbs in Kosovo mounted anti-Albanian demonstration

May 1986 Bosnian Serb Branko Mikulić became president of the federal government (Federal Executive Council)

April–May 1986 Milan Kučan and Slobodan Milošević are elected to lead their respective republican League of Communist organizations

24–25 September 1986 Belgrade daily *Večernje novosti* published excerpts of the *Memorandum Srpske akademije nauka i umjetnosti* (Memorandum of the Serb Academy of Arts and Sciences)

February 1987 *Nova Revija* published a Slovene National Program in its issue No. 57 demanding democracy and the independence of Slovenia

24 April 1987 Milošević proclaimed himself protector of the Serbs and Montenegrins of Kosovo

September 1987 Milošević took over the LC of Serbia and launched his "antibureaucratic revolution," a plan to dismiss all autonomy-oriented communist leaders of Yugoslav republics and autonomous provinces (he succeeded only in Vojvodina, Montenegro, and Kosovo)

15 December 1987 Milošević dismissed Ivan Stambolić

April–May 1988 Weekly magazine *Mladina* criticized Yugoslav Army

May 1988 Political proceeding against the counterrevolution in Slovenia started with the trial against the Gang of Four

20 August 1988 Mass protests of Milošević's followers in the Montenegrin capital of Titograd

September 1988 The first "mass demonstrations of truth" in Serbia and Montenegro in support of Milošević's proposed constitutional changes

18 September and 7 October 1988 Mass protests of Milošević's followers in the Montenegrin city of Nikšić

October 1988	Following huge demonstrations in Novi Sad, the leadership of the LC of Vojvodina resigned, to be replaced by nominees of Milošević
November 1988	Mass protests of miners of Trepča and Albanian students in Kosovo against the dismissal of Kosovo leaders (Kaçuša Jašari and Azem Vllasi)
19 November 1988	Almost one million people demanded the abolishment of Kosovo autonomy at the "Meeting of Truth"
30 December 1988	Branko Mikulić resigns as Prime Minister
11 January 1989	Leaders of the LC of Montenegro were compelled to resign under pressure from mass protests of Milošević's followers
19 January 1989	Ante Marković took office as the federal prime minister (President of the Federal Executive Council); the League of Communists of Slovenia, as the first reigning communist party, gave up their political monopoly in favor of democratic developments
20–28 February 1989	Strike of miners in Stari trg in Kosovo
27 February 1989	President of Yugoslavia declared martial law in Kosovo
28 February 1989	Croat Democratic Union (HDZ) was founded in Zagreb under the leadership of Franjo Tudjman
3 March 1989	Serb authorities arrested Albanian politician Azem Vllasi
28 March 1989	Parliament of the Republic of Serbia proclaimed a new Serb Constitution, which almost abolished the autonomy of Kosovo and Vojvodina; in mass protests by Kosovo Albanians, about 140 protesters were killed
8 May 1989	May Declaration in Slovenia (Majniška deklaracija)
9 May 1989	Slobodan Milošević was elected president of the Serb republic under the new constitution
15 May 1989	Janez Drnovšek of Slovenia took office as the president of the Presidency of the Yugoslav federation
28 June 1989	The 600th anniversary of the battle of Kosovo (Kosovo polje) was celebrated at Gazimestan;

Milošević spoke for the first time about the
possibility of armed fights

27 September 1989   Amendments made to the constitution of Slovenia
End of November 1989   Slovene opposition parties united into the
Democratic Opposition of Slovenia (DEMOS)

1 December 1989   Unsuccessful "meeting of truth" in Ljubljana

19 December 1989   Federal government announces its program for
the stabilization of the dinar (the Yugoslav unit of
currency)

27 December 1989   Communist-controlled Slovene Assembly
legalized a multiparty political system in Slovenia

January 1990   New convertible dinar (convertible into other
world currencies) was launched by the Marković
government

24 January 1990   Slovene communists left the Fourteenth
(Extraordinary) Congress of the LCY

February 1990   Serb Democratic Party founded

8 April 1990   First multiparty elections in Slovenia after World
War II

6 May 1990   HDZ won the first multiparty elections in Croatia

Significant People, Places, and Events

BAKALLI, MAHMUT (1936–) Albanian politician. Bakalli was assistant
professor of sociology at the University of Priština. In 1968 he was
elected a member of the Central Committee (CC) of the LC (League of
Communists) of Serbia. In 1971 he served as the president of the
provincial committee of the LC of Kosovo. From 1974 until 1981 he
was a member of the presidency of the CC of the LCY and a member of
the presidency of the CC of the LC of Serbia. Because he was not able
to predict early enough what was happening in Kosovo and to inform
the Belgrade government, he had to resign from all the positions he
held after the 1981 unrest in Kosovo.

BIJEDIĆ, DŽEMAL (1917–1977) President of the Yugoslav government,
Muslim. Bijedić studied law in Belgrade. He became a member of the
Communist Party of Yugoslavia (KPJ) in 1939. During World War II he
was one of the main organizers of the NLM in Bosnia and Herzegovina. During the postwar period he served as a secretary of justice and as
labor secretary, and from 1971 until his death in an airplane crash, he

served as the president of the Federal Executive Council (Savezno izvršno veče), that is, the, Yugoslav government.

BREGOVIĆ, GORAN (1950–) Yugoslav musician and composer. Born in Sarajevo to an ethnically mixed family (his mother was a Serb; his father was a Croat), Goran Bregović studied violin at the Music Academy in Sarajevo. In 1974 he established a rock band, Bjelo dugme (White Button), which was very successful until 1989. Then he composed music for films (e.g., for Kusturica's film *Dom za vešanje*) and ethnic music (music based on traditional folk/ethnic motifs). During the war he escaped to Paris. He spent much of the 1990s in Belgrade and today lives in Paris, New York, and Belgrade.

BROZ-TITO, JOSIP (1892–1980) Politician, after 1943, the Marshal of Yugoslavia. As an Austro-Hungarian soldier, Tito became a prisoner of war in Russia, and in 1917 he became a soldier in the Red Army. In Russia he became a communist. After he came back from Russia, he was a leading Yugoslav communist. From 1928 to 1934 he was imprisoned in Yugoslavia because of his communist activities. After he was released from the prison he went to Vienna and Moscow. After the Stalinist purges in the KPJ, in 1937 Tito formally became the secretary-general of the party. During World War II he organized and led the partisan army in its fight against the occupiers. In November 1943, at the second session of the AVNOJ (Anti-Fascist Council of National Liberation of Yugoslavia), he was named the president of the Temporary Revolutionary Government. After the Tito-Šubašić Agreement was signed, he became president of the unified Yugoslav government. During the period 1945–1953 he was the prime minister; from 1953–1963, he was the president of Yugoslavia; and from 1963 on, he was given the distinction of president for life.

After the conflict with the Cominform and a period of forced collectivization and purges of the followers of the Cominform, a new type of the communism (Titoism, self-management) was developed, and Yugoslavia became the first socialist country to open its borders to the West. There were 1.2 million Yugoslav temporary workers abroad (guest workers who worked abroad on the assumption that their employment was temporary). Tito was also one of the founders of the nonaligned movement. Tito became the symbol of the Yugoslav multinational state. However, this Yugoslav state proved unable to survive after his death.

COMINFORM (INFORMBUREAU) In September 1947, as the Cold War was descending upon Europe, Stalin established the Communist Information Bureau, or Cominform, an institution he would dominate. The purpose of the Cominform was to create cohesion among European communist parties, including those of Italy, France, and all Eastern European states. In Eastern Europe, where the communist parties were just coming to power, the Cominform required that parties follow the development model established by the Soviet Union, the only state where the communists had ruled before 1945. Although the KPJ (Communist Party of Yugoslavia) was initially among the USSR's enthusiastic and loyal emulators, it soon came into conflict with Moscow. On 28 June 1948, it was expelled from the Cominform.

CRVENKOVSKI, KRSTE (1921–) Macedonian politician. Crvenkovski served as a communist party functionary during World War II, beginning in 1941. He served as a member of the Federal Executive Council, a member of the CC of the LCY, a vice president of the Macedonian government, and the secretary of the CC of the LC of Macedonia.

DAPČEVIĆ-KUČAR, SAVKA (1923–) Professor of economics at the University of Zagreb; Croatian politician. Dapčević-Kučar participated in the NLM and was a member of the KPJ from 1943 on. In 1964 she became a member of the CC of the LCY. She served as a president of the Croat Parliament from 1967–1968 and then become the President of the CC of the LC of Croatia during the period 1969–1971. Because she "permitted" the development of liberalism and the spread of nationalist ideas in Croatia and also inside the Croat LC, she had to resign from all positions. She was also excluded from the LCY. During the period of the independence movement in Croatia in the 1990s, she cofounded a liberal political party in Croatia.

DOLANC, STANE (1925–2000) Slovene politician. During the period 1945–1960, Dolanc served in the Yugoslav People's Army; after that he served in the LCY. From 1969 until 1979 he was the secretary of the CC of the LCY. From 1982–1984 he served as the secretary for Internal Affairs and during 1984–1989 as a member of the joint presidency of the SFRY.

DRAGOSAVAC, DUŠAN (1919–) Serb politician from Croatia; President of the CC of the LCY. Dragosavac earned a Ph.D. in economics. During World War II he served in the KPJ. After World War II he occupied important positions in foreign trade. In 1978 he was a member of the CC and the LCY and the presidency of the CC of the LCY; later, he was secretary and president of the CC of the LCY.

FEDERAL EXECUTIVE COUNCIL (*Savezno izvršno veće*) The Federal Executive Council was the twenty-two-member government of Yugoslavia from 1963 on. Each republic had three representatives, and each of the autonomous provinces had two members on the council.

HODŽA, FADIL (1916–) Albanian politician. Although he was born in Kosovo, Hodža immigrated to Albania and finished teacher's college in Elbasan, Albania. Until 1941 he lived in Albania and helped Tito to establish the Albanian Communist Party. After he returned to Yugoslavia he joined the CPY and became one of the main organizers of the partisan movement in Kosovo. During the post–World War II period he served as a member of the Federal Executive Council. At the Seventh Congress of the LCY he became a member of the CC of the LCY and, in October 1966, a member of the presidency of the CC of the LCY. In 1987 he had to resign because he was condemned for overlooking the danger of Albanian nationalism and for protecting war criminals. He was excluded from the LCY and had to resign from politics.

KAVČIČ, STANE (1919–1987) Slovene politician. Kavčič was a member of the KPJ from 1941. During and after World War II he served in the communist youth organization and communist party and in trade unions. He served as the president of the Slovene Government during 1967–1972. As the prime minister he defended Slovene interests in Yugoslavia. As a liberal, he was later forced to resign and to retire. He described his life in a book, *Dnevnik in spomini* (*Diary and Memoirs*), published posthumously in 1988.

KIDRIČ, BORIS (1912–1953) Slovene politician. Kidrič served as leader of the Slovene communists during the interwar period. During World War II he was secretary of the KPS and political secretary of the Liberation Front– (OF). In 1945 he became the first president of the Slovene government after World War II. In 1946 he became a minister of industry in Yugoslavia and, as such, the creator of Yugoslav planning and economic policy. During the split with the Cominform he initiated workers' self-management.

KIŠ, DANILO (1935–1989) Serb writer and interpreter. Danilo Kiš wrote many novels on life in Serbia. The most important are *Peščenik* (*Sandy Watch*, 1972), *Grobnica za Borisa Davidovića* (*Tombstone for Boris Davidović*, 1976), *Čas anatomije* (*Anatomic Watch*, 1976), and *Enciklopedija mrtvih* (*Encyclopedia of Death*, 1983).

KOLIŠEVSKI, LAZAR (1914–) Macedonian politician. Koliševski was active in the KPJ during World War II. Soon after the capitulation of the Yugoslav armed forces, Koliševski prepared for armed resistance in Macedonia, which was under Bulgarian occupation. In November 1941, the Bulgarian authorities arrested and convicted him and sentenced him to death; however, the Bulgarians later changed the sentence to life in prison. After the communist takeover, he became the first president of the Macedonian government and, during the decade 1953–1963, the president of the Macedonian parliament (Narodno sobranie Narodne republike Makedonije). Koliševski was also active in party politics. He was a member of the presidency of the CC of the LCY and had numerous other functions in the federal parliament.

KRAIGHER, BORIS (1914–1967) Slovene politician. During the interwar period, Kraigher led the communist youth organization in Slovenia. After World War II (1953–1956) he served as a secretary of internal affairs; from 1953–1962 he was the president of the Slovene government, and during the period 1963–1967 he was a vice president of the Yugoslav government in charge of economic affairs.

KRAIGHER, SERGEJ (1914– 2001) Slovene politician. Sergej Kraigher was a member of the KPJ from 1934 on. During World War II he performed important functions in Slovene Styria; after World War II he became the governor of the National Bank of Yugoslavia (1951–1953), a member of the Yugoslav government, vice president of the Chambers of the Yugoslav Parliament, the president of the Slovene Parliament (1967–1974), the president of the presidency of the SRS (a multiperson presidency) (1974–1979), and a member and president of the presidency of the SFRY.

KUSTURICA, EMIR (1955–) Yugoslav film director, professor at Columbia University, New York. Kusturica began his career in TV and made an auspicious feature debut with *Sječaš li se Dolly Bell* (*Do You Remember Dolly Bell,* 1981). It won the Golden Lion award for the best first film at the Venice Film Festival. It was followed by the film *Otac na službenum putu* (*When Father Was Away on Business,* 1985), an absorbing portrait of provincial life and politics in 1950s Yugoslavia, partially seen through the eyes of a six-year-old child. It won the Palme d'Or at Cannes, five Golden Arenas awards (the Yugoslav Oscars), and an Academy Award nomination for best foreign film. Kusturica's third feature, *Vreme Cigana* (*Time of the Gypsies,* 1989), was inspired by a newspaper article about the inter-European trade in young gypsy children. It earned him the best director award at the Cannes Film Festival in 1989, the same year he was also awarded the Roberto Rosellini prize for lifetime achievement in film. Kusturica has taught film directing at Columbia University since 1988.

LEAGUE OF COMMUNISTS Yugoslavia was declared a republic in November 1945; after a brief period of coalition government, the communists, now in charge, initiated a series of revolutionary measures: for example, agrarian reforms, nationalization of industry, and the like. Political parties, except for the KPJ, were outlawed, and the country, although organized and run centrally, was divided into six socialist federal republics. In foreign relations the KPJ relied on guidance from Moscow and the Cominform, established in 1947, until Stalin expelled the Yugoslavs from the organization in 1948. Some Yugoslav internationalists, who put the interests of the international communist movement above the interests of Yugoslavia, sided with Moscow, and many were imprisoned.

In 1952 the KPJ embarked on a new course. Acknowledging the break with Moscow, and armed with an allegedly clearer understanding of Marxism, the Yugoslav communists set out to build socialism the "right way." The KPJ, in the spirit of renewed effort, renamed itself the League of Communists of Yugoslavia or LCY (Savez komunista Jugoslavije—Zveza komunistov Jugoslavije). Edvard Kardelj's brainchildren, Socialist self-management and the nonaligned movement, were endorsed at this time and became special features of Yugoslav Socialism.

Yugoslav Communism's survival ultimately depended on the willingness of ethnic groups and republic and provincial party organizations to cooperate. Nationalism, which had been proclaimed extinct by the party, reappeared openly in the 1960s, along with pressure for economic and political liberalization. By the end of the decade, Slovene and especially Croat communists pushed for greater autonomy in governing their respective republics. In applying policies, Tito alternated between federalism and centralism, generally siding with the less strong faction. Those in favor of federalism demanded decentralization of the federation and stronger autonomy of republics and provinces, and the centralists called for increased centralization, stronger federal authorities, concentration of all powers at the federal level, and reduced autonomy for republics and provinces. The 1974 constitution strengthened federalism in the party and the state, yet it also strengthened party authority (the communists intended to remain in control). The stage was set, however, for the disintegration of both the party and the state. After Kardelj's death in 1979 and Tito's death in 1980, the integrating forces in Yugoslavia disappeared. By 1986, the Great Serbian movement, attempting to gain control of both the LCY and the state, met with opposition from Slovenes, and eventually from Croats. In January 1990 the LCY collapsed.

LJUBIČIĆ, NIKOLA (1916–) Yugoslav general, Serbian. Ljubičić served in the army and was one of the main organizers of the uprising in Valjevo in Serbia, during World War II. In 1963, after finishing his studies at the Military Academy in Belgrade, he became a Colonel-General. In 1967 he became the federal secretary for people's defense (secretary of defense). He also served in the CC of the communist party and in the presidency of the CC of the LCY.

MAKAVEJEV, DUŠAN (1932–) Serb film director. Makavejev was the first Yugoslav director who filmed short films. His best-known films are *Čovjek nije tica* (*Man Is Not a Bird*, 1965), *Ljubavni slučaj ili tragedija službenice PTT* (*A Case of Love or Tragedy of a Postal Employee*, 1967) and *Nevinost bez zaštite* (*Virginity without Protection*, 1968). After 1973 he also became well known internationally with *Sweet Movie* (1974) and *The Coca-Cola Kid* (1985).

MAMULA, BRANKO (1921–) Admiral of the Yugoslav People's Army and minister of defense. During World War II Mamula served in the army. After he graduated from the Naval Academy he served as the chief of staff of the Yugoslav Navy and also as the undersecretary of defense. In August 1979 he became the chief of staff of the Yugoslav Army (he took over his post from Slovene general Stane Potočar). He also served as the secretary of defense and retained this position until 1988, when he was forced to retire. He was also elected the representative of the Army to the Central Committee of the LCY in 1978.

MARKOVIĆ, ANTE (1924–) Croatian politician. In the period 1982–1986, Marković served as the president of the Croat government, and in 1986 he became a member of the CC of the LCY. In 1989, after Branko Mikulić resigned, Ante Marković become the last president of the Yugoslav federal government. With financial and political aid from the West, he tried to prevent the dissolution of Yugoslavia. He tried first with constitutional and economic reforms (also with international convertibility of the national currency), and asked for financial aid from foreign countries. When Slovenia and Croatia opted for independence, he tried to preserve Yugoslavia with armed intervention. In the midst of armed conflicts in Yugoslavia, when he no longer controlled the situation, he resigned as prime minister in December 1991.

MEŠTROVIĆ, IVAN (1883–1962) Croatian sculptor. Ivan Meštrović combined the ideas of Viennese Secession (developed by a group of artists who seceded from the Society of Artists in Vienna in 1897) and the ideas of contemporary French sculptors with Croat national components. His sculptures show motifs from Croat people's poetry and from the Bible. He became especially well known with his monuments to Grgur Ninski (a Catholic bishop), Josip Juraj Strossmayer (a Catholic bishop of Djakovo and leader of the Illyrian movement), and Petar Petrović Njegoš (a Montenegrin poet and *vladika*). Among his other famous works are the sculpture of an unknown hero at Avala near Belgrade, and his monuments in Chicago. He also wrote a memoir, *Uspomene na političke ljude i dogadjaje* (Memoirs on Political Personalities and Events) in 1961 in which he described his political activities.

MIKULIĆ, BRANKO (1928–) Politician from Bosnia and Herzegovina, Serb. Mikulić joined the partisan movement when he was only fifteen years old. After the communist takeover he studied economics in Zagreb and worked in the communist party administration. In 1967 he became the president of Bosnia and Herzegovina, and in 1969, president of the CC of the LC of Bosnia and Herzegovina. He served also in the Presidency of the CC of the LCY. In October 1978 he was elected president of the Presidency of the CC of the LCY for one year. In 1985 he became the president of the Yugoslav government. During the deep economic and political crisis of Yugoslavia, he did not succeed in solving any problems, and he had to resign in December 1988.

NATIONALITIES (National Minorities) After the introduction of the system of self-management and following the traditional ethnic policy of the Yugoslav communists, a new concept of the protection of national minorities was developed. It was based on equality of all ethnic communities in a plural society and defined national minorities as equal actors that should enjoy adequate autonomy and play an active (equal) role in ethnic relations. To avoid possible negative connotations of the very term *minority* (a smaller, usually subordinate group), this concept introduced a new term, *nationality*. In practice, the term *nationalities* was considered a synonym of the term *national minorities*.

NIKEZIĆ, MARKO (1921–) Serbian politician and diplomat. In 1941 Nikezić joined the struggle of the partisans against the Fascists. After the communist takeover he at first worked in the communist party apparatus. From 1952 on, he served in the Foreign Secretariat of Yugoslavia, and from 1953, he served in the diplomatic service. He served as Yugoslav ambassador to the United Arab Emirates, Czechoslovakia, and the United States. In 1965 he become the foreign minister; he resigned in 1967, however, because he did not agree with Tito's foreign policy. In 1968 he was elected president of the LC of Serbia; in 1972 he was forced to resign, because he was condemned by the Yugoslav communists for anarcholiberalism, etatism, and technocratism. (In the vocabulary of the Yugoslav communists, anarcholiberalism meant rightwing ideological deviations from the official communist ideology of self-management; etatism meant the advocacy of the authority of the state in all fields including economy, culture, and science; and technocratism represented the attempt to increase the influence of experts, technicians, scholars, and scientists and their ways of operation on political leadership and the society.)

PAVLOVIĆ, ŽIVOJIN (1933–) Serb film director and writer. Pavlović's most important films are *Budjenje pacova* (*Waking Up of the Rats*, 1967); *Kad budem mrtav i beo* (*When I Am Going to Be "Death and White,"* 1967); *Zaseda* (*Ambush*, 1969); *Hajka* (*Hunt*, 1977); and *Dezerter* (*Deserter*, 1994). He became the leading author of the so-called new Yugoslavian film and the (pessimistic) "black wave." When his film *Zaseda* (*Ambush*, 1969) was criticized by the authorities, he went to work in Slovenia for a while. There he directed some films that were financed by Slovenes and in which Slovene was the language of communication: *Rdeče klasje* (*Red Ears*, 1970), *Let mrtve ptice* (*Flight of Death Beard*, 1973) and *Nasvidenje v naslednji vojni* (*Goodbye in the Next War*, 1980).

PEROVIĆ, LATINKA (1933–) Politician, Serbian. Perović was active in politics by the time she was a graduate student. She received an M.A. in political science. She was a member of the presidency of the Central Committee of the League of Youth of Serbia and a member of the presidency of the Central Committee of the League of Youth of Yugoslavia. In 1961 she became president of the Yugoslav Women's' Organization; she was also active as a member of the Federal Committee of the Socialist Alliance of Working People of Yugoslavia. She was elected a member of the CC of the LC of Serbia at its Fifth Congress of LC Serbia. In 1968 she was elected the secretary general of the CC of the LC of Serbia. In 1972 she had to resign and withdraw from politics, as she was accused of spreading "anarcholiberalist, etatist, and technocratic" ideas along with Marko Nikezić.

PLANINC, MILKA (1924–) Croatian politician. Milka Planinc was a graduate of the Higher Administration School in Zagreb. She joined Tito's partisans in 1941. After the war she pursued a full-time political career in the Croat Communist Party, specializing in agitation, propaganda, and education. In 1954 she became a party instructor in the Zagreb Municipal Party Committee, was later political secretary of the Trešnjevka (Zagreb) Municipal Party Committee, and, in 1957, president of the Trešnjevka People's Committee. After serving as the head of the Zagreb People's Committee Secretariat for Education and Culture, she became (in 1963) the organizational secretary of the Zagreb Municipal LC Committee and (in 1965) the republic's secretary of education. In

1966 she was elected to the Presidium of the Croat LC and in 1968 to its Executive Committee.

Planinc's real party career began in December 1971 after Tito purged the top Croat party and state leaders and she was elected president of the Central Committee of the Croat LC and helped Tito suppress Croat nationalism. She was confirmed in her offices both at the level of the republic at the Seventh Congress of the Croat LC (April 1974) and at the federal level at the Tenth (1974) and Eleventh (1978) LCY Congresses. In spring of 1982 she was elected the Yugoslav prime minister (president of the Federal Executive Council). Although she was quite successful in her attempts to revive the Yugoslav economy, she had to resign in 1985 because of the opinion of the leadership of the LCY that her promarket-oriented economic policy was not in accordance with the official line and economic policy of LCY.

POZDERAC, HAMDIJA (1923–) Muslim politician from Bosnia and Herzegovina. Pozderac joined Tito's partisan units in 1942. He graduated from the Philosophical Faculty and High Party School in Moscow. Both during and after his education, he occupied local party posts. In 1965 he was elected a member of the Central Committee of the Bosnian-Herzegovian LC and a member of its Executive Committee. At the Eleventh LCY Congress (1978), Pozderac was elected a member of the LCY Central Committee. At the sixth plenary session of the Central Committee in June 1979, he was elected to replace Cvijetin Mijatović (a Serb) as one of the three representatives of the Bosnian-Herzegovian LC on the LCY Presidium.

PRESIDENCY OF THE LEAGUE OF COMMUNISTS After the federalization of the state apparatus and then of the party apparatus, the communist party/League of Communist bodies became federalized also. Each of the republics sent three members and each autonomous province sent two members to a governing body of the LCY.

PRESIDENCY OF THE SFRY The Presidency was introduced as a collective head of state with the Constitutional Amendments of 1971 to ensure equality of the SRs and SAPs. According to the Constitution of the SFRY of 1974, this body consisted of nine members: in addition to one member of the federal presidency from each SR and SAP (elected by the respective republic or province assembly), one member of this body was also the president of the Presidency of the LCY. This arrangement, which was to formally ensure the leading social and political role of the LCY, persisted until 1988, when the Presidency was reduced to eight members—representatives of SRs and SAPs. The Presidency was headed by its president. President Tito was determined to be the president of the Presidency for life, and a vice president was elected for a one-year term from among other members. Following the death of Tito, presidents and vice presidents of the Presidency of SFRY were elected every year. Presidencies, as collective bodies, existed also in all SRs and SAPs.

ŠALAMUN, TOMAŽ (1941–) Slovene poet. Šalamun is representative of contemporary currents in Slovene poetry. His style includes Dadaism (an international movement in literature and plastic arts after World War I, developed as a protest against the bourgeoisie society and the aesthetics of the time); Surrealism (an artistic trend from the first half of the twentieth century that attempted to interpret reality through visions, hallucinations, and associations); and Ready Made (a style combining traditional spiritual values and banal objects in poetry). He mixes everyday anecdotes with esoteric, magic, and artistic experiences. He first became known with his books of poems, including Poker (1966), where he fights against mythology in Slovene poetry. His books of poems (twenty of them) are translated into many foreign languages.

SELF-MANAGEMENT Following the break with Stalin and the Soviet Union, but also based on some previously existing ideas in the Yugoslav communist leadership, a new ideology and system of self-management were introduced. This concept was first introduced as "workers' self-management" in the beginning of the 1950s. The initial idea was that workers themselves, through workers' councils in factories, should manage their own factories. However, self-management soon spread to all spheres of social and political life and became a universal ideology and system in Yugoslavia. The political system (called the political system of socialist self-management) was based on the "delegates' system," which required permanent communication and cooperation of assemblies at all levels (from communes as the basic units of local government, to SRs and SAPs, to the federation). The delegates in assemblies had to follow general instructions from their own delegate bases, to which they were responsible. Although delegates were elected for four-year terms, the possibility of recall existed if their delegate basis was unsatisfied with their performance in the assembly. (This power of recall was not used in practice.) The functioning of self-management, as it was introduced in practice, required active roles of the LCY and other social-political organizations (especially the Socialist Alliance of Working People), which were responsible for the coordination and internal cohesion of the system.

STAMBOLIĆ, IVAN (1936–2000?) Serb politician. After he finished law school at the University of Belgrade, Stambolić became a businessman. He was a director of the Tehnogas company in Belgrade and a president of the city's Chamber of Commerce. A member of the LCY since the age of eighteen, he served as the president of the city organization of Belgrade communists from 1982 to 1984, president of the CC of the LC of Serbia (1984–1986) and the president of Serbia (1986–1987). In December 1987 he was forced to resign from the latter post. His former protégé, Slobodan Milošević, accused him of being incompetent to deal with the situation in Kosovo. In mid-1988 he resigned from all political positions, became director of the Yugoslav Bank for International Economic Cooperation, and afterward was no longer involved in politics. In August 2000 every trace of him was lost; he disappeared while jogging in Košutnjak park in Belgrade. Rumors were spread that he was kidnapped. His remains were found in March 2003, and the police found that he was indeed kidnapped by four members of the Special Operations Unit of the Yugoslav army, who drove him to Fruška gora and killed him. According to Dušan Mihajlović, Serb Minister of the Interior (police), Slobodan Milošević ordered the killing of his longtime political mentor to prevent his candidacy for the presidency of the FRY in 2000.

STAMBOLIĆ, PETAR (1912–) Serb politician. Before World War II, Stambolić studied agriculture. During and after World War II he served in the communist party apparatus. He was one of the main organizers of the NLM in central Serbia. After December 1941 he was one of the leaders of the uprising in Serbia. He served as the agriculture secretary in the federal government of Yugoslavia. He belonged to the "conservatives" in the LCY and demanded a strong Serbia, which had to be defended from Albanian irredentists.

TRIPALO, MIKA (1926–) Lawyer and Croatian politician. During the NLM Tripalo served in the communist party apparatus in Dalmatia. After World War II he served as president of the Yugoslav student organization from 1953–1955. From 1957 until 1959 he was a secretary of the Yugoslav youth organization, then its president from 1957–1962. From 1962–1966, he was the secretary of the City Committee of the LC of Zagreb, and from 1966–1969, he was the secretary of the CC of the LC of Croatia. From 1969–1971 he was a member of the Executive Committee of the Presidency of the LCY. As a member of the "liberal wing" of the LC he had to resign from all political posts (together with Savka Dabčević-Kučar) because he did not succeed in preventing the spread of liberalism in connection with nationalist ideas in Croatia and inside the Croat LC.

VLLASI, AZEM (1948–) Albanian politician. Vllasi finished law school in Belgrade. A member of LCY after 1965, he was the president of the Provincial Committee of the League of Students of Kosovo and president of the League of Students of Yugoslavia. In 1971 he became a member of the presidency of the Socialist Alliance of Yugoslavia and secretary of the Provincial Conference of the Socialist Alliance of Kosovo. Later he became a member of the CC of the LCY and was the president of the CC of the LC of Kosovo. During the Milošević purges of 1988 he was forced to resign because he was accused of working against the Serb presidency's decisions. In July 1989 he was tried and acquitted. Since then he has written his memoirs and worked as a lawyer.

ŽIVOJINOVIĆ (BATA), VELIMIR (1933–) Serb film actor. At the young age of fifteen, Živojinović helped with scenery at the Academic Theatre in Belgrade. After he graduated from Belgrade Actor's Academy, he found employment in Belgrade theater, where he acted in 300 performances each year. He also acted in numerous films in Yugoslavia. After the dissolution of Yugoslavia, he became involved in politics. In autumn 2002 he was a candidate for president of the FRY on the list of the Socialist Party of Serbia.

Bibliography

Alexander, Stella. *Church and State in Yugoslavia since 1945.* (Cambridge, U.K.: Cambridge University Press, 1979).

Allcock, John B. "Montenegro." In Turnock, David, and Carter, Francis W. (eds.): *South-Eastern Europe.* Vol. 2, *The States of Eastern Europe.* (Aldershot, U.K.: Ashgate, 1999): 167–194.

Čović, Bože (ed.). *Izvori velikosrpske agresije* [Sources of Great-Serbian aggression]. (Zagreb, Croatia: Školska knjiga, 1991).

Dedijer, Vladimir. *The Battle Stalin Lost, 1948–1953.* (New York: Viking Press, 1970).

Djodan, Šime. "Gospodarska reforma i izbor optimalnog modela rasta" (Economic reform and choosing the optimal growth model). *Kolo 6*, no. 4 (April 1968): 306.

Friedman, Francine. "The Bosnian Muslims: The Making of a Yugoslav Nation." In Bokovoy, Melissa K., Irvine, Jill A., and Lilly, Carol S. (eds.): *State-Society Relations in Yugoslavia, 1945–1992.* (New York: St. Martin's Press, 1997): 267–290.

Kavčič, Stane. Igor Bavčar and Janez Janša (eds.). *Dnevnik in spomini, 1972–1987* (Diary and memoirs 1972–1987). (Ljubljana, Slovenia: Časopis za kritiko znanosti, 1988).

Kocbek, Edvard. *Dnevnik 1951–1952* (Diary, 1951–1952). (Zagreb, Croatia: Globus, 1986).

Lampe, John R. *Yugoslavia as History: Twice There Was a Country.* (Cambridge, U.K.: Cambridge University Press, 1996).

Lees, Lorraine M. *Keeping Tito Afloat: The United States, Yugoslavia, and the Cold War* (University Park: Pennsylvania State University Press, 1997).

Miller, Nicholas J. "Reconstituting Serbia, 1945–1991." In Bokovoy, Melissa K., Irvine, Jill A., and Lilly, Carol S. (eds.): *State-Society Relations in Yugoslavia, 1945–1992.* (New York: St. Martin's Press, 1997), 291–314.

Novak, Bogdan C. *Trieste 1941–54: The Ethnic, Political, and Ideological Struggle.* (Chicago: University of Chicago Press, 1970).

Pirjevec, Jože. *Jugoslavija 1918–1992: Nastanek, razvoj ter razpad Karadjordjević-eve in Titove Jugoslavije* (Yugoslavia 1918–1992: The creation, development, and dissolution of Karadjordjević's and Tito's Yugoslavia). (Koper, Slovenia: Založba Lipa, 1995)

Ramet, Sabrina P. *Beyond Yugoslavia: Politics, economics, and culture in a shattered community.* (Boulder, CO: Westview Press, 1995).

———. *Nationalism and Federalism in Yugoslavia, 1962–1991.* (Bloomington: Indiana University Press, 1992).

Remington, Robin A. "Ideology as a resource: A communist case study." In Bartelsen, J. S. (ed.): *Nonstate nations in international politics.* (New York: Praeger, 1977).

Repe, Božo. "Historical consequences of the disintegration of Yugoslavia for Slovene society." *Österreichische Osthefte 43,* no. 1–2 (2001): 5–26.

Rusinow, Dennison. *The Yugoslav Experiment, 1948–1972.* (Berkeley: University of California Press for Royal Institutional Affairs, 1977).

Savez komunista Hrvatske (League of Communists of Croatia). *Izveštaj o stanju SKH u odnosu na prodor nacionalizma u njegove redove,* 21. sjednica, 8. maj 1972 (Report on the situation in the LCC in relation with nationalism inside it, 21st session, 8 May 1972). (Zagreb, Croatia: Informativna služba CK SKH, 1972.

Silber, Laura, and Little, Allan. *Yugoslavia: Death of a Nation.* (New York: Penguin, 1997).

Smole, Joža. *Spomini Titovega sekretarja, 1968–1970* (Memoirs of Tito's Secretary, 1968–1970). (Ljubljana, Slovenia: Založba Delo, 1992).

Šuvar, Stipe. *Nacionalno i nacionalističko* (National and nationalistic). (Split, Croatia: Marksistični centar, 1974).

Tripalo, Mika. *Hrvatsko proljeće* (Croat Spring). (Zagreb, Croatia: Globus, 1990).

Troebst, Stefan. "Yugoslav Macedonia, 1943–1953: Building the Party, the State, and the Nation." In Bukovoy, Melissa K., Irvine, Jill A., and Lilly, Carol S.

(eds.): *State-Society Relations in Yugoslavia 1945–1992.* (New York: St. Martin's Press, 1997): 243–266.

Žagar, Mitja. "Yugoslavia: what went wrong? Constitutional aspects of the Yugoslav crisis from the perspective of ethnic conflict." In Spencer, Metta (ed.). *The Lessons of Yugoslavia* (*Research on Russia and Eastern Europe*), vol. 3. (Amsterdam: Elsevier Science JAI, 2000): 65–96.

CHAPTER SEVEN

The Region of
the Former Yugoslavia after 1990
New States and a New Situation

I N 1992 the international community officially recognized the independence of Slovenia, Croatia, Bosnia and Herzegovina, and (the Former Yugoslav Republic of) Macedonia, which meant the end of the former Yugoslavia. However, this was not the end of the Yugoslav crisis and drama. The tragic wars that followed in the territory of the former Yugoslavia, especially in Croatia and Bosnia and Herzegovina, colored the whole world's history in the last decade of the twentieth century. The Federal Republic of Yugoslavia (which is to be formally reorganized as the Union of Serbia and Montenegro based on the 14 March 2002 agreement, although the constitutional arrangements of this union are still to be decided), was another successor state of the SFRY that played a key role in the tragic developments of the 1990s. This country, internationally isolated during the regime of Slobodan Milošević, was welcomed into the international community again at the end of 2000 when democratic changes there took place.

This chapter briefly presents the dissolution of the former Yugoslavia and focuses on the history of the successor states of the SFRY in the last decade of twentieth century and at the beginning of the third millennium.

The Dissolution of Yugoslavia

The beginning of the 1990s marked the end of the Socialist Federative Republic of Yugoslavia (SFRY) and the collapse of its socialist/communist regime. At the end of the 1980s, the inability of the existing regime to address key problems and worsening social and political crisis in Yugoslavia,

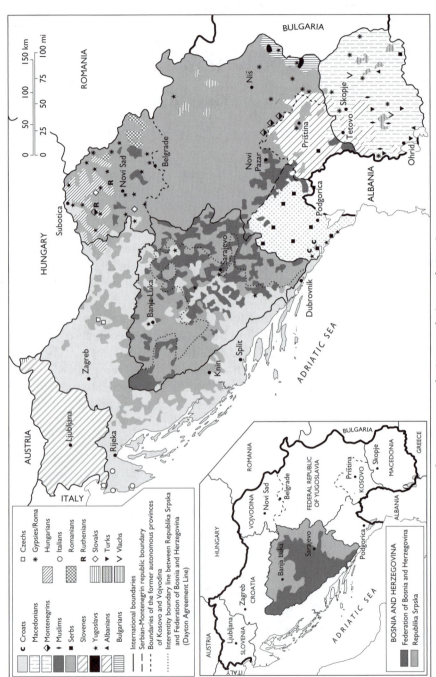

The Former Yugoslavia: Population and New States

Legend:

Croats
Macedonians
Montenegrins
Muslims
Slovenes
Yugoslavs
Albanians
Bulgarians

c — Croats
Czechs
Gypsies/Roma
Hungarians
Italians
R — Serbs
Romanians
Ruthenians
Slovaks
Turks
Vlachs

International boundaries
Serbian-Montenegrin republic boundary
Boundaries of the former autonomous provinces of Kosovo and Vojvodina
Interentity boundary line between Republika Srpska and Federation of Bosnia and Herzegovina (Dayton Agreement Line)

BOSNIA AND HERZEGOVINA
Federation of Bosnia and Herzegovina
Republika Srpska

AUSTRIA
HUNGARY
ROMANIA
BULGARIA
ITALY
ALBANIA

Ljubljana
Rijeka
Zagreb
Subotica
Novi Sad
Belgrade
Niš
Banja Luka
Sarajevo
Knin
Split
Dubrovnik
Novi Pazar
Priština
Podgorica
Skopje
Tetovo
Ohrid

ADRIATIC SEA

Inset map:
AUSTRIA
SLOVENIA
ITALY
HUNGARY
ROMANIA
BULGARIA
CROATIA
Ljubljana
Zagreb
VOJVODINA
Novi Sad
Belgrade
FEDERAL REPUBLIC OF YUGOSLAVIA
Banja Luka
Sarajevo
Priština
KOSOVO
Podgorica
Skopje
MACEDONIA
GREECE
ALBANIA
ADRIATIC SEA

150 km
100 mi
0 25 50 75 100
0 50 100 150

especially conflicts between Serbia and Slovenia and the crisis in Kosovo, reached its peak. Also, relations between the Serbs and Croats dangerously worsened. One could not be surprised that the Fourteenth Extraordinary Congress of the League of Communists of Yugoslavia (20–26 January 1990) developed into a quarrel about every question of political and economic life in Yugoslavia. When Slovene delegates left the Congress in protest on 23 January, the LCY dissolved.

Once the LCY fell apart, the Yugoslav People's Army (Jugoslovenska narodna Armija, JNA), in which Serb officers prevailed, started to interfere in the Yugoslav political scene. The JNA considered itself the heir to Tito's idea of Yugoslavia, based on brotherhood and unity. From the very beginning of the Yugoslav crises of the modern era, the JNA stated that it would fight "counterrevolutionary" tendencies and defend Yugoslavia's unity and territorial integrity at any cost. However, once they sided with the Serb position, this reduced the political space for a compromise. They proclaimed reform proposals of the Slovene and Croat communist authorities to decentralize the country and introduce a multiparty political system. Retrospectively, one could say that the JNA was among the key factors that prevented a peaceful solution of the Yugoslav crises.

Yugoslav Prime Minister Ante Marković was an optimist when he predicted that Yugoslavia would be able to survive without the LCY. Marković prepared a package of economic reforms that included liberalization of the economy, a stable Yugoslav currency (the dinar), and privatization of the economy, but also a stronger role of the central federal authorities in leading monetary policy. Marković devalued the dinar and, with monetary measures, succeeded in reducing inflation from 2500 percent to zero. He even declared convertibility of the dinar, which was the last symbol of Yugoslav unity. Although all deputies in the federal parliament applauded when Marković declared convertibility of the dinar on 19 December 1989, there was no necessary consensus to implement and further develop the proposed reforms.

Although Marković continued to fight for his reforms, he did not succeed in implementing most of them because Yugoslavia and its political system had already started to dissolve. By then, the conflicts between two diametrically opposed concepts of the future development of post-Tito Yugoslavia paralyzed the existing political system completely. To make the situation worse, people started to see these basically ideological and political conflicts as predominantly ethnic conflicts—initially between the Serbs and Slovenes. The reason for this was that the Serb (communist) political leadership advocated a unitaristic, centralized, and communist-

led Yugoslavia, but the Slovene (communist) political leadership demanded decentralization (later confederalization), democratic political
reforms (including the introduction of a multiparty political system), and
a market-oriented economy—both in the name of the nationalist interests of their respective nations, which they saw as the basis for the common Yugoslav interest. These differences, which were growing over time
and were rooted in specific historic, cultural, economic, social, and political developments and experiences of different parts of the former Yugoslavia, also produced different political orientations of the communist political leaders in Serbia and Slovenia as well as in other parts of the
country. When the conflicts between the communist leaders of Serbia and
Slovenia escalated, people started to perceive them as conflicts between
republics and, consequently, nations. (The perception of these conflicts as
ethnic conflicts took on a new dimension later when Croatia, Bosnia and
Herzegovina, and Macedonia sided with Slovenia and Montenegro supported Serbia, which had by then established its complete control over
both autonomous provinces.)

The situation became even more complicated after the first free and
democratic elections brought opposition parties to power in Croatia and
Slovenia in April 1990. The situation worsened, especially in Croatia,
where the "nationally" oriented Croat Democratic Union (Hrvatska
demokratska zajednica, HDZ), under the leadership of Franjo Tudjman,
came to power. Slogans like "Croatia has to assure its historic boundaries"
(claiming Herzegovina and Bosnian Posavina, a region in northern Bosnia and Herzegovina along the Sava River—see chapters 4 and 5) and the
decision to abolish the red star in the flag of Croatia and replace it with an
old Croat symbol, the red and white chessboard (also used by the Ustaša
and NDH), drew furious reactions among the Serbs in Croatia, who considered the HDZ a Croat nationalistic party. The growing ethnic tensions
between the Serbs and Croats paved the way for the later escalation of the
ethnic conflict and war in Croatia.

In Slovenia a coalition of the whole spectrum of political parties, from
Christian-Democrats to Social-Democrats, which established the DEMOS
(Democratic Opposition of Slovenia), won the elections against the governing communists and formed a new government. However, the reformist former communist leader in Slovenia, Milan Kučan, became the
president of the Republic.

Milošević, who in 1987 became the president of the LC of Serbia and
who until then had been fighting for the unity of the federation and for
the one-party system, started to think about the independence of Serbia.

He also spoke about the destiny of the one-quarter of the Serb nation that lived outside of Serb borders, mostly in Bosnia and Herzegovina and Croatia. Such slogans as "Serbia is everywhere that Serb graves are!" (Reuter, 1990, 586) gave courage to the Serbs in Croatia, who, with the help of the JNA, started to arm themselves in order to protect their identity and ensure their "ethnic" interests.

While Milošević tried to build the cornerstones of the Great Serbia, the JNA became more and more worried about the events in Croatia and Slovenia. In April and May 1990, the JNA confiscated most of the weapons stored for the territorial defense (a kind of National Guard) of both republics. Slovenia reacted, rescuing some weapons and making its territorial defense independent from the JNA. It also announced a plebiscite "on Slovene independence" that was to determine the future status of the republic and its (possible) links and arrangements with Yugoslavia. Croatia answered with the restructuring of its police forces into military units, from which the Croats removed all ethnic Serbs. To make up for the confiscated weapons, both republics had to buy weapons abroad, which brought protests from the JNA and the Yugoslav federation.

At the end of 1990, the League of Communists organization inside the JNA was renamed the League of Communists–Movement for Yugoslavia, and some politicians (e.g., Stipe Šuvar, Raif Dizdarević, and Mirjana Marković, the wife of Slobodan Milošević) joined it. They hoped that it could become a leading political force in the state in a few months. On 22 December 1990, a new constitution was proclaimed in Croatia, according to which the Croats had the sovereign right to decide upon their destiny.

In a plebiscite of 23 December 1990 in Slovenia, 90 percent of voters opted for the independence of Slovenia. After the plebiscite Slovenia started the process of implementing its independence from Yugoslavia, scheduled for June 1991. The Croats joined them in trying to leave the Yugoslav state. At the same time, a constitutional crisis occurred in Yugoslavia: Stipe Mesić (a Croat member of the Presidency of the SFRY) was due to become its president, but the Serbs and their allied members of the presidency did not want to elect him because they considered him a Croat nationalist who would do anything to help the dissolution of Yugoslavia.

In the multiparty parliamentary elections in Bosnia and Herzegovina, Serbia, and Montenegro in 1990, nationalist politicians and political parties came to power; and it became clear that there would be no peaceful solution to the crisis. The Serbs in the territory near the city of Knin in Croatia declared their independence from Croatia on 28 February 1991. On 12 May 1991 they declared that their communities would become a part of Serbia. The Serbs in Bosnia and Herzegovina also started to demand autonomy. In March 1991 the first armed conflicts between the Croat Serbs and the JNA on the one side and the newly established Croat army on the other occurred in Croatia (on 2 March in Pakrac, and on 31 March in Plitvice; see the section on Croatia in this chapter).

The situation became even more complicated after students' demonstrations in Belgrade in March 1991. The JNA wanted to proclaim martial law in the entire country. This idea was supported by the then-president of the SFRY, Borisav Jović. However, the Slovene, Croat, Bosnian-Herzegovian, Macedonian, and even Kosovo members of the presidency, which was the supreme commander of the armed forces, voted against it, and the JNA was not able to act on its own. Simultaneously, the army could not count on the support of their traditional allies from Moscow, as the Soviet army had too many problems of its own upon the dissolution of the Soviet Union.

In the first half of 1991, the presidents of the Yugoslav republics tried in a series of meetings to find solutions to some problems. For example, at the beginning of April 1991 in Brdo near Kranj (in Slovenia, where presidents George W. Bush and Vladimir Putin met in 2001), they put forward two blueprints for the future of Yugoslavia. While Slovenia and Croatia tried to find a solution within different forms of a loose confederation of independent states, Serbia insisted on a centralized federation with a strong federal government. The Serbs had the support of the JNA, and they also counted on the support of Marković's government. The leaders of Bosnia and Herzegovina and Macedonia joined the cause of the Slovenes and Croats, as they did not plan to stay in Yugoslavia if Slovenia and Croatia seceded. They knew that the Serbs would have an absolute majority in such a "rump" Yugoslavia and feared the Serbs' hegemonic aspirations. They were afraid that the equality and "national" rights of Bosniaks, Macedonians, and Bosnian Croats might be threatened and reduced.

The decisions of both Slovenia and Croatia to declare independence caused unrest in the West, which still wanted to preserve Yugoslavia's territorial integrity, unity, and independence. On 21 June 1991, the then U.S. secretary of state, James Baker, on the occasion of his visit to Belgrade, declared that the United States did not intend to recognize Slovenia and Croatia as independent states. These words were taken as U.S. support for any action against the "secessionist" republics.

Military intervention in Slovenia after it declared its independence on 25 June 1991 by the JNA in an attempt to force Slovenia not to secede was the final blow to Yugoslavia and led to its dissolution. By the end of 1991,

Bosnia and Herzegovina and Macedonia had also proclaimed their independence on the basis of plebiscites. On 15 January 1992, the European Union recognized Slovene, Croat, and Bosnian-Herzegovian independence. The United States's official recognition of Slovenia, Croatia, and Bosnia and Herzegovina followed on 7 April 1992. (When Slovenia had been promised its recognition by Germany before Christmas of 1991, Lawrence Eagleburger, the acting U.S. Secretary of State, in a conversation with Dimitrij Rupel, the Slovene foreign minister, had said that Slovenia would receive its recognition sooner or later. The actual recognition by the United States might have been an attempt to prevent a war in Bosnia and Herzegovina.) All these states became members of the United Nations on 22 May 1992.

Bloody wars accompanied the dismantling of the former Yugoslavia. Ethnic cleansing and 4 million refugees completely changed the ethnic structure of some regions.

Reactions of Diasporas from Yugoslavia to the Events in Their Homelands in the 1990s

In the 1990s as in the past (during World Wars I and II), diaspora communities from the former Yugoslavia played an important role in the developments, especially in advocating for international recognition of the independence of the Yugoslav successor states. Traditional divisions between "progressive" left (procommunist and Yugoslav) and "conservative" right (often nationalist) diaspora circles were somewhat decreasing after the death of President Tito in 1980. In the mid 1980s ideas of establishing independent states of individual Yugoslav nations started to strengthen. Most Slovene, Croat, and Macedonian emigrants supported democratization in their respective home republics and supported their efforts to establish independent states. The majority of Serb emigrants supported the policy of Slobodan Milošević and Serbia, which meant that initially they supported centralization of the Yugoslav federation and, later, the Great Serbia idea.

Following the homogenization of individual ethnic diaspora communities in the late 1980s and 1990s, cooperation between left- and right-wing emigrants and their organizations intensified. There was also cooperation between different emigrant communities, especially between the Croats and Slovenes, who organized several demonstrations (in the United States, Australia, Canada, Argentina, etc.) in 1991 and demanded the international recognition of the Slovene and Croat states. Sometimes

Albanian and Macedonian diaspora communities joined them. These activities strengthened during the war in Slovenia and Croatia.

Many immigrants wrote letters and petitions to newspaper editors, presidents of governments, and parliamentarians in their new homelands. A "War of Words" (Taylor, 1992, 6) among ethnic diaspora communities from the former Yugoslavia characterized the early 1990s. Diaspora communities hoped to receive support for their requests, especially from politicians of the same ethnic origin—for example, Helen Delich-Bentley, a congresswoman from Maryland, worked to aid the "Serb cause" in the United States and asked Serb immigrants to write to members of the U.S. Congress ("Bentley Calls Serbian/Americans to Arms" 1990); James Oberstar, a congressman from Minnesota; and Dennis Eckart, a congressman from Ohio, supported the Slovene cause. Diaspora communities established several organizations in support of independence and recognition of their countries of origin, and these groups were often active in collecting economic and humanitarian aid. Among these organizations were the United Americans for Slovenia, Conferences of the Slovene World Congress, the Serb National Federation (which, with its Serbia.net, aided propaganda activities of Serbia in the world), the Croat Congress, the United Macedonian Organization, and the Macedonian Patriotic Organization.

In some cases, newly established states invited some emigrants from the former Yugoslavia to take offices in their governments. The best known was Milan Panić, the owner of a pharmaceuticals factory in Los Angeles, who became the prime minister of Serbia with the permission of the U.S. State Department in 1992. Other such officials are Andrej Bajuk, a descendant of a Slovene political émigré from Argentina, who became the prime minister of Slovenia in 2000; and Gojko Šušak, a restaurant owner from Canada who was minister of defense in the Croat government of President Franjo Tudjman in the 1990s. In the case of George J. Perpich, the former governor of Minnesota, his request for dual Croat-U.S. citizenship was denied by the United States in 1990 (Secretary of State James Baker thought that the national interests of the the United States would not be best served by granting this demand), so he was unable to accept an opportunity to become minister of foreign affairs of Croatia.

Slovenia after 1990

The Slovenes consider their independent statehood a major historic achievement. As the Preamble of the Constitution of the Republic of Slovenia of 1991 explains, the proclamation of sovereignty and independence of the Republic of Slovenia was based on human rights and freedoms and the "fundamental and permanent right of the Slovene nation to self-determination" (confirmed by the plebiscite in December 1990), and it was a result of "the historical fact that in a centuries-long struggle for national liberation we Slovenes have established our national identity and asserted our statehood." The constitution establishes a "democratic republic" of "all its citizens" (regardless of their ethnic origin or other characteristics) that is a "social state" governed "by the rule of law"; citizens exercise power vested in the people "directly and through elections, consistent with the principle of the separation of legislative, executive and judicial powers" (Articles 1, 2, 3).

The Ethnic Situation

The territory and the international borders of the Republic of Slovenia with Italy, Austria, and Hungary were determined after World War II, and the republic's new international border with Croatia follows the border that existed in the former Yugoslavia (and is yet to be confirmed officially by a bilateral agreement). These borders meant that more than 200,000 ethnic Slovenes remained outside the borders of Yugoslavia after World War II as national minorities in Austria, Hungary, and Italy. A new situation and status for the Slovenes in the other countries established after the dissolution of the former Yugoslavia and immigrants from those countries in Slovenia are consequences of the independence of the new countries.

After most of the Germans, who had stayed after World War I, and many Italians decided to emigrate or were forced to emigrate from the country following World War II, Slovenia became the most ethnically homogeneous republic in Yugoslavia. Its largest autochthonous national minorities were the Hungarians, who settled the regions along the Hungarian-Slovenian border in Prekmurje, and the Italians, who lived in Slovene Istria on the coast. The Roma, some of them still nomads/travelers, were more concentrated in the regions of Dolenjska and Prekmurje.

Nonetheless, the natural increase of the population, and especially internal economic migrations, in Yugoslavia were most important factors in the changes of the ethnic structure in Slovenia after World War II. As the most economically developed Yugoslav republic, Slovenia attracted many immigrants from other parts of Yugoslavia. Because of immigration, the number and percentage of members of all the Yugoslav nations (but especially Croats, Serbs, and Muslims) and of Albanians from Kosovo increased. Most of these newcomers settled down in industrial centers and in Slovene Istria. From the 1970s on, the number and percentage of people the census designated as "other" and "ethnically or nationally un-decided" increased also. As a result of these internal economic migrations in Yugoslavia in the post–World War II period one can observe a gradual decrease in the share (percentage) of ethnic Slovenes, Italians, and Hun-garians in the population of Slovenia, while the share of "immigrants" in-creased substantially.

This trend continued almost until Slovenia declared independence. The main impact of the Yugoslav crisis of the 1980s on the ethnic struc-ture of the population in Slovenia was a decreased number and share of (ethnic) "Yugoslavs," while the number of Italians and "nationality un-known" people increased significantly. Also significant in this period was the decrease in the number and percentage of Hungarians.

Although the share of ethnic Slovenes in the population of the Republic of Slovenia decreased from 95.6 percent in 1961 to 87.6 percent in 1991, Slovenia remained the most ethnically homogeneous Yugoslav republic. The percentage of Slovenes in Slovenia remained unchanged also in the 2002 census. Additionally, there was no sizable Serb national minority in Slovenia. For these reasons Milošević and the JNA gave up on their at-tempts to keep Slovenia within Yugoslavia early in the process of Yugo-slavia's dissolution.

Democratization in the Beginning of the 1990s

It is important to note that the process of democratization in Slovenia had already started in the early 1980s and had been gradually progressing for almost a decade by the beginning of the 1990s. This process that had started with the emergence of new social movements and alternative poli-tics, especially within the Slovene youth organization, escalated in the sec-ond half of the 1980s and culminated at the end of the 1980s with the official introduction of a multiparty system, the establishment of opposi-tion political parties, and a dialogue between the ruling regime and the opposition.

The first democratic elections after World War II meant a new stage in this process. They took place in Slovenia in April 1990, according to a new electoral law that was passed by a communist-dominated parliament. On 8 and 22 April the parliamentary coalition DEMOS (the Slovene demo-cratic opposition, representing a coalition of six newly formed democratic parties [from Christian democrats to Environmentalists]), won more than 55 percent of the votes altogether. Apart from the parties gathered in the DEMOS coalition, three other political parties emerged from already-existing political structures on the Slovene political scene: the largest single party, the reformed former communists, with 17.3 percent of the vote; the Socialist Party as the successor of the Socialist Alliance of Working People with 5.4 percent of the vote; and the Liberal Democratic Party, which emerged from the Slovene Youth Organization, with 14.5 percent of the vote. The first freely elected Slovene government, led by Christian Democrat Lojze Peterle, was formed from the members of the DEMOS coalition parties. On the other hand, the former president of the League of Communists of Slovenia, Milan Kučan, won the presidential election as the candidate of the reformed communists and Socialist Party.

In the plebiscite of 23 December 1990 a vast majority of citizens of Slovenia voted for an independent Slovenia. Initially, the Slovene political leadership tried to negotiate new confederal Yugoslav arrangement with the federal government and other Yugoslav republics. After these attempts failed and the six-month transition period determined by the plebiscite (within which the future federal or confederal arrangements in Yugoslavia should have been negotiated and agreed upon) ended, Slovenia declared its independence on 25 June 1991. This act was followed by an attack of the JNA on Slovenia, with the goal being to overthrow the Slovene proindependence government and gain control over the territory and especially the border crossings in Slovenia. The JNA, however, was trapped at barricades that the Slovene Territorial Defense had constructed out of buses and trucks. With the help of mediators from the European Community, the so-called Brioni Declaration, also known as the three months' moratorium, was signed on 8 July 1991. This was an agreement between the Slovene authorities and the Yugoslav federal government for freezing the implementation of Slovenia's independence.

The JNA lost the war on Slovene soil. The attack on Slovenia had been immediately followed by the desertion from the JNA of the non-Serb and non-Montenegrin soldiers, that is, draft soldiers of Muslim, Kosovo Albanian, Croat, and Macedonian nationality, who did not want to fight against the Slovenians. The Brioni Declaration prevented further air raids on Slovenia as well as any kind of larger military activity by the JNA on Slovene territory. Mediators from the European Community quickly negotiated an agreement between Slovenia and the JNA because the European Community did not want a war on its borders; they still hoped that a war in what used to be Yugoslavia could be prevented. Initially, they still hoped that Slovenia might act as a democratizing force in Yugoslavia, but they soon realized that this scenario was not possible.

After its defeat, the (Serb-controlled) JNA and its supreme commander, the presidency of Yugoslavia, decided to retreat from Slovenia along with all its equipment and machinery. They did this because controlling or absorbing Slovenia was never a Serb goal, unless it could be done with Slovene acquiescence and thus without major fighting. The initial Slovene resistance made it clear this would not happen. Serbia was concerned primarily with Croatia and Bosnia and Herzegovina, not to mention Kosovo and Vojvodina. Slovenia would have been nice as a bonus, but it was never a primary goal. For the Serbs to devote their military strength to fighting in Slovenia would have made war in Croatia—which, in fact, had already started with the uprising of the Croat Serbs in the summer of 1990 and with the first armed fighting in spring 1991—that much harder.

As soon as the three-month moratorium determined by the Brioni Declaration was over on 8 October 1991, Slovenia resumed the implementation of its independence process by introducing its own currency. By the end of October 1991, the last soldier of the JNA, considered by Slovenes to be a Serb communist occupation force, had left Slovene soil. By the end of October 1991, Slovenia had gained control over the territory of its state, had established a new currency, and had clearly defined its boundaries. By then Slovenia had fulfilled all preconditions for its international recognition, including the adequate protection of the rights of national minorities within its borders. Slovenia also showed that it was prepared to work for a peaceful dissolution of Yugoslavia. Yet it was not until 15 January 1992 that recognition came from the European community. Soon after that Slovenia became a full member of the Conference of Security and Cooperation in Europe and the Council of Europe.

On 7 April, the United States officially recognized the independence of Slovenia, Croatia, and Bosnia and Herzegovina. On 23 May all three states became new members of the United Nations. The process of international recognition of Slovenia was in a way completed by the establishment of a diplomatic relationship with the United States on 27 August 1992.

The Independent Slovenia

Slovenia was the first republic that experienced a war in the process of disssolution of the Yugoslav federation in the 1990s. However, the consequences of the "ten-day war" were not as grave as those of the wars in Croatia or in Bosnia and Herzegovina. There were some sixty-one people killed in the Slovene war, among them some forty soldiers of the JNA, eight members of the Slovene Territorial Defense, and thirteen civilians (most of them were foreign truck drivers killed on the highways during air raids). During the battles and air raids some factories and private houses were destroyed or damaged, there was some damage to Ljubljana's airport and some planes (of the Slovene airline) parked there, and also some roads were damaged by the JNA tanks. As mentioned, the JNA withdrew from Slovenia soon after the war.

The war in Slovenia did not result in any major changes in its ethnic structure. The Law on Citizenship of the Republic of Slovenia (Zakon o državljanstvu Republike Slovenije), adopted as a part of the legislation on independence in June 1991, enabled special naturalization for all citizens of the former Yugoslavia who were not citizens of Slovenia but had their permanent residences in Slovenia at the time of the plebiscite. Consequently, most economic immigrants in Slovenia originating from other parts of Yugoslavia applied, and almost all of them (more than 170,000) were naturalized and became Slovene citizens. Only a small number of non-Slovenes, mostly officers and employees of the JNA and the federal customs service, emigrated from Slovenia, in some cases with their families.

The war in Slovenia also did not produce a refugee crisis. However, at the peak of fighting in Croatia and Bosnia and Herzegovina, up to 70,000 people from warring regions there found refuge in Slovenia as temporary refugees. Most of them later returned to their homes or emigrated to western Europe, the United States, Canada, or Australia. In the beginning of 2002 only some 2,300 refugees, mostly elderly people and some families from Bosnia and Herzegovina, still lived in Slovenia; they could not return to their homes because of non-implementation of the Dayton Agreement (see the section on Bosnia and Herzegovina), which, among other things, provided for the return of refugees from Bosnia and Herzegovina to their homes regardless of their ethnic background. During the crises in Kosovo in 1999 Slovenia also accepted 1,600 ethnic Albanians. Most of them returned home after the NATO intervention and restoration of peace in this province.

Although direct war damages in Slovenia were not enormous, economic consequences of the dissolution of the former Yugoslavia were substantial. Slovenia, at least temporarily, lost a relatively large (and for Slovenia's economy very important) Yugoslav market. Additionally, the dismantling of the former Yugoslavia meant that some production chains were broken. Although Slovenia's exports to the West were the largest in the former Yugoslavia, some Slovene companies depended on this home market. This was especially true for the companies that produced goods for the army (the so-called defense industry complex) and for those companies that for various reasons could not compete in the West and were selling their products mostly on the Yugoslav market. Consequently, many big companies that were important in the former Yugoslavia went bankrupt or had to undergo extensive restructuring (i.e., Litostroj in Ljubljana, which produced turbines and other components for electrical power plants; TAM in Maribor, an automobile factory; etc.); this increased the unemployment rate, which rose from 3.5 percent in December 1990 to more than 14 percent in December 1993. Economic crises in Slovenia reached their peak in 1993. However, intensive international economic cooperation—especially with central and western European countries—and a rapid integration in the global economy made it possible for the Slovene economy to recover by the mid-1990s. By then the GNP as well as the personal income of the population started to increase, and inflation and unemployment rates started to decrease.

The laws on denationalization and privatization, adopted by Slovene parliament in 1992, meant important changes in Slovenia's economic policy and brought important changes into the Slovene economy. The former provided for the return of private property that had been nationalized after World War II, and the latter enabled privatization of formerly public enterprises. This legislation provided the basis for the transformation of ownership that was considered necessary for the development of a market economy. However, the introduction of "liberal capitalism" also showed some bad sides. While the rich were becoming even richer, social problems, poverty, and uncertainty among the lower socioeconomic classes increased.

Also by mid-1992 the international community realized that the political, economic, and social situations and development in Slovenia were rather different from those in other states that emerged from the former Yugoslavia. Already in the 1990s Slovenia started to integrate into the European Union and NATO. In the context of the (first) eastern enlargement of the EU and considering its success in adaptation of its legal, judicial, political, and economic systems to the EU standards and criteria, Slovenia was considered one of the leading countries among ten candidate countries (Czech Republic, Cyprus, Estonia, Hungary, Latvia, Lithuania, Malta, Poland, Slovakia, and Slovenia). At the end of 2002 Slovenia successfully concluded negotiations with the EU and was invited to join the organization. On 23 March 2003, in a referendum in Slovenia, 89.6 percent of participating voters (actually more than two-thirds of all voters) supported EU membership. Slovenia signed the treaty with the EU at the EU summit meeting in Athens, Greece, in May 2003, which at this writing still needed to be ratified by all existing EU member states. It is expected that Slovenia will become a EU member state by May 2004, just in time for the election for the European Parliament.

The disappointment was substantial when Slovenia had not been invited to join NATO in 1997. However, Slovenia continued its efforts to join this alliance, and at the Prague summit in December 2002, Slovenia was invited to join NATO. In the meantime a decrease in the public support for Slovenia's NATO membership was seen as a consequence of certain international developments, such as the war in Iraq, and as a consequence of the activities of some nongovernmental organizations that opposed Slovenia's membership in the alliance. Just before the referendum on NATO membership, held simultaneously with the EU referendum, the government launched a strong pro-NATO campaign and 60.4 percent voted for the accession of Slovenia to NATO. When the protocol on Accession Treaties to NATO was signed, George Robertson, the NATO Secretary General, he said: "Membership in NATO brings . . . a seat in the company at the table, in which we deliver key decisions regarding European security . . . The country that becomes a member of NATO does not have to worry to have to solve security problems by itself. . . ." (Robertson, 2003, 5).

Croatia after 1990

The Republic of Croatia declared its independence simultaneously with Slovenia's declaring its; however, Croatia's independent development was impaired substantially by the rebellion of Croat Serbs and by the war that followed.

Ethnic Map of Croatia before Its Declaration of Independence

The ethnic structure of Croatia before its declaration of independence was quite heterogeneous. According to the population census of 1991, taken a just few months before the declaration of Croatia's independence, twenty-five ethnic groups lived on its territory; eleven of them numbered more than 5,000 people.

Until 1971 the Croat ethnic map was stable; 80 percent of its inhabitants were Croats, 15 percent were Serbs, and the remaining 5 percent were members of other ethnic groups. After 1971 the ethnic map began to change, due to the introduction of new categories in the population census such as "Yugoslavs" and "Did not declare themselves under Article 170 of the Constitution of the SFRY of 1974." Until 1971 the percentage of Croats, Serbs, and most minority groups (Czechs, Italians, Hungarians, Slovaks, Ruthenians, and Ukrainians) declined. As in the entire post–World War II period, the number and percentage of Albanians, Montenegrins, and Muslims increased through immigration. Most of these economic immigrants settled in larger Croat towns and cities along the Adriatic coast.

During the 1970s the number of those who declared themselves Yugoslavs increased sharply, due to the politics of the Yugoslav state and to many ethnically mixed marriages. However, the number and percentage of "Yugoslavs" sharply declined in the second half of the 1980s due to worsened economic and political conditions, growing ethnic tensions, and divisions in Yugoslavia, while simultaneously the numbers and percentages of those who "Did not declare themselves under Article 170 of the Constitution of the SFRY" and those who "Declared no nationality" increased sharply, as did the number of people who declared themselves by regional identity (e.g., "Istrians," "Dalmatians," etc.). Until 1991 one could notice a small increase of Serbs, Macedonians, Montenegrins, and Muslims; with the exception of the Italians and Albanians, the numbers and percentages of other minority groups declined.

The case of the Serbs in Croatia was a special one; according to the Constitution of 1974 they had the status of a nation-building nation (i.e., a constitutive nation of the Croat Republic). The majority of Croat Serbs lived in the Dalmatian coast hinterland, Lika, Banija, Kordun, Slavonia, Western Srijem, Baranja (which were the regions of the autochthonous settlement of the Serbs in the "Military Frontier Region"), and in large cities such as Zagreb, Rijeka, Dubrovnik, etc.).

Even though the regions where Serbs settled in Croatia were economically underdeveloped, the main trade routes of Croatia (and the former Yugoslavia) were situated in those regions—from Zagreb toward the Dalmatian coast and from Zagreb toward Belgrade. Also, the Serb population produced numerous communist political leaders in Croatia, who occupied many political posts as well as positions in cultural life and in the state-run economy. Once it was certain that Yugoslavia would be dissolved, one of the main aims of Milošević's policy was to incorporate into Greater Serbia the regions where Croat Serbs lived.

Croatia's Emancipation and Independence

In the spring of 1990, the HDZ (Hrvatska demokratska zajednica—Croat Democratic Union) won the elections. The new Croat president, Franjo Tudjman, started to implement the political promises the HDZ had made during the electoral campaign, especially the one to build a Croat national state. This provoked unrest among the Serbs in Kninska Krajina, who often still remembered and feared the ethnic cleansing by the Ustaša regime during World War II. Fearing new exterminations and influenced by Serb nationalist propaganda, these Serbs were attracted by the Great Serbia nationalist ideas of Slobodan Milošević to unite all the Serbs in a common state.

Under these conditions the decisions of the new Croat authorities did not seem to be calming their fears. In fact, it was exactly the opposite: the new Croat authorities threw numerous Serbs out of the jobs they held in public service and the police (this even happened in the territories where the Serbs were a majority). The flag of Croatia was changed, so that the red five-pointed star on the flag was replaced with a red and white chessboard, the historic coat of arms of Croatia. Although this was a traditional medieval Croat coat of arms, Ante Pavelić and the Ustaša had used it as the symbol of the Independent State of Croatia (NDH) during World War II. In addition, as suggested by the new authorities, Croatia's new constitution no longer declared the Serbs in Croatia to be a constitutive nation, which meant that they became a national minority in Croatia. The Serbs found this very disturbing, as all previous Croat republic constitutions after World War II had mentioned them a constituent nation.

These actions provoked unrest among the Croat Serbs. Moderates such as Jovan Opačić and Jovan Rašković, who demanded cultural autonomy for the Serbs of Croatia, lost support, and Milan Babić, whose aim was the secession of the Serb-populated territories from Croatia, gained in reputation and followers. Supported by Milošević's statement that republican borders were only administrative division lines and that only nations, and not republics, had the right to secede from the Yugoslav federation, the Croat Serbs started to organize. On 25 July 1990, the Serb parliament in the city of Srb introduced its Declaration on Sovereignty and Autonomy of the Serb Nation, and on 18 August, in spite of a ban issued by the Croat constitutional court, it organized a referendum on the cultural and political autonomy of the Serbs in the territory of Kninska Krajina. A day before the referendum took place on 17 August, units of the Croat police tried unsuccessfully to forbid the referendum by force. Under the leadership of Milan Babić, the Serb population armed itself, put up barricades, and staged an uprising. In the referendum 99.9 percent of Croat Serbs supported the declaration. The Belgrade authorities also intervened with Zagreb authorities on behalf of the Serbs of Kninska Krajina, gaining for them the status of a para-state divided by the barricades from the rest of Croatia.

As the Croat authorities were unable to make the Serbs obey their decisions, the Serbs of Kninska Krajina continued to create their own "state." On 30 September 1990, the Serb National Council declared autonomy for Kninska Krajina (Northwest Dalmatia; later, communes of Lika, Gorski Kotar, Bania, and Kordun also joined) and built new barricades. On 3 October, with the help of the new barricades, they interrupted all rail and road traffic with the rest of Croatia. On 21 October, a special Statute of SAO Krajina was officially proclaimed by the Serb National Council, and the Serb Autonomous Authority of Krajina, or Srpska autonomna oblast Krajina (SAO Krajina), was declared. In this territory the Serbs comprised between 50 and 97.5 percent of the local population.

A few months later, in January 1991, the Serbs in Slavonia organized in accordance with the same principle. The Serbs of Slavonia, Baranja, and Western Srijem organized a Serb National Council for their territories in Šidski Banovci. This Serb National Council issued a Declaration of the Serb Nation at the end of February 1991. In this territory the Serbs comprised between 20 and 50 percent of the local population.

Croatia found itself in very difficult circumstances. On the one hand, because of the preparations for its secession from Yugoslavia, the JNA threatened to proclaim martial law in Yugoslavia to prevent Slovenia and Croatia from seceding; on the other hand, the Serb rebels now controlled large parts of Croatia. In February 1991 the rebels even declared and published a Resolution on Dissolution from Croatia and Remaining in Yugoslavia. In an attempt to prevent JNA intervention, the Croat president, Tudjman, had a secret meeting in Karadjordjevo with Slobodan Milošević. (Later, rumors spread that they even talked about the division of Bosnia and Herzegovina.) Whatever they talked about and decided at this meeting, however, was moot. In March 1991 the first armed clashes occurred between the rebel Serbs and the Croat police units. In order to prevent further clashes, the Yugoslav Presidency ordered the JNA to intervene and separate the warring sides.

The intervention of the JNA and the further worsening of conditions in the federation convinced the Croat leadership to progress with the independence process for Croatia. The Croat leadership contacted the Slovene leadership to coordinate their actions for independence. On 19

May 1991, they organized a referendum in which almost 83 percent of the voters participated, and 94.17 percent of those who voted opted for Croat independence. The Croat government had now gained the people's support for the independence of Croatia. On 25 June 1991 (simultaneously with a similar declaration in Slovenia), the Croat Parliament (Sabor) declared the independence of Croatia. However, the conditions for implementing Croatia's independence were rather different from those in Slovenia.

The "War for the Homeland"

Its declaration of independence provoked new troubles for Croatia. Milošević did not oppose the independence of Slovenia and Croatia, but at the same time he declared that the Croat Serbs also had the right to secede from Croatia. He supported the right of Croat Serbs to change republican administrative borders, so that the border of Croatia should be the ethnic Serb border, allowing Kninska Krajina and Slavonia to remain out of Croatia.

In the middle of July 1991, a large-scale-war now broke out, in which the Serb insurgents at first provoked fights with the Croat forces and the intervention of the JNA followed "to separate the fighting sides." The Croat army was not powerful enough to fight both the Serb insurgents and the JNA, and every day the JNA controlled a greater part of Croatia. Dalmatia was soon cut off from the rest of Croatia, and the shells of the JNA and the Serb insurgents were even directed on the city of Dubrovnik, which was under the protection of UNESCO (the United Nations Educational, Scientific, and Cultural Organization) as a historic architectural landmark. A special, tragic chapter in the history of Croatia belongs to Vukovar, a city on the Serb border in the most eastern part of Croatia, which fell after three months of siege.

The plan of Slobodan Milošević and his co-visionaries for a "New Yugoslavia" was for the Serbs and the JNA to occupy all the territories of Croatia east of the Virovitica-Karlovac-Karlobag line. This plan changed when the strength of the Croat army increased by the end of 1991. Financial contributions of Croat émigré communities and the arms seized from the JNA barracks enabled this strengthening of the Croat army. The new plan of Slobodan Milošević was to occupy the territory within the Croat-Serb ethnic borders. The front line of the war followed the Croat-Serb ethnic borders, so that three separated Serb regions in Croatia were created. These Serb regions were separated by the territories controlled by the Croat army, and the connections among them existed only over the territories of Bosnia and Herzegovina controlled by the Serbs. The largest and best organized was the region of Kninska Krajina. The second was the region around Glina and in western Slavonia; the third region was eastern Slavonia and Baranja (Croat Podunavlje), which bordered on Serbia. These regions were unified into the Republic of Serb Krajina (Republika srpska Krajina, or RSK) on 19 December 1991, and Milan Babić became its first president. Its territory had been "ethnically cleansed" of the Croats by then. The Croats, as refugees or displaced persons, had to leave for parts of Croatia controlled by the Croat army, in addition to European countries and countries overseas.

After the Serb rebels and the JNA had occupied most of the desired territories, the leadership of rump Yugoslavia demanded on 9 November 1991 that the United Nations (UN) Security Council send peacekeeping forces to Croatia. The UN Security Council agreed, and it adopted Resolution No. 743 to this effect on 21 February 1992. This meant that the Serb desires and accomplishments were now temporarily secured.

Although the new state of Croatia was recognized by the European Union (15 January 1992) and the United States (7 April 1992) and was accepted into the UN on 23 May 1992, the situation at the battleground did not change. Daily fights could not be prevented—neither by the diplomatic missions of Lord Peter Carrington, the first EC peace envoy (1991–1992) and former foreign secretary in the British conservative government in the 1980s, and Lord David Owen, the EC mediator and cochair of the Peace Conference on the former Yugoslavia (1992–1995); nor through the peacekeeping missions of the UN. The front line remained unchanged until spring 1995. At that point Croatia, with financial help from its émigré communities around the world, succeeded in building a powerful army that, in a blitzkrieg in May 1995, first regained the territories of Western Slavonia. In August 1995, the Croat army, with its Operation Storm (Oluja), regained control over most of the territories of the RSK, and more than 200,000 ethnic Serbs fled the region. Croatia was again unified, with the exception of Baranja and Eastern Slavonia (Croat Podunavlje).

Consequences of the War

Four years of war in Croatia had severe consequences for the Croat economy and social situation. The territories where the military fights had taken place (especially some regions of the former Serb settlements) were almost deserted because people had fled to escape the war and ethnic cleansing.

Refugee crises started as early as 1990, when the first fights occurred between the Croat paramilitary forces and armed Serb rebels from Krajina. From the territories at the border of Croatia with Bosnia and Herzegovina, SAO Krajina, and western Slavonia, a few thousand inhabitants of Croat nationality emigrated. Most of them found temporary sanctuary in Croatia; a few of them found refuge with relatives in Slovenia or in Western Europe. In the second half of 1991, Croat armed forces forced many thousands of Serbs from Grubišino Polje and Virovitica to leave. They found refuge in Serbia or in Eastern Slavonia (Croat Podunavlje) around Vukovar, which was then under the control of the Serb authorities. During the period of armed battles in 1992, the number of Croat refugees increased dramatically. The Croat refugees fled west, and the Serb refugees fled east. More than two-thirds of the ethnic Croats who fled, predominantly from the regions around Dubrovnik, Šibenik, Zadar, Banija, and Eastern Slavonia, remained in Croatia as internally displaced persons (internal refugees). Around 150,000 immigrated to Western European countries, but also to the United States, Canada, and Australia. The Serb refugees predominantly moved to Serbia (around 163,000) and Serb-controlled parts of Bosnia and Herzegovina (around 93,000).

From 1992 until May 1995 almost no forced migrations occurred, as there were almost no changes in the front line. However, in May 1995, after a blitzkrieg by the Croat army that first liberated the regions of Western Slavonia, 20,000 Serbs emigrated from this region (Serb sources claim as many as 60,000–70,000). Because of the fear of Croat revenge, even more Serbs felt compelled to leave their homes in August 1995, when Croat forces took over the region of the RSK. Almost all the Serbs left (around 150,000–180,000), so that the region was almost completely deserted. Most of them (more than 100,000) immigrated to Serbia and to the regions under Serb control in Bosnia and Herzegovina (around 50,000); some of them found refuge in the last remaining part of "Krajina" in Croat Podunavlje.

In addition to tens of thousand of killed and wounded soldiers and civilians and hundreds of thousands of refugees, the war in Croatia also caused substantial property damage. Numerous industrial enterprises, houses, and apartments, in addition to much infrastructure (roads, electric lines, etc.), were destroyed or badly damaged. However, these were not the only damages and unpleasant consequences of the war. The war also slowed down or even stopped democratic developments in Croatia.

Additionally, it hindered Croatia in its attempts to join the Euro-Atlantic society of nations.

Other tragic consequences of the war were numerous war crimes committed by the Serbs in the regions that they controlled, as well as by Croats. In this context, crimes against the civilian Serb population during the liberation of Kninska Krajina in 1995 should be mentioned. The Croat army burned quite a few Serb settlements and confiscated the Serbs' property. Some civilians were tortured and killed. Because of that, some Croat generals (Ivan Čermak, Ante Gotovina, Mirko Norac, Petar Stipetić, and others) were indicted by the Hague Tribunal. It is believed that the Hague Tribunal would also have indicted the Croat president, Franjo Tudjman, had he not died of cancer in 1999. In September 2002 the Hague Tribunal indicted another Croat war "hero," General Janko Bobetko, who was the commanding general of the Croat army in the 1990s. This provoked an uproar among Croats. Considering the importance of the "War for the Homeland" in Croat nation-building, these issues are especially difficult for Croatia and are still exploited in Croat daily politics. Many Croats are quite critical toward the Hague Tribunal, especially members of the HDZ and numerous active participants in the war. They reproach the Hague Tribunal because it started to indict the defenders of Croatia before the Serb aggressors and war criminals who had spread Great Serbian nationalism. Some Croats were also upset when, in March 2003, Croat General Mirko Norac was sentenced by a Croat court in Rijeka to twelve years in prison for crimes against humanity committed against the Serb civilians during the War for the "Homeland."

Croatia after the War for the Homeland

By the end of summer 1995, Croatia controlled all the territories in its borders, with the exception of Podunavlje (4.5 percent of the state's territory), which was under the control of the UN peacekeeping mission. The Croat authorities tried to revitalize the country's impoverished economy as soon as possible, especially tourism, which had been the most profitable part of the Croat economy during the period of the former Yugoslavia. Tudjman, who was the undisputed leader of Croatia, and the HDZ, tried to put Croatia on the international scene and normalize relations with all neighboring countries. They even made a diplomatic connection with the Federal Republic of Yugoslavia, although this did not lead to mutual recognition. It took until September 1996 for both countries to exchange ambassadors, but the "normalization" of Croat-Serb relations did not bring significant changes. It did not hasten the return of the Serb refugees to Croatia or the return of the Croats, who had fled from Vojvodina to Serbia, even though the memorandum of diplomatic ties formally allowed for the safe return of around 200,000 Serbs who had escaped from the region of Krajina.

The Croat authorities did not like the idea of Serb refugees being allowed to return to Croatia, and they did everything in their power to make the return of these refugees more difficult. This worsened the international situation of Croatia. Until the beginning of 1998, only 12,000 Serbs returned to their homes in western Slavonia and Kninska Krajina; a mere 8,000 Serbs returned to Croat Podunavlje (one-tenth of the Serb refugees). Relations with the international community were further worsened by Croat interference in the internal political affairs of Bosnia and Herzegovina. In August 1995, during Operation Storm, the Croat army was accused of violating human rights, especially those of Croat Serbs, and there were threats of sanctions by the international community. There were also a few unsolved questions in Croatia's relations with Italy, Slovenia, and Montenegro.

In 1995 the Croat Podunavlje was peacefully reintegrated into Croatia, after President Tudjman had specified this at the negotiations in Dayton, Ohio, as a precondition for his support of the Agreement regarding Bosnia and Herzegovina. The international peace mission of retired U.S. general Jacques Klein, when he administered Croat Podunavlje before it was peacefully reintegrated into Croatia, also deserves mention in this context. In spite of the peaceful reestablishment of Croat authority in this region, however, quite a few thousand Serbs still emigrated.

Croatia after the Death of Franjo Tudjman

President Franjo Tudjman died of cancer on 11 December 1999. Two months after his death political conditions in Croatia changed completely. At the elections in the beginning of 2000, a coalition of six political parties (from liberals to former communists) defeated the HDZ (which, until then, had been the leading party), and the coalition's candidate, Stipe Mesić, became the president of Croatia. After the nationalist, autocratic regime of Tudjman and the HDZ was replaced, the image of Croatia in the world became more positive. The new government of Prime Minister Ivica Račan, a reformed communist and leader of the

Social-Democrats, struggled for a better positioning of Croatia in the international community and also struggled to improve Croatia's economy.

Although Croatia reached some of its goals in international politics (membership in the Council of Europe, World Trade Organization, and NATO's Partnership for Peace), it still has to deal with the consequences of the "war for the homeland." The country was expected to enable the Serbs of Krajina, who had fled into Bosnia and Herzegovina and the Federal Republic of Yugoslavia during the war, to return to their homes. This provoked sharp political fights, however. Also, its relationship with the International Court Tribunal in The Hague is still unclear, particularly because of the opposition (especially of the HDZ) toward extradition to the Court of those Croats who are indicted for war crimes. The current Croat government is often accused of not working in accordance with Croat national interests, especially in dealing with the Hague Tribunal, but also in dealing with Slovenia and Italy. The critics point to the Stabilization Association Agreement with the European Union, which, among other things, establishes Croatia's obligation to cooperate with its Balkan neighbors. This is too much for many Croats, who are stubborn in their decision to defend their historical rights and national interests, which they see reflected in the Catholic West rather than in the Balkan region. They are convinced that Europe is sending them "back to the Balkans," from which they just "escaped."

Bosnia and Herzegovina after 1990

Bosnia and Herzegovina was the only republic of the former Yugoslavia where none of the Yugoslav ethnic nations had an absolute majority in the population. The constitutive nations of Bosnia and Herzegovina were the Bosniaks (i.e., Bosnian Muslims), Serbs, and Croats. This situation was the result of a centuries-long historic development of this territory. However, past censuses did not reveal the whole and exact picture of Bosnia and Herzegovina's ethnic patchwork. The main reasons for this were problems in defining who the Muslims were and, after 1961, the introduction of ethnic "Yugoslavs" and "Other, nationality unknown" categories in the census.

In general, however, it is known that the ethnic structure of the population of Bosnia and Herzegovina changed rapidly in the 1960s and then again in the 1980s, with the numbers and percentages of Serbs and Croats decreasing. In 1981, Muslims had the second highest birth rates in Europe, with an increase rate of 14.8 per thousand. At the same time, the birth rate was 7.7 per thousand for the Serbs and 8.9 per thousand for the Croats.

For the first time in the post–World War II period, the number of Serbs in Bosnia and Herzegovina decreased in 1971. During the period of homogenization of population according to ethnic identity (during the first period of the sharpening of the Yugoslav crisis in the late 1960s), the number and percentage of declared "Yugoslavs" in Bosnia and Herzegovina decreased sharply as well, while at the same time the number and percentage of Muslims increased substantially, due to the census manipulations described in previous chapters. The number and percentage of (ethnic) "Yugoslavs" rose again during the 1970s, while the census of 1991 showed a sharp decrease in this group. In the 1981 census the numbers and percentages of both the Serbs and, for the first time, the Croats, decreased in comparison with the previous census. This trend continued for the Croats in the 1991 census, but the number of Serbs increased that year. However, the relative percentage of Serbs in the total population of Bosnia and Herzegovina decreased again.

During the end of the 1980s one could not ascertain larger changes in areas of settlement of individual ethnic groups. The Muslims had a majority in central Bosnia, in northeastern Bosnia (south of Tuzla), in Cazinska krajina (western Bosnia), and in northern Herzegovina. The Serbs had the majority in Bosanska krajina, Semberija, and eastern Herzegovina. Croats were the majority in western and central Herzegovina, in parts of Posavina, and in some parts of central Bosnia.

In many ways the ethnic makeup of Bosnia and Herzegovina has much in common with the ethnic makeup of an American city such as Los Angeles, where members of many ethnic groups can live side by side peacefully, even in the same housing complexes. In Bosnia and Herzegovina, the Serbs, Croats, and Muslims traditionally lived together in the same way.

Ideas of nationalistic ethnic politicians that Bosnia and Herzegovina be reorganized into homogenous national territories inevitably required the division of ethnically mixed territories into their Serb, Croat, and Muslim parts. To a certain extent this was formalized after the Dayton Agreement was signed. In Bosnia and Herzegovina, according to the 1991 population census, 44 percent of the population were Muslims, 31 percent were Croats, 17 percent were Serbs, and 6 percent were "Yugoslavs." Many people (regardless of nationality) in Bosnia and Herzegovina were happy under the old regime, which, by its dictatorship, suppressed ethnic hatred. That is why even today one can see many pictures of the late Marshal Tito (Josip Broz) in Sarajevo. "Ethnically cleansing" mixed areas in such a way that the Serb territory would be 100 percent Serb, the Croat territory would be 100 percent Croat, and so forth would mean dividing ethnically mixed families, houses, villages, and towns. Sarajevo would become like the divided Berlin.

Such divisions seemed unthinkable in Bosnia and Herzegovina before 1992. The only alternative for the Serbs, Croats, and Muslims (Bosniaks) seemed to be to live together in one state that would be neither Serb nor Croat nor Muslim and in which all three constituent nations would have the same rights. However, Croat and Serb nationalists in Bosnia and Herzegovina, Croatia, and Serbia dreamed of dividing the country into three ethnically homogenous units, with the Bosniak unit being very small.

Bosnia and Herzegovina and the Dissolution of Yugoslavia

Conditions in Bosnia and Herzegovina worsened rapidly after the first free and multiparty elections, held on 18 November 1990. Then candidates of respective nationalistic parties won 202 out of the 240 deputy seats in the new Bosnian-Herzegovian parliament. The Muslim Party of Democratic Action (Stranka demokratske akcije, SDA) gained 87 seats; the Serb Democratic Party (Srpska demokratska stranka, SDS), 71 seats; and the Bosnian affiliate of the Croat Democratic Union (Hrvatska demokratska zajednica, HDZ), 44 seats in the parliament. At first it seemed that the multiparty system would work hand in hand with power sharing among the individual ethnic groups, a system already introduced by the communists. Alija Izetbegović, a Muslim, was elected president of the presidency of Bosnia and Herzegovina; Momčilo Krajišnik, a Serb, was elected speaker of the parliament; and Jure Pelivan, a Croat, became the prime minister.

In spite of this spirit of cooperation, conditions in Bosnia and Herzegovina started to worsen with the dawn of the Croat and Slovene declarations of independence. First, the Bosnian Serbs declared "their right" to live in Yugoslavia (i.e., the state where most of the Serbs of the world lived). However, President Izetbegović declared in February 1991 that Bosnia and Herzegovina would declare its independence from Yugoslavia if Slovenia and Croatia did the same. In this sharpened political standoff, no one was ready to compromise. The last chance for a peaceful solution disappeared in March 1991 when Milošević and Tudjman, without including Izetbegović in their discussions, discussed the possibility of dividing Bosnia and Herzegovina between Croatia and Serbia. Consequently,

Izetbegović started to strengthen ties with Islamic countries. During a visit to Turkey, he even asked for membership for Bosnia and Herzegovina in the Organization of Islamic States, causing the Bosnian Serbs to accuse him of trying to make the country an Islamic republic.

Under these conditions of general mistrust the SDS began to hinder governmental operations of the Bosnian government. At the same time the Serb population started to establish so-called Serb Autonomous Authorities (SAOs) in the regions where Serbs were a majority: SAO Bosanska Krajina with its seat in Banja Luka, SAO Romanija with its seat in Sarajevo, and SAO Eastern Herzegovina with its seat in Nevesinje. In October 1991, as the situation became more and more complicated, members of the parliament from SDA and HDZ decided to suggest independence for Bosnia and Herzegovina. After a series of thunderous discussions, deputies of the SDS decided to leave the parliament, and on October 25 they established their own parliament. This Serb parliament of Bosnia and Herzegovina consisted only of the deputies of Serb nationality—members of SDS.

Bosnian Serb politicians, with the help of the Serb-dominated regime of Slobodan Milošević, started to implement a plan to forcibly prevent the international recognition of Bosnia and Herzegovina's independence. In accordance with secret orders from Milošević, they began to move into Bosnia and Herzegovina from other parts of Yugoslavia all the ethnic Serb officers and soldiers of the JNA who were, or whose ancestors were, from Bosnia and Herzegovina. With this military support, the Bosnian Serbs declared their own Serb Republic of Bosnia and Herzegovina (Srpska republika Bosna i Hercegovina) on 9 January 1992 and proclaimed it to be a part of the Yugoslav federation.

By the end of 1991 it had became clear that Slovenia and Croatia would achieve international recognition for their independence. On 20 December 1991, the presidency of Bosnia and Herzegovina also decided to ask the European Union to recognize Bosnia and Herzegovina as an independent state. Both Serb members of the Bosnian presidency voted against this decision.

In a referendum on 29 February and 1 March 1992, 99.45 percent of those who participated voted for the independence of Bosnia and Herzegovina, and 1.2 million eligible voters (36.96 percent) abstained. Voting against the independence of Bosnia and Herzegovina were only 5,997. A total of 5,070 (0.16 percent) of the ballots were invalid. The majority of the Serb population abstained, as their ethnic political leaders had already declared their own Serb Republic of Bosnia and Herzegovina (Srpska Republika Bosna i Hercegovina).

From then on it became clear, even to the greatest optimists, that the Bosnian crisis would and could not be solved peacefully. Only the international peacemakers still tried to reach a compromise among the leaders of all sides (i.e., Muslim Alija Izetbegović, Serb Radovan Karadžić, and Croat Mate Boban) in an effort to come to a peaceful solution. Fighting broke out only a week after the referendum, first near Bosanski Brod and then also near Zvornik and Bjeljina. Tensions were also increasing in Sarajevo. Under these tense and complicated circumstances, the European Union recognized the independence of Bosnia and Herzegovina on 6 April 1992. The United States followed on 7 April 1992. However, the Bosnian Serbs continued to act independently from the rest of Bosnia. The "Assembly of the Serb Nation in Bosnia and Herzegovina" soon declared the independence of the Serb Republic of Bosnia and Herzegovina (later renamed Republika srpska/Serb Republic). In the middle of April, President Izetbegović and Speaker of the Parliament Krajišnik met to talk about the chances for peace once more in secret in Sarajevo, but the fights could not be prevented any longer.

The War and Ethnic Cleansing, 1992–1995

In the spring of 1992, one of the bloodiest wars in the history of Europe began in Bosnia and Herzegovina, the most ethnically mixed of all the republics of the former Yugoslavia. Because it was so mixed, every clash on the battlefield provoked forced migrations of the populations of all ethnic groups. The Serbs, who were supported by the JNA as early as August 1992, controlled 70 percent of the territory of the Republic of Bosnia and Herzegovina, and they wanted to get rid of all non-Serbs in this territory. They started with a policy of ethnic cleansing. In the first year of the war, the Serbs succeeded in ousting the Muslims and Croats from eastern Bosnia (Zvornik, Višegrad, Foča), Posavina (Bosanski Brod, Derventa), and Banja Luka. Most of the Croats escaped to Croatia and Herzegovina, which was under Croat control (after July 1992 Herzegovina was renamed Herceg-Bosna). The Muslim refugees moved to the regions around Tuzla and Sarajevo, which were under Muslim control, but some of them also moved to Croatia, Slovenia, and some Western European countries. At the beginning of 1992 there were already some peacekeeping forces on the ground in Bosnia and Herzegovina; these troops were supposed to protect civilians. Their lack of success can be shown by the fact that by August of 1992, 1.7 million people in Bosnia and Herzegovina had to leave their homes.

From the very beginning of the war, the international community tried to stop the fighting and to find a peaceful solution to all issues, especially because of the many refugees the war produced. All the peace plans suggested by the United Nations and European Union were based on the condition that Bosnian Muslims would not be forced to leave their homes in those territories where they had been a majority before the war. They also demanded that the international borders of Bosnia and Herzegovina remain unchanged, but they failed to demand a nationally unified state. The January 1993 plan of former U.S. Secretary of State Cyrus Vance and former British Foreign Secretary Lord David Owen—the so-called Vance-Owen Plan—foresaw the division of Bosnia and Herzegovina into ten regions—three for every ethnic group plus the neutral region of Sarajevo. Neither this nor many of the later peace plans put forward until the year 1995 were able to stop the fighting, because none of the sides involved in the war was prepared to give up its plans for an ethnically divided Bosnia and Herzegovina.

Until April 1993, the Serbs were fighting the Muslims and Croats. However, in April 1993 fighting also began over how to divide territories between the Croats and Muslims, formerly allies; as a result there was now ethnic cleansing in regions where it had not taken place before. In spring 1993 the Croats began to force the Muslims out of the Herzegovian towns of Stolac, Čapljina, Ljubuški, and towns in central Bosnia (Busovača, Kiseljak). In revenge the Muslims began to force the Croats out of Jablanica and Konjic along the river of Neretva, as well as from the regions of Vareš and Bugojno in central Bosnia. The Muslim refugees found refuge primarily in the Western European countries, and the Croat refugees found refuge in Livno (Herzegovina) and in Istria (Croatia).

During this period, fights between the Croats and Serbs, who both were preoccupied with fighting against the Bosnian Muslim army, nearly stopped. In spring 1993 it seemed possible that the Serbs and Croats would succeed in dividing Bosnia. At the same time the Muslims also started to fight each other. Fikret Abdić, a regional leader in Bihać in Western Bosnia, did not recognize the central Bosnian government of Alija Izetbegović anymore, and on 27 September 1993 he declared Western Bosnia (with 350,000 inhabitants) to be an autonomous region, with its capital in Bihać. He made an agreement with the local commanders of the Bosnian Serbs and Croats and started to fight the army of Alija Izetbegović with a force of 6,000 soldiers.

The international community did not intervene in Bosnia and Herzegovina until May 1993, when the Serb forces surrounded some towns where the Bosnian Muslims were a majority of the local population. The UN Security Council proclaimed the towns of Sarajevo, Bihać, Goraž de, Srebrenica, Tuzla, and Žepa to be "safe havens," and the forces of UN-PROFOR (the United Nations Protection Force) were sent to them. On 2 March 1994, international mediators practically forced the Muslims and Bosnian Croats to sign the Washington Framework Agreement, which unified the territories under their control into the Federation of Bosnia and Herzegovina. In August 1994 the international community, with the help of the Russians, forced the Federal Republic of Yugoslavia to close its borders with the regions of Bosnia and Herzegovina that were under Serb control and to sever its ties with Karadžić. This, however, did not stop the war. Despite seventy-seven cease-fires from March 1992 until May 1994 and numerous diplomatic missions, in particular by Richard Holbrooke, the assistant secretary of state for European and Canadian affairs during the Clinton administration) ethnic cleansing continued in Bosnia and Herzegovina. In July 1995 the Serb forces captured Srebrenica and Žepa, where they killed almost 8,000 Bosnian Muslims. Consequently, NATO intervened with air raids on the Serb positions, and the Serbs agreed to start peace negotiations in August 1995. On 8 September 1995, the foreign ministers of Bosnia and Herzegovina, Croatia, and the Federal Republic of Yugoslavia, meeting in Geneva, agreed that Bosnia and Herzegovina would remain a country but would be divided into two entities, a Croat-Muslim entity and a Serb one. In October of the same year the cease-fire (temporary peace) started, and on 1 November 1995 peace negotiations started at an American Air Force base near Dayton, Ohio. Those peace negotiations ended with the signing of a peace agreement (the Dayton Agreement) in December 1995 in Paris.

The Dayton Agreement consists of a general document, 11 annexes, and 102 maps. It states the following:

1. Bosnia and Herzegovina shall stay as a unified, internationally recognized state in its prewar borders. It will have a constitution that envisions Bosnia and Herzegovina as a federal state. It shall have a bicameral parliament, federal constitutional court, common presidency, unified currency, and central government.
2. The state shall consist of two units: a Bosniak-Croat Federation, which shall consist of 51 percent of the territories of Bosnia and Herzegovina, and Serb Republic (Republika Srpska), which will control the remaining 49 percent of the territory. The Serb part will encompass the cities of Srebrenica, Žepa, and Pale, which shall be

*Srebrenica refugees arrive in Tuzla, Bosnia, which was declared a "safe haven"
by the UN Security Council. (Corbis/Sygma)*

the seat of the leadership of the Republika srpska. The Serb entity
shall have access to the Adriatic coast.

3. The capital, Sarajevo, shall remain united with the Bosniak-Croat
   federation; the Serbs of Sarajevo shall have special rights in the
   school system and local self-management.

4. The territorial corridor that connects the Serb territories shall be
   five kilometers wide. On the status of the city of Brčko,
   international arbiters shall decide.

5. Members of the presidency and the parliament of Bosnia and
   Herzegovina shall be elected at free and democratic elections by all
   the citizens of voting age in Bosnia and Herzegovina. Elections
   shall take place under the control of the international community;
   citizens shall vote in places where they have permanent residence.

6. The refugees shall be permitted to return to their homes. Citizens
   shall be allowed free and unhindered movement in the whole
   territory of Bosnia and Herzegovina.

7. Convicted war criminals shall not be permitted to serve in the
   armed forces or occupy positions in state structures.

8. It is agreed that 60,000 peacekeeping forces will be stationed in
   Bosnia and Herzegovina.

Serbian President Slobodan Milošević, Croatian President Franjo Tudjman, and Bosnian President Alija Izetbegović sign the Dayton Peace Agreement. Six other world leaders look on as witnesses to the historic agreement, which was intended to end the bloodshed and vicious fighting that began after the fall of communism in 1989–1990 in the republics of the former Yugoslavia. (Peter Turnley/CORBIS)

9. Serbia and the Federal Republic of Yugoslavia will recognize Bosnia and Herzegovina.
10. Consequently, the United States will suggest that the UN Security Council pass a resolution to end economic sanctions against the Federal Republic of Yugoslavia (Pirjevec, 2003, 450–453).

The signatories of this agreement were Alija Izetbegović of Bosnia and Herzegovina, Slobodan Milošević of Serbia, and Franjo Tudjman of Croatia.

The Consequences of the War

More than three years of war entirely changed the ethnic structure of this once ethnically mixed former Yugoslav republic. As a result of ethnic cleansing, the country of Bosnia and Herzegovina was divided into more or less ethnically homogeneous regions. The region of Serb settlement

Demonstrators demand a stop to the ethnic cleansing that victimized Albanians.
(Goran Sivaki/Corbis Sygma)

now covers the lands of the Republika Srpska; the region of the Croat and Muslim settlement covers the lands of the Federation of Bosnia and Herzegovina.

The extent of the consequences of ethnic cleansing is shown by data on the changes in ethnic structure in some cities of Bosnia and Herzegovina during 1991–1995. The percentage of Serbs in Banja Luka rose from 52 percent in 1991 to 90 percent in 1995; in Doboj, from 32 percent to 90 percent; in Mostar, the percentage of Serbs fell from 18 percent to 3 percent. The number of the Serbs also substantially decreased in Bihać (from 29,398 to about 1,000); in Tuzla (from 82,235 to about 15,000); in Zenica (from 79,233 to about 16,000); and in western Herzegovina and central Bosnia (from 43,595 to about 5,000). Similar trends of ethnic homogenization can be seen also in Sarajevo; in the part controlled by the Federation of Bosnia and Herzegovina, the percentage of Muslims has risen from 52 percent to 85 percent.

More than 2 million refugees had to leave their homes as a result of the war. According to the UN High Commissioner for Refugees and various government institutions, most of the refugees had originally lived within Bosnia and Herzegovina (1.2 million). Many settled in the successor states of the former Yugoslavia. In November 1995 there were 453,000 refugees from Bosnia and Herzegovina in Croatia, 38,600 in Montenegro, 28,000 in Macedonia, 405,000 in Serbia, and 24,000 in Slovenia. As for other European countries, most of the refugees settled in Germany (320,000), Italy (90,000), Switzerland (33,000), Austria (20,000), France (15,000), Sweden (50,000), and the Netherlands (33,000). For the most part, the Muslims found refuge in Turkey (52,000), Saudi Arabia (7,000), and Libya (3,500).

In spite of all peace agreements, most refugees still had not been able to return to their homes as of late 2003. Consequences of the war, including the changed ethnic situation, continuing ethnic hatred, lack of security, and poor economic conditions were among the key reasons that the refugees of Croat and Muslim nationality who were forced to emigrate from the Republika Srpska, the Serb refugees who left regions in the Federation of Bosnia and Herzegovina, and the Muslims who left Mostar in Herzegovina have not been able to return to their homes.

Bosnia and Herzegovina after the Dayton Agreement

After three years of war, peace came to Bosnia and Herzegovina again. The reactions to the signing of the Dayton Agreement were most euphoric in Belgrade, where the people honored Slobodan Milošević as a visionary, and in Zagreb, where Franjo Tudjman evaluated the agreement as a "victory of Croat diplomacy" because the Croats lost the least of all the three fighting sides in the conflict. In Bosnia and Herzegovina there were many who had doubts about the peace, though.

With the exception of the Bosnian Serbs, most of the parties concerned were in agreement that Bosnia needed peace. However, every ethnic group wanted as much territory as possible and was unhappy with the proposed situations. For this reason the Bosnian Serbs opposed the agreement. The most critical was the president of the self-proclaimed Serb parliament in Pale, Momčilo Krajišnik, who claimed that the agreement did not fulfill even the least of the Serb interests. He threatened that he would not respect the agreement, as the Bosnian Serbs had not signed it; Slobodan Milošević had signed it for them.

In spite of all doubts about the agreement, the fighting in Bosnia and Herzegovina ended, and conditions improved. The implementation of the Dayton Agreement has been overseen by 50,000 soldiers of the IFOR (Implementation Forces) and later the SFOR (Stabilization Forces), who came to take the places of the United Nation Forces (UNPROFOR). Being under the command of NATO, the IFOR and SFOR had the approval of the UN Security Councel. Implementation of the agreement was not an easy task, because each side respected only those points of the Dayton Agreement that were in its favor.

In reality, none of the parts of the Dayton Agreement has been fulfilled fully. For example, although in Bosnia and Herzegovina all structures and organs necessary for the state to survive have been put in place, they have experienced major problems in their functioning. In everyday life, each of the entities has lived its own separate life. In order to stop the "life of three states in one state," the Organization for Security and Cooperation in Europe (OSCE) organized elections in September 1996. Inhabitants of Bosnia and Herzegovina elected a three-member presidency and parliament for the country as a whole. Citizens of each of the two constituent entities also elected regional parliaments. Bosnian Alija Izetbegović was elected the president of the three-member presidency, and Serb representative Momčilo Krajišnik and Croat representative Krešimir Zubak became members of the presidency.

The elections showed that the refugee crisis could not be solved any time soon. In accordance with the Dayton Agreement, citizens had to vote in the places of their permanent settlement. Even though there were 1.5 million refugees, only 14,500 Bosniaks who lived as refugees in the territories of the Federation of Bosnia and Herzegovina participated in the elections in the Republika Srpska; while only 1,500 Serbs who lived as refugees in the territories of the Republika Srpska voted in the elections in the Federation of Bosnia and Herzegovina. This meant that the intentions of the Dayton Accord to assist the return of refugees by including them in the political process, registered in the place of their previous permanent residence, did not materialize. Most refugees abstained out of fear, but also because they were not informed about the election or because of bad organization in transfers to the polling places. In spite of the troubles mentioned here, the international observers' reactions to the election process were positive. The elections of 2001 were organized again by the international community and went smoothly; although refugees were still in the country, more of them were able to vote.

Even before the elections took place in 1996, all those who were indicted as war criminals by the Hague Tribunal had to withdraw from political life. Radovan Karadžić left the political scene on 28 June 1996 (St. Vitus's Day, a commemorative day in Serb history). The new president of the Republika Srpska, Biljana Plavšić, decided to respect the Dayton Agreement by issuing a statement of support. This meant that the Republika Srpska would not fight against the arrest of Radovan Karadžić, who

Bosnian Serb president
Biljana Plavšić,
during a press conference,
5 September 1997
(AFP Photo/Saša Stanković/Corbis)

was indicted as a war criminal. However, when the international community's forces tried to arrest Karadžić, his guards fought back and fifty people were killed. Another result of the 1996 elections was a schism among the politicians of the Republika Srpska. The most radical faction, the so-called Karadžić faction, slowly but surely began to lose its influence also, because of its leader's indictment.

Events took another course in the Croat part of Bosnia and Herzegovina, in the so-called Croat Republic of Herceg-Bosna (although it was officially a part of the Muslim-Croat federation). Its political representatives, who were functionaries of the HDZ and who had 90 percent support from their voters, did not want to transfer power to the Croat-Muslim Federation, which they were required to do in accordance with the Dayton Agreement. They had the open support of Franjo Tudjman, who still hoped that Milošević would succeed in annexing a part of Bosnia so that Croatia could annex another part of Bosnia.

Neither the death of Franjo Tudjman and the fact that the HDZ lost the elections in Croatia in 2001, nor the suspension of financial help to Herceg-Bosna by the new Croat authorities, changed the situation. Furthermore, at the beginning of March 2001, the Bosnian HDZ proclaimed local self-management and threatened that it would not recognize the common institutions and authority of the state organs of Bosnia and Herzegovina. Wolfgang Petritsch, the UN administrator of Bosnia and Herzegovina, had to intervene. He forced five functionaries of the HDZ in Bosnia to resign from all political positions; among them was the president of the Bosnian-Herzegovian HDZ, Ante Jelavić, who was also an elected member of the presidency of Bosnia and Herzegovina.

Although the situation was calming down, the nationalists from all parties still had considerable influence. For example, when the international community tried to rebuild mosques in Trebinje and Banja Luka in spring 2001, the Bosnian Serbs protested. The intention of those who organized the demonstrations was not only to prevent the building of the mosques. It was, instead, a question of keeping these territories ethnically cleansed and ready for annexation to Greater Serbia in the near future.

The governments of both entities acted together for the first time during a dispute with Croatia that, in 2002, had threatened the flow of oil and gasoline into Bosnia by hindering its transportation on Croat roads from Slovenia for "ecological reasons."

On a final note, the Constitutional Court of Bosnia and Herzegovina decided that all inhabitants of both national entities in Bosnia and Herzegovina should have equal rights as citizens. This decision is now being implemented slowly but surely.

The Federal Republic of Yugoslavia and of Serbia-Montenegro after 1990

After Slovenia, Croatia, Bosnia and Herzegovina, and Macedonia declared independence, the Socialist Federative Republic of Yugoslavia (SFRY) ceased to exist. In addition to the abovementioned new states on the ruins of the SFRY, another new federal state came into being: the Federal Republic of Yugoslavia or FRY (Savezna republika Jugoslavija). The former socialist republics of Serbia and Montenegro decided to establish the FRY in April 1992. The FRY was divided into two administrative units, the Republic of Serbia and the Republic of Montenegro.

The FRY proclaimed itself the legal successor of the SFRY—a status similar to that of the Russian Federation after 1990. The difference was, however, that this status was not recognized by the other successor states of the former Yugoslavia in the way that the successor states of the former Soviet Union recognized the Russian Federation. Additionally, the Russian Federation was by far the largest part of the region in which the majority of the former Soviet Union's population lived. This was not the case with the FRY.

In 2002 under the auspices of the international community, Serbia and Montenegro were again negotiating the transformation of the existing federation into a new State of Serbia and Montenegro, which is seen by many as a transitory stage in the final dismantling of the former Yugoslavia and the establishing of the independent states of Serbia and Montenegro. The negotiations between Serbia and Montenegro were concluded by the adoption of an agreement in the parliaments of Serbia and Montenegro as well as in the federal parliament of the FRY in March 2003. By this agreement a new official name for the country was introduced: Serbia and Montenegro.

The Ethnic Situation in the Territory of the FRY before the Dissolution of the SFRY

The territory of the FRY is around 39,451.4 square miles (40 percent of the territory of the former SFRY). According to the census of 1991, 10.4 million people lived in the territory of the FRY. Two constitutive nations of the former Yugoslavia that lived in this territory were the Serbs, who, with 62.3 percent of the population, comprised an absolute majority of the population in the FRY, and the Montenegrins, with only 5 percent of the population. National minorities comprised a substantial percentage of all inhabitants, most notably the Albanians at 16.6 percent, but also the Hungarians with 3.3 percent and the Muslims with 3.1 percent of the total population in the FRY.

Most of the ethnic minorities in the FRY lived in the territories of the Autonomous Provinces of Vojvodina and Kosovo. Before Milošević almost completely abolished their autonomous position, both provinces had enjoyed substantial autonomy according to the Constitution of the SFRY of 1974. As a result, their development differed considerably from the development of so-called Serbia Proper. Thus this book will present separately the ethnic composition of the populations of Serbia Proper, Kosovo, Vojvodina, and Montenegro.

However, one cannot help but put a question mark on the accuracy on some data in the ethnic statistics of Yugoslav censuses in this territory. The change of the existing categories and the introduction of new ethnic categories in the censuses created some confusion, but this cannot explain substantial differences that exist between the results of different censuses regarding the numbers and percentages of Muslims, Vlachs, or Roma; these differences can be explained partially by the fact that some people, especially those belonging to marginal communities (e.g., Roma), in different situations have decided to change their ethnic affiliation hoping for some social or other gains. However, one can also not exclude the possibility of falsification of census data for certain political needs. Additionally, it is known that the Albanians of Kosovo on some occasions boycotted the censuses.

Serbia Proper

For the region of Serbia Proper (i.e., the Republic of Serbia, not including Vojvodina and Kosovo), there was a substantial decrease in the percentage of the Serb population, mostly due to the fast rise in the numbers and percentages of Muslims, Albanians, Gypsies (Roma), and (after 1961) ethnic "Yugoslavs." The reasons for that development are threefold. First, there is the (un)reliability of the Yugoslav statistics, especially when dealing with the Muslims, Gypsies, and Vlachs. The second reason is the low natural increase (birth rate) of the Serb population, in contrast with the much higher natural increase rates of some minority groups such as the Albanians, Muslims, Gypsies, and Vlachs. Third, mass migrations, both emigrations and immigrations, also changed the ethnic structure in Serbia Proper. This territory was a magnet for immigration of Serbs from the other regions of the former Yugoslavia, not only for those who wanted jobs in the federal Yugoslav institutions, but also for those from less developed regions in the former Yugoslavia (Kosovo, Macedonia, Montenegro, etc.) who had moved to developing industrial centers in Serbia after World War II; on the other hand, numerous Serbs emigrated for economic reasons or because they found employment in the administration and army in other parts of the former Yugoslavia or abroad.

All these reasons especially affected the central and eastern regions of Serbia Proper, where an ethnically homogeneous Serb population prevailed, as well as the southern and eastern regions of Serbia Proper, where there was an ethnically mixed population. Significantly ethnically mixed regions in Serbia Proper were Sandžak (a border region with Montenegro), which had many Muslims, and the region on the border with Kosovo (Bujanovac, Medvedja, Kreševo), with a large number of Albanians.

Traditionally, especially unsettled relations with the Albanians of Kosovo and the Muslims from Sandžak were the main problems in ethnic relations in Serbia Proper. If one recognizes that ethnic conflicts are normal phenomena in plural societies, one could conclude that tensions and conflicts that escalated especially from the 1980s and afterward were because the Serb (but also Yugoslav) authorities were unable to deal with problems in ethnic relations promptly and effectively in a peaceful and democratic way. This inability of the authorities to deal with problems in ethnic relations might be named one of the important factors for the collapse of the former Yugoslavia.

Vojvodina

Vojvodina has been traditionally, and is still today, one of the most ethnically mixed regions in Europe. Censuses show that the ethnic structure of Vojvodina changed slowly but surely after World War II. The numbers, and especially percentages, of Hungarians, Croats, and most other national minorities decreased, while the numbers and percentages of Montenegrins, Serbs, "Yugoslavs," and Roma (Gypsies) significantly increased.

These changes had already provoked the development of two blocs of ethnic groups by the 1970s. One consisted of Serbs, Montenegrins, and "Yugoslavs"; the other comprised the Hungarians, Croats, and members of the other numerous minorities. It is interesting to note that until the mid-1980s both groups demanded from Belgrade the widest autonomy possible.

Until the 1990s individual minorities were mostly concentrated in certain narrow regions. Most of the Hungarians lived in northern Bačka, the Romanians in southern Banat, the Slovaks in some smaller regions in central Banat and Bačka, the Ruthenians in a smaller region in central Bačka, and the Croats in the northern region of Bačka (since the seventeenth century) and in some regions of Srijem. Larger Croat communities also lived in Novi Sad and in central Bačka (near Kula and Vrbas).

In the decade 1981–1991 Vojvodina was the only federal unit of the former Yugoslavia where the total population decreased. This phenomenon requires some explanation. The census data showed that Vojvodina, as the most developed region of Serbia, contained an aging population that had a very low birth rate which, during the period 1980–1984 alone, decreased from 2.7 per thousand to 1.4 per thousand. Also, immigration to Vojvodina, traditionally an important factor in the changes in the ethnic structure of the region, mostly stopped after the mid-1970s, when the influx of economic immigrants from other regions decreased substantially. Immediately after World War II the new colonists, mostly from Montenegro and Herzegovina, replaced the Germans (members of a traditionally large German minority in Vojvodina) who had left; later immigration—especially of Serbs and Montenegrins—further changed the existing ethnic structure. As a consequence, the numbers and percentages of Serbs and Montenegrins increased substantially in Vojvodina. On the other hand, the percentage of Hungarians and other traditional minorities was decreasing. In the 1980s the percentage of Hungarians increased slightly, although their total number decreased. This was because the decrease in their number was smaller than the decrease in other populations in Vojvodina. Most significant was the decrease in the number and percentage of Croats; their birth rates were among the lowest, and many emigrated to Croatia and elsewhere, especially when the Yugoslav crises reached its peak.

In the mid-1980s many Serbs, Montenegrins, and "Yugoslavs" who came to Vojvodina after World War II became the main supporters of Great Serbian nationalism and of Milošević. During the Yugoslav crisis, Vojvodina, due to its relatively better standard of living in comparison with other parts of Serbia, again became very attractive for Serb immigrants, especially richer ones, from Croatia and Bosnia and Herzegovina—which further increased the region's support for Serb nationalism. On the other hand the "old settlers"—the autochthonous Serbs and especially "non-Serbs," members of diverse minorities in Vojvodina—hoped for the restoration of Vojvodina's autonomy and actively took part in, or at least supported, the opposition to Milošević. All this deepened the gap between the "old settlers" and the new immigrants.

Kosovo

The main characteristics of the demographic development of Kosovo during past decades had been the high birth rate and natural increase of Albanians, which was, at 28.3 percent, the highest in Europe, and the mass emigrations of the Serbs and Montenegrins as well as the Albanians—caused by difficult economic, social, and political conditions in the region. Most Serbs and Montenegrins from Kosovo went to Serbia and Montenegro, while the Albanians emigrated to all of the more economically developed regions in the former Yugoslavia and also abroad. Many Albanians left Kosovo for Macedonia, where they settled in the larger Macedonian towns. Albanians from Montenegro also migrated into Kosovo, and these numbered more than the Montenegrins from Kosovo who migrated into Montenegro. Those migrations would have been insignificant if they had not helped decrease the numbers and percentages of Serbs and Montenegrins in Kosovo.

Also significant was the increase in the numbers and percentages of Muslims and Gypsies and the sharp decrease in number and percentage of Turks, which is partially also due to the abovementioned problems with the Yugoslav censuses.

Due to the fast decrease in the numbers and percentages of Serbs and Montenegrins in Kosovo, and, as mentioned above, due to the high birth rate of the Albanians, the proportion of Albanians increased by 15 percent (from 67.2 percent in 1961 to 82.2 percent in 1991). By 1991 the Albanians had an absolute majority in all the regions of Kosovo, with the exception of those in the most northern parts of Kosovo (formerly the Leposavić commune). However, the Serb population had been living in smaller or larger groups in all the communes until the crisis of 1998 (to be discussed in a following section of this chapter). Larger groups of Montenegrins lived in Peć, Priština, Djakovica, and Istok, while in the region of Lipljan and Vitina a few thousand Croats lived.

This was the situation until 1998, when the crisis in Kosovo led to new migrations and changes in the ethnic composition for which the data are not yet available. In spite of the efforts of the international community to "rehabilitate" the multiethnic society of Kosovo, which had been destroyed during the crisis, the numbers of Serbs and Montenegrins—but also the Roma, whose situation is especially difficult—continued to decrease in Kosovo into the early 2000s.

Montenegro

In 1991 Montenegro had only one-third the population of Kosovo. However, 380,000 Montenegrins had their own republic in the former Yugoslavia, while Kosovo remained an autonomous province of Serbia and 1.6 million Albanians in Kosovo officially remained a national minority. This situation showed the nature of Yugoslav "national politics" and also some of its problems.

Although Montenegro was the smallest federal unit in the former Yugoslavia, its population was ethnically diverse. According to official data there were 387 Muslims in Montenegro in 1948, but their number "increased" significantly after 1961—mostly by the account of the Montenegrins. Obviously before 1961 many Slav Muslims in Montenegro had declared themselves Montenegrins—as was the case in Sandžak. The number of Albanians also increased, especially in the border regions with Albania and the Autonomous Province of Kosovo. It is also interesting to note the decrease in the Croat and Serb populations, which was mostly due to the large increase of "Yugoslavs." According to the census in 1991,

Montenegrins represented less than two-thirds of the population in their own republic.

The changes in the numbers and percentages of individual ethnic groups in the population of Montenegro were influenced by migrations from different regions of the former Yugoslavia. At the same time, others, especially the Montenegrins, kept emigrating from this republic. Because of the abovementioned changes in the population of Montenegro, the question of minority rights of the Albanians and even Croats surfaced very early.

"Serboslavia," or Great Serbia–The Dilemma that Finally Caused the Dissolution of the Socialist Federated Republic of Yugoslavia

On 28 June 1989 at Gazimestan, on the occasion of the 600th anniversary of the battle of Kosovo, when Slobodan Milošević mentioned for the first time "a possibility of armed battle in the near future" (Silber and Little, 1997, 72), he did not speak without reason. He must have been aware that it would be extremely difficult to realize his dream of a Yugoslavia, or as some called it "Serboslavia," in which Serbia and the Serbs would have a leading role, because the Albanians, Slovenes, and Croats were against it. The fate of this vision could be predicted by analyzing the events at, and the fate of, the Fourteenth Extraordinary Congress of the LCY (20–26 January 1990), which resulted in the dissolution of the LCY. The Slovene and Croat delegates left the congress after any productive compromise proved impossible.

In spite of the debacle of the party congress, Milošević did not give up his plans, and he continued to strengthen his own position in Serbia. In the middle of July 1990 he changed the name of the League of Communists of Serbia to the Socialist Party of Serbia (Socialistička partija Srbije, SPS). He retained for himself both the presidency of the Republic of Serbia and the presidency of the SPS. He gathered even more power into his hands when the new constitution of the Republic of Serbia was passed in the Serb parliament on 28 September 1990. This constitution gave Milošević—who, as president of the Republic of Serbia, became supreme commander of its armed forces—the right to also name the prime minister of Serbia.

The new constitution (re)defined relations between Serbia and the federation, thereby actually derogating the existing constitution of the SFRY of 1974. As a constitution of Great Serbia, it proclaimed, among other things, the right of the Republic of Serbia to take care of the interests of all Serbs who were living outside Serbia. In other words, following the scenario presented in the so-called Memorandum of the Serb Academy of Sciences and Arts, Serbia would claim control over its own historic and ethnic regions if the Yugoslav federation changed its nature into a confederation or dissolved. The Serbs were interested in protecting their own ethnic minorities outside Serbia, but at the same time, they would not give the same rights to their own minorities within the Republic of Serbia. The new Serb constitution did not give any protection to the Albanians in Kosovo. These Albanians' already unsecured position worsened after mid-May 1990, when Serbia took direct control over Kosovo. The situation worsened further after 5 July, when the parliament of Kosovo and the provincial government of Kosovo dissolved themselves under pressure of the Serb authorities, and printing of any materials in the Albanian language was prohibited. At the same time 15,000 ethnic Albanians lost their jobs, as they were forced to give up all leading positions in politics, culture, science, education, and the state-run economy. The Serb government gave those jobs to ethnic Serbs, which provoked mass protests from the Albanian population.

Fired delegates to the Albanian parliament met secretly in Kačanik on 7 September 1990 and proclaimed the independence of the Republic of Kosovo from the Yugoslav federation. With the so-called Kačanik Constitution they proclaimed the independence of the Republic of Kosovo as "a democratic state of Albanian people and of members of other nations and national minorities who are its citizens: Serbs, Montenegrins, Croats, Turks, Romanians and others living in Kosovo" (Vickers, 1998, 245). The Serbs did not recognize the Kačanik Constitution and reacted by arresting members of the provincial parliament, who were accused of undermining state unity. The authorities also fired another 45,000 ethnic Albanians from their jobs in state-run enterprises. This time the Albanians did not react with mass demonstrations; a period of passive resistance (*pasivni otpor*) began. It lasted through 1997.

Pursuant to the ideal of a Great Serbia, elections were held. Milošević still left open the question of whether his "New Yugoslavia" would be formed within or outside of the SFRY. In two election rounds on 9 and 23 December 1990, the population of Serbia voted unconditionally for the SPS, while in Montenegro the League of Communists won. Slobodan Milošević and Momir Bulatović were elected presidents of Serbia and Montenegro, respectively. These election results did not come as a surprise, because most of the Serbs, in reality, supported Milošević's policy.

At the last moment—after other political parties threatened to boycott the elections—he allowed the opposition to introduce their candidates in the media and to participate in the counting of the election votes. Exploiting the existing system of the state-run economy, he also gave the people of Serbia a raise in their salaries and pensions (almost all enterprises were state-run at the time.) The money was not available for that, however, so without letting the federal authorities know, he ordered the printing of 18 billion dinars ($1.8 billion U.S.). The result was hyperinflation in Yugoslavia, which provoked rage in other republics. With the help of these measures and an election law that also helped gain deputies for the SPS, Milošević's party succeeded in winning 194 of the 250 seats in the Serb parliament and in winning the presidency of Serbia. He received 65 percent of the presidential votes.

The 1990 elections in Serbia brought a severe defeat for the opposition parties, especially for Vuk Drašković's Serb Movement for Renewal (Srpski pokret obnove—SPO) and Vojislav Šešelj's Serb Radical Party (Srpska radikalna stranka—SRS), which at the beginning of the election campaign were almost equal in popularity to Milošević's SPS. The Albanians of Kosovo boycotted the elections. The results of the elections were welcomed by Yugoslav Minister of Defense Veljko Kadijević, because the JNA had its own plans. According to these plans, Yugoslavia would be saved by the League of Communists—Movement for Yugoslavia (Savez komunista-Pokret za Jugoslaviju, as the LC inside the JNA was renamed in November 1990). Although this organization, which had plans to become a leading force in the Republic of Serbia, got only a small percentage of the votes, its influence in the political life of Serbia was very large because of the support that Mira Marković, the wife of Slobodan Milošević, gave to it.

In spite of all these successes for Milošević, not everyone was happy with his adventuristic and radical policy as the "protector of the Serb nation." At the beginning of March 1991 under the leadership of Vuk Drašković, the opposition parties organized mass demonstrations in Belgrade against the "red mafia." The demonstrators, joined by students, were attacked by the police forces; two students and one police officer were killed. Approximately 90 people were wounded. Because the authorities were not able to calm down the demonstrators, the JNA, with its tanks, was sent into the streets. The Yugoslav minister of defense, General Veljko Kadijević, and the commanding officers of the JNA wanted to introduce extraordinary measures and declare a state of emergency in Yugoslavia. They hoped that this would not only calm down the demonstrations in Belgrade, but also enable them to take control over Slovenia and

Slovenian president Milan Kučan (right) meets with U.S. president Bill Clinton at the presidential palace in Ljubljana, Slovenia, 21 June 1999. It was the first visit to Slovenia by a U.S. president. (AFP/Corbis)

Croatia. However, they did not succeed in getting the votes they needed from the presidency of Yugoslavia to proclaim extraordinary emergency measures in Yugoslavia.

After the March demonstrations and some strikes in Serb textile and metallurgical industries, Milošević went on to fire up nationalist passions among the Serbs in Croatia and Bosnia and Herzegovina, where the first armed clashes took place in which the JNA was also involved. In Belgrade during that period, Milošević, together with Šešelj and Drašković, loudly advocated hatred of the other nations in Yugoslavia. His followers were singing, "*Slobodane, pripremi salate, bit će mesa, klat ćemo Hrvate*" ("Slobodan, get the salad ready, there shall be meat, we are going to slaughter the Croats") (Pirjevec, 1995, 415).

The chaos in which the SFRY found itself started to be clear. After the "ten-day war" in Slovenia, it became clear that the SFRY was dead, and the Serbs started to create a Great Serbia. This led to wars in Croatia and Bosnia and Herzegovina. Slovenia, Croatia, Bosnia and Herzegovina, and Macedonia became independent states, while Serbia and Montenegro were united in the so-called Federal Republic of Yugoslavia (Savezna republika Jugoslavija, FRY).

The FRY during the Wars in Croatia and Bosnia and Herzegovina (1992–1995)

The first ideas on the unification of Serbia and Montenegro into a new federal state came to fruition after Slovenia and Croatia became independent states. Already during the winter of 1991–1992, federal bodies of what remained from Yugoslavia began to create documents for the establishment of a "third" Yugoslavia, which was set up by the end of April 1992. It came into being under the name of the Federal Republic of Yugoslavia (FRY).

This state became a country where Slobodan Milošević and the Serb ethnic nation had a leading role. The FRY experienced severe economic and social problems from the very beginning. Its formal legal international status was questionable after it failed to ask for international recognition (as required by the EU) until 23 December 1991. The FRY declared itself a legal successor to the SFRY, but the newly independent former Yugoslav states and the international community opposed this status. Because the FRY was involved in the wars in Croatia and Bosnia and Herzegovina, the international community took the legal position, expressed in decisions of the Badinter Commission. This Commission, established in November 1991 by the EC to study the problems of the succession of the SFRY, came to the conclusion that all successor states that came into being in the territories of the former SFRY were equal successors of the SFRY. The international community did not succeed in reaching an agreement with Slobodan Milošević on a cease-fire, which should have been a condition for the search for a solution to other open issues. The UN introduced economic sanctions against the FRY with the Security Council's Resolution no. 757/1992, which isolated the FRY from the rest of the world.

The "third Yugoslavia" soon got new political leadership. During a period when the world was accusing Milošević of carrying on the war in the former Yugoslavia, he did not want to provoke the international community any further. Instead, he installed other people (albeit ones who were still loyal to him) in the highest government positions. The first president of the FRY was the "spiritual father of the Serbs," Dobrica Ćosić, while an American businessman of Serb descent, Milan Panić, became the new president of the federal government. The choosing of Panić was a surprise for everyone. Milošević had chosen him because he thought Panić would be the right man to help to fight the international isolation of the FRY, and the U.S. government counted on Panić to find a solution to the crisis in the former Yugoslavia. So the State Department gave permission for Panić, an American citizen, to head the government of the FRY, although it had not given similar permission for the former governor of Minnesota, Rudolph G. Perpich, to become a foreign minister of Croatia.

Ćosić's term in office as president of the FRY ended in summer 1993, and Zoran Lilić, who followed him, obeyed Milošević's orders until the end of his term in office. In spite of the fact that, legally, the decision makers in the FRY were federal office holders (like the president of the FRY, the president of the federal government, and the federal parliament), in reality the greatest role in decision making was played by the president of Serbia, Slobodan Milošević. Later on (in February of 2002), Milošević repeatedly denied this role in his defense in front of the Hague Tribunal. He said that he only executed what these other office holders were ordering him to do. In spite of this, he played a major role in the peace process, because international peace makers in the territory of the former Yugoslavia (e.g., Richard Holbrooke, former Secretary of State Cyrus Vance, and former British Foreign Secretary Lord Peter Carrington) were aware of his great influence. These international peacemakers put pressure on Milošević, who, nevertheless, still followed the plans for the creation of a Greater Serbia.

The international sanctions, which were destroying the economy of the FRY and were bringing the Serb people in the FRY to the lowest level of poverty seen during the twentieth century, started to threaten the political position of Milošević. During the parliamentary elections in Serbia, many prominent intellectuals who at first had supported his Serb national program began to criticize Milošević. Later he was deserted even by the Serb Orthodox Church, which as a rule during the course of history has supported Serb national leaders. Now it supported the idea of a return of the Karadjordjević dynasty to the throne of Serbia, urging that Prince Aleksandar, the son of the last king of Yugoslavia, Peter II Karadjordjević, and successor to the throne, should become King of Yugoslavia.

When Milan Panić became the president of the federal government, he supported the attempts of the international community to find a peaceful solution to the Yugoslav crisis at the Conference in London held in the second half of 1992. This especially angered the followers of Slobodan Milošević's SPS and Vojislav Šešelj's Serb Radical Party, who tried to get rid of Panić as soon as possible, before he and the united opposition, the Democratic Movement of Serbia (Demokratski pokret Srbije, DEPOS) could play an important role in the approaching elections.

The elections for the federal and republican parliaments of Serbia and Montenegro and the election for president of Serbia on 20 December 1992 showed the strength of Milošević's regime, which controlled the media. With the help of election manipulations, Milošević won a second term as president of Serbia with 56 percent of the vote, while his opponent, Milan Panić, received 34 percent of the popular vote. Milošević's SPS became the most represented party in the federal and Serb parliaments. Under pressure from Milošević and being refused the support of his SPS, Panić had to resign as president of the federal government only a few days after the elections. Although other nationalist and democratic opposition political parties were emerging in Serbia, they were still marginalized.

The FRY paid a high price for its involvement in the wars in Croatia and Bosnia and Herzegovina. After the introduction of international economic sanctions, the FRY's industrial output fell to 20 percent of that of the year before, and the unemployment rate increased to 50 percent in 1993. The printing of money without backing resulted in a world record inflation rate of 13 million percent per year. The breakdown of the economy reduced many people to poverty, but it also created new elite of war profiteers. Thousands of intellectuals, looking for a better life or fleeing a likely draft into the Yugoslav army (which still fought wars in Bosnia and Herzegovina and Croatia), left the country.

Pressed by conditions in his country in 1994, Milošević had to support a peace plan proposed by the Contact Group of high representatives of the United Kingdom, Russia, France, Germany, and the United States. He hoped that the international community would cease sanctions because of his support of the Contact Group's plan. In August 1994 Milošević finally stopped his direct support of Radovan Karadžić and agreed to participate in the negotiations at Dayton. After many unsuccessful attempts to find a lasting solution for peace in the former Yugoslavia, Milošević's cooperation became, in the eyes of the West, the most promising hope for reaching peace and stability in this region. After the Dayton Agreement was signed, the idea of a Great Serbia seemed to fade into history. However, Milošević stayed in power for another six years.

Kosovo–The Main and Durable Serb Problem

After the Dayton Agreement was signed in December 1995, it became clear that Milošević would try to introduce Serb rule in Kosovo. He declared that Kosovo, which was a part of the first Serb state, Raška and which was considered to be a holy place for the Serb people because of the

Ibrahim Rugova served as president of the largest party of Kosova Albanians, the Democratic League of Kosova and was elected president of Kosova. (G. Mastrullo/Grazia Neri/Corbis Sygma)

battle of Kosovo polje that took place there, ought to become Serb again. Thus, the Serb government tried to direct the flow of Serb refugees from Croatia and Bosnia and Herzegovina into Kosovo. In January 1995, the Serb government even proclaimed an edict on the settlement of 100,000 Serbs, especially Serb refugees from Croatia and Bosnia and Herzegovina in Kosovo, which caused new tensions in this already-uneasy province. Even though the Albanians of Kosovo did not react to Serb pressures with mass demonstrations, they continued with their so-called "passive resistance," and because of the peaceful resistance the army even took the tanks off the streets.

Very few people believed in the possibility of a peaceful solution to the question of Kosovo. The greatest optimist was Ibrahim Rugova, the president of the largest party of Kosovo Albanians, the Democratic League of Kosovo (Lidhja Demokratike e Kosovës, LDK)]. There was a great political, ideological, and cultural gap between the Albanians and Serbs in Kosovo, especially because soon after Slovenia and Croatia declared their independence, the Kosovo Albanians started to construct a parallel structure of government to the existing Serb government in Kosovo. As early as 22 September 1991, the Kosovo Albanian leadership introduced a Declaration on Independence and Sovereignty of Kosovo. During 26–30 September 1991, a secret referendum took place in which more than 87 percent of the eligible voters of Kosovo participated; 99.87 percent of them chose sovereignty and independence for Kosovo. Only 164 voters were against, and 933 ballots were declared invalid.

On the basis of the results of this referendum and the amended Kačanik Constitution, the Kosovo parliament (that is, the Albanian members of the provincial parliament that had been dissolved in July 1990) declared the independence of the Republic of Kosovo on 19 October 1991, and named Dr. Bujar Bukoshi the prime minister. Predictably, the Serb state did not recognize the results of the referendum. The Kosovo Albanians held parliamentary and presidential elections on 24 May 1992. The LDK got 76.4 percent of the vote and had an absolute majority in the 130-member parliament, with 96 deputies. Dr. Ibrahim Rugova got 99.5 percent of the presidential vote (Vickers, 1998, 261). So, in mid-1992 the Kosovo Albanians organized, parallel to the existing Serb authorities, their new state, which operated relatively successfully in education at all levels. They also developed their own Albanian economy, to a large extent dependent on the help of the Albanian emigrant communities in the west. The Kosovo Albanians succeeded in organizing their own "parallel state" in spite of the fact that in all vital segments (the economy, financial structure, etc.) it did not have anything to do with the "official" FRY. The FRY and the Kosovo Serbs did not recognize this Albanian parallel state in Kosovo and wanted to destroy it. Simultaneously, the Albanians ceased paying taxes to the Serb authorities and the FRY. Instead they financed the Albanian parallel state and army; Albanian emigrants contributed up to 10 percent of their income for these purposes. This all deepened the differences between the Serbs and Albanians.

In May 1992 the then-president of the Serb government, Radovan Božović, invited all the political parties of Kosovo to a series of talks about a peaceful solution to the problems. FRY President Dobrica Ćosić proposed a solution according to which 40 percent of Kosovo's territory would become a part of Serbia. Also, Priština and Kosovska Mitrovica, the two largest cities of Kosovo, and all the mines, including Trepća (a mine for zinc, lead, silver, and gold), would become part of Serbia. Eight hundred thousand Albanians living in the "Serb" part would have to emigrate in a "peaceful" ethnic cleansing. The Albanians offered a countersuggestion that 10 percent of Kosovo's territory would be ceded to Serbia, and the territory of communes (as basic units of local government) of Preševo and Bujanovac, which were at that time part of Serbia Proper, would again became part of Kosovo. Those districts were 70 percent Albanian. The Albanians offered ethnic minority rights to the 150,000 Serbs who lived in major cities of Kosovo (Priština, Mitrovica, and Gnjilane). The Kačanik Constitution of September 1990, according to which the Serbs of Kosovo were a "nation" and not only a national minority, should have guaranteed the special ethnic rights of the Serbs. This Albanian proposal could have prevented the total Albanization of Kosovo. A third proposal offered to the Serbs 20 percent of Kosovo's territory, including the mines of Trepća, the electricity plant of Obilić, Serb monasteries, and the historical seat of the Serb Orthodox Church organization, the Patriarchy in Peć in the west. The main towns, Priština, Mitrovica, Gnjilane, and Peć, were to be on the border of this new Kosovo, which would become an independent state. According to a statement by the German ambassador to the FRY, Gerth Aarens, who at the Geneva Convention on Yugoslavia presided over a group responsible for national minorities, Slobodan Milošević had agreed to the third proposal. However, the talks did not succeed because Milošević changed his position.

Later, different solutions were discussed: autonomy for Kosovo (which would not be less than that already gained in the constitutional arrangements of 1974), independence of Kosovo, Kosovo as a part of Albania, division of Kosovo (the abovementioned three versions), an international protectorate, etc. When Milošević and Rugova signed an agreement on 2 September 1996 to include the Albanians again into the official education system in Kosovo, a compromise solution seemed possible: The Albanians of Kosovo could be given the right to govern Kosovo, which would remain a part of Serbia. However, there were at least two interpretations of the agreement. The Serbs insisted that the Albanians would have to return to the regular educational system, and the Albanians claimed the accord should allow their students to use regular school facilities under their own, separate curriculum (Sell, 2002, 278). The fact that a compromise was not reached caused the gap between the Albanians and Serbs to grow deeper and deeper.

The Albanians continued to patronize their own parallel Albanian school system at all levels of education in spite of the abovementioned Milošević-Rugova agreement. The Albanians also maintained their own administration in the province. The Serbs, who lived in "ghettos," felt even more compelled to emigrate than ever. However, the Serb authorities in Belgrade prohibited any real estate transactions between the members of the Serb and Albanian ethnic groups, making it impossible for these Serbs to sell their land in order to emigrate. In Kosovo, which was under a special administration of the Serb state and the FRY, the Albanians were facing brutal police repression. On the other hand, numerous murders and bomb attacks also occurred for which the Liberation Army of Kosovo (Ushtria Çlirimtare e Kosovës, UÇK) took responsibility.

Simultaneously, important political changes took place in the FRY. Although the coalition of the leftist parties—the SPS of Slobodan

Milošević, the Yugoslav Left (Jugoslavenska levica, JUL) of Milošević's wife, and the New Democracy (Nova Demokratija)—won 46 percent of the popular vote, a coalition of opposition parties Zajedno (Together) was the winner of the local elections, achieving majorities in the thirteen largest Serb cities. Slobodan Milošević—with the help of the judges of the Belgrade municipal court, who were faithful to him—nullified the results of these elections in Belgrade, which caused demonstrations by the followers of the opposition. After three months of mass protests, at which, according to some reports, from 300,000 to one million people gathered in daily demonstrations, Milošević recognized the results of the elections and the victory of the opposition in February 1997. For the first time in the post–World War II history of Yugoslavia, Belgrade got a non-communist mayor, Zoran Djindjić.

As Milošević could no longer run for president of Serbia after two terms in office, he got himself elected president of the FRY by the federal parliament. The election of Milošević as the president of the FRY and mass arrests of Albanians accused of membership in the UÇK foreshadowed the next developments in Kosovo.

The Kosovo Crisis

Due to extremely bad economic conditions in the FRY as a whole, the relations among the Serbs of Kosovo, Serb authorities in Kosovo, and the Serb state on the one hand and the Albanian population in Kosovo on the other deteriorated even further. Ibrahim Rugova could not find a common language with the Serb authorities. Young Albanians (70 percent of the Albanians of Kosovo were younger than 30 years of age) were unhappy with Rugova's willingness to search for compromise. Instead, younger people, who did not have any opportunity for employment or any other perspective, were willing to follow leaders who demanded action against Serb violence. Adem Demaçi, who spent more than 27 years in Yugoslav jails and was named "the Kosovo Mandela," gained popularity. The main opponent of Rugova's search for a peaceful solution, Demaçi demanded that the UÇK act, which soon led to the first fights. In the Klina and Drenica region these developed into a full-blown war at the beginning of 1998.

Escalation of armed conflicts in Kosovo caused new headaches for the international community, because the international leaders were afraid that the widening of the conflict could endanger the implementation of the Dayton Agreement in Bosnia and Herzegovina. Therefore, the Contact

Group accepted a special plan in London on 9 March 1998, in which they demanded from Milošević the retreat of his Serb special forces from Kosovo and a beginning of dialogue between Serbs and the Kosovo Albanians. The EU also got actively involved in negotiations between Serb and Kosovo Albanian leaders and wanted to send an EU diplomatic mission to Priština to observe events in the province.

In spite of all its attempts, however, the international community did not succeed in opening a dialogue between Serb and Kosovo Albanian leadership. The fights continued, and Milošević opposed all attempts by the international community to observe events in Kosovo. On 23 April 1998, he even organized a referendum in the FRY in which 75 percent of the eligible voters participated; 94.73 percent of them voted against allowing foreign observers to come to Kosovo.

Six days later, the international community agreed to new sanctions against the FRY. In July, the Kosovo Albanians formed a secret parliament; during the summer of 1998, the Serb armed forces were cleansing Kosovo of UÇK troops. On 24 September NATO gave Milošević an ultimatum, to stop the violence in Kosovo or face air strikes. In October, Richard Holbrooke suggested giving Milošević some time to stop the offensive against the Kosovo Albanians. The UN Security Council demanded that observers be allowed to go to Kosovo to stop the violence, hoping that the very presence of the international observers would be enough to stop the oppression by the Serb apparatus and the violence against the Albanians there. At the same time the Serb troops started to retreat.

After many months of attempts, the Contact Group finally gathered representatives from both sides in Rambouillet Castle near Paris. The Contact Group wanted "extensive autonomy" for Kosovo, short of outright independence; free movement for all international persons under the auspices of the UN High Commissioner for Refugees (UNHCR); the suspension of federal authority in matters injurious or discriminatory to the Kosovo Albanians; and the stationing of NATO troops in the province. The Rambouillet Agreement offered a plan for wide autonomy for Kosovo and demanded an immediate cease-fire. On 23 February 1999 after days of negotiations, representatives of the Kosovo Albanians conditionally accepted a draft of the Rambouillet Agreement on the future status of Kosovo; Serb representatives, however, did not accept it and labeled it as an attack on the sovereignty of their state. The two sides in the conflict were then offered an alternate agreement under which Kosovo would become an international protectorate. For the security of the members of all the ethnic groups there, an international peacekeeping force would be

Ethnic Albanian negotiators at the Kosovo peace talks at the International Conference Center in Paris, 18 March 1999. From the left, sitting at the table, Veton Surroi, Ibrahim Rugova, Hashim Thaci, and Rexhep Qosja sign a draft accord, hammered out in the Rambouillet Agreement. The accord called for self-rule for Kosovo, plus the deployment of a NATO-led peacekeeping force. (AFP/Corbis)

stationed in Kosovo. Three years later, a new referendum on the future status of Kosovo was foreseen.

During the negotiations in Rambouillet, on 16–17 February 1999, American diplomat Christopher Hill went to visit Milošević and threatened him with air strikes if he did not allow the deployment of NATO peacekeepers in Kosovo. However, Milošević rejected the deployment of the NATO peacekeepers. Two day later Milošević said: "We are not going to give up Kosovo, even if they bomb us" (Z. R., 1999, 5). Western diplomats started to leave the FRY. At the end of February, the Serb forces occupied the entire province of Kosovo. On 1 March 1999 Milošević rejected international negotiatiors for Kosovo, and one day later Adem Demaçi resigned as political leader of the UÇK, which withdrew his signature from the Albanian side on the Rambouillet Agreement. However, after the United Stated agreed to add a provision that "the will of the people" was among issues to be considered by an international conference after three years, the Kosovo Albanians signed the agreement again on 18 March, while the Serbs boycotted the event. The international observers left Kosovo on 20 March 1999, when they realized that their mission to prevent Serb violence against the Albanians through peaceful means had failed. Richard Holbrooke, the U.S. special envoy, tried for the last time to convince Milošević to sign the agreement, but Milošević reportedly said to him: "You're a great country, a powerful country. You can do anything you want. We can't stop you. Go ahead and bomb us, but you will never get Kosovo" (Sell, 2002, 299). On 23 March the Serb parliament voted against stationing NATO troops in Kosovo, and on 24 March, NATO started air strikes on the FRY.

At the same time the air strikes began on the FRY, a mass exodus (i.e., forced emigration) of Albanians and others from Kosovo also began. This caused a new international refugee crisis. According to the UNHCR, 831,000 people were forced to leave their homes, including more than 400,000 during the first days of the NATO air strikes. The majority of refugees were ethnic Albanians. Approximately one-third of them were hiding in the woods in Kosovo and with their relatives and friends in Serbia. Others escaped to Albania (270,000), Macedonia (130,000), Montenegro (35,700), and Bosnia and Herzegovina (around 8,000). Because the burden of refugees on Albania and Macedonia was so high, other countries agreed to receive some refugees from Kosovo who escaped these two countries. Many refugees later emigrated to Turkey and the United States (20,000 each); Spain (more than 7,000); Romania, Norway, and Denmark (6,000 each); and Greece, Sweden, and Austria (5,000 each).

Soon after the air strikes began, attempts to find a solution for the Kosovo crisis continued. On 6 May 1999, representatives of the western European countries and Russia met in Bonn, Germany, where they discussed strategies to end the crisis. A few days later, the western European countries named Finland's president, Marti Ahtisaari, a special envoy to Kosovo. The G-8 Group (Russia and the most developed countries of the West) wrote a draft of a UN resolution that would end the war. In spite of air strikes, the FRY authorities were still not ready to withdraw their military units from Kosovo. By the end of May, the FRY authorities even started to send new troops to Kosovo.

On 3 June 1999, after the air strikes intensified and the situation in the FRY worsened, Milošević accepted a peace proposal that was brought to him by Ahtisaari and the former Russian prime minister, Viktor Černomerdin. The plan called for the complete withdrawal of the FRY's armed forces from Kosovo and the setting up of international troops there under UN command. On 9 June 1999 in Kumanovo (Macedonia), representatives of the FRY's army and NATO signed a technical plan for withdrawal of the Yugoslav troops, and NATO stopped its attacks on the FRY the next day. On 10 June 1999, the UN Security Council accepted a resolution on Kosovo, which established legal grounds for peacekeeping forces to be stationed in Kosovo. The UN Security Council's Resolution

No. 1244 also determined that the FRY had to immediately stop the violence and repression in Kosovo. The international forces, in which civilians as well as soldiers were to serve, would be stationed there for a period of twelve months, with a possible extension of the mandate subject to the Security Council's approval.

This resolution also foresaw a temporary civil administration of Kosovo in which its inhabitants would have wide autonomy and would develop their own democratic institutions. Albanian refugees were able to return to Kosovo under the control of the UNHCR. Members of the UÇK and other armed Albanian groups were required to stop fighting and to give up their weapons. Negotiations on the future of Kosovo were required to begin among the Serbs, the remaining Yugoslav state, and the Albanians of Kosovo. The resolution also guaranteed the territorial integrity of the FRY and neighboring countries. This resolution also demanded that all parties concerned cooperate with the Hague Tribunal.

While the Western powers were getting ready to divide Kosovo into five sectors, a small unit of Russian soldiers from Bosnia and Herzegovina quickly moved into Kosovo and captured the strategically important airport in Priština, thereby showing Russia's interest in serving as the special protector of the Serbs of Kosovo. The Russians simply stayed at the airport as a part of the international forces in Kosovo and Kosovo was divided into five sectors, in which representatives of the French, English, Italian, German, and U.S. military and civilian authorities started to renew the local administration. Peace in Kosovo meant, according to some media, "the beginning of the end of the Serb myth about Kosovo and the myth of the nation from heaven." ("Konec Mita," 1999, 37–38). According to this historic myth, Kosovo was a "holy Serb land" that should have been included into the greater Serbia at all costs.

After the peace agreement was signed, most of the Albanians returned to their homes, and mass emigrations of the Serbs and Montenegrins began. Kosovo experienced ethnic cleansing again. The Serb population remained only in the northern part of Kosovska Mitrovica, some cities and villages north of Kosovska Mitrovica, and some enclaves in the Priština area. Under the circumstances, there were many within both emigrating ethnic groups who did not like the peace. Bloody unrest began in Kosovska Mitrovica at the beginning of February 2001. In March, fights also began in Preševo Valley, in the regions of southeastern Serbia (near the administrative border between Kosovo and Serbia), where the Albanian population prevails. A part of this territory was a demilitarized zone, which came under the complete sovereignty of the FRY again. After some days of fighting, under international peacekeeping forces' surveillance, both sides signed a cease-fire, then fighting erupted in neighboring districts in Macedonia. The Balkan tragedy still continued.

In spite of resistance from the Albanians of Kosovo, Hans Haekkerup, the civilian administrator for Kosovo, signed along with the representatives of the FRY a document of cooperation that was intended to mean "a beginning of return of Serbia and Yugoslavia to its territory" ("Za tri leta odložena neodvisnost Kosova," 2001, 4) as official Yugoslav sources commented on the event. The Albanians, who at the time were getting ready to hold elections for their provincial parliament, accepted this development with discontent. All opinion polls were predicting that the LDK and Ibrahim Rugova would be absolute winners of the elections. Rugova's LDK did win a majority of seats in the 120-member Kosovo provincial parliament. However, Rugova did not get the necessary number of votes (two-thirds of all members of the provincial parliament) to be elected president of Kosovo. The deputies of the Democratic Party of Kosovo (PDK) and the Union of the Future of Kosovo were boycotting the elections. Similar events happened on 10 January 2002, during the second and third rounds of elections. After the new civil administrator, Michael Steiner, intervened, the Kosovo parliament, with eighty-eight votes (three deputies voted against; fifteen deputies abstained), finally elected Rugova as the president of the province. In his intervention Steiner pointed out that the constitutional provisions on the election of the president (also those regarding the independence of Kosovo) should be respected and supported. At the same time Bajram Rexhepi was elected prime minister of the ten-member Kosovo government.

Although Kosovo, since Rugova and Rexhepi were named to their positions, had all the administrative bodies needed for the functioning of the state, these bodies had limited competencies. The real master in the province was still the civil administrator, who administered the province in the name of the international community. He had veto power over any decision that would violate UN Resolution no. 1244 on the mission of the UNMIK (United Nations Mission in Kosovo) and KFOR (Kosovo force). At this writing, the status of Kosovo is not expected to change for some years to come.

The Political "Death" of Slobodan Milošević and the New Beginning in Serbia

After he had to admit defeat in Kosovo, Milošević started to lose popularity very quickly. At the beginning of 2000, he changed the federal consti-

Belgrade celebrates the defeat of Slobodan Milošević.
(Bernard Bisson/CORBIS Sygma)

tution and ran for president of the FRY. He organized elections in October 2000. The people of Serbia were dissatisfied because of worsened economic conditions as well as because Milošević's policy did not serve the interests of the Serb nation, especially in Kosovo. The opposition to Milošević was still divided, but they succeeded in uniting into the Democratic Opposition of Serbia (Demokratska opozicija Srbije, DOS). They also agreed to a common platform for the elections against Milošević and his regime. Dr. Vojislav Koštunica, a "moderate" Serb nationalist, a lawyer, and an ardent negotiator, became the presidential candidate of the united opposition.

Koštunica won the election of 22 September 2000. He got 48.2 percent of the popular vote, Milošević received 40.23 percent, and all other candidates got the rest—most of them less than 1 percent of the votes. A DOS representative claimed in a statement to independent radio station B2-92 that the election commission had stolen 400,000 of Koštunica's votes and had added 200,000 votes to Milošević's total. (Milošević, meanwhile, was getting ready for the runoff elections.) Although officially Koštunica was not declared a winner, he had been receiving his first congratulations from foreign dignitaries and representatives of the Serb Orthodox Church. People reacted to the news about the stealing of the votes with a general strike and with protests. After seemingly all of Serbia protested, Milošević officially admitted that he had lost the elections. After that the

Yugoslav president Vojislav Koštunica casts his vote for the Serbian parliamentary elections in Belgrade, 23 December 2000. (AFP Photo Epa/Srdjan Suki/Corbis)

election commission "admitted its mistake," and the Yugoslav Constitutional Court accepted Vojislav Koštunica as the new president.

The victory of Koštunica was happily accepted in foreign countries; people were also happy about it in Kosovo, although the Kosovo Albanians were skeptical, especially because Koštunica was a Serb nationalist. There were also reservations toward Koštunica in Montenegro, where only followers of the Socialist National Party of Momir Bulatović participated in the elections and all others who advocated the independence of Montenegro boycotted elections for president and for the federal parliament.

Milošević's defeat meant the normalization of political life in the FRY; visits from foreign heads of state followed after the new FRY and Serb governments took over. Carla del Ponte, the General Prosecutor of the Hague International Tribunal, visited Belgrade in the second half of January 2001. Milošević was arrested on 1 April 2001, allegedly for financial fraud and for killings of his opponents while he was in office. On 28 June 2001 (St. Vitus Day), the FRY authorities handed Milošević over to the Hague Tribunal. In protest, Milošević's followers in Belgrade and other towns in Serbia held demonstrations, but they soon ended. The handing over of Milošević also caused a crisis within the government, because FRY president Koštunica declared that surrendering Milošević to the Hague International Tribunal "was still illegal and unconstitutional, and as such threatened the existence of the FRY" (Mašanović, 2001, 1). This statement reflected the differences within the DOS. Although Djindjić demanded a radical reform and settlement of the accounts with Milošević's Serbia and the FRY, Koštunica advocated gradual and "peaceful" transition. Consequently, the reform of the legislation adopted by the Milošević's regime was very slow and slowed down democratization of the society.

In spite of all the problems inside the government, the FRY still tried to strengthen the ties between the Yugoslav state and the rest of the world. Its representatives also soon signed a succession agreement on the inheritance of the federal wealth and debts of the SFRY among the successor states. Negotiations on division of the wealth of the former common federation began.

Until February 2002, theories and discussions on how to solve the economic crisis in the former Yugoslavia were the main topic of interest in Serbia. For a while in February 2002, almost everyone in Serbia watched the trial against Milošević that began before the Hague Tribunal; however, the interest did not last long. People were burdened by problems of everyday life and disappointed with the actual progress of reforms, and the corruption and criminal activities continued to grow. Clashes among criminals and criminal organizations, murders of high state officials, and attempts on the lives of some Serb politicians became a part of everyday life and remained mostly unpunished because of links between the police and judiciary and organized crime. Unhappy with such conditions, people lost their interest for participating in democratic political life. Consequently, the 2002 elections for a new president of Serbia failed in accordance with the existing electoral legislation because less than one-half of the electorate participated. When the term of office of Milutinović, a loyal Milošević collaborator indicted by the Hague Tribunal, had expired and three attempts to elect a new president of Serbia by general elections had failed, the Constitutional Committee of the Parliament of Serbia declared on 30 December 2002—in accordance with the constitution—Nataša Micić to be the president of the republic parliament, and also the acting pro tempore president of Serbia.

Under the pressure from the EU and its High Representative for the Common Foreign and Security Policy, Javier Solana, negotiations on future arrangements between Serbia and Montenegro continued during 2002. Following long, uncertain, and difficult negotiations a compromise was found and confirmed by authorities of both republics; on 4 February 2003 the federal parliament voted for new constitutional documents

(Constitution and Executive Law) of a new state of Serbia-Montenegro. This act started a process of creation of new state institutions for Serbia-Montenegro (a 126-member parliament, Council of ministers, etc.).

By the creation of this state, the name *Yugoslavia* was officially abolished and disappeared from political maps. Some newspapers sarcastically named the new state Solania, referring to the desperate attempts of Javier Solana to create this state entity (Potočnik, 2003a, 4) Though some reactions to the creation of this new entity were positive, Vojislav Koštunica, the president of the FRY (who remained in office), reproached the new arrangement. Simultaneously, forty-two representatives of the Kosovo parliament initiated a resolution "to proclaim independence of this South Serb province" (B. J., 2003, 1). However, the Proclamation of the Independent state of Kosovo announced on 13 February 2003 was cancelled, at least temporarily, due to the pressure of the international community.

The international community continued to press Serbia-Montenegro to follow the demands of the Hague Tribunal. Vojislav Šešelj, indicted by the Hague Tribunal for war crimes, decided to turn himself in voluntarily and leave for Hague. At his "goodbye meeting" in Belgrade on 23 February 2003 he declared that after he left, "Serbia is going to burn. . . ." (Potočnik, 2003b, 28).

On 18 March 2003 the murder of Zoran Djindjić, the prime minister of Serbia, shocked Serbia and the international community. This successful attempt on his life was condemned by the people of Serbia and by foreign, especially European, politicians, who declared that "they shall do everything to fulfill the idea of the late Prime Minister on European Serbia-Montenegro. . . ." (Potočnik, 2003c, 1). The same day Nataša Micić, the acting president of Serbia, signed a law on the introduction of extraordinary measures that suspended some human rights and gave the police broad authority in fighting organized crime. Simultaneously, the parliament of Serbia elected a new prime minister, Zoran Živković, previously a deputy prime minister in Djindjić's government.

The Serb police reacted immediately against the criminal organizations that committed Djindjić's murder, and in a few weeks they had interrogated more then 6,000 people and imprisoned 2,000 suspects. Two main suspects and known criminals (Dušan Spasojević-Šiptar and Mile Luković-Kum) were killed when they refused to surrender. The infamous Red Berets, a "special unit for special operations" (apart from the police and army) established by Milošević and instrumental in the attempt on Djindjić's life, were abolished; their main organizer, Milorad Luković-Legija, a former commander of the Red Berets, had still not been arrested at the time of this writing. The police investigation showed that the successful attempt on the prime minister's life was part of an attempted coup d'etat and shed light on numerous murders of high state functionaries committed in the past. It also explained the disappearance and murder of Ivan Stambolić, a former president of Serbia, whose remains were found at Fruška Gora. Dušan Mihajlović, the Serb Minister of the Interior, stated that the order to kill Stambolić was given by Slobodan Milošević to prevent Stambolić's candidacy for the presidency of the FRY in 2000. The investigation showed links between organized crime and Milošević's regime, links that in some cases continued after the fall of this regime. It is believed that Djindjić was killed because he tried to cut these links and suppress organized crime.

In spite of such extraordinary events, on 18 March 2003 the parliament of the state of Serbia-Montenegro elected its first government, a five-member Council of Ministers proposed by the prime minister, Svetozar Marković. On 4 April 2003 Serbia-Montenegro officially became a member of the Council of Europe.

Montenegro

The destiny of Montenegro was not yet quite clear when Yugoslavia started to collapse in 1991. In November 1991, when negotiations took place in The Hague under the presidency of Lord Peter Carrington about the future destiny of Yugoslavia, Montenegro was one of the republics of Yugoslavia. Lord Carrington foresaw the same level of independence for it as for other former Yugoslav republics. Initially the president of Montenegro, Momir Bulatović, accepted Carrington's proposal. Later he had to withdraw from this decision under pressure from Milošević and had to accept Milošević's proposal to create the FRY as a union between Montenegro and Serbia. Bulatović was under so much pressure from Milošević because Milošević needed the new federation to claim rights as the only successor of the former Yugoslavia (SFRY). Also, the people of Montenegro were still supportive of Milošević's policy.

Montenegro remained a part of the "third" Yugoslavia, the FRY, which was proclaimed with the adoption of the Constitution at Žabljak in Montenegro on 27 April 1992. In accordance with this constitution, Montenegro retained an equal position with Serbia and was also fairly well represented in federal institutions; in reality it had as much autonomy as Milošević permitted. Montenegro shared the destiny of the rest of the

FRY when the economic sanctions of the international community were imposed on Yugoslavia. For Montenegro, whose economy lagged behind the other Yugoslav republics even before 1991, this meant even greater poverty. At this time a majority of Montenegrins were still supporting Milošević.

In the second half of the 1990s, the deepening economic crisis, widening social gaps, and political instability in the FRY brought changes in Montenegrin politics. Within the leading political party, the Socialist Party of Montenegro, a group of politicians demanded more rights and equality for Montenegro inside the Yugoslav federation. The future president of Montenegro and then-prime minister, Milo Djukanović, said, "Montenegro was not forced to enter Yugoslavia. . . . It did not enter Yugoslavia to be threatened by the state, nor to flee Yugoslavia." The president of the Montenegrin parliament, Svetozar Marović, was even more direct when he declared: ". . . the Montenegrin president will not be chosen any more by staffs of some hired Montenegrins in Belgrade, nor the dukes, nor the wives, nor *Politika Express* [the Belgrade regime's newspaper] . . . Montenegro wishes to have its own president and not a deputy installed by decree at a secret dinner in Dedinje [the government villa quarter in Belgrade] . . . (Vasović, 1997, 34–35). Bulatović did not care much about dissatisfaction among Montenegrins. He paid, however, for his unconditional following of Milošević's policy by being defeated in the next election. Djukanović won the election for the presidency of Montenegro in September 1997 with a margin of 5,488 votes. Bulatović admitted defeat at first; later, at Milošević's request, he accused Djukanović of stealing votes. In January 1998 he even tried to come to power by force. General demonstrations and unrest were organized by followers of Bulatović (and Milošević); 13 demonstrators were arrested, and 100 people were wounded. In spite of uncertain conditions, Djukanović succeeded in retaining power. For the first time in the FRY, a party won that supported reforms and the opening of the country to the world. Also for the first time, Slobodan Milošević got a political opponent worthy of the title.

The change of power in Montenegro took place under very tense circumstances, as the rise of radicalism in neighboring Serbia brought new violence in Kosovo. Because of different points of view toward this "life and death issue" of what to do in Kosovo for Yugoslavia and Milošević, Montenegro and Serbia found themselves at a very crucial crossroads. The new Montenegrin leadership demanded opening toward the world, especially in the economy, with participation in the International Monetary Fund and other international financial institutions. At the same time,

they demanded a quick solution to the Kosovo problem. The Montenegrin leadership also demanded the development of an open multinational
and democratic society, although the current society was being more and
more constricted by Milošević's policy of deepening the conflict with the
international community. Eventually, Milošević's policy even provoked
an attack by NATO against the FRY.

This brought a change in the formerly positive public opinion regarding the continuation of the FRY in Montenegro, which was not ready to
lose time while waiting for democratic change in Serbia. Montenegrin
politicians even offered Serbia some suggestions on how to change relations in the federation. If Belgrade had given Montenegro enough freedom and independence to enable Montenegro to continue its democratic
reforms, even if Serbia was not willing to change its society, Montenegro
would have stayed in the federation with Serbia. However, as the regime
of Slobodan Milošević continued its policy of stifling the development of
Montenegro, Montenegrin leaders started openly to demand independence. The governments of the EU countries and the U.S. administration
were against Montenegro's independence because they were afraid of the
eruption of another armed conflict. However, Montenegrin president
Djukanović did not succumb to their pressure to stay in the FRY. He
warned the EU and the United States that Montenegro, which was being
affected by the NATO bombardment and international sanctions, would
leave the FRY if Milošević did not resign.

Montenegro had already been executing a plan in secret. By the sum-
mer of 1999, the FRY's federal institutions had already lost control over
Montenegro. The Montenegrin police, faithful to the Djukanović administration, controlled the borders with Albania and Croatia and the Adriatic coast. Montenegro had its own unofficial representatives in Western
European capitals; it issued its own visas and had its own foreign minister.
Only the inflated dinar and the Yugoslav army, which was still faithful to
Milošević, connected Montenegro with Serbia. Although Milošević had
to leave the presidency of the FRY after the September elections of 2000,
the Montenegrin leadership did not change their position on the issue of
independence for Montenegro. Incidentally, Djukanović and his followers
almost helped Milošević to stay in power because they boycotted the September 2000 elections.

The right of Montenegro to be an independent state was explained
with quite a few arguments by the Montenegrin leadership. They pointed
to the fact that Montenegro had been an internationally recognized state
before 1918 and that Montenegro was one of the Yugoslav republics

recognized by the Badinter Commission at the beginning of the 1990s as having a right to independence. They also called attention to their experiences after 1990, which showed that it was impossible to work for the development of Montenegro from inside the third Yugoslavia. At the end of 2000, Djukanović even announced a referendum on independence of Montenegro because he was convinced that more than 60 percent of the inhabitants of Montenegro would vote for independence. It should have been held by the first half of 2001 but was not because of the election discussed below. The Serb authorities were very skeptical about the Montenegrins' proposal for Serbia and Montenegro as internationally recognized states. Zoran Djindjić, who later became the Serb prime minister, foresaw the possibility of negotiations, but the president of the FRY, Vojislav Koštunica, still insisted on the FRY staying intact and was against the Montenegrin position.

Montenegrin parliamentary elections followed on 22 April 2001. This was the first test of Djukanović's aspirations toward independence. His coalition, Victory of Montenegro (Pobjeda Crne gore), won slightly more than 50 percent of the votes. At the same time, the coalition United for Yugoslavia (Zajedno za Jugoslaviju) received slightly less than 50 percent of the votes. The latter side was pleased because this narrow result meant that a referendum on Montenegrin independence would be postponed: Djukanović's coalition got only two deputies more in the Montenegrin parliament than the opposition; holding a referendum on the independence of Montenegro would have meant that the pro-Yugoslav half of the population would not support the independence of Montenegro, or, under the worst scenario, it could even have meant a civil war. An important explanation of why the Socialist National Party of Momir Bulatović was so successful in Montenegro is that it deserted Slobodan Milošević and entered the federal government of Dragiša Pešić of the DOS. Also, the international community's pressure against Montenegrin independence played a role, since the Montenegrin state could not survive without external help.

It became clear that all misunderstandings would have to be solved with negotiations, even though those in favor of Montenegrin independence were still convinced that the conflict on the future destiny of the FRY could be solved only with a referendum. At the end of 2001, experts began to negotiate on how to change the FRY, and they continued into January 2002. The EU joined the negotiations in February 2002. In Brussels, Montenegrin and Serb experts in economic, monetary, and social issues met and discussed integrating the FRY into the European structure, especially from the perspective of the Stabilization Association (the first phase of cooperation between the EU and nonmember states) agreement between the FRY and the EU. The EU intended to sign such an agreement with all the states of southeastern Europe except Slovenia, which was already on its way to full EU membership.

The EU wanted the Yugoslav Federation to remain in existence, simply changing its name to the Union of Serbia and Montenegro. Javier Solana, the EU representative at these talks, proposed that instead of a federal government the new state would have a president elected by the parliament and a "coordination body" with specifically determined and limited powers. Montenegro would even have the right to establish the Euro as its currency. The Montenegrins would serve in the Serb-Montenegrin army on Montenegro's territory. After five years (the EU's proposal) or one year (the Montenegrin proposal), Serbia and Montenegro would have the right to decide on their own future status by a referendum.

Djukanović now found himself in a bad situation. His coalition partners (the Social Democratic Party and Liberal Union) declared that if Djukanović accepted the EU proposal, they would enter the opposition, which would bring new parliamentary elections. This would divide Montenegrins even more. Negotiations on the reconstruction of the FRY continued. According to Djukanović the so-called Belgrade Agreement on starting points for the reconstruction of the FRY of 14 March 2002 "does not negate the basic right of Serbia and Montenegro to—after a certain period of time—reconsider their common future . . . No one could deny to the Montenegrin nation the right to referendum, which shall be postponed for three years. . . ." (Jokić, 2002, 1). As mentioned in the previous section of this chapter, the negotiations resulted in a compromise, which enabled the adoption in the parliament of the FRY of constitutional documents for a state of Serbia-Montenegro on 4 February 2003.

The outcome of the situation in Montenegro remains to be seen. Montenegro remains an interesting society that, in many ways, combines structures and ideas of modern democracy with those of a traditional tribal society; this mixture continues to play an important role in Montenegrin politics.

Sandžak: Is a New Balkan War Possible There?

During the search for a solution on Serb-Montenegrin relations, the question of Sandžak was surfacing again. Sandžak encompasses the mountainous region of northern Montenegro (districts of Rožaj, Plav, Ivangrad, Bijelo Polje, Plevlja) and southwestern Serbia (districts of Novi Pazar, Tutin, Sjenica, Prijepolje, Priboj) settled by the Muslims. Today its people think of themselves as Bosniaks. Sandžak lies between the regions of settlement of the Serbs in the north and Montenegrins in the south. During the Turkish rule it represented a special administrative-political unit (Yeni Pazar Sanjak). After the Turks had to leave the Balkan Peninsula in 1912 it was divided between Montenegro and Serbia. The border has remained unchanged until today.

The Muslims of Sandžak did not gain a special status either during the period of Karadjordjević's Yugoslavia or during Tito's Yugoslavia. Until the Muslims in Tito's Yugoslavia were denied the status of a "constitutive nation," the Muslims of Sandžak did not demand any type of autonomy or special status inside the Yugoslav society. Demands for a change in their status became louder only after the Yugoslav crisis sharpened, and they began demanding cultural autonomy. The SDA in Sandžak was also involved in those demands (Ramet, 1992, 244).

Serb politicians reacted strongly against these attempts at autonomy by the Bosniaks of Sandžak. The Serb regime accused the leaders of the Sandžak SDA, Dr. Sulejman Ugljanin and his collaborators, of an attempt at armed resistance. Under these circumstances, the Serb and Muslim sides broke contact and ceased all cooperation on the political level. The Yugoslav army occupied all strategic points in Sandžak. Because of the repression and complicated inter-ethnic relations in the region, many Muslims even started to consider independence for Sandžak, while others were considering the annexation of Sandžak to Bosnia and Herzegovina; still others emigrated to Turkey because they were afraid of possible violence.

In spite of all the violence, Muslims did not back down from their demands for autonomy. During 25–27 October 1991, they even held a referendum in which the people of Sandžak voted for its autonomy; on 11 January 1992, they successfully organized a referendum on a special status for Sandžak. The Muslims of Sandžak even established their own parliament a few months later to represent the Muslims to Serbia. Milošević did not want to negotiate the demands of the Bosniaks of Sandžak. For him, it was part of Serbia. Any autonomy would mean a hindrance for Serbia's entry to the Adriatic Sea, as autonomy in the Balkans often meant the first step toward independence. The Serbs were nervous about the fast increase in the Muslim population—in Serb as well as in Montenegrin parts of Sandžak—where their numbers during 1961–1991 had more than doubled.

Parallel with the fast increase in the Muslim population, the number of Serbs and Montenegrins during the period 1961–1991 decreased very fast. In the 1990s the Muslims already represented a majority of the inhabitants of Sandžak. When studying the changes in the ethnic composition of Sandžak a careful observer will notice an almost complete disappearance of the Turks. Most of the "Turks" after 1961 identified themselves as Muslims, and a few thousand emigrated to Turkey (especially to Istanbul). The Muslims, Serbs, and Montenegrins of Sandžak clearly defined themselves as such. Therefore, the numbers and percentages of "Yugoslavs," "Unknowns," and other categories for whom nationalities were not identified were small and did not comprise a significant part of the population.

Because of constant tensions among the Serbs and Montenegrins on the one side and the Muslims on the other side, the first attempts at peaceful cooperation between the Muslims of Sandžak and the Serb authorities started after the end of the war in Bosnia and Herzegovina, in the first half of 1995. The SDA even entered the race for the federal parliament in November 1996. However, the names of many voters of this party were not to be found in the election lists of those eligible to vote, and they were hence not allowed to vote.

After the fall of the regime of Slobodan Milošević, cooperation between the Serb state and the Muslims of Sandžak improved. A member of the Coalition for Sandžak (a party of Muslims from Sandžak), Rasim Ljajić, became a member of the Yugoslav federal government and later the minister for minorities and human rights in the government of Serbia-Montenegro. However, as of this writing in 2003, Sandžak, and the ethnic relations there, still represent a potential danger for future interethnic conflict. Quite often in Serb-Montenegrin disputes, the question arises as to what would happen to Sandžak if Montenegro should become independent.

Macedonia after 1990

Macedonia was, after Vojvodina, ethnically the most heterogeneous region of the former Yugoslavia. One of its characteristics was also the fast growth of its population. Until the beginning of the 1980s, the actual increase was more than 2 percent annually; then, until the beginning of the 1990s, it remained at 0.6 percent annually. Also, the ethnic structure of the population changed. The percentage of ethnic Macedonians dropped from 71.2

percent in 1961 to 64.6 percent in 1991, although during the same period the actual number of the Macedonians increased at a rate of 0.8 percent annually. The reason was the faster increase in the numbers of Albanians, Gypsies, and Muslims in Macedonia. In addition to the percentage of Macedonians, the percentage of Serbs also decreased, mostly because of their low birth rate and high rate of emigration, mostly into Serbia.

The number of Turks also dropped until 1981, in spite of their high birth rate. Mass emigration of Turks in the time of Aleksandar Ranković could be traced only from the eastern and central parts of Macedonia, while in western Macedonia (in the districts of Debar, Kruševo, and Gostivar), the drop in the Turkish population could be explained by a large increase of Muslims. Those Slav Muslims who identified themselves as Turks in the previous censuses started to identify themselves as Muslims in the censuses of 1981 and 1991. Also with regard to Macedonia, the question arises as to how valid the censuses in the FPRY and SFRY were, especially when one studies the numbers and percentages of Muslims, Turks, and Albanians. Often people declared their identities differently in different censuses, depending on their perception of the current political situation.

According to the census, the ethnic Macedonians retained an absolute majority in almost every district in 1991. The Albanians had a majority only in some districts in the western part of Macedonia (Tetovo, 71.1 percent; Gostivar, 62.7 percent; Debar, 44.0 percent; and Kičevo, 45.9 percent). This region of continuous Albanian settlement in western Macedonia, which continues to the north into Kosovo, is getting more and more Albanized due to the constantly increasing percentage of Albanians and a dropping percentage of Macedonians, who traditionally lived there. In this region, tensions have arisen between the Albanians and Macedonians numerous times from the 1960s on.

Macedonia and the Dissolution of Yugoslavia

During the dissolution of the former Yugoslavia, the Macedonian dilemma was even greater then ever. The Macedonians were aware of the fact that they could not remain in the new incarnation of Yugoslavia, which the Serbs would rule in all spheres of life if Slovenia and Croatia became independent. On the other hand, it was not clear what the reaction of the neighboring countries would be upon the declaration of the independence of Macedonia, as in the past the other nations had many times shown aspirations toward Macedonian territories. The Serbs, Greeks, and Bulgarians for a long time denied the Macedonians their distinct ethnic identity. In the past, Albania had also shown aspirations toward the western part of Macedonia, which had Albanian settlers. It was also not clear what the reaction of numerous members of the Albanian minority in Macedonia would be regarding the independence of Macedonia. A major issue was also whether this southernmost and economically least developed republic of the former Yugoslavia would be able to survive economically as an independent state.

During this tense period, the Macedonians organized their first free and independent multiparty elections, held on 25 November 1990, at which more then 1,000 candidates from 16 parties fought for 120 seats in the Macedonian parliament (*sobranie*). The elections did not bring a decisive victory to any of the contenders. After the elections, a government was formed from a coalition of the League of Communists-Party of Democratic Change (they had the support of thirty members of the parliament of Macedonia) and members of a coalition of six parties, the Alliance of Reform Forces (Savez reformskih snaga, with nineteen members of the parliament), who fought for Yugoslavia to remain in one piece and for the reform program of Yugoslav prime minister Ante Marković. The most successful group at these elections (thirty-seven deputies) was the Internal Macedonian Revolutionary Organization-Democratic Party for Macedonian National Unity (Vnatrešna makedonska revolucionarna organizacija, MRO-DPMNE), which was united under interwar period nationalist programs for an independent Macedonian state that would unite "all three Macedonias" (Vardar Macedonia in Yugoslavia, Aegean Macedonia in Greece, and Pirin Macedonia in Bulgaria).

Against these Macedonian ethnic parties, the Albanians in Macedonia chose to create and vote for separate ethnic parties, the largest of which, the Party of Democratic Prosperity (PDP), gained twenty-four seats. In January 1991 the newly elected parliament elected a new president of Macedonia. On 27 January 1991, Kiro Gligorov, who had served as the president of the LC of Macedonia for many years, took this office.

The results of the elections showed that, during this decisive period of the deepening Yugoslav crisis, the Macedonians were more afraid of the Serbs than of economic downfall, the Albanian minority, or Bulgarian and Greek pressure. Consequently, many of them voted for Macedonian nationalist political parties.

Under these uncertain conditions it was clear that due to their weak economy the Macedonians were at first more interested in saving the former Yugoslavia than they were in their independence. Macedonian president Kiro Gligorov, together with president of Bosnia and Herzegovina Alija Izetbegović, tried in May 1991 to suggest an "asymmetric confederation"—which was based on a former Slovene proposal that was not agreed upon—at one of the last meetings of the presidents of the Yugoslav republics. In accord with this proposal, Serbia and Montenegro would become the nucleus of a new Yugoslav confederation; Bosnia and Herzegovina and Macedonia would be half-independent, but they would still be constitutive republics of this new entity; Croatia and Slovenia would be allowed to have, while staying inside the confederation, as much independence as they would feel feasible. Gligorov and Izetbegović were convinced that this proposal would, on the one hand, fulfill Serb wishes to live in one state; on the other hand, it would fulfill Croat and Slovene wishes toward independence and sovereignty. This proposal failed because of a complete failure of the Yugoslav economic and political system and because of interethnic conflicts, in spite of the fact that the western European countries and the United States supported it.

Once Slovenia and Croatia declared independence, Macedonia started to get ready for a referendum. The Macedonian parliament released on 25 January 1990 the Declaration on the Sovereignty of the Republic of Macedonia. This declaration was confirmed by a referendum on 8 September 1991 in which almost 71.85 percent of the 1,495,626 registered voters participated, of whom 95.09 percent voted in favor of the declaration. The Albanian and Serb populations (comprising about 23 percent and 2.3 percent of the population, respectively) boycotted this referendum. Independence was declared on the basis of the results of the referendum on 19 November 1991. Macedonia was, according to its constitution, ". . . the national state of the Macedonian people in which full equality as citizens and permanent coexistence with the Macedonian people is provided for Albanians, Turks, Vlachs, Roma and other nationalities living in the Republic of Macedonia . . ." (Jokić, 2001,4). However, the Macedonian Albanians, who were guaranteed minority protection, nevertheless felt neglected, because they were not recognized as a constituent nation of the new independent Macedonian republic.

A New Independent State in the Balkans: The Former Yugoslav Republic of Macedonia

When Macedonia declared independence, it was widely expected that another war would erupt, as wars had in Slovenia, Croatia, and Bosnia and

Herzegovina. This did not happen, due to the diplomatic efforts of Macedonian president Kiro Gligorov, who succeeded in making an agreement with the Yugoslav army, so that the army peacefully withdrew from this southernmost former Yugoslav republic.

Macedonia had, however, many problems to deal with in the international arena. Although the Badinter Commission recommended the recognition of Macedonia's indepence, the county had to wait for this international recognition for some time. Greece was most opposed to the international recognition of Macedonia because the Greeks did not like the Macedonian state symbols (especially the flag) and the name "Macedonia." Greece believed that the name of Macedonia was the exclusive property of the Greeks and that even the use of this name by a new state showed irredentist plans by this former Yugoslav republic toward Aegean Macedonia. Because the two states were not able to solve these problems, Greece (the only ally of the Serbs in the Balkans) in 1992 introduced economic sanctions against Macedonia and in fact stopped the formation of an EU policy toward Macedonia. In 1995, the United Nations intervened, and the foreign ministers of Greece and Macedonia met in New York and signed an agreement (on 13 September 1995) in which Greece gave up economic sanctions, but Macedonia had to change its state flag because it had previously contained Greek symbols. (By 1993 they had been able to some extent to solve their disagreements on the name of the new state. Greece accepted a temporary name for Macedonia—the Former Yugoslav Republic of Macedonia—and Macedonia became a member of the UN in 1993 under this name.)

There were also quite a few unsolved questions in the new Macedonian state's relationship with the FRY. The question of the border of the new state was especially burdensome. The border was not clearly marked at the mountainous region of Šar planina with Kosovo and in the regions near Djeneral Janković, Kumanovo, and Kriva Palanka. At the request of the Macedonian government, because of the spread of the wars in Croatia and Bosnia and Herzegovina, a NATO peacekeeping force of 1,000 American soldiers was stationed at the border of Macedonia with the FRY to prevent spreading of the wars into Macedonian territories (Security Council Resolution 795, 9 December 1992). The United States and the western European countries were aware that the eruption of military fighting in Macedonia could provoke a wider crisis in southeastern Europe, into which Serbia, Albania, Bulgaria, and NATO members Turkey and Greece could get involved due to historic ties. Therefore, the international community could not allow destabilization of Macedonia.

The international community was also aware of the unrest and dissatisfaction of the Albanians of Macedonia, who were making the Macedonian government unstable and unhappy with their new demands. At first the Albanians demanded that the official language of administration in schools situated in the territories where the Albanians were in a majority should be Albanian. New demands followed. The Albanians even demanded the establishment of a new university where the language of instruction would be exclusively Albanian. The Macedonian government did not comply with this demand, as it claimed that the Albanians already had Albanian as the language of instruction at the University of Skopje and University of Bitola. The Albanians did not stop their action for a university that would use the Albanian language exclusively and, in 1995, they established a private university in the village of Rečica near Tetovo. Because the Macedonian authorities tried to prevent its operation, mass demonstrations of the Albanians in Tetovo and neighboring settlements erupted. This reaction actually was an eruption of the general unhappiness of the Albanians, which had smoldered since the Macedonian constitution was approved in November 1991. The Albanians started to ask political questions and to demand their human rights and freedoms as citizens. The wish to establish a "Great Albania" was often hidden behind those demands.

Macedonian-Albanian relations also influenced the results of the parliamentary elections that took place on 16 October and 30 October 1994. The leading party, the Coalition for Macedonia, won 89 of 120 parliamentary seats. Albanian parties gained only eleven parliamentary seats, while the largest opposition party, VMRO-DPMNE, boycotted the elections. Kiro Gligorov was reelected president with 52.44 percent of the popular vote, and the VMRO-DPMNE candidate, Ljubčo Georgijevski, received only 14.47 percent of the popular vote. The Albanians of Macedonia did not like the outcome of the elections because the victorious Coalition for Macedonia wanted to change the constitution to enact the idea of "Macedonia, the state of Macedonians," which would lessen the level of constitutional rights of the Albanians; it would especially mean denial of their demands for federalization of Macedonia.

The numerous problems in Macedonian-Albanian relations and many unsolved questions with neighboring Greece, the FRY, Albania, and also Bulgaria might have been the reasons for an attempt that was made to assassinate the Macedonian president, Kiro Gligorov, on 3 October 1995. He was injured, but he survived. Although police and criminal investigators interrogated 36,000 people and searched 19,000 private homes and more

Macedonian president Boris Trajkovski
addresses parliament in Skopje,
8 June 2001.
(Reuters/Ognen Teofilovsk/Corbis)

than 31,000 cars, they were not able to find either the organizers or the direct motive for this attempt. Gligorov, who lost one eye in the attack, finished his presidential term. Boris Trajkovski, a member of VMRO-
DPMNE, was elected president of Macedonia in the presidential elections
in November 1999. He received 52.6 percent of the popular vote; his major competitor, Tito Petkovski, a member of the Social Democratic Union,
gained 43.7 percent. VMRO-DPMNE held all the power, though, because
it had won a majority, in coalition with Democratic Alternative, in the
parliamentary elections of 1998. Each of the two Albanian parties gained
twenty-four seats in the parliament.

The tensions in Albanian-Macedonian relations continued. Some leaders of the Albanians in Macedonia kept saying that the Macedonians were
traditionally anti-Albanian. Albanian demands were ignored all the time,
they accused, while the Macedonians tried to create the illusion of a
multinational society that included Albanian political parties in the government. Albanian-Macedonian tensions deepened further during the
Kosovo refugee crisis in 1999, when 130,000 Albanians from Kosovo fled
to Macedonia to escape from ethnic cleansing in Kosovo. Most of these
refugees were returned to Kosovo a few weeks after conditions calmed
down when NATO intervention ended successfully.

Although conditions in Macedonia were very tense, Macedonian
politicians, with the help of foreign diplomats, kept the situation more or
less under control. It looked as if the Former Yugoslav Republic of Macedonia would succeed in avoiding the wars that had come during the

independence movements in all other former Yugoslav republics. These optimistic expectations might have seemed realistic at first, especially when the situation in Kosovo settled down under the control of the KFOR and once Slobodan Milošević had to leave power in Serbia following his defeat in the elections. Those wishes ultimately remained unfulfilled, however. The growing ethnic distance between the Macedonians and Albanians in the second half of the 1990s, when examined by some scholars, showed the actual developments and escalation of conflicts.

Another War in the Balkans

The situation in Macedonia started to worsen after KFOR came to Kosovo, but especially after November 2000, when groups of Albanian extremists also started to "solve" the Albanian question in the territories of the south Serb districts of Bujanovac and Preševo. It was only a question of when the violence would also erupt among the dissatisfied Albanians in western Macedonia, who were not happy with their status of a national minority and were demanding new solutions from the Macedonian government with regard to their status in Macedonia.

Macedonian politicians who had not listened to Albanian demands for many years tried, on the eve of the danger of an "Albanian revolution," to solve as many open questions with neighboring countries as possible. Negotiations with the FRY on border issues were especially successful. Authorities signed an agreement determining 161.5 miles of the FRY-Macedonian border. The Albanians were against the agreement because this border divided them from other Albanians, and staying connected with other Albanians was one of the cornerstones of their desired Great Albania. The Macedonian state was seen as one of the main handicaps for this project to come into being because it hindered complete geographic, cultural, and territorial ethnic homogenization of the Albanian "national" space in this part of the ethnic territory of the Albanians.

The first fights between Albanian rebels, a majority of whom came from Kosovo, and the Macedonian army erupted during the last days of February 2001 in the mountainous region north of Tetovo, at the border with Kosovo.

The crisis soon started to follow the already well-known scenario in the Balkans. Albanians first called attention to themselves with some armed attacks. What followed was the reaction from the Macedonian army and police. Because none of the sides involved was ready to compromise, the fights spread in the wide region from Kumanovo to Gostivar. Functionaries of Albanian political parties as well as leaders of extremist groups kept saying that the aim of their uprising was not the secession of any part of Macedonia but the betterment of their national rights and human rights as well as changes to the 1991 constitution.

The international community tried to stop the armed fights and to force the fighting sides to the negotiating table. The war lasted for more than six months, however. There were hundreds of deaths, many villages were burned down, cultural monuments were destroyed, and the already-weak economy collapsed. The fights stopped only after a new, wide-based government coalition—in which the two most important opposition parties to the previous government, the Social Democratic Union and the Albanian PDP (Party of Democratic Prosperity), also joined—was formed; this new government coalition promised to study the demands of the rebel Albanian Liberation National Army. The negotiations soon started in Ohrid, ending with the signing of the Ohrid Agreement. Under the Ohrid Agreement, signed on 13 August 2001, the Macedonian authorities were obliged to recognize Albanian as a second official language in the work of the parliament and in the western part of the country. Also, Albanians were required to be represented in the police force in accordance with their percentage in the population (there were more than 80 percent Albanians in some regions in the western part of the country). The agreement also foresaw disarmament of the Albanian rebels. UN peacekeepers were sent to collect arms from Albanians, who gave up only old weaponry, prompting the director of the Macedonian National Museum to say that he would need most of the weapons collected for his displays. The UN peacekeepers collected more than three thousand weapons.

The Ohrid Agreement did not satisfy the Macedonian authorities, so they tried to postpone realization of its regulations. This caused a new eruption of unhappiness among the Albanian population. Although in Tetovo and Kumanovo new incidents of fighting occurred, in neutral circles the opinion prevailed that the crisis could be solved by consistent enforcement of the Ohrid Agreement and with the operation of a lawful and democratic country. Albanians did not have enough soldiers or international support to bring about the establishment of a Great Albania, which would need to, in addition to Kosovo, include southern Serbia, half of Macedonia, part of Montenegro, and even part of Greece. However, it is possible that Albanian guerillas could continue their partisan warfare,

Macedonian president Boris Trajkovski (right) begins a session of crisis talks on Western peace proposals with prime minister Ljubče Georgijevski (second from right), Macedonia's foremost Albanian politician, Arben Xhaferi (left), and other party leaders, 28 July 2001. U.S. envoy James Pardew and European Union negotiator Francois Leotard met with Macedonia's polarized politicians in the lakeside resort of Ohrid for a last-ditch effort to secure agreement on a plan to avoid a slide toward civil war. (Reuters/Goran Tomasevic)

and Albanian nationalism could completely ruin relations between Albanians and Macedonians and break up the state of Macedonia.

One thing is certain: At the beginning of the third millennium, as before, the Balkans remain Balkanized (in the truest sense of this word).

Culture in the Countries of the Former Yugoslavia after 1990

The process of dissolution of the former Yugoslavia and the wars that took place during this process in the beginning of the 1990s almost completely cut cultural connections among the individual ethno-nations of the former Yugoslavia. However, although the wars—depending on their intensity and length—in some territories almost put cultural creativity to death, it did not stop completely. Even in the surrounded Sarajevo, some artists, especially writers and actors, continued with their performances, and thus helped people for a short period of time to forget the war. Many internationally known artists left their homelands, though.

Monuments of cultural heritage were quite often targets for destruction by grenades and other weapons. According to data from the Ministry of Culture and Education of the Republic of Croatia, by September 1992 many thousands of monuments of cultural heritage in Croatia had been destroyed. The grenades of the Yugoslav army and Montenegrin paramilitary units were also aimed at old Dubrovnik, which is under the protection of UNESCO as a cultural treasure of the world, and old Zadar and Šibenik. Also, the well-known stone bridge in Mostar, which was built in 1557–1566, was destroyed. Many times, religious objects of all denominations were made into targets during fights, because rendering freedom of religious expression impossible was one of the methods of building "ethnically pure and large Balkan tribal states." In Banja Luka alone, sixteen mosques were put into ruins, among them the well-known Ferhadija Mosque from 1579. Some monuments of cultural heritage were rebuilt after the war, but it will take some time and money before most of them are rebuilt.

Popular music often served as propaganda for different ideologies during this time. War "pop-nationalism" developed mostly in Serbia and Croatia. Although Serb pop musicians glorified the Great Serbia idea and stimulated interethnic hatred in their performances, Croat (as well as Bosnian and Macedonian) pop musicians mainly called for peace in their performances. During the war in Croatia, musicians cooperated in different projects, regardless of their age and genre (from punk rockers to chansonniers).

The music of the Kosovo Albanians was mostly nationalistic. Albanian songs with nationalistic content were forbidden by the Serb authorities and were never performed on radio or TV. They nevertheless spread among the people. The Albanians put these songs on videos and sold them in different shops (not only in music stores). The best-known Albanian singer of this period was Shkurte Fejza.

Pop-nationalism was the least developed in Slovenia because the war in Slovenia was very short. It is, however, interesting to note that during this period music from the other Yugoslav republics (regardless of content) continued to be present in Slovene radio and TV programs.

Once the fights ceased in different parts of the former Yugoslavia, pop-nationalism disappeared. Music and other cultural activities went back to normal. In the development of art and culture the influence of the consumer society was seen. Art is becoming more and more commercialized. Also, literature and the film industry have adjusted to the new circumstances. Many books have been published and many films made on the absurdity of war in the former Yugoslavia. The Oscar-winning 2002 film *Ničija zemlja (No Man's Land)* from Bosnian director Danis Tanović is one example.

In the new millennium, cultural connections among the ethno-nations of the former Yugoslavia have started to be renewed. The laws of a market economy support connections among the cultures of the different post–Yugoslav states.

Timeline

28 March 1989   The Republic Assembly (parliament) of the (Socialist) Republic of Serbia adopted and proclaimed a new Serb constitution that almost abolished the autonomy of Kosovo and Vojvodina; in mass protests of Kosovo Albanians, about 140 protesters were killed

27 September 1989   The adoption of the Amendments to the Constitution of the Republic of Slovenia (of 1974)

20–26 January 1990   The fourteenth extraordinary Congress of the LCY (League of Communists of Yugoslavia); dissolution of the LCY after Slovene delegates left the Congress in protest

April 1990   Multiparty elections in Slovenia and Croatia

May 1990   Serbia took direct control over Kosovo

5 July 1990   The Provincial Assembly and Provincial Executive Council of Kosovo dissolved themselves under pressure from the Serb regime

25 July 1990   The Republic Assembly (Sabor) of Croatia adopted amendments to the constitution of the Republic of Croatia that introduced controversial "new" republic state symbols; following a demonstration of 100,000 people in the village of Serb in Kninska krajina, the Serb National Council was formed, and it proclaimed the Declaration on Sovereignty and Autonomy of the Serb Nation

17 August 1990   Serb militias in Kninska krajina set up barricades on roads in the area of Benkovac

18 August 1990	Referendum on autonomy of the Serb regions in Croatia (Kninska krajina)
7 September 1990	At a secret meeting in Kačanik, the Albanian representatives of the dissolved Kosovo assembly proclaim the Kačanik Constitution for the "Republic of Kosovo"
28 September 1990	Adoption of the new constitution of the Republic of Serbia, which abrogated the autonomy and powers of the former autonomous provinces of Kosovo and Vojvodina
30 September 1990	The Serb national Council in Croatia proclaims the autonomy of Kninska krajina
3 October 1990	The Serb population in Kninska krajina interrupted all traffic by rail and road with the rest of Croatia
21 October 1990	The Serb National Council proclaimed the Statute of SAO Krajina and declared the Serb Autonomous Authority Krajina (Srpska autonomna oblast Krajina—SAO Krajina)
18 November 1990	The first multiparty elections in Bosnia and Herzegovina
25 November 1990	The first multiparty elections in Macedonia
9 and 23 December 1990	The first multiparty elections in Montenegro and Serbia: Slobodan Milošević elected president of Serbia with an overwhelming majority in the first round
22 December 1990	The Sabor adopted the new constitution of the Republic of Croatia
23 December 1990	Referendum on Slovene independence
7 January 1991	The Serb National Council for Slavonia, Baranja, and Western Srijem is formed in Šidski Banovci
25 January 1991	The Republic Assembly Sobranje (Macedonian parliament) proclaimed the Declaration on the Sovereignty of the Republic of Macedonia
27 January 1991	Kiro Gligorov is elected president of Macedonia
20 February 1991	The Assembly of the Republic of Slovenia adopted the Constitution of the Republic of Slovenia—a new constitution of an independent state
26 February 1991	The Serb National Council for Slavonia, Baranja, and Western Srijem issued the Declaration of the Serb Nation
28 February 1991	The authorities of the SAO Krajina declared the

	Resolution on Secession from Croatia and Remaining in Yugoslavia
2 March 1991	Fighting broke out in the Slavonian town of Pakrac; the Yugoslav Presidency ordered the Yugoslav People's Army (JNA) to intervene and separate the sides
9 March 1991	Mass demonstrations in Belgrade; the JNA was sent into the streets with tanks
25 March 1991	At a meeting in Karadjordjevo, Milošević and Tudjman discussed the possibility of the division of Bosnia and Herzegovina
31 March 1991	Armed conflict between the Croat security forces and local Serb militia in the Plitvice area
12 May 1991	At a plebiscite, a majority of the Serbs in Croatia voted in favor of remaining in Yugoslavia
19 May 1991	Croat referendum on independence
3 June 1991	Kiro Gligorov and Alija Izetbegović announced a joint proposal for a confederal Yugoslavia of independent republics
21 June 1991	The U.S. Secretary of State, James Baker, visited Belgrade
25 June 1991	Slovenia and Croatia declared their independence; the JNA moved into Slovenia to restore the federal authority and the Ten-Day War commenced
8 July 1991	The Brioni Declaration formally ended the war in Slovenia
August-September 1991	The Serb population established the so-called Serb Autonomous Authorities (SAO Bosanska Krajina, SAO Romanija, SAO Eastern Herzegovina)
8 September 1991	Referendum on independence of the Republic of Macedonia
22 September 1991	The Kosovo Albanian leadership introduced the Declaration on Independence and Sovereignty of Kosovo
26–30 September 1991	The Albanian population of Kosovo conducted a secret referendum on independence from Yugoslavia, and returned a massive vote in favor of independence
15 October 1991	Representatives of the Party of Democratic Action (SDA) and Croat Democratic Union of Bosnia and

Herzegovina (HDZ) decided to suggest the independence of Bosnia and Herzegovina

19 October 1991   The Kosovo parliament (the Albanian members of the dissolved former provincial parliament) declared the independence of the Republic of Kosovo

25 October 1991   The last soldier of the Yugoslav army left Slovene soil; deputies of the Serb Democratic Party (SDS) decided to leave the parliament of Bosnia and Herzegovina and established their own Serb parliament

25–27 October 1991   Referendum on the autonomy of Sandžak

9 November 1991   The leadership of the remaining Yugoslavia demanded that the UN Security Council send peacekeeping forces to Yugoslavia

18 November 1991   The siege of Vukovar ended with the fall of the town to the Serb forces after 86 days' defense

19 November 1991   Macedonia declared its independence

19 December 1991   The SAO Krajina introduced its constitution and was renamed the Republic of Serb Krajina; Milan Babić became its first president

20 December 1991   Federal prime minister Ante Marković resigned; the presidency of Bosnia and Herzegovina (without Serb members) decided to ask the European Union to recognize Bosnia and Herzegovina as an independent state

9 January 1992   An assembly representing the Serb population of Bosnia and Herzegovina renounced the Bosnian government and declared their own Serb Republic of Bosnia and Herzegovina (Srpska republika Bosna i Hercegovina); this formation declared itself a part of the Yugoslav federation

11 January 1992   Referendum on special status for Sandžak

15 January 1992   The EU officially recognized the independence of Slovenia and Croatia

21 February 1992   UN Security Council Resolution 743 on "blue helmets"

9 March 1992   The advance party of UNPROFOR arrived in Croatia and Bosnia and Herzegovina (commanded by Lt. Gen. Satish Nambiar)

29 February–1 March 1992   Referendum on the independence of Bosnia and Herzegovina

5–7 April 1992	Armed clashes began in Sarajevo; the siege of Sarajevo started
6 April 1992	The EU officially recognized the independence of Bosnia and Herzegovina
7 April 1992	The United States officially recognized the independence of Slovenia, Croatia, and Bosnia and Herzegovina; the "assembly of the Serb nation in Bosnia and Herzegovina" declared the independence of the Srpska Republika of Bosnia and Herzegovina; Serb offensives began in eastern Bosnia and the Krajina
27 April 1992	The "new" Yugoslav federal government endorsed a new constitution of the Federal Republic of Yugoslavia, consisting of Serbia and Montenegro
8 May 1992	Representatives of Kosovo Albanians rejected the invitation of Serb prime minister Radovan Božović to a meeting on open questions of Kosovo
12 May 1992	The Muslims of Sandžak established their own parliament to represent all the Muslims in Serbia
23 May 1992	Slovenia, Croatia, and Bosnia and Herzegovina accepted into the UN
24 May 1992	The unofficial Albanian government of Kosovo organized parliamentary and presidential elections; Ibrahim Rugova was elected president of the Republic of Kosovo
30 May 1992	The UN Security Council adopted Resolution 757, imposing mandatory sanctions against the Federal Republic of Yugoslavia
11 December 1992	The UN Security Council adopted Resolution 795, sending peacekeeping forces to the territory of Macedonia
2 January 1993	Lord David Owen and Cyrus Vance presented the "Vance-Owen Plan" for a new constitutional settlement in Bosnia and Herzegovina
8 April 1993	The Republic of Macedonia was admitted to the UN under a provisional name: the Former Yugoslav Republic of Macedonia
16 April 1993	Fights between the forces of the Croat Defense Council in Bosnia and Herzegovina (HVO) and the army of Bosnia and Herzegovina began in Mostar
6 May 1993	The UN Security Council adopted Resolution 824 proclaiming the towns of Sarajevo, Bihać, Goražde,

	Srebrenica, Tuzla, and Žepa to be "safe havens" protected by the UNPROFR
24 August 1993	The Croat Republic of Herceg-Bosna was proclaimed
27 September 1993	A local Muslim leader, Fikret Abdić, declared the Autonomous Region of Western Bosnia (in Cazinska krajina)
2 March 1994	The Muslims and Bosnian Croats signed the Washington Framework Agreement to unify the territories under their control into the Federation of Bosnia and Herzegovina
26 April 1994	The Contact Group was formed, superseding Lord David Owen and Cyrus Vance
4 July 1994	The Federal Republic of Yugoslavia declared an economic embargo against the Bosnian Serbs
4 August 1994	The Federal Republic of Yugoslavia closed its borders with regions of Bosnia and Herzegovina under Serb control
16 January 1995	The government of the Republic of Serbia issued an edict requiring the settlement of 100,000 Serbs in Kosovo
1–2 May 1995	The Croat army launched Operation Flash (Bljesak) in western Slavonia and regained this territory
25–26 May 1995	Large air strikes were launched by NATO against the Bosnian Serb forces in response to increasing Serb pressure on the safe areas
7–11 July 1995	The Bosnian Serb forces captured Srebrenica; massacre of Bosnian Muslims at Srebrenica
14–26 July 1995	The Bosnian Serb forces captured Žepa
4–9 August 1995	The Croat army, with its Operation Storm (Oluja), regained control over most of the territories of the Republic of Serb Krajina
7 August 1995	Units of Fikret Abdić capitulated to the army of Bosnia and Herzegovina; Abdić's autonomous region of Western Bosnia ceased to exist
30 August 1995	The Bosnian Serb assembly delegates negotiated with Milošević
8 September 1995	The foreign ministers of Bosnia and Herzegovina, Croatia, and the Federal Republic of Yugoslavia, at a meeting in Geneva, agreed that Bosnia and Herzegovina would remain a country divided into two entities, Croat-Muslim and Serb

13 September 1995	In New York, representatives of the governments of Macedonia and Greece signed an agreement by which Greece agreed to lift the embargo against Macedonia after the change of certain Macedonian state symbols
3 October 1995	An attempt to assassinate the Macedonian president Kiro Gligorov in Skopje failed
12 October 1995	A general cease-fire came into effect in Bosnia and Herzegovina
1 November 1995	Peace talks (on Bosnia and Herzegovina) concluded in Dayton, Ohio
12 November 1995	The agreement between the Croat government and Serb authorities in western Slavonia for the peaceful reintegration of Slavonia into Croatia
14 December 1995	The agreements reached at Dayton were formally signed in Paris
April–May 1996	Mass demonstrations against the government in Serbia
25 June 1996	Radovan Karadžić, in accordance with Dayton Agreement, resigned from politics
15 August 1996	An agreement was signed in Zagreb bringing to an official end the Republic of Herceg-Bosna
2 September 1996	The agreement between representatives of the Kosovo Albanians (Ibrahim Rugova) and Serb president Slobodan Milošević to restore education of Albanian children within the official educational system of Serbia in Kosovo
14 September 1996	Parliamentary elections in Bosnia and Herzegovina at the federal (Federation of Bosnia and Herzegovina, Republic of Srbska) and common state (Bosnia and Herzegovina) levels
3 November 1996	Serb parliamentary and municipal elections
20 November 1996	The Supreme Court of Serbia in Belgrade annulled local elections in the thirteen largest Serb cities where the opposition won a majority; mass demonstrations of opposition followers began
11 February 1997	Milošević accepted results of local elections held in November 1996
spring 1997	Increasing activity by the Kosovo Liberation Army (UÇK)

28 June 1997	The conflict within the ruling Democratic Party in the Republika Srpska deepened when Biljana Plavšić dismissed her minister of interior, accusing him of supporting Radovan Karadžić
15 July 1997	The Yugoslav federal parliament elected Milošević president of the FRY
20 October 1997	Milo Djukanović won the presidential election in Montenegro; Momir Bulatović admitted defeat
16 January 1998	Croatia regained control in Podunavlje (Eastern Slavonia)
28 February 1998	Fights between the UÇK units and Serb Police in Drenova in Kosovo began; more than eighty people killed
9 March 1998	The Contact Group, at a meeting in London, demanded that Milošević remove special forces from Kosovo in ten days and begin a dialogue with the Kosovo Albanians
23 April 1998	In a referendum, citizens of the FRY rejected the interference of the international community in Kosovo
29 April 1998	The Contact Group, at a meeting in Rome, agreed to new sanctions against the FRY
22 July 1998	Underground parliament of the Kosovo Albanians acknowledged UÇK
24 September 1998	The NATO Council gave Milošević an ultimatum to stop the violence in Kosovo or face air strikes
13 October 1998	Holbrooke, in negotiations with Milošević, demanded cessation of the offensive against the UÇK
24 October 1998	The UN Security Council voted for the placement of international observers in Kosovo
27 October 1998	Serb forces started to retreat from Kosovo; NATO repealed its threats of air strikes
6 February 1999	Negotiations between the Kosovo Albanians and Serbs began in Rambouillet Castle near Paris
1 March 1999	Milošević refused international negotiators for Kosovo
18 March 1999	The leadership of the Kosovo Albanians signed the Rambouillet Agreement, while the Serbs boycotted the event

22 March 1999   Holbrooke tried for the last time to convince Milošević to accept the Rambouillet Agreement

23 March 1999   The Serb parliament voted against stationing NATO troops in Kosovo

24 March 1999   NATO launched air strikes against the FRY, in a campaign of seventy-eight days of continuous bombing

6 May 1999   Foreign ministers of the G-8 Group adopted common principles on solving the Kosovo crises

3 June 1999   Milošević accepted a peace proposal brought to him by the president of Finland, Marti Ahtisaari, and former Russian prime minister Viktor Černomerdin

9 June 1999   In Kumanovo representatives of the Yugoslav army and NATO signed a technical plan on withdrawal of the Yugoslav troops

10 June 1999   NATO stopped attacks on the FRY

10 July 1999   The UN Security Council adopted Resolution 1244 on Kosovo, declaring the conditions for the resolution of the crisis and establishing legal grounds for stationing peacekeeping forces in Kosovo; Serb forces began their retreat from Kosovo

14 November 1999   Boris Trajkovski was elected president of Macedonia

11 December 1999   The president of Croatia, Franjo Tudjman, died

January 2000   Defeat of the Croat Democratic Union (HDZ) in elections in Croatia; Stipe Mesić became president of Croatia

22 September 2000   Parliamentary and presidential elections in the FRY; Vojislav Koštunica defeated Slobodan Milošević

4 October 2000   The Constitutional Court of the FRY annulled the results of the September elections; general strikes and mass demonstrations against Milošević's regime began

6 October 2000   The Constitutional Court of the FRY accepted the results of the September elections; Milošević admitted electoral defeat

November 2000   Armed activities of extremist Albanian groups in the South of Serbia began

February–August 2001   Fights between the Albanian rebels and Macedonian army in the mountains regions north of Gostivar-Kumanovo line

1 April 2001	Yugoslav authorities arrested Slobodan Milošević
28 June 2001	The Yugoslav authorities handed Milošević over to the Hague Tribunal
13 August 2001	The Ohrid Agreement was signed
22 August 2001	NATO started the "Urgent Harvest" to collect the weapons of the rebel Albanians in Macedonia
13 December 2001	The first parliamentary elections in Kosovo
13 February 2002	The trial before the Hague Tribunal against Slobodan Milošević began
4 March 2002	Kosovo parliament elected Ibrahim Rugova as president of the province
14 March 2002	The Belgrade Agreement on the transformation of the FRY into a new state of Serbia-Montenegro was signed

Significant People, Places, and Events

ABDIĆ, FIKRET (1940–) Until 1990 Abdić was a member of the republican parliament and also a functionary of the SK of Bosnia and Herzegovina. In 1990 he became a member of the presidency of Bosnia and Herzegovina. At the end of the summer he ceased to acknowledge the authority of Izetbegović's presidency and on 27 September 1993, declared the independence of Western Bosnia (350,000 inhabitants; 90 percent Muslims). He renamed it the Autonomous Region of Western Bosnia. After this he started to fight the central government's troops with his army of 6,000. Those fights continued until August 1995, when his troops capitulated. Abdić left for Croatia, where in July 2002 he was sentenced to twenty years in prison for crimes committed during the war.

ADŽIĆ, BLAGOJE (1927–) JNA general. Adžić graduated from the Military Academy in Belgrade and also studied at the Russian and French Military Academies. In 1991 he became Chief of General Staff of the JNA and, in 1992, minister of defense of the rump Yugoslavia. For him, the existence of Yugoslavia was a precondition for the existence of the JNA. He is also well known for his statement, "If some thousands of people are killed, so what? The world will shake for a week and then forget."

BABIĆ, MILAN (1956–) Leader of the uprising of Krajina Serbs of Croatia. Milan Babić was not known as a politician until 1989. He resigned from the LCY in 1989 and organized a new local party, the Knin

Democratic Union. During the dissolution of Yugoslavia he soon took over all the powers in Kninska krajina. He was forced to resign from all positions in 1992 because he did not accept the Vance-Owen Plan. In 1995 he served as foreign minister of Kninska Krajina. He fled Croatia after Kninska krajina fell into Croat hands.

BAJUK, ANDREJ (1943–) Professor of economics, international financial official, Slovene politician, president of the Slovene government in 2000. Andrej Bajuk spent his childhood in refugee camps in Austria before his family emigrated to Argentina in 1948. He taught economics at the University of Mendoza and later served in the Inter-American Development Bank in Washington and in Paris. On his return to Slovenia in 1999 he was elected vice president of the united SLS+SKD Slovene People's Party, and he led the Slovene government as prime minister from May until November 2000. Before the elections of 2000 he established a new party, Nova Slovenija-Krščanska ljudska stranka (New Slovenia-Christian People's Party), and became its president.

BULATOVIĆ, MOMIR (1956–) Montenegrin politician, president of Montenegro 1990–1997. Bulatović pursued an academic career at the School of Economics of the University of Titograd in 1970s. In the 1980s he started to establish himself in politics. During the "anti-bureaucrat revolution" in Montenegro, supported by Milošević, he became president of the LC of Montenegro, and in 1990, he became president of the Republic of Montenegro. He lost the election for the Montenegrin presidency in 1997. Until 2000 he was president of the Federal Yugoslav government.

CRVENKOVSKI, BRANKO (1952–) Soon after Crvenkovski graduated from the Faculty of Electromechanics and Information Studies he started his political career. In December 1990 he was elected to the Macedonian parliament (*sobranie*). In 1992 he was elected president of the Social Democratic Union of Macedonia; in September of the same year, he was elected president of the government. At the elections in 1994 he was elected president of the Macedonian government again. He served as prime minister until 1998; he is still president of the Social Democratic Union of Macedonia.

DEMAÇI, ADEM (1936–) Writer and one of the leaders of Kosovo Albanians. Adem Demaçi, known as the "Kosovo Mandela," spent twenty-eight years in prison of the former Yugoslavia. Already as a teenager he had actively joined the movement for unification of Kosovo with Albania. After he left prison in 1990, he was president of the Committee for Protection of Human Rights in Priština until 1996. In December 1996 he joined the Party of Kosovo. He was first among the leaders of the Kosovo Albanians to admit the existence of the UÇK. He resigned from political life in autumn of 1998 because he did not agree with the stance of Christopher Hill, American negotiator in the Albanian-Serb negotiations.

DJINDJIĆ, ZORAN (1952–2003) Serb politician, president of the Serb government after 2000. After Djindjić returned to his homeland after studying philosophy at the University of Konstanz at the end of the 1970s, he lectured at the University of Novi Sad. He was one of the cofounders of the Democratic Party, from which (because of numerous misunderstandings with the other leading members of the party) almost all Serb democratic parties developed. In 1994 he became the first democratically elected mayor of Belgrade, and later one of the main leaders of the united Serb opposition. In 2000 he was elected prime minister of Serbia. He fought for democratization of Serbia and economic reforms, including the stabilization of the Yugoslav currency and privatization. Being aware of the power of organized crime in Serbia, he tried to limit its power, which resulted in his assassination in March 2003.

DJUKANOVIĆ, MILO (1962–) Montenegrin politician, president of Montenegro after 1997. After Djukanović finished his studies in the field of economics he served in the Federation of Socialist Youth of Yugoslavia and then became a member of the CC LCY (Central Committee of the League of Communists of Yugoslavia). During the period from 1989–1991, he was secretary of CC LC (Central Committee of the League of Communists) Montenegro; he was elected prime minister of Montenegro in 1991. He was elected president of Montenegro in 1997 and has, since 2002, again been prime minister of Montenegro. He fought for independence for Montenegro but accepted the European Union proposal for a loose union between Serbia and Montenegro in 2002.

DRAŠKOVIĆ, VUK (1946–) Serb writer and politician, leader of the Serb Party of Renewal (Srpski pokret obnove). After Drašković finished his studies at Belgrade Law School he became a member of the SKJ and found employment with TANJUG, the Yugoslav press agency. For two years he served as journalist in Lusaka (Zambia). On returning to his homeland he became cabinet chief for the president of the Yugoslav Trade Unions, Mika Špiljak. He openly praised the Chetnik leader from the World War II period, Draža Mihailović, and started to fight for the Chetnik program of Great Serbia, as leader of his party, Srpski pokret obnove. Although his party was in the opposition until the NATO attack on Yugoslavia he served as vice president of the Serb government during the attacks.

DRNOVŠEK, JANEZ (1950–) Slovene politician, president of the SFRY presidency, president of the Slovene government, president of the Republic of Slovenia. After Janez Drnovšek received his doctorate in economics he served for a few years in industry and then in the Yugoslav diplomatic corps. He was elected a member of the presidency of the SFRY in 1988, and later he became president of the presidency of the SFRY for a one-year term ending 15 May 1990. During the crucial period of Slovenia's gaining independence, he was a member of the presidency of the SFRY. In independent Slovenia he became president of the Liberal-Democratic Party in 1992; from 12 March 1994, he was president of the united Liberal Democracy of Slovenia (LDS). From May 1992 until December 2002 (with the exception of April–November 2000) he has served as prime minister of Slovenia. In December 2002 he was elected president of the republic of Slovenia.

GANIĆ, EJUP (1946–) Professor of mechanical engineering, Bosnian Muslim politician, vice president of the Federation of Bosnia and Herzegovina. Ganić earned a doctorate from MIT. At the beginning of his political career he joined Ante Marković's Union of Reform Forces (Savez reformnih snaga) and was elected a member of the presidency of Bosnia and Herzegovina in 1990. As a member of the presidency he was supposed to represent "Yugoslavs" and ethnic minorities. His candidacy was also supported by the SDA. At the beginning of the war in 1992, he led the crisis staff. As vice president of Bosnia and Herzegovina he was the deputy of Alija Izetbegović; during 1994–1996 he also performed the duties of president of the Bosnian-Croat Federation (Federacija Bosna i Hercegovina).

GLIGOROV, KIRO (1917–) Macedonian politician and president of the Former Yugoslav Republic of Macedonia (1991–1999). After he finished law school at Belgrade University, Kiro Gligorov worked in private banking until the beginning of World War II. In 1941 he joined the partisan movement and was accepted into the KPJ in 1944. After World War II he became the Yugoslav finance minister (1962–1967), vice president (1967–1969), a member of the Yugoslav presidency (1969–1972), and president of the Yugoslav Parliament (1974–1978). He was elected president of the presidency of Macedonia in 1990, reelected in 1994, and then badly wounded in an attempt on his life on 3 October 1995. He retired in 1999.

HADŽIĆ, GORAN (1958–) President of Srem-Baranja District (Srbsko-baranjska oblast). During the period of dissolution of Yugoslavia, Hadžić became president of the Regional Committee of the Serb Democratic Party for Slavonia, Baranja, and western Srijem. In January 1991 he became president of the regional Serb National Council; he later became president of the Serb Region of Slavonia, Baranja, and western Srijem. In 1996 he became president of the Srem-Baranja District (eastern Slavonia). After peaceful reintegration of those regions into Croatia, he resigned from politics and immigrated to Šid in Vojvodina.

IMERI, IMER (1943–) Albanian politician from Macedonia. As leader of the Albanian opposition Party of Democratic Welfare, Imer Imeri became known especially during the Albanian uprising in Macedonia, when he openly supported the ideas of the rebels and articulated their demands (European integration, open borders, equality of the Albanian population with the Macedonian population, and acceptance of the Albanian language as a second official language in the state). He even declared the possibility of revenge if Macedonian politicians would not listen to these demands.

IZETBEGOVIĆ, ALIJA (1925–) Bosnian politician, president of the presidency of Bosnia and Herzegovina (1990–1998). Izetbegović was never a member of the SKJ. Because he criticized the Yugoslav communist regime, he was imprisoned many times. During the period of dissolution of Yugoslavia he led the establishment of the Muslim Party of Democratic Action (Stranka demokratske akcije—SDA) and became its first president. In 1990 he was elected the first president of the presidency of Bosnia and Herzegovina. Although Izetbegović was among the least inclined toward the independence of Bosnia and Herzegovina, Bosnia found itself in one of the bloodiest wars after its declaration of independence—a war that lasted until the Dayton Agreement was signed on 14 December 1995. He won reelection in September 1996, but he did not finish his term; he resigned in 1998 due to ill health.

JANŠA, JANEZ (1958–) Slovene politician and journalist. After he finished military studies at the Faculty of Political Science in Ljubljana, Janša took a position as a journalist for *Mladina,* a Slovene youth journal. As a candidate for president of the Slovene Youth Organization, he was arrested and condemned in a military trial in 1988 (in the famous "Process against the Gang of Four"). He became the first Slovene defense minister in 1990 in Peterle's government. He was later voted out of this position because it was alleged (later successfully contested in

court) that the army police had violated its mandate. After 1993 he was
president of the SDSS (Social Democratic Party of Slovenia) and leader
of the Slovene opposition.

JELAVIĆ, ANTE (1963–) Croat politician in Bosnia and Herzegovina, Croat
member of the presidency of Bosnia and Herzegovina. Jelavić was a nationalist backed by Croatia. In the 1998 elections he defeated the more
moderate Krešimir Zubak, who broke with the ruling nationalist party
to embrace the Dayton Agreement. The party was led by ethnic separatists and long had a stronghold on political and economic life in
Croat-held portions of Bosnia. The party was widely regarded as a
pawn of Franjo Tudjman, the wartime Croat president who favored
annexation of Croat Bosnian areas. At the beginning of March 2001,
Wolfgang Petritsch, a high representative of the international community to Bosnia and Herzegovina, forced him to resign from all functions on charges of ruining the constitutional order of Bosnia and
Herzegovina and the Dayton Peace Agreement.

KADIJEVIĆ, VELJKO (1925–) Yugoslav general and politician, minister of
defense 1988–1992. Veljko Kadijević was of mixed Serb-Croat parent-
age and has generally been identified as "Yugoslav." At the young age of
sixteen, he joined the partisan movement in 1941; he became a member of KPJ in 1943 and performed important duties almost immediately. He stayed in active military duty after World War II. He graduated from the Military Academy in Belgrade and was deputy chief of
the general staff of the JNA and deputy of Branko Mamula, who was
secretary of defense. After 1988 he was secretary of defense. He advocated the existence of Yugoslavia and in January 1992 resigned as secretary of defense and retired.

KARADŽIĆ, RADOVAN (1945–) Serb politician in Bosnia and Herzegovina,
president of Republika Srpska 1992–1996. After he studied at the Medical Faculty in Sarajevo, specializing in psychiatry (he also studied in
the United States), Karadžić served as a psychiatrist at Koševo Hospital
in Sarajevo. In 1990 he established the Serb Democratic Party in Bosnia
and Herzegovina and was political leader of the Bosnian Serbs during
the forty-three-month siege of Sarajevo. He was president of Republika
Srpska 1992–July 1996. He was forced to resign because of pressure
from the international community and was indicted as a war criminal.
He is wanted by the Hague War Tribunal as the main ideologue, together with Milošević and Mladić, of Bosnian ethnic cleansing.

KOŠTUNICA, VOJISLAV (1944–) President of the FRY. After earning his
Ph.D. at Belgrade Law School, Koštunica became assistant professor of

law at the school. Because he opposed the framework of the Constitution of 1974, he lost his job. He was active in the Committee for Protection of Freedom of Thought and Expression. In 1989 he established the Democratic Party at a meeting in his apartment. Because of differences with other party leaders (especially with Zoran Djindjić), in 1992 together with a group of Serb legalists, he established his own Democratic Party of Serbia, of which he is still the president. From 2000 to 2003 he was president of the FRY.

KUČAN, MILAN (1941–) President of the Republic of Slovenia. Kučan received his law degree from Ljubljana Law Faculty. Kučan served as a member of the secretariat of CC LCS (Central Committee of the League of Communists of Slovenia) (1969–1973) and as secretary of the Republican Committee of the Socialist Alliance of Working People of Slovenia (1973–1978). During 1978–1982 he served as president of the Slovene parliament. From 1982–1986, Kučan was a member of the presidency of CC LCY (Central Committee of the League of Communists of Yugoslavia); and from 1986–1990, president of LCS (League of Communists of Slovenia). He was elected president of the presidency of the Republic of Slovenia (a collective head of state) in April 1990 and president of the independent Republic of Slovenia in 1992. In 1997 he was reelected president, and his term expired in December 2002.

MARTIĆ, MILAN (1945–) President of the Republic of Srpska Krajina. Martić graduated from the police academy in Zagreb and was employed as police inspector in Knin. In May 1991 he became Minister for Internal Affairs in the Republic of Srpska Krajina, and in 1993 he became president of the Republic of Srpska Krajina. In 1995, after operation Oluja (Storm), he escaped (together with 200,000 Serbs) to Bosnia and Herzegovina. He has been indicted for crimes against humanity by the Hague Tribunal.

MESIĆ, STJEPAN (STIPE) (1934–) Croat politician, after 2000 president of the Republic of Croatia. Mesić graduated from law school in Zagreb. For his activities in the so-called Croat Spring, he was imprisoned for a year in Stara Gradiška. After the victory of the HDZ in the elections in 1990, he became president of the Croat government. He also served as the last president of the presidency of the SFRY (until 5 December 1991). In 1992 he was elected president of the Croat parliament. In 1994, because he was not satisfied with HDZ policy (especially with the active Croat policy in Bosnia and Herzegovina), he established his own party. At the beginning of 2000 he was elected president of the Republic of Croatia for a term of five years.

MILOŠEVIĆ, SLOBODAN (1941–) Serb politician, president of Serbia (1990–1997), president of the FRY (1997–2000). Milošević started his political career in 1982 when he became a member of the presidency of CC LC Serbia. In 1990 he was elected president of the presidency of Serbia. In July 1990 he established the Socialist Party of Serbia, which won the parliamentary elections in December 1990. He retained his position as president of Serbia after the 1992 elections, continuing in office until 1997. During this period he also signed the Dayton Agreement. In 1997 he became president of the FRY. In 1998 he crushed the Albanian nationalist movement in Kosovo and forced the international community and NATO into military intervention. He lost the presidential elections in September 2000. On 1 April 2001, the new Yugoslav authorities arrested him, and on 28 June 2001, they extradited him to the Hague international tribunal. His trial is still in progress and is not expected to be completed until 2005.

MLADIĆ, RATKO (1943–) Serb general and commander of the army of Republika Srpska. After he graduated from the Military Academy in Belgrade, Ratko Mladić served in different places all over Yugoslavia. He became well known in Yugoslavia after the war in Croatia erupted in 1990, when units of the Knin Corps under his military command were active in the execution of widespread military operations. As a Bosnian Serb, Mladić was first named commander of the JNA troops in Bosnia and Herzegovina and later became military commander of the troops of Republika Srpska. He commanded Serb troops until November 1996, when he withdrew from public life after being indicted as a war criminal by the Hague Tribunal.

PETERLE, LOJZE (1948–) Slovene politician. In March 1989 Lojze Peterle became president of the Slovene Christian Democratic Party. He led the party until it united with the SLS in April 2000. He was elected the first president of the Slovene democratically elected government, serving until May 1992. After the elections in 1992 he became vice president of the Slovene government and its minister of foreign affairs. He resigned in September 1994. From 1996–1999 he was vice president of the European Union of Christian Democrats. He joined Andrej Bajuk in establishing the New Slovenia-Christian People's Party and is currently serving as its vice president and as a member of the Slovene parliament.

PLAVŠIĆ, BILJANA (1930–) Professor of biology, Serb politician from Bosnia and Herzegovina, president of Republika Srpska. After the 1990 elections Plavšić became a member of the presidency of Bosnia and

Herzegovina. In 1992 she resigned from the presidency and switched to the presidency of the self-proclaimed Serb Republic of Bosnia and Herzegovina (later Republika Srpska). In 1995 she became vice president of Republika Srpska and, after Karadžić was forced to resign from politics, she was elected president. In 1996 she decided to follow the Dayton Agreement and was excluded from the SDS in July 1997. Indicted by the Hague Tribunal for war crimes, she turned herself in and was sentenced to eleven years in prison for crimes against humanity.

POP-NATIONALISM Pop-nationalist music developed as nationalistic and entertaining music, mostly in Serbia and Croatia, during the period of the dissolution of Yugoslavia. Various themes were used that served to propagate different ideologies. Although Serb pop-nationalism praised the ideal of a Great Serbia and was even used to stir up interethnic hatred, Croat (and Bosnian and Macedonian) pop-nationalism called for peace. This type of music was popular during the period of war; after the wars ended, it disappeared from radio and TV programs.

RAČAN, IVICA (1944–) Croat politician. In 1986 Račan was elected a member of the CK SKJ, later also a member of its presidency. Together with Slovene communists, he fought for political pluralism and joined Slovenes in deserting the Congress of SKJ in 1989. After the first democratic elections in 1990, as leader of League of Communists of Croatia (which was renamed the Party of Democratic Changes), he remained in the opposition. After the victory of a coalition of the democratic parties in 2000 (after the death of Franjo Tudjman), he became president of the Croat government.

RAŠKOVIĆ, JOVAN (1929–1992) Serb politician in Croatia. After he received his doctorate in psychiatry at the University of Zagreb, Rašković served in Šibenik as a clinical psychiatrist. A splendid orator, he became a political leader of Serbs in Croatia. Together with Jovan Opačić he established the Serb Democratic Party. Because he fought "only" for cultural autonomy of Serbs in Croatia, he was soon replaced by Milan Babić as leader of the Croat Serbs. After the war in Croatia he moved to Belgrade.

RAŽNJATOVIĆ-ARKAN, ŽELKO (1953–2000) Commander of Serb paramilitary units. Želko Ražnjatović-Arkan was convicted for murders (many in the service of the Yugoslav communist secret service in the mid-1970s) and for blackmail and was sentenced to a twenty-year prison term in seven different European states. He succeeded in avoiding the international judiciary. During the period of dissolution of Yugoslavia he established the Serb paramilitary volunteer guard "Arkan's Tigers," which actively participated in the war. Arkan and his "Tigers" murdered and robbed non-Serbs in Croatia, Bosnia and Herzegovina, and Kosovo, for which he was indicted by the Hague War Tribunal. Arkan was also president of the Party of Serb Unity and a deputy to the Serb parliament. He was killed in "mafia" fights in the lobby of the Belgrade Intercontinental Hotel.

RUGOVA, IBRAHIM (1944–) Albanian politician of Kosovo, first president of the Kosovo parliament, first president of Kosovo. Rugova earned his doctorate at the University of the Sorbonne in Paris. He pursued an academic career at the University of Priština in the history of literature. In 1989 he became leader of the largest party of Kosovo Albanians, the Democratic League of Kosovo. After the Kosovo Albanians organized their parallel state in Kosovo, Rugova was elected president of the "Republic of Kosovo" in 1992. Milošević did not accept those elections, however. At the beginning of March 2002 he was elected president of Kosovo by the Kosovo parliament.

ŠAĆIRBEJ (ŠAĆIRBEGOVIĆ), MOHAMED (1950–) Bosnian ambassador to the UN, foreign minister of Bosnia and Herzegovina. Because his father was accused of antigovernment and anti-communist activities, the family of Mohamed Šaćirbej had to emigrate from Yugoslavia in 1963. After that they lived in Italy, Turkey, and Libya; in 1967, they settled in the United States. After he finished law school at Tulane University in New Orleans, he graduated with a degree in economics from Columbia University in New York. He became special advisor to Izetbegović in 1991; in 1992, he became first ambassador of Bosnia and Herzegovina to the UN. He retained his position until 1999, and for a short period of time even served as Bosnian foreign minister.

ŠEŠELJ, VOJISLAV (1954–) Serb politician, leader of the Serb Radical Party (Srpska radikalna stranka), vice president of the Yugoslav government. After he received his doctorate in sociology, Šešelj pursued his academic career at the Sarajevo Law Faculty. He wrote an article in which he suggested the idea of a Great Serbia. Because of his ideas, in 1984 Šešelj was sentenced to twenty-two months in prison. After his prison term, he moved to Belgrade, where he established the Serb Radical Party (Srpska radikalna stranka), which based its ideas on tradition on the Chetnik movement in Serbia. Later he established paramilitary Chetnik units within his party that cooperated in ethnic cleansing in Croatia and Bosnia and Herzegovina. Šešelj and his party were supported by a great part of the Serb people, because of their Serb nationalist policy. Later his political influence waned. Šešelj, who was indicted by the Hague Tribunal, decided to turn himself in voluntarily and leave for the Hague. His request to be released pending the trial was denied.

SILAJDŽIĆ, HARIS (1945–) Muslim politician, president of the government of Bosnia and Herzegovina (1993–1996), cochair of the government of Bosnia and Herzegovina 1997–1999. Silajdžić graduated with a degree in Islamic studies from the University of Benghazi in Libya. At the Priština Faculty of Philosophy, he obtained his Ph.D., writing a dissertation on relations of the United States toward Albania from 1912–1939. Together with Alija Izetbegović, Silajdžić established the SDA. After the 1990 election he became president of the Committee of Bosnia and Herzegovina for International Cooperation, which later transformed into the foreign ministry. In September 1993 he became Bosnian-Herzegovian prime minister. He was the first to demand armed intervention by the West against Serbia and was the greatest opponent of the division of Bosnia and Herzegovina. In December 1996 he was elected cochair of the Bosnian-Herzegovian government; he preformed duties every other week, alternating with Boro Bosić, the Serb representative. In September 2001 he resigned from all political functions due to ill health.

TANOVIĆ, DANIS (1969–) Bosniak film director, Oscar award winner. During the war in Bosnia and Herzegovina (1992–1994), Tanović gathered films for the film archive of the Bosniak army. In 1994 he immigrated to Belgium, where he got a degree in film production; in 2001 he became a naturalized Belgian citizen. He became famous with his film *Ničija zemlja* (*No Man's Land*), for which he won the Palme d'Or at Cannes and an Oscar for Best Foreign Film in 2002.

THAÇI (ALSO THAQUI), HASHIM (1968–) Political and military leader of the UÇK. After abolishment of Kosovo's autonomy, Thaçi immigrated to Zürich, where he studied politics and international law. In 1993 he established an army organization of Kosovo Albanians from which the UÇK developed. His influence grew with the military successes of the UÇK. He became leader of the Albanian negotiating group in Rambouillet in France. Soon he became prime minister of the temporary government of Kosovo as established after the Rambouillet negotiations. After the peacekeeping forces of KFOR were deployed and Kosovo became relatively stable, he was leader of the Democratic Party of Kosovo.

TRAJKOVSKI, BORIS (1956–) Lawyer and politician, after 1999 president of the Former Yugoslav Republic of Macedonia. Trajkovski established himself in politics at the beginning of the 1990s when he became a member of the leadership of VMRO-DPMNE. In 1998 he became deputy foreign minister. He became well known in Macedonia after he demanded greater efforts from representatives of NATO and the western European countries to find a solution to the Kosovo refugee crisis. In November 1999, he was elected president of the Former Yugoslav Republic of Macedonia with 52.6 percent of the votes. His term ends in 2004.

TUDJMAN, FRANJO (1922–1999) Croat politician, first president of the Republic of Croatia. By 1941, Franjo Tudjman had already joined the partisan movement. After World War II he remained on active military duty until 1961 and was the youngest general of the JNA at age 38. After he finished his doctoral studies in history, he served as associate professor at the Faculty of Political Science at the University of Zagreb. He also served as director of the Institute for the Study of the History of the Workers' Movement in Croatia. Because he advocated the idea of an independent Croatia, he was imprisoned for many years; until 1989 he could not participate in political life. In 1989 he established a political party, Hrvatska Demokratska zajednica (Croat Democratic Union), which received a majority of the votes in the 1990 election. From May 1990 he served as president of Croatia; he declared the independence of Croatia in 1991 and was successful in the War for the Homeland. In June 1997 he was reelected president of Croatia.

XHAFERI, ARBEN (1950–) Journalist and leader of Macedonian Albanians. After Macedonia declared independence, Xhaferi became a leader of the Macedonian Albanians. As of this writing he is demanding that Macedonian authorities declare Albanians a second constitutive nation of Macedonia and that Albanian be an official language of Macedonia; that education be provided at all levels in the Albanian language; that the Albanian University in Tetovo be legalized; and that proportional representation of Albanians in administration be established, based on the percentage of Albanians in Macedonia. His demands will soon be addressed in negotiations, with the help of international negotiators and the international community. He is respected as the most important personality in interethnic relations in Macedonia.

Bibliography

Allcock, John B. "Macedonia." In Turnock, David, and Carter, Francis W. (eds.): *The States of Eastern Europe, vol. 2: South-Eastern Europe.* (Aldershot, U.K.: Ashgate, 1999): pp. 141–166.

Benson, Leslie. *Yugoslavia: A Concise History.* (New York: Palgrave, 2001).

"Bentley Calls Serbian/Americans to Arms." *American Srbobran*, vol. 84, no. 15999 (27 June 1990): 1.

B. J. "Kosovo hoče neodvisnost" (Kosovo demands independence). *Delo* 45, no. 29 (5 February 2003): 1.

Cohen, Lenard J. *Broken Bonds: Yugoslavia's Disintegration and Balkan Politics in Transition.* (Boulder, CO: Westview, 1995).

"Did You Contact Your Member of Congress?" *American Srbobran 83* no. 15961 (October 11, 1989): 1.

Holbrooke, Richard. *To End a War.* (New York: The Modern Library, 1999).

Jokić, Branko. "Mešani občutki Črnogorcev na beograjski sporazum" (Mixed feelings of Montenegrins on the occasion of the Belgrade Agreement). *Delo* 44, no. 61 (15 March 2002): 1.

———. "Vojna le zaradi preambule" (The war only because of preamble). *Delo* 43, no. 76 (2 April 2001): 4.

Klemenčič, Matjaž. "Slovenia at the Crossroads of the Nineties: From the First Multiparty Elections and the Declaration of Independence to Membership in the Council of Europe." *Slovene Studies* 14, no. 1 (1992): 9–34.

"Konec mita" (The end of the myth). *Mladina* 24 (14 June 1999): 37–38.

"Kronologija kosovskega zapleta." (Chronology of Kosovo conflict). *Delo* 41, no. 69 (25 March 1999): 5.

Lampe, John R. *Yugoslavia as History: Twice there Was a Country.* (Cambridge, U.K.: Cambridge University Press, 1996).

Mašanovič, Božo. "Milošević izročen haaškemu sodišču" (Milošević extradited to Hague Tribunal). *Delo* 43, no. 147 (29 June 2001): 1.

"MPO Releases Statements to International Community." *Macedonian Tribune* 73, no. 3276 (April 22, 1999): 3.

Pirjevec, Jože. *Jugoslovanske vojne 1991–2001* (Yugoslav Wars 1991–2001). (Ljubljana, Slovenia: Cankarjeva založba, 2003).

Potočnik, Peter. "Ceneje za Srbijo, draže za Črno goro (Cheaper for Serbia, more expensive for Montenegro). *Delo* 45, no. 30 (6 February 2003a): 4.

———. "Pospremila ga je množica" (Accompanied by a crowd). *Delo* 45, no. 44 (24 February 2003b): 28.

———. "Srbija zavita v žalost" (Serbia wrapped into sadness). *Delo* 45, no. 60 (14 March 2003c): 1.

Ramet, Sabrina P. *Nationalism and Federalism in Yugoslavia, 1962–1991.* (Bloomington: Indiana University Press, 1992).

Ramet, Sabrina P. "The Macedonian Enigma." In Ramet, Sabrina P., and Adamović, Ljubiša Š. (eds.): *Beyond Yugoslavia: Politics, Economics, and Culture in a Shattered Community* (Boulder, CO: Westview, 1995): 208–229.

Reuter, Jens. "Vom Ordnungspolitischen zum Nationalitaenkonflikt zwischen Serbien und Slowenien" (From political to ethnic conflict between Serbia and Slovenia). *Suedosteuropa* 39, no. 10 (1990): 571–586.

Robertson, George. "Podpis protokola je še en zgodovinski dan" (The signature of Protocol is another historic day). *Delo* 45, no. 70 (26 March 2003): 5.

Sell, Louis. *Slobodan Milošević and the Destruction of Yugoslavia.* (Durham, NC: Duke University Press, 2002).

"Seven Countries sign NATO treaty," *Herald International Tribune* (27 March 2003): 7.

Silber, Laura, and Little, Allan. *Yugoslavia: Death of a Nation.* (New York: Penguin Books, 1997).

Tanner, Marcus. *Croatia: A Nation Forged in War.* (New Haven, CT: Yale University Press, 1997).

Taylor, Charles. *Multiculturalism and "The Politics of Recognition": An Essay.* (Princeton, NJ: Princeton University Press, 1992).

Taylor, Mark. "A War of Words." *American Srbobran 83* no. 15965 (4 November 1992):6.

Vasović, Svetlana. "Očesi gledata v različni smeri" (The eyes looking into different directions). *Mladina* 43 (28 October 1997): 34–35.

Vickers, Miranda. *Between Serb and Albanian: A History of Kosovo.* (London: Hurst, 1998).

Woodward, Susan L. *Balkan Tragedy: Chaos and Dissolution after the Cold War.* (Washington, DC: The Brookings Institution, 1995).

"Za tri leta odložena neodvisnost Kosova?" (Independence of Kosovo postponed for three years?). *Delo* 43, no. 256 (7 November 2001): 4.

Zimmermann, Warren. "The Last Ambassador Tells the Story of the Collapse of Yugoslavia." *Foreign Affairs* 74, no. 2 (March–April 1995): 2–20.

Z. R. "Kronologija kosovskega zapleta" (Chronology of Kosovo conflict). *Delo* 41, no. 69 (25 March 1999): 5.

Bibliography

Atlases

A Concise Atlas of the Republic of Croatia and of the Republic of Bosnia and Herzegovina. (Zagreb: Miroslav Krleža Lexicographical Institute, 1993).

Atlas svetovne zgodovine–dopolnjena izdaja za Jugoslavijo (Atlas of world's history: Revised edition for Yugoslavia). (Ljubljana: Cankarjeva založba in Državna založba Slovenije, 1989).

Magocsi, Paul Robert. *Historical Atlas of East central Europe, vol. 1: A History of East Central Europe.* (Seattle: University of Washington Press, 1993).

Books

Alexander, Stella. *The Triple Myth: A Life of Archbishop Alojzije Stepinec.* (New York: Columbia University Press, Eastern European Monographs, 1987).

Allcock, John B., Horton, John J., and Milivojević, Marko (eds.): *Yugoslavia in Transition.* (New York: BERG, 1992).

Allcock, John B. *The Dilemmas of Independent Macedonia.* (London: ISIS Briefing, 1994).

Avakumović, Ivan. *History of the Communist Party of Yugoslavia, I.* (Aberdeen, U.K.: Aberdeen University Press, 1964).

Banac, Ivo. *With Stalin against Tito: Cominformist Splits in Yugoslav Communism.* (Ithaca, NY: Cornell University Press, 1988).

Barker, Elisabeth. *British Policy in South-East Europe in the Second World War.* (London: Macmillan, 1976).

Bartelsen, J. S. (ed.): *Nonstate Nations in International Politics.* (New York: Praeger, 1977).

Bass, Robert H., and Marbury, Elizabeth (eds.): *The Soviet-Yugoslav Controversy, 1948–1958: A Documentary Record.* (New York: Prospect Books, 1959).

Benderly, Jill, and Kraft, Evan (eds.): *Independent Slovenia: Origins, Movement, Prospects.* (New York: St. Martin's Press, 1994).

Biber, Dušan (ed.): *Konec druge svetovne vojne v Jugoslaviji* (The end of World War II in Yugoslavia). (Ljubljana, Slovenia: Borec, 1986).

Bićanić, Rudolf. *Economic Policy in Socialist Yugoslavia.* (Cambridge: Cambridge University Press, 1973).

Bieber, Florian, and Dzemal, Sokolović (eds.): *Reconstructing Multiethnic Societies: The Case of Bosnia-Herzegovina.* (Burlington, VT: Aldershot, 2001).

Boban, Ljubo. *Sporazum Cvetković-Maček* (The Cvetković-Maček Agreement). (Beograd, Serbia-Montenegro: Institut društvenih nauka, 1965).

Bokovoy, Melissa K., Irvine, Jill A., and Lilly, Carol S. (eds.): *State-Society Relations in Yugoslavia, 1945–1992.* (New York: St. Martin's Press, 1997).

Bugajski, J. *Ethnic Politics in Eastern Europe: A Guide to Nationality Policies, Organizations, and Parties.* (Armnok, NY: M. E. Sharpe, 1994).

Burg, Steven. *Conflict and Cohesion in Socialist Yugoslavia.* (Princeton, NJ: Princeton University Press, 1983).

Burks, R. V. *The National Problem and the Future of Yugoslavia.* (Santa Monica, CA: Rand Corporation, 1971).

Čakić, Stefan. *Velika seoba Srba 1689/90 i patrijarh Arsenije III Crnojević* (The great migration of Serbs 1689–1690 and the patriarch Arsenije III Crnojević). (Novi Sad, Serbia-Montenegro: Dobra vest, 1990).

Carter, April. *Democratic Reform in Yugoslavia: The Changing Role of the Party.* (Princeton, NJ: Princeton University Press, 1982).

Ćirković, Sima. *Istorija srednjevekovne bosanske države* (*The History of Medieval Bosnia*). (Beograd, Serbia-Montenegro: Srpska književna zadruga, 1964).

Dedijer, Vladimir. *The Road to Sarajevo.* (New York: Simon and Schuster, 1966).

Djilas, Aleksa. *The Contested Country: Yugoslav Unity and Communist Revolution, 1919–1953.* (Cambridge, MA: Harvard University Press, 1991).

Djilas, Milovan. *Conversations with Stalin.* (New York: Harcourt Brace Jovanovich, 1962).

Djilas, Milovan. *Wartime.* (New York: Harcourt Brace Jovanovich, 1977).

Donia, Robert J. *Islam under the Double Eagle: The Muslims of Bosnia and Herzegovina, 1878–1914.* (New York: Columbia University Press, 1981).

Dragnich, Alex N. *Serbia, Nikola Pašic, and Yugoslavia.* (New Brunswick, NJ: Rutgers University Press, 1974).

Dvornik, Francis. *The Slavs in European Civilization.* (New Brunswick, NJ: Rutgers University Press, 1962).

Dyker, David A. *Yugoslavia: Socialism, Development, and Debt.* (London: Routledge, 1990).

Estrin, Saul. *Self-Management: Economic Theory and Yugoslav Practice.* (Cambridge, U.K.: Cambridge University Press, 1983).

Ferfila, Bogomil. *The Economics and Politics of the Socialist Debacle.* (Lanham, MD: University Press of America, 1991).

Fine, John V. A., Jr. *The Early Medieval Balkans.* (Ann Arbor: University of Michigan Press, 1983).

Gačeša, Nikola. *Agrarna reforma i kolonizacija u Jugoslaviji, 1945–48* (*Agrarian reform and colonization in Yugoslavia, 1945–1948*). (Novi Sad, Serbia-Montenegro: Matica srpska, 1974).

Gestrin, Ferdo, and Melik, Vasilij. *Slovenska zgodovina od konca osemnajstega stoletja do 1918* (Slovene history from the end of the eighteenth century to 1918). (Ljubljana, Slovenia: Državna založba Slovenije, 1966).

Gianaris, Nicholas V. *Geopolitical and Economic Changes in the Balkan Countries.* (Westport, CT: Praeger, 1996).

Glenny, Misha. *The Fall of Yugoslavia: The Third Balkan War.* (New York: Penguin, 1992).

Gounaris, B. C. *The Events of 1903 in Macedonia as Presented in European Diplomatic Correspondence.* (Thessaloniki, Greece: Museum of the Macedonian Struggle, 1993).

Grafenauer, Bogo. *Ustoličevanje koroških vojvod in država karantanskih Slovencev* (Coronation of Carinthanian dukes and the state of Carantanian Slovenes). (Ljubljana, Slovenia: Slovenska akademija znanosti in umetnosti, 1952).

———. *Zgodovina slovenskega naroda 1: Od naselitve do uveljavljenja frankovskega fevdalnega reda* (History of the Slovene Nation 1: From the settlement to the Frank Feudal Order). (Ljubljana, Slovenia: Državna založba Slovenije, 1964).

———. *Boj za staro pravdo v 15. in 16. stoletju na Slovenskem* (Peasant risings in the territory of Slovenia in the fifteenth and sixteenth centuries). (Ljubljana, Slovenia: Državna založba Slovenije, 1974).

Grafenauer, Bogo, Perović, Dušan, and Šidak, Jaroslav (eds.): *Zgodovina narodov Jugoslavije 1: Do zacetka 16. stoletja* (History of the nations of Yugoslavia 1: Until the beginning of the sixteenth century). (Ljubljana, Slovenia: Državna založba Slovenije, 1953).

Grafenauer Bogo, Đurđev, Branislav, and Tadić, Jorjo (eds.): *Zgodovina narodov Jugoslavije 2: Od začetka 16. stoletja do konca 18. stoletja* (History of the nations of Yugoslavia 2: From the beginning of the sixteenth century to the end of the eighteenth century). (Ljubljana, Slovenia: Državna založba Slovenije, 1959).

Graham, Stephen. *Alexander of Yugoslavia.* (London: Cassel, 1938).

Guldescu, Stanko. *The Croatian-Slavonian Kingdom, 1526–1792.* (The Hague: Mouton, 1970).

Hadži–Jovanović, Duška (ed.): *The Serbian Question in The Balkans.* (Beograd, Serbia-Montenegro: Faculty of Geography University of Belgrade, 1995).

Hammond, Thomas T. (ed.): *Witnesses to the Origins of the Cold War.* (Palo Alto, CA: Stanford University Press, 1982).

Holton, Milne, and Mihailovich, Vasa D. *Serbian Poetry from the Beginning to the Present.* (Columbus, OH: Slavica Publications, 1988)

Horvat, Branko. *Kosovsko pitanje* (The Question of Kosovo). (Zagreb, Croatia: Globus, 1988).

Huttenbach, Henry R., and Vodopivec, Peter (eds.): *Voices from the Slovene Nation, 1990–1992* (*Nationalities Papers* 21, no. 1 [Spring 1993]). (New York: Association for the Study of the Nationalities of the USSR and Eastern Europe, 1993).

Janša, Janez. *Premiki: Nastajanje in obramba slovenske države, 1988–1992* (Movements: The coming into being and defense of the Slovene state movements, 1988–1992). (Ljubljana, Slovenia: Mladinska knjiga, 1992).

Jelavich, Charles, and Jelavich, Barbara (eds.): *The Balkans in Transition: Essays on the Development of Balkan Life and Politics since the Eighteenth Century.* (Berkeley: University of California Press, 1963).

Jelić-Butić, Fikreta. *Ustaše i Nezavisna Država Hrvatska, 1941–1945* (Ustaša and the independent state of Croatia, 1941–1945). (Zagreb, Croatia: Školska knjiga, 1977).

Jireček, Konstantin. *Istorija Srba 1: Do 1537. godine: Politička istorija* (History of Serbs 1: Until 1537–Political history). (Beograd, Serbia-Montenegro: Prosveta, 1984).

Johnson, Ross A. *The Transformation of Communist Ideology: The Yugoslav Case, 1948–1953.* (Cambridge, MA: MIT Press, 1972).

Jurukova, Nada. *Osnovnoto vospitanie i obrazovanie vo Makedonija, 1944–1950* (Elementary education in Macedonia, 1944–1950). (Skopje, Macedonia: Institut na nacionalna istorija, 1990).

Kadijević, Veljko. *Moje vidjenje raspada: Vojska bez države* (My view of the collapse: An army without a state). (Beograd, Serbia-Montenegro: Politika 1993).

Kann, Robert A., Kiraly, Bela, and Fichtner, Paula S. (eds.): *The Habsburg Empire in the First World War.* (New York: Columbia University Press, East European Quarterly, 1977).

Kardelj, Edvard. *Reminiscences, the Struggle for Recognition, and Independence: The New Yugoslavia, 1944–1957.* (London: Blond & Briggs with Summerfield Press, 1982).

Katardžiev, Ivan. *Makedonsko nacionalno pitanje, 1919–1930* (The Macedonian national question, 1919–1930). (Zagreb, Croatia: Globus, 1983)

Kennan, George F. (ed.): *The Other Balkan Wars: A 1913 Carnegie Endowment Inquiry in Retrospect, with a New Introduction and Reflections on the Present Conflict.* (Washington, DC: Carnegie Endowment, 1993).

Kiraly, Bela, and Djordjević, Dimitrije (eds.). *East Central European Society and the Balkan Wars.* (New York: Columbia University Press, Social Science Monographs and Atlantic Research and Publications, 1987).

Klaić, Nada. *Srednjevjekovna Bosna* (Medieval Bosnia). (Zagreb, Croatia: Grafički zavod Hrvatske, 1989).

Klemenčič, Matjaž. *Ameriški Slovenci in NOB v Jugoslaviji. Naseljevanje, zemljepisna razprostranjenost in odnos ameriških Slovencev do stare domovine od sredine 19. stoletja do konca druge svetovne vojne* (American Slovenes and the National Liberation Movement in Yugoslavia: Settlement, geographical diffusion, and the attitude of American Slovenes toward the Old Country from the mid-nineteenth century to World War II). (Maribor, Slovenia: Založba Obzorja, 1987).

————. *Slovenes of Cleveland: The Creation of a New Nation and a New World Community, Slovenia and the Slovenes of Cleveland, Ohio.* (Novo Mesto, Slovenia: Dolenjska založba, 1995).

Kostovicova, Dana. *Parallel Worlds: Response of Kosovo Albanians to Loss of Autonomy in Serbia, 1986–1996.* (Keele, UK: Keele University European Research Centre, 1997).

Koštunica, Vojislav, and Čavoški, Kosta. *Party Pluralism or Monism? Social Movements and the Political System in Yugoslavia 1944–1949.* (New York: Columbia University Press, East European Monographs, 1985).

Krizman, Bogdan. *Raspad Austro-Ugarske i stvaranje jugoslavenske države* (The Dissolution of Austria-Hungary and the creation of the Yugoslav state). (Zagreb, Croatia: Školska knjiga, 1977).

Kržišnik-Bukić, Vera. *Bosanska identiteta med preteklostjo in prihodnostjo* (Bosnian identity between the past and the future). (Ljubljana, Slovenia: Inštitut za narodnostna vprašanja, 1996).

Lampe, John R., and Jackson, Marvin R. *Balkan Economic History, 1550–1950.* (Bloomington: Indiana University Press, 1983).

Lampe, John R., Prickett, Russell O., and Adamović, Ljubiša. *Yugoslav-American Economic Relations since World War II.* (Durham, NC: Duke University Press, 1990).

Libal, Wolfgang. *Das Ende Jugoslawiens. Chronik einer Selbstzerstörung* (The end of Yugoslavia: Chronicle of a self-destroying policy). (Wien, Austria: Europaverlag, 1991).

Litvinoff, Miles, et al. (eds.): *World Directory of Minorities.* (London: Minority Rights Group International, 1997).

Lydall, Harold. *Yugoslavia in Crisis.* (Oxford, U.K.: Clarendon Press, 1989).

Macan, Trpimir. *Povijest hrvatskog naroda* (The history of the Croat nation). (Zagreb, Croatia: Nakladni zavod Matice hrvatske, Školska knjiga, 1992).

Macartney, C. A. *The Habsburg Empire, 1790–1918.* (London: Weidenfeld and Nicolson, 1968).

Maček, Vladko. *In the Struggle for Freedom.* (University Park: Pennsylvania State University Press, 1957).

Magaš, Branka. *The Destruction of Yugoslavia: Tracking the Breakup 1980–1992.* (London: Verso, 1993).

Milenkovitch, Deborah. *Plan and Market in Yugoslav Economic Thought.* (New Haven, CT: Yale University Press, 1971).

Moačanin, Fedor, and Valentić, Mirko. *Vojna krajina u Hrvatskoj* (The military frontier in Croatia). (Zagreb, Croatia: Povijesni muzej Hrvatske, 1981).

Palmer, Stephen E., and King, Robert R. *Yugoslav Communism and the Macedonian Question.* (Hamden, CT: Archon Press, 1970).

Pandev, K. *Borbite v Makedonija i Odrinsko, 1878–1912* (Battles and wars in Macedonia and Odrin, 1878–1912). (Sofia, Bulgaria: Balgarski Pisatel, 1981).

Paulova, Miladina. *Jugoslavenski odbor* (Yugoslav Committee). (Zagreb, Croatia: Prosvjetna nakladna zadruga, 1925).

Perović, Latinka. *Zatvaranje kruga. Ishod politickog rascepa u SKJ 1971–1972* (The closing of the circle: A way out from the political split within the LCY 1971–1972). (Sarajevo, Bosnia and Herzegovina: Svijetlost, 1991).

Petričević, Jure. *Nacionalnost stanovništva Jugoslavije. Nazadovanje Hrvata i manjina, napredovanje Muslimana i Albanaca* (Ethnic structure of Yugoslavia: Lagging behind of Croat and minorities, positive development of Muslims and Albanians). (Brugg, Switzerland: Verlag Adria, 1983).

Petrovich, Michael B. *A History of Modern Serbia, 1804–1918.* (New York: Harcourt Brace Jovanovich, 1976).

Petrović, Ruža. *Migracije u Jugoslaviji i etnički aspekt* (Ethnic aspect of migrations in Yugoslavia). (Beograd, Serbia-Montenegro: Izdavački centar SSO Srbije, 1987).

Pleterski, Janko. *Prva odločitev Slovencev za Jugoslavijo: politika na domačih tleh med vojno 1914–1918* (The first decisions of Slovenes for Yugoslavia: Policy at home during the war 1914–1918). (Ljubljana, Slovenia: Slovenska matica, 1971).

Pogačnik, Jože, and Zadravec, Franc (eds.): *Istorija slovenačke književnosti: Književnost i civilizacija* (The history of Slovene literature: literature and civilization). (Beograd, Serbia-Montenegro: Nolit, 1973).

Popović, A. *L'Islam balkanique* (Islam in the Balkans). (Berlin, Germany: Osteuropa-Institut an der Freien Universität Berlin, 1986).

Pribichevich, Svetozar. *Macedonia: Its People and History.* (University Park: Pennsylvania State University Press, 1989).

Purivatra, Arif (ed.): *Muslimani i Bošnjaštvo.* (The Muslims in Bosnia). (Sarajevo, Bosnia and Herzegovina: Svjetlost, 1991).

Rabel, Roberto G. *Between East and West: Trieste, the United States, and the Cold War, 1941–1954.* (Durham, NC: Duke University Press, 1988).

Rajšp, Vincenc, Gestrin, Ferdo, Marolt, Janez, and Mihelič, Darja (eds.): *Grafenauerjev zbornik* (Collection of scientific papers in honor of Grafenauer). (Ljubljana, Slovenia: Slovenska akademija znanosti in umetnosti, 1996).

Ramet, Sabrina P., and Adamović, Ljubiša Š. (eds.): *Beyond Yugoslavia: Politics, Economics, and Culture in a Shattered Community* (Boulder, CO: Westview, 1995).

Repe, Božo: *Jutri je nov dan: Slovenci in razpad Jugoslavije* (Tomorrow is a new day: Slovenes and the dissolution of Yugoslavia). (Ljubljana, Slovenia: Modrijan, 2002).

Reuter, Jens. *Die Albaner in Jugoslawien* (Albanians in Yugoslavia). (Munich, Germany: R. Oldenbourg Verlag, 1982).

Rich, Norman. *Hitler's War Aims: The Establishment of the New Order.* (London: Andre Deutsch, 1974).

Risteski, Stojan. *Sozdavanjeto na sovremeniot makedonski literaturen jazik* (Development of the modern Macedonian literary language). (Skopje, Macedonia: Studentski zbor, 1988).

Risteski, Stojan. *Sudeni za Makedonija, 1945–1985* (Destined for Macedonia, 1945–1985). (Skopje, Macedonia: Vreme, 1993).

Roksandić, Drago. *Srbi u Hrvatskoj* (Serbs in Croatia). (Zagreb, Croatia: Vjesnik, 1991).

Rupel, Dimitrij. *Skrivnost države. Spomini na domače in zunanje zadeve 1989–1992* (Secret of the State: Memoirs on internal and foreign affairs 1989–1992). (Ljubljana, Slovenia: Cankarjeva založba, 1992).

Sachs, Stephen R. *Self-Management and Efficiency: Large Corporations in Yugoslavia.* (London: George Allen & Unwin, 1983).

Sekelj, Laszlo. *Yugoslavia: The Process of Disintegration.* (New York: Columbia University Press, Atlantic Research and Publications, 1993).

Shoup, Paul. *Communism and the Yugoslav National Question.* (New York: Columbia University Press, 1968).

Simoniti, Vasko. *Turki so v deželi že: turški vpadi na slovensko ozemlje v 15. in 16. stoletju* (Turks are already in the country: Turkish incursions in the territory of Slovenia in the fifteenth and sixteenth centuries). (Celje, Slovenia: Mohorjeva družba, 1990).

Simoniti, Vasko. *Vojaška organizacija na Slovenskem v 16. stoletju* (Military organization in the territory of Slovenia in the sixteenth century). (Ljubljana, Slovenia: Slovenska matica, 1991).

Spencer, Metta (ed.): *The Lessons of Yugoslavia.* (*Research on Russia and Eastern Europe,* vol. 3.) (Amsterdam: Elsevier Science JAI, 2000).

Stambolić, Ivan. *Rasprave o SR Srbiji 1979–1987* (Discussions on SR Serbia 1979–1987). (Zagreb, Croatia: Globus, 1988).

Štih, Peter, and Simoniti, Vasko. *Slovenska zgodovina do razsvetljenstva* (Slovene history until the Age of Enlightenment). (Ljubljana, Slovenia: Mohorjeva družba, 1995).

Stoianovich, Traian. *Balkan Worlds: The First and Last Europe.* (Armonk, NY: M. E. Sharpe, 1994).

Tomasevich, Jozo. *Peasants, Politics, and Economic Change in Yugoslavia.* (Palo Alto, CA: Stanford University Press, 1955).

Tomiak, Janusz (ed.): *Schooling, Educational Policy, and Ethnic Identity.* (New York: New York University Press, European Science Foundation, 1986).

Turnock, David, and Carter, Francis W. (eds.): *South-Eastern Europe,* vol. 2 of *The States of Eastern Europe.* (Aldershot, U.K.: Ashgate, 1999).

Vishninski, B. (ed.): *The Epic of Ilinden.* (Skopje Macedonia: Macedonian Review Editions, 1973).

Voje, Ignacij. *Nemirni Balkan: Zgodovinski pregled od 6. do 18. stoletja* (The rest-less Balkans: Historic overview from the sixth to the eighteenth century). (Ljubljana, Slovenia: DZS, 1994.)

Vucinich, Wayne S. *Serbia between East and West: The Events of 1903–1908.* (Palo Alto, CA: Stanford University Press, 1954).

———. (ed.): *Contemporary Yugoslavia.* (Berkeley: University of California Press, 1969).

Vujović, Dimitrije-Dimo. *Ujedinjenje Crne gore i Srbije* (The unification of Montenegro and Serbia). (Titograd, Serbia-Montenegro: Istorijski institut NR Crne gore, 1962).

Vukčević, Nikola. *Etnicko porijeklo Crnogoraca* (Ethnic descent of Montenegrins). (Beograd, Serbia-Montenegro: Sava Mihić, 1981).

Vukmanović-Tempo, Svetozar. *Struggle for the Balkans.* (London: Merlin Press, 1990).

Wilson, Duncan. *Tito's Yugoslavia.* (Cambridge, U.K.: Cambridge University Press, 1979).

Winkler, Wilhelm. *Statistisches Handbuch der europäischen Nationalitäten* (Statis-tical manuals of European nationalities). (Wien, Austria: Wilhelm Braumüller Universitäts-Verlagsbuchhandlung, 1931).

Zgodovina Slovencev (History of Slovenes). (Ljubljana, Slovenia: Cankarjeva založba, 1979).

Živojinović, Dragoljub. *America, Italy, and the Birth of Yugoslavia, 1917–1919.* (Boulder, CO: East European Monographs, 1972).

Zografski, Dančo, Stojanovski, Aleksandar, and Todorovski, Gligor (eds.): *Istorija na makedonskiot narod* (The history of the Macedonian nation). (Skopje, Macedonia: Institut na nacionalna istorija, 1972).

Zotiades, G. B. *The Macedonian Controversy.* (Thessaloniki, Greece: Etaireia Makedonikon Spoudon, 1961).

Žuljić, Stanko. *Narodnostna struktura Jugoslavije i tokovi promjena* (Ethnic struc-ture of Yugoslavia and currents of changes). (Zagreb, Croatia: Ekonomski in-stitut, 1989).

Zwitter, Fran (in collaboration with Šidak, Jaroslav, and Bogdanov, Vaso). *Na-cionalni problemi v habsburški monarhiji* (National Problems in the Habsburg Monarchy). (Ljubljana, Slovenia: Slovenska matica, 1962).

Articles

Andrejevich, Milan. "The Sandžak: The Next Balkan Theater of War?" *Radio Free Europe Research Report* (27 November 1992): 26–34.

Crkvenčić, Ivan. "Croatian Ethnic Territory and the Multiethnic Composition of Croatia as a Result of Population Migrations." *Društvena istraživanja* 7, nos. 1–3 (1998): 109–126.

Djodan, Šime. "Gdje dr. Stipe Šuvar pronalazi nacionalizam, a gdje ga ne vidi" (Where does Dr. Stipe Šuvar find nationalism, and where he does not see it). *Kolo* 7, no. 7 (July 1969): 695.

Gompert, David. "How to Defeat Serbia." *Foreign Policy* 73 (July/August 1994): 30–42.

Hadžić, Adem. "Etničke promjene u sjeveroistočnoj Bosni i Posavini u XV i XVI veku" (Ethnic changes in northeastern Bosnia and Posavina in the fifteenth and sixteenth centuries). *Jugoslovenski istorijski časopis* 4 (1969): 31–37.

Handžić, Adem. "O islamizaciji u sjeveroistočnoj Bosni u XV i XVI vijeku" (Islamization in southeastern Bosnia-Herzegovina in the fifteenth and sixteenth centuries). *Prilozi za orijentalnu filologiju* 16–18 (1970): 5–45.

Inić, Slobodan. "Serbia's Historic Defeat." *New Politics* 4, no. 2 (summer 1993): 161–166.

Klemenčič, Matjaž. "To Fellow Americanists: A Letter from Slovenia." *Journal of American History* 80, no. 3 (1993): 1031–1034.

Klemenčič, Vladimir. "Spreminjanje nacionalne strukture prebivalstva Jugoslavije v novejšem razdobju" (The changes in ethnic structure of Yugoslavia in the recent period). *Geografija v šoli* 1, no. 1 (1991): 7–22.

———. "National Minorities as an Element of the Demographic and Spatial Structure of the Alpine-Adriatic-Pannonian Region." *GeoJournal* 30, no. 3 (1993): 207–214.

Krizman, Bogdan. "The Croatians in the Habsburg Monarchy in the Nineteenth Century." *Austrian History Yearbook* 3, no. 2 (1967): 116–158.

Pavličević, D. "A review of the historical development of the Republic of Croatia." *GeoJournal* 38 (1996): 381–391.

Pavlowitsch, Stevan K. "Society in Serbia, 1791–1830." In Clogg, Richard (ed.): *Balkan Society in the Age of Greek Independence.* (Totowa, NJ: Barnes and Noble, 1981): 137–156.

Todorović, Desanka. "Okupacijata na Strumica 1919 godina" (The occupation of Strumica in 1919). *Institut za nacionalna istorija: Glasnik* 10, no. 1 (1966): 50–51.

Voje, Ignacij. "Procesi migracij na južnoslovanskem prostoru pod turško oblastjo" (Migrations in the territory of South Slavic settlement under the Turkish rule). *Zgodovina v šoli* 1, no. 1 (1992): 20–27.

Index

About the Authors

Matjaž Klemencic, Ph.D., is a professor of history at the University of Maribor (Slovenia) and is president of the scientific board at the Institute for Ethnic Studies (IES) in Ljubljana, Slovenia. He also teaches at the University of Ljubljana. With Professor Mirko Jurak, he cofounded a graduate program in American studies at the University of Ljubljana. Professor Klemencic was a Fulbright scholar at Yale University and received several research grants from the University of Minnesota Immigration History Research Center; the JFK Institute for North American Studies in Berlin, Germany; Volkswagenwerk Stiftung, and the Roosevelt Study Center in the Netherlands. He specializes in the history of American immigration and in the history of nationalism in the former Yugoslavia and its neighbors. His books include *Slovenes of Cleveland: The Creation of a New Nation and a New World Community: Slovenia and the Slovenes of Cleveland, Ohio* and *Jurij Trunk med Koroško in Združenimi državami Amerike ter zgodovina slovenskih naselbin v Leadvillu, Kolorado in San Franciscu, Kalifornija* (Jurij Trunk between Carinthia/Austria and the United States and the History of the Slovene Settlements in Leadville, Colorado, and San Francisco, California). He has written a number of articles in scholarly journals and collections of essays in Slovenia and abroad. He is a member of the editorial board of *Journal of American History, Dve domovini–Two Homelands* and *Treatises and Documents: Journal of Ethnic Studies.* He organized several international conferences, most notably one on ethnic fraternalism in 1994.

Mitja Žagar, Ph.D., a jurist and political scientist, is director of the Institute for Ethnic Studies (IES), in Ljubljana, Slovenia, and associate professor at the University of Ljubljana (Faculty of Social Sciences and Faculty of Law). At the Faculty of Social Sciences he coordinates a graduate program in political science/ethnic studies. He is also a chair of the International Center for Interethnic Relations and Minorities in South-Eastern

Europe (at the IES), established within the Stability Pact for South Eastern Europe. An expert with some international organizations (Council of Europe, Organization for Security and Co-operation in Europe), he is also a chair of the Task Force on Human Rights and Minorities of the Stability Pact for South Eastern Europe. He was a Fulbright scholar and visiting professor at Wayne State University, a visiting scholar/researcher in Norway (Norwegian Institute of International Affairs), and a fellow at the East-West Institute. His main fields of research and work are ethnic studies, international (public) law and human rights, constitutional and comparative constitutional law, comparative government and politics. He has published extensively in Slovenia and abroad. He coedited several books, among them *Liberal Democracy, Citizenship & Education* and *Changing Faces of Federalism: Political Reconfiguration in Europe* (forthcoming 2004). As a speaker he has participated in several international scholarly conferences, colloquia, and symposia in Europe, Africa, and North America. He also coorganized several international conferences, including four international scholarly conferences on the constitutional and political regulation and management of ethnic relations in Ljubljana (1996, 1997, 2000, and 2002). He is a member of the editorial board of the *Journal of Ethno-development, Treatises and Documents: Journal of Ethnic Studies,* and *Peace and Conflict Studies, A Journal of the Network of Peace and Conflict Studies.*